Twenty Years with the Jewish Labor Bund

A Memoir of Interwar Poland

Shofar Supplements in Jewish Studies

Zev Garber, Editor
Los Angeles Valley College

Bernard Goldstein (1889–1959). From the Archives of the YIVO Institute for Jewish Research, New York.

Twenty Years with the Jewish Labor Bund

A Memoir of Interwar Poland

Bernard Goldstein

Translated by Marvin S. Zuckerman

Preface by
Victor Gilinsky

Introduction by Emanuel Sherer,
General Secretary, Jewish Labor Bund

Purdue University Press
West Lafayette, Indiana

© Copyright 2016 by Marvin Zuckerman. All rights reserved.
Printed in the United States of America.
Originally published in Yiddish by Unser Tsait, New York, 1960.

Library of Congress Cataloging-in-Publication Data

Names: Goldstein, Bernard, 1889- author.
Title: Twenty Years with the Jewish Labor Bund: A Memoir of Interwar Poland
 /by Bernard Goldstein; translated by Marvin S. Zuckerman; preface by Victor Gilinsky;
 introduction by Emanuel Sherer, PhD, General Secretary, Jewish Labor Bund.
Other titles: Tsvantsig yor in Varshever "Bund." English.
Description: West Lafayette, Indiana: Purdue University Press, [2016] | © 2016 | Series:
 Shofar Supplements in Jewish Studies | Includes bibliographical references and index.
Identifiers: LCCN 2015048692| ISBN 9781557537492 (pbk. : alk. paper) |
 ISBN 9781612494470 (epub) | ISBN 9781612494463 (epdf)
Subjects: LCSH: Ogólny Żydowski Związek Robotniczy "Bund" w Polsce. |
 Jews—Poland—Warsaw.
Classification: LCC HD8537.O42 G6513 2016 | DDC 305.892/4043841—dc22
LC record available at http://lccn.loc.gov/2015048692

Cover image: Poster stating, "There where we live, there is our country! A democratic republic! Full political and national rights for Jews! Ensure that the voice of the Jewish working class is heard at the constituent assembly!" Kiev, ca. 1918. The poster further urges Jews to vote for the Bund candidates, Slate 9, in an election following the Russian Revolution, when non-Bolshevik parties were still being tolerated by the Communist regime. From the Archives of the YIVO Institute for Jewish Research, New York.

*This volume is gratefully dedicated to
Leo Melamed
in appreciation of his generous contribution to this project
and
to his beloved parents
Faygl and Itzchok Melamdovitch
ardent Bialystok Bundists, both.*

I have always regarded memoirs as source material.
A memoir provides a record not so much of the memoirist as of the memoirist's world.

—Arthur Golden

Figure 2. The flag reads "BUND." Artist unknown. From the translator's private collection.

Contents

Foreword	xi
Translator's Preface	xiii
Acknowledgments	xxvii
Bernard Goldstein: A Chronology	xxix
Translator's Note	xxxi
Original Introduction by Dr. Emanuel Sherer, General Secretary of the Jewish Labor Bund	1
1. I Go Home	9
2. Back in Warsaw	15
3. Praga	21
4. The Seven Lions	27
5. The First of May Demonstration in Praga, 1920	31
6. Pogrom at the Praga Bund Club	35
7. Janek Jankelewicz	37
8. The Cracow Convention	41
9. A Hail of Persecutions	47
10. Illegal Work—Once Again	53
11. The Danzig Convention	57
12. Coming to the Defense of the Movement	63
13. Organizing the Bund Militia	65
14. The Communists and the Underworld	71
15. The 1922 Election Campaign	75
16. Unifying the Trade Union Movement	83
17. The Slaughterers Union	89
18. Three Slaughterer Dynasties	95

19. The Transport Workers Union: Back Porters	101
20. Back Porter Types	105
21. Rope and Handcart Porters	111
22. The Food Workers Union	115
23. The Bakers Union	123
24. Bagel Bakers and Peddlers	129
25. A Day in a Slaughter House	133
26. Jewish and Polish Meat Workers	137
27. At Parties and Celebrations	141
28. Resistance: The First of May Demonstration, 1923	143
29. Struggles over the Saturday Edition of the *Folkstsaytung*	149
30. Commissar Cechnowski	153
31. Kalmen the Bootmaker's Death	155
32. The Piłsudski Coup, the PPS, and the FRACs	159
33. The FRAC Militia	163
34. A New Gang of Communist Strong-Arms	167
35. Communists Shoot at a Workers Convention	171
36. *Morgnshtern*	175
37. The Labor Sports Olympiad in Prague	185
38. Ominous Dark Clouds on All Sides	189
39. Concerns about Self-Defense	195
40. A Wave of Wildcat Strikes	197
41. An Attempted Murderous Assault on Me	205
42. In Zakopane	209
43. Attacks on a Night School	215
44. The Medem Sanitarium Attacked	219
45. Another Attempt on My Life	227
46. Krochmalna Street	231
47. Fat Yosl	235
48. Khaskele	241
49. "Malematke"	245

50. Yukele	249
51. Troubles with Cultural Awakening	253
52. The Militia Comes to the Aid of Bundist Members on the Warsaw City Council	265
53. First of May Demonstrations Under the Piłsudski Regime	273
54. A Joint First of May Demonstration with the PPS	287
55. In Red Vienna	289
56. Street Fights with the Polish Hitlerites	295
57. Battles over the Boycotting of Jewish Businesses	301
58. The "Ghetto Benches" in the Universities	303
59. My Son at the SKIF Camp	307
60. The Bakers Union Turns Away from the Communists; The Murder of Neuerman	311
61. Nathan (Nokhem) Chanin's Visit to Warsaw	315
62. Three Bloody Attacks in One Day	319
63. Temptations and Doubts	323
64. Shloyme Mendelson	327
65. In the Trap of the Shetshke Gang	331
66. The FRACs Try to Take Over the Newspaper Deliverers Union	333
67. The FRAC Transport Workers Union and Itshe "Zbukh"	337
68. Returning Stolen Goods to a Leather Merchant	341
69. Among the Retail Clerks; Another Worker Murdered	343
70. Auctioning off the *Folkstsaytung*	349
71. A Defeat for the Priest, Father Trzeciak	355
72. Przytyk and the Protest-Strike on March 17, 1936	359
73. The Pogrom in Minsk-Mazowiecki	363
74. Antisemitic Hooligans Kill a Jewish Child during a First of May Demonstration	367
75. *Oenerowcy* Leaders Are Taught a Lesson	369
76. Guarding the *Folkstsaytung*	371
77. The Pogrom in Brisk	373

78. The Bund's Warsaw Locales	379
79. A Bombing of the Bund Offices— And Our Answer to the *Oenerowcy*	383
80. An *Oenerowcy* Attempt to Murder Comrade Henryk Erlich	387
81. December 18, 1938	391
82. A Final Look at Our Youth	395
Glossary of Terms, Names, and Acronyms	397
References	411
Index	413

Foreword

Some memoirs transcend their detailed recollections of an individual's experience to illuminate a time past in a way that historical accounts cannot do. That is what Bernard Goldstein's memoir does for the Jewish world in Poland between the world wars.

The Jewish community in Poland was at the time the largest single concentration of Jews in the world, the heartland of the East European Yiddish-speaking cultural world. It was also the capital of the Jewish Socialist labor movement, the most popular Jewish movement—more so than Zionism—on the eve of World War II. It produced remarkably energetic and creative people, some of whom came to the United States and played key roles in the American labor movement and in the Democratic Party.

All this was of course utterly destroyed by Hitler's Germany. In the end, Zionism prevailed, led by early emigrants from the Jewish community in Poland. But in their struggle to create a new nation in Palestine their public narrative emphasized the bravery of Israel's defenders in contrast with the defenseless Jews who perished in the Holocaust. The reality of the vibrant, rough and tumble pre-World War II Jewish world in Poland has been submerged by the subsequent Holocaust literature and the subsequent focus on Israel.

The picture Bernard Goldstein paints of Jewish life in Poland before World War II is a very different one from the widely held caricature of timorous Jews. It was a time of struggle but also of optimism, greater assertiveness, and self-confidence. It is important to bring that earlier period back to life to balance the historical account. Jewish readers with roots in Eastern Europe will find much here to be proud of.

Between the wars, Goldstein was head of the Militia of the Bund, as the Jewish Social-Democratic Labor Party was called. He provides an unparalleled street-level view of the political struggles for the Jewish masses in Poland, then emerging into the secular modern world, and the fights to organize the Jewish workers. Goldstein and his tough operatives got involved with a broad cross-section of the Jewish and Polish societies, including their seamy sides, all of which he writes about with a keen eye. His sketches of the Jewish underworld in Warsaw recall Isaac Babel's descriptions of the Jewish criminal world in Odessa.

"Comrade" Bernard, as he was known, organized street demonstrations and protests. Against great odds he gained union rights for Jewish workers such as the slaughterers, bakers, and teamsters, and battled for higher pay and better working conditions. He knew the workers well, as he was the one they went to with their complaints and even their personal problems. Throughout, and in line with his party's directives, he maintained and taught a high ethical standard of behavior.

Goldstein's book consists of a series of short anecdotal chapters based on what he personally witnessed and played a part in—fighting off an armed attack by the Jewish Communists; defending a street demonstration; attending a gangster wedding; repulsing Polish hooligans attacking Jews in Warsaw's park; protecting a prostitute from her pimp so she could get off the street and marry; making peace between knife-wielding Jewish and Polish butchers; and joining Jewish Socialist youths at their summer camp right before the war, little imagining that these young people would then come to lead the heroic and tragic Warsaw Ghetto Uprising in 1943. Goldstein himself later fought in the Warsaw Ghetto and survived.

—Victor Gilinsky

Figure 4. A pre-World War II Bund Rally in a Warsaw Courtyard.

Translator's Preface

In October 1897, under cover of the Jewish high holy days, in the attic of a small, rundown house on the outskirts of Vilnius, thirteen Jewish intellectuals, writers, and workingmen gathered together, illegally, from five different cities of the Pale, to form what they decided to call *Der Algemeyner Yidisher Arbeter Bund fun Rusland un Poyln* (The General Jewish Labor Bund of Russia and Poland)—which came to be known by the one word—"BUND."

The organization which they formed came to play a large role in East European Jewish life for the next close to 50 years, until it was destroyed by the two great destroyers of our time: Hitler and Stalin, Nazism and communism.

Together with the Zionist movement, the Bund led the masses of East European Jewish life into the modern era, with their heads held high, full of pride, unafraid, and ready to do battle.

And what was the Bund ready to do battle for? For Jewish honor, for cultural autonomy, social-democracy, Yiddish language and literature, full civil rights in the lands in which they lived, and a trade union movement to fight for better working conditions and decent pay.

In the course of time, they drew tens of thousands of Jewish working people to their organization, as well as thousands of Jewish youths, intellectuals, and students—young men and women who abandoned the *kheydorim* and *yeshivas* on the one hand, or left the *gymnasiums* and universities on the other, to enter into, build, and work together with the poor laboring Jewish masses in the new free, fighting atmosphere of the Bund, where they could express themselves, not only as Socialists, but as Jews.

And in the course of time, the Bund organized Jewish trade unions, built schools for children, published scores of newspapers and magazines, and organized *zelbst-shuts* (self-defense) organizations to fight off pogromists and fascist, anti-Semitic hooligans. It built a summer camp and sanitorium for children. It created choral groups, sports organizations, evening classes, consumers' and

Figure 5. Thirteen delegates representing Jewish labor organizations from Vilnius, Warsaw, Bialystok, Minsk, and Vitebsk met illegally in the attic of this house in Vilnius from October 7–9 to found the Jewish Labor Bund. From the Archives of the YIVO Institute for Jewish Research, New York.

producers' co-operatives, libraries, dramatic groups, literary clubs, schools for children, and other institutions which served the poor, working-class Jews of Eastern Europe.

Here is how the revered Bund leader, Vladimir Medem, expressed himself in 1919 on the meaning of the Bund:

> Listen carefully to the word "bund." It comes from the word "to bind." To bind together into one complete entity all separate things with a tie. To join feeble energies into one huge power. Put your ear to the chest of the Jewish worker and listen: his heartbeat is strong and steady. Look into the eyes of the comrade: they are wide open and clear. Take his hand: it is strong and hardened. How come? How is it that a single person, a grain of sand in this huge desert of a world, a tiny drop in the turbulent sea of life which surrounds you with thousands of brutal enemies, which destroys a whole world, grinding countries and states into dust, drowning in its depths countless human existences, how is it that in the middle of this enormous whirlwind stands a person with sparkling eyes, undaunted by the storm? Look, comrade, into your own soul. There you will read the answer: you have a home, a family, a basis to stand on; you can feel that around you, above you, and within you there is a great force that supports, embraces, and carries

you, makes you strong, and does not let you fall. Do you know, comrade, the name of this enormous force? Do you know what is the name of your home, your family, your existence, your hope? Stand up comrade! Lift up your head and sing the old "Shvue"! This is the Bund![1]

The Bund led successful strikes throughout the Pale—strikes among the weavers of Lodz, the brushmakers of Warsaw, the leather workers of Lublin, slaughterers, coachmen, porters, garment workers, etc., all over the Pale.

The Bund played a leading role in the 1905 revolution throughout the Russian empire.[2]

And also in that year, in 1905, the Bund organized the Jewish working people of Czarist Russia into armed bands of *zelbst-shuts* (self-defense) units which successfully fought off pogromists who were attacking Jewish towns and neighborhoods all over the Pale.[3] Listen to Zalmen Shazar's (the third President of Israel) account of how, in his youth, the Bund and the Zionist *zelbst-shuts* together fought off pogromists in his *shtetl*, Stolpce:

> This time we were ready. We knew that agitators had come from afar. We saw peasant women coming into town with empty wagons, and we knew they were coming to loot and wanted to be able to take the stolen goods home. In the morning, our comrades were on the street ready with iron rods, lead bars, and whips with rounded pieces of lead at their tips. The commandants of the units of ten, armed with revolvers, stationed themselves at many points in the marketplace. At noon, when the peasants poured out of the white church, rabid and worked up, ready to assault the Jews, one of the outside agitators gave the signal and started to lead the peasants to break into the shops. Then all at once our unit commanders fired their revolvers—in the air, not hurting anyone. The shots came from all sides of the marketplace, creating panic and confusion among the crowd of attackers. The horses broke wild, the peasant women began screaming as though they were being slaughtered. One wagon collided with another. With what seemed their last gasp, the peasants ran in fear from the Jews firing all over the marketplace. It took only a few minutes before the marketplace was emptied of the aroused pogromists.
>
> No, Stolpce, pride of my youth, I cannot believe that you were led like sheep to the slaughter.[4]

The Bund attracted some of the finest leaders, spokesmen, and intellectuals the Jewish people, or for that matter, any people, possessed: Vladimir Medem, Henryk Erlich, Victor Alter, Arkady Kremer, and Noyekh Portnoy, to name a few. The Bund gave rise to a movement that fostered ethics, honesty, and democratic values—and its leaders displayed these virtues at the head of their mass, a mass that inspired them, and who were, in turn, inspired by their remarkable leaders.

Figure 6. Delegates to the 1908 Czernowitz Language Conference in Romania, where Yiddish was declared a Jewish National Language. Bundists were heavily represented. Some great Yiddish writers were present and in this group portrait: I. L. Peretz, Sholem Asch, Avrom Reisin—and others. From the Archives of the YIVO Institute for Jewish Research, New York.

The Bund was the only Jewish party which made the advocacy of the Yiddish language and literature part of its program. It was the only party to argue that Yiddish was a language on a par with all the other modern European languages, possessing a grammar and a syntax, and with as much right to status as all the other recognized languages of the world.

And many of the Yiddish writers repaid the Bund with their loyalty and creativity. Listen to this account by Mark Schweid (my translation) of an episode in the life of I. L. Peretz. It was during a celebration of Peretz's 25th jubilee as a writer, in his home at the address that had become famous throughout the new Yiddish literary world, No.1 Ceglana Street, Warsaw:

> The guests were in an elevated mood when there was ring at the door and two young, unknown personages let themselves in. They were poorly dressed workingmen. They spoke quietly with Peretz and asked him to go with them into another room. Peretz excused himself from the committee and went into another room with the two young people. A few minutes later he emerged with his face alight with enthusiasm; in his hand was an old

book. The workers quietly left, and then Peretz called out, "Do you know who that was? A delegation from the Bund. They sent me an official greeting with this gift." The Polish-speaking guests grew pale with fright and looked towards the door. In the word "Bund" they smelled Siberia and the gallows. Dineson calmed them with a quiet act. The official greeting of the Bund he cautiously removed from Peretz's hand and burned in the lighted candle on the table. He gathered the ashes carefully on a piece of paper and threw them into an ashtray. The book, a copy of Peretz's Yiddish Library, Peretz hid deep among his most precious documents that he held dear his whole life.

The book, greasy, smeared, torn-up from use, came from the Tenth Pavilion of the Citadel Prison where it had been secretly circulated from one

Figure 7. I. L. Peretz, from an old postcard. The words beneath his portrait are lines from his famous verse drama, *Di Goldene Keyt*. From the Archives of the YIVO Institute for Jewish Research, New York.

political prisoner to the next. Many single letters were underlined with pencil which encoded messages from one prisoner to the next. After this event, Peretz would write with deep sincerity: "I belong to no party, but I feel closest to the Bund." And years later he would say: "I found my socialism in the Prophets of the Bible."[5]

The Bund forged a mass movement which struggled against the Leninist-Bolshevik line on the one hand, and against what it conceived of as a narrow, chauvinistic, unrealistic, nationalist dream on the other.

Let me deal with the question of the Bund vis-à-vis the Communist movement first.

In 1898 it was the Bund that organized the first Russian Social-Democratic Federation meeting from which Dan, Martov, Lenin, Plekhanov, Axelrod, Zasulich, and all the other founders and shapers of the coming Russian revolution were to play such an important role on the world stage. The historian Bertram D. Wolfe calls the Bund at that time, "the largest and best organized body of workingmen inside the Russian empire."[6]

It is a matter of interesting historical fact that it is because of the Bund that the Leninist/Communist faction in the Russian Social-Democratic Federation was able to acquire the name "Bolshevik," or majority-faction. Remember that the Bund had actually organized the first meeting of the RSDF in 1898. In 1903 at the second convention of the RSDF, Lenin, who was chairing the meeting at the time, knew that the Bund wanted to propose that the it be recognized as the representative in the Federation of the specifically Jewish Socialist labor movement in the Russian empire. He also knew that the Bund representatives would vote against him and his group on issues important to him, and that they, together with the Dan and Martov group, would constitute a majority that would outvote him on his program. And because he knew further that the Bund would walk out of the convention if its proposal should be defeated, and because he knew the Dan-Martov group would vote against the Bund on this one issue, thus insuring the defeat of the Bund proposal, he made sure to place the Bund's proposal for autonomy on Jewish matters first on the agenda. Sure enough this strategy worked. The Dan-Martov group voted against the Bund's proposal for Jewish autonomy, and the Bund walked out, leaving Lenin's group with a majority—thus enabling him to name his group the Bolsheviks, the majority, and leaving the label Menshevik, the minority, for the Martov-Dan group. Thus it was due to the Bund's insistence on Jewish autonomy within the Russian Social-Democratic Federation, and Lenin's unscrupulous parliamentary maneuvering, that Lenin was able to arrogate the name Bolshevik for himself and his group.[7]

The Bund participated in a significant way in the first 1917 Revolution, its leaders and members playing a prominent role.[8]

As for its antipathy to the Communist Party, the Bund was always in opposition to the antidemocratic, dictatorial approach of Lenin and his followers.

Here are the words of another greatly revered leader of the Bund, Henryk Erlich, speaking on that subject in 1918:

> Is the Soviet government a workers' government? No! It has no right to call itself a workers' government. It has no right to speak in the name of the Russian working class.⁹

Another Bundist leader, Vladimir Medem, put it this way:

> Socialism is the rule—the true rule, not the fictional rule—of the majority, which must in the end take its fate into its own hands. A socialism based on the rule of the minority, however, is absurd . . . [The Bolsheviks] stay in power only because their terror has destroyed and made powerless all of their opponents.¹⁰

And a 1921 convention of the Bund put it still another way:

> The difference between us and the Communists lies in the fact that they believe in the rule by the party and we believe in rule by the whole working class. We say the working-class government must be answerable to the whole class; the Communists, on the other hand, say that if the working class doesn't like the Communist Party government, the working class must still accept the will of the government and not the reverse. The chief error of the Communist Party lies in its effort to turn the might of the working class into a dictatorship of the central committee of the party over the proletariat.¹¹

As for its struggle with the Zionists, let me begin by saying that both Bundism and Zionism, from our point in time, can be viewed as two sides of the same coin. And that coin is the Jewish response to the nationalist, revolutionary ideas and movements sweeping Europe in the nineteenth century. It began in the Jewish East European world in that same century with the *haskole*, the Jewish enlightenment, which brought the first breath of modernism into the closed off, medieval world of East European Jewry. From the haskole, from the Jewish enlightenment movement, a straight line can be drawn to the emergence of modern Zionism and that peculiar blend of Jewish nationalism and socialism called the Bund. The Bund, being a Socialist, Marxist party, disavowed any nationalistic programs. On the other hand, the Bund expressed a form of nationalism by championing Jewish civil rights, cultural autonomy, Yiddish language and literature, a modern Yiddish school structure, and all the other things I've already mentioned that addressed specifically Jewish needs and concerns. In that sense the Bund was also nationalistic. As the great Russian early Social Democrat, Lenin's teacher, Plekhanov, once wittily put it—"Bundists?—Zionists who suffer from seasickness."

The Bundist argument with the Zionists was a simple one. We are here, not there, in Palestine. The Jews are a world people now, like it or not. All the Jews of the world will never fit into Palestine. There will always be a Jewish diaspora. To deflect the energy and passion of the Jewish people away from the struggle here for our civil rights and a decent socialist world here, is the wrong thing to do. We are here, and we need to struggle here. As I. L. Peretz once put it,

> Zionism cannot be the solution for the whole Jewish people. We can't return to the cradle. We have grown in the Diaspora. And the Diaspora is our battlefield. We do not run away from the battlefield.[12]

This attitude was articulated by Medem with his "Do-i-kayt" program—his "hereness" program. Since we are not there, but here, we have to fight for a better "here"—a socialist world with dignity and rights for every minority, every people or ethnic group, every language and culture, including the Jewish people and their language, Yiddish. And as the great Bund leader, Henryk Erlich, said, writing in 1938 about the Zionist dream for a Jewish nation in Palestine:

> What can a Jewish Palestine be, *under the best of circumstances*? If a Jewish state should arise in Palestine, its spiritual climate will be: eternal fear of the external enemy (the Arabs); and eternal struggle for every foot of ground and for every bit of work with the internal enemy (Arabs). . . . Is this a climate in which freedom, democracy, and progress can grow? Indeed, is it not the climate in which reaction and chauvinism ordinarily flourish? Even . . . Zionist publicists who visit the Holy Land affirm the tremendous influence of clericalism, despite the fact that manual workers play such a prominent part in the Zionist organization. An eventual Jewish state cannot offer itself as a spiritual center to the Jewish masses of the *goles* [diaspora] lands, and as a center for immigration. . . . The Zionists themselves have already significantly reduced their ambitions today: in a memorandum submitted by the representatives of the Jewish Agency to the Council of the League of Nations during its September session in 1937, they speak of Palestine as only a partial solution to the Jewish question [emphasis in original].[13]

How prophetic and insightful his words seem now.

History decided this quarrel, or rather Hitler and Stalin decided it for them. Who was right? Perhaps they were both right. From our perspective now, it is clear that they both fought a brave, honorable fight for Jewish pride and worth and life.

In the 1930s the Bund organized mass protest demonstrations and walkouts in Poland. During these years preceding the war and the Holocaust, Polish anti-Semitism bore down hard on the Jews of Poland. The Bund "rallied multitudes to strikes, protests, and demonstrations against the violence of pogroms and the denial of Jewish rights. On March 16, 1936, for example, after a pogrom in Przytyk in which four Jews were killed and several score wounded, the Bund called a general strike:

Three and a half million Jews went out on strike. At noon all Jewish workers left their work; all Jewish stores shut down; Jewish pupils walked out of school. The streets of Poland were filled with a fiery people, proud, and battle ready.[14]

A year later, the anti-Semitic Polish government issued a decree that all Jewish students attending Polish universities must sit on separate, segregated benches on the left side of the classroom. In response, in October 1937, "all Jewish parties joined [with the Bund] in issuing a general strike call to protest the infamous introduction of ghetto-benches for Jewish students at the universities."[15]

And the Bund was repaid by the loyalty and devotion of the Jewish working masses of Poland. By 1938, on the eve of the Holocaust, in the municipal elections in Poland of that year, in 89 Polish cities and towns, the Bund received 55% of the votes cast for all Jewish parties. The Bund's greatest strength was, of course, in the large industrial centers, like Lodz and Warsaw—but the Bund drew support from a wide range of Jews now—from Chassidim on the right to proletarians on the left.[16] It was in the municipalities of Poland that the subsidies for health and educational institutions were allocated—and as a result of their strength on these governing bodies, the Bundist representatives "became communal spokesmen and aggressive advocates of financial aid to all Jewish institutions, including yeshivas and religious institutions."[17]

When the war came at the end of 1939, the Bundists found themselves caught in a vise: Nazi hangmen on the west, Communist torturers and executioners on the east. Where to run? There was no escape. Stay in place, and the German Gestapo and SS arrested, tortured, and killed you; run to the east and the Russian NKVD arrested, tortured, and killed you. And thus it was for those Bundist leaders who could not successfully hide or manage to escape to Shanghai, or America, or wherever. Thus it was that the two great leaders of the Bund in interwar Poland, Erlich and Alter, were arrested and tortured and killed by the Communist regime with the horrible defamation that they were Nazi spies. And there were many other Bundist leaders who met the same fate from the NKVD.

During the Holocaust, the years of Bundist underground, illegal, conspiratorial work stood them in good stead. The Bund took a leading role in the resistance to the Nazi criminals. Couriers were sent all over occupied Poland with money, messages of encouragement, food, and weapons.[18] Resistance groups were organized in all the ghettos. A united fighting organization with the Zionists and the Communists was eventually formed to fight together for Jewish lives and honor. The Bund played a leading role in the Warsaw ghetto uprising, in Vilnius, in Bialystok, in Czenstochowa, and elsewhere.[19] During the Nazi occupation the Bund managed to illegally publish scores of underground newsletters and flyers, encouraging the people, urging resistance, and warning the Jews of where the transport trains were taking them. In 1942, the Bund sent one of its members, Zalmen Friedrych, to determine exactly where the transports from

Warsaw were taking the Jews and what was happening to them there. Through the cooperation of a Polish Socialist railway worker, Friedrych smuggled himself close to Treblinka, where he met Azrel Wallach, Maxim Litvinov's nephew, who had just escaped from Treblinka. Wallach described the gas chambers there. Friedrych came back to report to the Bund. The Bund lost no time in informing the ghetto population through its illegal publication, *Sturm*.[20]

The first public resistance to the Nazis was made by a leader of the Bund in Warsaw—Artur Zygielbojm (also transliterated as Ziglboym, Zygielbaum, Zyglboym, etc.). When the Nazis formed the Judenrat in October 1939, Ziglboym among them, they instructed the Judenrat to tell the Jewish populace of Warsaw to cooperate in moving within the new ghetto to be walled off. Artur was the only representative among the Judenrat to push the Judenrat to defy this order. He said under no circumstances should the Jews voluntarily submit to this order. Here are his own words addressed to the Judenrat in October 1939:

> You have taken an historic decision. It appears that I have been too weak to convince you that we cannot permit ourselves to do this. I feel, however, that I do not possess the moral strength to participate in the execution of this decree. I also feel that I would no longer have the right to go on living if a ghetto were set up and my head remained whole. Therefore, I must relinquish my mandate as a member of the Council. I realize it is the Chairman's duty to inform the Gestapo immediately of my resignation, and I am ready to accept the consequences of this action, but I cannot act otherwise.[21]

Figure 8. "Artur" Zygielbojm (Shmuel-Mordkhe, 1895–1943). From the Archives of the YIVO Institute for Jewish Research, New York.

Outside the Judenrat Building a crowd of more than 10,000 Jews had massed, agitated and panicked. Addressing the crowd, Artur urged the people to maintain their courage and dignity; he called upon them to refuse to go into a ghetto; he urged them to remain in their homes and resist if they were forced to leave. No one, he said, should go willingly into a ghetto.[22]

His defiance did not succeed in keeping the ghetto from being formed, and of course he had to go into hiding. He then smuggled himself across Nazi Germany and occupied Europe to England, where he occupied the post of Bundist representative in the Polish government in exile in London. There he struggled tirelessly to make the allied governments aware of the terrible atrocities being committed against the Jews under the Nazis. His attempts to get the allied governments to act in some way as to save the Jews from the Holocaust having failed, when the news of the Warsaw ghetto uprising reached him in London in 1943, he decided to take his own life in protest, hoping in this way to succeed in death where he had failed in life. He left this famous open letter to the world:

> With these, my last words, I address myself to you, the Polish Government, the Polish people, the Allied Governments and their peoples, and the conscience of the world.
>
> News recently received from Poland informs us that the Germans are exterminating with unheard-of savagery the remaining Jews in that country. Behind the walls of the ghetto is taking place today the last act of a tragedy which has no parallel in the history of the human race. The responsibility for this crime—the assassination of the Jewish population in Poland—rests above all on the murderers themselves, but falls indirectly upon the whole human race, on the allies and their governments, who so far have taken no firm steps to put a stop to these crimes. By their indifference to the killing of millions of hapless men, to the massacre of women and children, these countries have become accomplices of the assassins....
>
> Of the three and a half million Polish Jews (to whom must be added the 700,000 deported from the other countries) in April, 1943, there remained alive not more than 300,000 Jews, according to news received from the head of the Bund organization and supplied by government representatives. And the extermination continues.
>
> I cannot remain silent. I cannot live while the remnants of the Jewish people in Poland, whom I represent, continue to be liquidated.
>
> My companions of the Warsaw Ghetto fell in a last heroic battle with their weapons in their hands. I did not have the honor to die with them, but I belong to them and to their common grave.
>
> Let my death be an energetic cry of protest against the indifference of the world which witnesses the extermination of the Jewish people without taking any steps to prevent it. In our day and age human life is of little value; having failed to achieve success in my life, I hope that my death may jolt the

indifference of those who, perhaps even in this extreme moment, could save the Jews who are still alive in Poland.

My life belongs to my people in Poland and that is why I am sacrificing it for them. May the handful of people who will survive out of the millions of Polish Jews achieve liberation in a world of liberty and social justice. . . .

I take my leave of all those who have been dear to me and whom I have loved.[23]

After the Holocaust, after the war, the few remaining remnants of what had been a proud, strong, mass movement among Jews, picked themselves up and began again—as the Yiddish poet and Bundist Leivik put it, *"Ikh heyb zikh oyf vider un shpan avek vayter"* (I pick myself up again and stride on farther). They assembled in Poland, in Paris, in the Displaced Persons (DP) camps, in New York, Buenos Aires, Mexico City, Montevideo, wherever they managed to get to, and, yes, in Israel. And in these cities and places the Bund lives on. A powerful mythos, movement, ethic, like the Bund—an *ecclesia militanta* as one historian dubbed it[24]—cannot just disappear. It lives on in small but devoted groups; it manages to publish newspapers and magazines and continues to publish position papers and articles analyzing world events and politics from a Bundist perspective.[25] Its attitude toward Israel is a positive one—it is for a strong and prosperous Israel. But because of its anti-chauvinistic background, a belief-system grounded in internationalism and fairplay and justice for all peoples, it does not allow its positive attitude towards Israel to prevent it from being critical when Israel needs criticism. It is an attitude of which most American Jews, including the Zionist movement here and elsewhere, have finally come to see as wisdom. And the Bund has a devoted following inside Israel itself. They are loyal Bundists. And the Bundist comrades there are just as loyal and devoted to the future of Israel as the most nationalistic right-wing Israeli—but, ah, what a wonderful difference between them.

So the Bund, in spite of everything, has a present, a vastly diminished present, but it lives, nevertheless. But does the Bund have a future? Perhaps not. Not as it did, certainly. But so many of its ideas, so many of its ideals, are still relevant today. Do-i-kayt—being here, now, with our Jewishness, figuring out how to be Jewish here and now, not there—because we are not there. Social Democracy— more relevant than ever—is the only answer, I believe, to the injustice, poverty, and *umentslikhkayt* (inhumanity) of the world—an undogmatic, flexible social democracy that places justice and common sense above doctrine and dogma. Social democracy has saved the democratic industrialized nations of the world from collapse and chaos and has brought a degree of social justice and decency to the working classes of these nations. And, finally, cultural, secular Jewishness that draws on the religious past for its rich moral tradition, folk-history, and folk-celebrations. The Jews of the diaspora cannot sustain a Jewish life by simply facing toward Jerusalem. We are here, they are there. What is to become of us here?

The Bund long struggled with this question, and perhaps modern, acculturated Jewry here and elsewhere in the Diaspora can learn from the Bund.

Over one hundred years ago the Bund launched a new Jewish answer to anti-Semitism, poverty, and the question of how to be Jewish. For over one hundred years, it has struggled, fought, overcome, and written a glorious chapter in the history of the Jewish people. Nothing can take that away. It remains forever. The Hitlerites and the Stalinists crushed it. But the Bund and its approach to Jewish life and to the world live on.

—Marvin S. Zuckerman

Notes

1. "Bulletin of the Bund Archives of the Jewish Labor Movement," *New Series*, no. 7–9 (Winter 1988): 35–37, 1.
2. Bernard K. Johnpoll, *The Politics of Futility: The General Workers Bund of Poland, 1917–1943* (Ithaca, NY: Cornell University Press, 1967), 32: "The discontent flared into open rebellion in 1905 . . . the . . . Bund played a vital role . . . it organized the March anti-Czar demonstration in Warsaw, the strike and open rebellion in Lodz, and the uprising in Bialystok. The general uprising in October was under the leadership of the Social Revolutionaries, the Social Democrats (mainly the Menshevik wing), and the Bund." Hereafter cited as Johnpoll.
3. Johnpoll, 33: ". . . Czarist officials. . . . blamed the Jews for the [1905] uprising, and instigated pogroms throughout the Pale. The Bundists answered these new and bloody onslaughts with armed resistance by newly organized self-defense units."
4. Lucy S. Dawidowicz, *The Golden Tradition: Jewish Life and Thought in Eastern Europe* (New York: Holt, Rinehart and Winston, 1967), 388. Hereafter cited as Dawidowicz. From *Shtern Fartog: Zikhroynes, Dertseylungen*, (Buenos Aires, 1952), 152–62; translated from Yiddish by Lucy Dawidowicz.
5. Marvin Zuckerman, "Biographical Sketch" in *The Three Great Classical Writers of Modern Yiddish Literature, Volume III: I. L.Peretz* by Zuckerman & Herbst (Los Angeles: Pangloss Press, 1996), 43. Translated from Yiddish by Marvin Zuckerman from Mark Schweid, *Treyst Mayn Folk: Dos Lebm fun Y.L.Perets* (New York: Farlag Perets, 1955), 239–40.
6. Bertram D. Wolfe, *Three Who Made a Revolution* (Boston: Beacon Press, 1948), 232. Hereafter cited as Wolfe. Also, p. 233: "The Bundists soon discovered that the Jewish workers were far ahead of the Russian in organization and in consciousness." And, Johnpoll, 30: "At the 1903 congress of the RSDRP . . . any Russian Socialist group, however small it might be, had the right to send a delegate; the Bund, with tens of thousands of members, and many times larger than all the Russian groups combined, was allowed only five." Finally, from Ezra Mendelsohn, *Class Struggle in the Pale* (Cambridge: Cambridge University Press, 1970), 156, from Georgii Plekhanov's report to the 1896 Congress of the Socialist International in London: "From a certain point of view the Jewish workers may be considered the vanguard of the labor army in Russia."
7. Wolfe, 226, 243.
8. Johnpoll, 56: "One of the leaders of the Petrograd Soviet was Henryk Erlich, Polish-born leader of the Bund. He was chosen in June [1917] as emissary of the Soviet to an international Socialist conference in Stockholm."

9. Johnpoll, 63–64.
10. Johnpoll, 65.
11. Johnpoll, 137.
12. Joseph Leftwich, *The Book of Fire* (New York: Thomas Yoseloff, 1959, 47.
13. Samuel A. Portnoy, *Henryk Ehrlich and Victor Alter* (Hoboken and New York: KTAV and the Jewish Labor Bund, 1990), 258.
14. Dawidowicz, 80.
15. Dawidowicz, 80.
16. Dawidowicz, 80.
17. Dawidowicz, 80.
18. Vladka Meed, *On Both Sides of the Wall*, trans. from Yiddish, *Fun Beyde Zaytn Geto Moyer* (1948), (Israel: Ghetto Fighters' House and Hakibbutz Hameuchad, 1973).
19. Goldstein Meed and Marek Edelman, *The Ghetto Fights* (New York: Bund, 1946) and J. S. Hertz, ed., *Zygelboim Bukh* (New York, Undzer Tsayt, 1947).
20. Milton Meltzer, *Never to Forget* (New York: Dell Publishing, 1976), 125–26.
21. Aviva Ravel, *Faithful unto Death: The Story of Arthur Zygielbaum* (Montreal: Workmen's Circle, 1980), 85. Based on J. S. Hertz, ed., *Ziglboym Bukh* (New York: Undzer Tsayt, 1947). Cited hereafter as Ravel.
22. Ravel, 64.
23. Jacob Glatstein et al., *Anthology of Holocaust Literature* (New York: Atheneum, 1976), translated from the Yiddish, 329–31.
24. Johnpoll, 6.
25. *Undzer Tsayt*, 25 East 21st Street, 3rd Floor, New York, NY 10010.

Acknowledgments

I want to thank Pablo Capra and Savannah Daniels for their invaluable help and support in scanning and locating and organizing the illustrations. I could not have done it without them. My deepest thanks also to the archivists at the YIVO Institute for Jewish Research, and especially Vital Zajka, for his help in locating and providing the illustrations in a usable form. Thanks also to Dan Opatoshu for going to bat for me when I needed it. Thanks to J. Hoberman, author of that wonderful book on the Yiddish cinema, *Bridge of Light,* for help with a few of the stills I wanted from the Bund's documentary about their Medem Sanitarium, *Mir Kumen On.* Finally, a great big "thank you" to Leo Melamed: this book would have had a paucity of illustrations if not for his magnanimous generosity.

Most of all, I am extremely grateful to Dr. Jack Jacobs for his invaluable and generous help. He suggested many, many emendations to my typescript, saving me from some grievous errors in several places. Any such errors still existing, large or small, are of course solely my own.

Victor Gilinsky, who wrote an introduction to this book, contributed some editorial suggestions and comments, for which I am also grateful. He was the one who urged me to translate this book. If not for that, I may not have done it.

Bernard Goldstein: A Chronology

- Born 1889 in Shedltze, three hours from Warsaw
- 1905: At the age of 16, arrested at a revolutionary forest meeting of 400; wounded by saber from mounted police
- 1906: Arrested in Kalushin while helping striking fur workers
- 1908: Exiled for organizing painters, ironmongers, and carpenters; escaped exile
- 1911–12: Imprisoned in jail on Danilowiczowska Street.
- 1913: Helped organize the general protest strike against the trial of Mendl Beylis for ritual murder
- 1914: Elected by the Warsaw Bund as one of two delegates to attend the Socialist convention in Vienna in 1914; outbreak of World War I canceled the convention
- 1915: Arrested at a secret meeting of trade union leaders in Warsaw and exiled deep inside Russia; escaped to Kiev; captured and exiled again, this time to Siberia
- 1917: Freed by Revolution; elected to the Ukrainian Soviet; organized a Jewish militia which helped overthrow Hetman Skoropadskyi
- 1919: Returned to Warsaw; elected to the presidium of the Warsaw Bund and to the Executive Committee of the Trade Union Federation
- 1919–1939: Organized the bakers, transport workers, and slaughterers—tough, uncohesive elements, difficult to organize; was in charge of all large political demonstrations, mass meetings, and street demonstrations; was in constant contact with Polish labor leaders and other Poles prominent in public life
- 1920–1921: Organized and led self-defense militias to fight off attacks by fascist Polish anti-Semites and Communist thugs
- 1929: Survived a shooting attack by a band of Communists; shot back and wounded one of the attackers

- 1933–1939: Led militia in fighting off anti-Semitic attacks on Jewish university youth
- 1936: Enlisted help of Jewish underworld in Lodz to fight off attacks by Polish fascist anti-Semites in their attempt to keep Jews away from the polls
- 1939–1945: Played a leading role in the Bundist underground and resistance during the Nazi Holocaust and the Warsaw Ghetto uprising
- 1945: Came to America
- 1946–47: Wrote *Finf Yor in Varshever Geto,* first published by the Bund in New York in 1947, then translated into English as *The Stars Bear Witness*, published by Viking Press in New York in 1949
- 1959: Died in New York
- 1960: His book *Tsvontsik Yor in Varshever Bund (Twenty Years In the Warsaw Bund)* was published in Yiddish in New York by the Bund press, Undzer Tsayt

Figure 3. Bernard Goldstein. From the Archives of the YIVO Institute for Jewish Research, New York.

Translator's Note

Footnotes written by the author, Bernard Goldstein, are marked "—BG"; footnotes provided by Dr. Martyna Rusiniak-Karwat are marked "—MR"; footnotes written by me are marked "—MZ."

Wherever possible, and in almost every case, I followed the YIVO convention for transliterating Yiddish words.

I have once in a while translated rather freely, departing somewhat from Goldstein's literal text. As every translator knows, hewing too closely to the words and phrases of the original will often result in obscurity, unintelligibility, and awkward expression.

I have generally spelled place names and the names of individuals who lived in interwar Poland as they would have been spelled in Polish. However, I have not consistently followed this guideline, especially when a different spelling is already standard in English (e.g., Warsaw), or in specific cases involving Bundists who ultimately moved to the US (such as Sherer and Goldstein) and who Anglicized their names.

In Yiddish, Polish place names and the names of individuals are most often pronounced differently from the way they are pronounced in Polish. Since Yiddish spells these names phonetically, there is no way to tell from the Yiddish original how these names are spelled in Polish. To render them with the proper Polish spelling, I had the great help of Zenon Neumark and Dr. Martyna Rusiniak-Karwat, to whom I want to express my deepest appreciation and thanks (if there are still misspellings, the fault is mine, not theirs). Dr. Rusiniak-Karwat was also able to update the names of streets, where they had changed, and to indicate what other changes had taken place to some of the locations mentioned. These changes are noted in the footnotes.

Introduction

We have now placed in your hands a new book by Bernard Goldstein: his experiences in Warsaw in the fighting ranks of the Bund from 1919–1939.[1]

The various periods in the history of the Bund are represented in the literature in very unequal measure. Most numerous, relatively, are the books about the first two decades of the Bund—about the Bund in Czarist Russia; much smaller is the number of Bundist publications dealing with the years during the Second World War. And least of all has been written about the history of the Bund in independent Poland.

This last period amounts to over twenty years—the time from the First to the Second World War. It is a period during which the Bund surpassed itself in its Socialist struggle and in its national-cultural work. Despite that, even the Bundist publications have not devoted much space to this period.

It is no accident that such an important part of Bundist history—and of modern Jewish history in general—has received such relatively little attention in the world of books. One of the factors that caused this dearth is certainly our great Catastrophe.

The tragic mass murder of Polish Jewry throws a bloody veil over the years leading up to the Holocaust. It is not an easy task to tell now about the long, courageous, and often heroic fight against the antisemitism of the Polish reactionary forces—now, when all the wild antisemitic excesses, boycotts, and pogroms pale next to murderous Hitlerism. A handful of Jewish victims fell in Przytyk, in Mińsk Mazoviecki, and in Brześć nad Bugiem (Brisk or Brest-Litovsk)—what kind of "theme" is that when compared to the mass murders in the Warsaw and other ghettos, and in Treblinka, Auschwitz, Maidanek, Bergen-Belson, Buchenwald, and other death camps.

The Jewish community in Poland went through a unique evolution. It was sharply divided socially, politically, and ideologically. It shimmered with all sorts of political colors: black, blue-white, red. In this community, the Bund had a

Figure 9. Emanuel Sherer (1901-1977). From the private collection of Marvin Zuckerman.

firm, broad, and enduring working-class base which none of its opponents could take from it. On the other hand, it did succeed in broadening its base by attracting many of its opponents' followers to itself. In the last, difficult years leading up to the Catastrophe, a majority of those in the Jewish community who had previously placed their trust in the parties of the Orthodoxy and the Zionists, turned to the Bund—the heretical, anti-Zionist, anticapitalist, anti-Communist, and consistently Socialist Bund. The victories at the ballot box of the Bund for representation to the Kehillahs [community councils], the fortress of traditional Jewishness, and to the city councils of the biggest cities in Poland, including Warsaw—this was a unique phenomenon in the history of the Bund and in the history of the Jewish people. But how does one go about setting down this instructive historical development, after Polish Jewry was so suddenly and brutally and murderously cut down?

"Jews, remember! Jews write it down!"[2]—is a cry that pervades our contemporary, Jewish, post-Holocaust epoch. But this cry must not be interpreted too narrowly; it must not apply exclusively to the Holocaust and to Jewish resistance during the Second World War. The unprecedented Nazi genocide—carried out against over six million Jews, with the Jewish community of Poland in the front ranks of those murdered—will become starker in the eyes of the world, and more painful for future Jewish generations, if Jewish life—and that means to a significant degree the life of the Jewish working class—at the moment of its impassioned rise, is so cruelly and totally cut down. Only in the light of such a broader historical perspective will it become really clear exactly what it was that the Jewish people and future generations of Jews have lost. And only in such a broader historical account can the inner vitality, national-cultural creativity, and developmental talent of the Jewish people in the circumstances of the so-called "Exile" be appreciated to its fullest extent.

It must be noted: No internal Jewish factors put an end to these new developments in Jewish life, but an external, devilish, murdering hand brought it about. The liquidation of Jewish life by an external force did not occur only in our "exile," but the same tragic liquidation would also have occurred in the land of Israel by the invasion of the Jew-killing Hitler horde—a deadly, militarily superior force—had it not been defeated by the mighty (not Jewish) Western armies at El-Alamein.

No matter from which perspective one may consider the matter, there is no objective rationale for covering over or minimizing the liquidated Jewish Diaspora life in Eastern Europe up to the time of its deadly annihilation by our national Catastrophe. And also the over twenty-year period of Bundist activity in independent Poland must not be lost to Jewish social memory.

This book by Comrade Goldstein covers this little-described epoch. By doing just this much, it accomplishes an important task.

This book, with few exceptions, is limited to Warsaw, the city the author lived in during the 20 years he writes about. It is a work of memoir, telling about people, events, battles and encounters worth chronicling that the author had personal, direct experience with.

"Comrade Bernard," as he is still known in Bundist circles, was one of the most engaged activists in the Warsaw Bund. During the Nazi occupation, he was a member of the Central Committee of the underground Bund in the Warsaw Ghetto. In prewar Poland, he was a member of all the leading bodies of the Bund in Warsaw: the Warsaw Committee of the Bund; the Bund Presidium; and the Bund Secretariat. He was a member and activist in the Executive Committee of the organized labor movement of the Jewish workers in Warsaw—the "Central Council," as it was called. He was in the leadership of the Bund sports organization, "Morgenstern." He lived his work passionately in the largest Bund organization in Poland. He was a delegate to all the Bund conventions in Poland. He was active in many of the Bund's political struggles, shows of strength, and demonstrations. Anything that had anything to do with the Bund was (and still is) very, very dear to him.

Nevertheless, Comrade Bernard limits himself in this book only to those things he himself experienced during the years he is writing about. About all the many battles, activities, events, tasks, problems, discussions the Bund and Bundists were undergoing, he says nothing, or very little—only as much as is necessary to clarify his narrative and make it understandable.

For example:

The Bund held seven conventions in Poland in the years Comrade Bernard writes about (1920–1921, 1924, 1929–1930, 1935, and 1937). Every one of them was a milestone in the development of the Bund, and for months on end drew the attention of broad Bundist (and even non-Bundist) circles. Comrade Bernstein writes only about the first two conventions, and only briefly, without going into any detail on the issues dealt with.

During the 20 years that are included in Comrade Bernard's memoirs, there were also seven general conventions of the Jewish trade unions in Poland, represented by their executive leadership from "The National Council of the Jewish Working Class Trade Union Federation." In addition to these, many conventions were held by individual Jewish trade unions, as well as by the entire trade union movement, including non-Jewish Polish unions with which the Bund had close relations. These were important events in the Bundist and general labor movement. In the 1930s, the Jewish trade unions numbered about 100,000 members—one fourth of all the workers who were organized in the general trade union movement in Poland. This was the biggest Jewish mass movement in Poland, and it was under the leadership of the Bund. Comrade Bernard tells in this book about the alliance of the Jewish trade unions with the non-Jewish Polish trade unions. He describes interestingly and in great detail the specifics, the activities, and the problems of several of the unions with which he had particularly close ties. He also relates, when necessary for clarity, about other unions. But the life of the whole Jewish trade union movement and its many problems, battles, and conferences, is not discussed in this book.

The Polish Bund possessed a large youth movement with an intense program, many public performances, and with specific tasks, problems, and discussions. It was the strongest youth movement in the Polish-Jewish world, and relatively one of the biggest in the general Socialist Youth Internationale, of which it was a member.

The Bund built a network of Yiddish-secular day schools, children's homes, and evening schools. The Polish government did not support these institutions: quite the opposite, it persecuted and impeded their development. Battling for the rights of the children, caring for their material well-being, their educational attainment, struggling for Yiddish and Yiddish secular culture—these were the tasks of the Bund. They required, day to day, a great deal of effort, energy, and work. In addition, there was the political enlightenment and cultural activity systematically conducted every week among thousands of Jewish workers. Again, an undertaking with many unique tasks, problems, and difficulties.

There were many other branches and areas of Bundist activity. They were all permeated with the same worldview and ideology. In general, ideological questions occupied a large place in the life of the Bund and the Bundists. Bundists often fevered about contemporary world problems, as well as questions of general, Socialist, and Jewish politics.

All these various other important aspects of the Bundist movement are only touched on lightly in this book, and some are not even mentioned.

But this is not a fault in the book; it is a virtue. Comrade Bernard did not set himself the task of describing all the events and activities of the Warsaw Bund with which he was involved. He wanted to describe, and describe in detail, only a part of Bundist life and struggle, only those tasks he himself carried out, only those events and labor struggles in which his role was decisive and with which no one was as well acquainted as he. The positive result of such an approach is that his descriptions are interesting, accurate, and show an intimate knowledge of the specifics. Instead of touching on many subjects and saying little about each, he deals with fewer subjects—no less important—and tells us a lot about them. The reader, therefore, acquires a clear picture about important parts of Bundist life and struggle in Warsaw before the Second World War.

A great many of the organizations and individual types described in this book were located at the fringes of Warsaw's Jewish working masses and the Jewish Labor Movement. Some of the Jewish trade unions, so interestingly and vividly described in this book, were distinctly different, and it was an achievement to bring these workers into the labor movement, and thus lift them to a higher social and cultural level.

Before they came to the Bund, some of these fringe organizations and types often found themselves between two worlds: on the one hand, that of the underworld; and on the other, the world of the "overworld," the world of Socialist idealism, of the struggle for higher ends, the world to which they were being uplifted. It wasn't easy to lead the average Jewish worker to the level of a fighter, revolutionary, and idealist. How much harder was it to do so with the people "on the fringe"? And how much longer was the path to their getting there? The chapters in this book that describe the obstacles on that path and the psychological difficulties occurring even after overcoming them ought to be interesting, not only for historians, but also for social psychologists.

Many of these "fringe" types, their ways and their milieu—the various kinds of porter trades, slaughterhouse workers, bakers, and others—are little known to the general reader. Through the descriptions of Comrade Bernard, important elements of Jewish folklore and ways of life have been recorded and rescued from obscurity.

A large and very important part of Comrade Bernard's book is devoted to the Bundist "zelbst-shuts," or self-defense militia.

The self-defense militias—active resistance against pogroms and other physical attacks on Jewish individuals and on the Jewish people—were an important aspect of the revolution the Bund brought into Jewish life. The self-defense militias fighting off the Czarist *pogromchiks* have long had a place in the glorious pages of the history of the Bund and the Jewish people.

In independent Poland the warding off of antisemitic attacks remained an important national task of the Bundist self-defense militia. But it was not its only task. The battle line of self-defense was broadened. Added to it was the task of protection and defense against the anti-Bundist terrorism of the Communists.

Later still a third self-defense task presented itself—that against the "proletarian" fascists who supported and received the support of the ruling Pilsudski regime and wanted to disrupt, also with physical terror, the Socialist labor movement, including our Jewish one. And at times we had to defend ourselves also against attacks from certain religious-orthodox segments of the Jewish people who didn't want to tolerate our secular Jewishness, and physically attacked—in certain instances—the various manifestations of Bundist, Jewish-secular, cultural activity.

Not always did all these various self-defense tasks present themselves to our movement at the same time or with the same sharp urgency. Some of them fell away in later years from our daily agenda: the Communists in Poland halted (around the mid-1930s) their physical attacks on the Socialist and labor movement, and later Stalin disbanded and liquidated the whole Communist movement in Poland. From the other direction, in the internal Jewish world, many of the orthodox got used to the existence and spread of Jewish secularism, and many realized the positive role the Bund played in the battle for the security and defense of Jewish life. But one of the tasks of self-defense became, with time—and continued in this way up to the end—more exigent, more pressing: self-defense against and resistance to the Polish antisemites and their antisemitism.

We are today [1960] far, far from that time. True, by the calendar, it is "only" 20 or 25 years. But according to our experience and our tragedy, it is more than a hundred. We ourselves do not fully credit the significance and importance in the most difficult circumstances of the Bundist self-defense and resistance to the attacks of the antisemitic hooligans. Comrade Bernard documents—for the first time for the general public—much important information and many of the events in this struggle that the Bund in Poland then conducted for the rights and the security of the Jews. It was the last basic training school for that which happened later.

Comrade Bernard describes interestingly and in some detail the organization of the self-defense groups, that is, the Bundist party militias in Warsaw. Such groups also existed in many other big and small cities throughout Poland. In many cases they consisted of thousands of comrades. But no matter how large they were in number, or how well organized, or how well disciplined for battle, it was only the *passion* for self-defense, the "soul that seethed" and that summoned and suffused the whole Bundist movement in all its various activities—it was that fervor that made it possible for the Bund to accomplish its various tasks, and in particular, those described in Comrade Bernard's book.

This book bears witness to that passion. In this too resides its value. Being a firsthand account about various cross-sections of Bundist life in Warsaw, it reveals in a much clearer way than is or can normally be known, the atmosphere of battle and exaltation that the Bund brought into Jewish life.

After *Finf Yor in Varshever Geto* [*Five Years in the Warsaw Ghetto*, translated into English as *The Stars Bear Witness*], this is the publication of Comrade

Bernard's second book. Naturally, it is quite different from the first one. . . . But there is a connection between them.

Memoirs are not history. But they can be an important source and material for history. We hope that this is and will remain the value of Comrade Bernard's memoir.

—Emanuel Sherer, PhD
General Secretary, Jewish Labor Bund
New York, 1960

Notes

1. Goldstein's first book was *Finf Yor in Varshever Geto* (New York: Farlag Unser Tsait, 1947); translated as *The Stars Bear Witness* (New York: Viking Press, 1949).—MZ
2. Reported to be the last words of Simon Dubnow, Jewish historian, before being shot to death by Nazi assassins.—MZ

CHAPTER 1

I Go Home

Kiev, Ukraine, 1918: The Ukrainian labor parties readied themselves for an armed uprising against the pro-German Skoropadskyi regime.[1]

Each of the labor parties created its own armed battle unit. We of the Bund assembled an armed unit of several hundred comrades. I was put in command, becoming a member of the Executive Committee (*Ispolkom*[2]) of the uprising.

The Bundist armed unit fought in the center of the city, occupying the quarter between the following streets: Kreshtchatik, Male Vasilkovske, and Fundekleyevske.

The success of the uprising brought the Ukrainian nationalist Vasylyovych Petliura[3] to power, and, officially, the various political parties disbanded their armed party detachments. But in fact, every party—including the Bund—kept an organized core of its battle unit intact, just in case, as well as its store of arms.

The joyous mood of the Socialist parties after the uprising didn't last long. The Petliura government lost no time in turning away from the labor parties that had helped bring it to power.

A telling incident: When Rosa Luxemburg and Karl Liebknecht were murdered in Germany, the Bund committee organized an open meeting to mourn and honor their memories. The Petliura administration forbade the gathering. I went to the offices of the administration to intervene, and to my great surprise met there with an official who had sat with me on *Ispolkom* just a short time ago. He ultimately withdrew the ban, but it left me with a very unpleasant feeling. Not very long ago we had fought side-by-side for the same goal; now we each of us stood opposed to the other.

The internal situation within the Bund itself also embittered our mood. The Bolsheviks were marching on Ukraine and approaching Kiev. The closer they came, the more our comrades appeared to give themselves over to the pro-

Bolshevik view. But this was no longer simply a change of opinion, something we in the Bund were long accustomed to. This shift was something altogether new, and it was the chief cause of our bitterness. The Bundist comrade who became pro-Bolshevik did not simply change his opinion. He suddenly became unrecognizable, an altogether different person. In the factional fight, betrayal, trickery, and disloyalty became his weapons. Painfully we witnessed how the Bund spirit of comradeship, the feeling of belonging to one family, began to dissipate. In its place came distrust and suspicion.

In this situation and in this depressed mood, I attended a party meeting and listened to a report by Comrade Emanuel Nowogrodzki[4], on a short visit from Warsaw. He talked about the revived Bundist movement in the new, independent Poland, and specifically, in Warsaw. He spoke about how the trade unions, now operating legally, had, as if overnight, branched out and grown. He told about the leading role the Bund played in these trade unions, about the Warsaw Labor Council and the important part the Bund played in that, and about the Bund's many-branched cultural activities, centering around our Grosser Club.[5] In passing, he spoke of comrades, the mere mention of whose names brought them vividly to mind for me. These were people with whom I was bound by many unforgettable moments of illegal activity during Czarist times.

Figure 10. Emanuel Nowogrodzki (1947–1961). From the Archives of the YIVO Institute for Jewish Research, New York.

The picture that Comrade Emanuel painted captivated me. I imagined it all. I suddenly felt that the place Emanuel was describing was, after all, my home, and I was filled with a longing to return.

After the meeting, my mood, this sudden homesickness, grew even stronger. The report of a revived Bund in Poland sounded to me—here, in Kiev—like an idyll. The more I thought about it, the stronger my inner voice grew: Go home—now! Work in your own hometown Bund! Go where you will be battling with enemies of the working class, not with those who were your comrades only yesterday!

I decided to return to Warsaw. I went to the Kiev Bund offices to give my notice, submitting a report to the committee, and turning over all the bookkeeping items and party materials I had accumulated. I started preparing for the journey. My wife, Lucia, had just recovered from an illness. A very severe influenza epidemic was raging, and Lucia had contracted the disease. She had just started recovering, when we decided to go back home to Warsaw. Travel on the trains at that time was terribly risky for her. She was too weak to attempt such a difficult journey. We began to look for some other, more comfortable way for her to travel the distance, and suddenly, just such an opportunity presented itself.

Felye Kasel—the wife of the Yiddish writer, Dovid Kasel—and her sister, Pola, were living in Kiev at the time. They both worked for a large German company with a branch in Kiev. The company was leaving Kiev and arranging comfortable railroad cars for its staff. These two sisters were Lucia's close relatives. After much effort they obtained permission for her to travel on this special train with them, so she was able to travel home quite comfortably. I remained in Kiev for a few more weeks, until I was able, as a Polish citizen, to obtain legal travel papers. I then started packing for the trip.

Actually, there was nothing to pack. I was dressed in an old military uniform, a long alpaca, and a pair of boots. Aside from those, I had only some underwear. I also took along a teakettle, a little sugar and tea, a spoon (just in case there was an opportunity to eat something hot), and a piece of soap. That was it. It was not a very heavy load. I did, however, end up carrying quite a heavy load, and one that was not even mine.

Right before my departure, Shuel Kahan, a brother of our comrade Virgili Kahan[6]—a one-time "United,"[7] now a Bundist—approached me and requested that, since he had heard I was traveling to Warsaw, and since his family members, who were in Lodz, were also traveling back home to Warsaw, would I please help them out with some luggage? I agreed. These people—I forget their names, Silverberg or Silvermintz—had two very heavy valises. I helped by carrying one of their valises as my own luggage. We couldn't all fit into one railroad car, so I went off by myself with my small bundle and their heavy valise. They sat separately in another compartment.

The journey was difficult. Trains were few and far between and ran irregularly. The individual train cars were also few, unheated, broken down, and packed full of people. Entire families with all their belongings were traveling in all directions, running from city to city, seeking some out-of-the-way, secure spot to settle. When the steam locomotives ran out of fuel, as happened often, the trains would stop in the middle of nowhere. The stokers would run over to a nearby forest, chop some wood, feed the locomotive, and then proceed a bit farther. Trains would often have to stand waiting for a long time. If the passengers were lucky, another train would come they could transfer to and continue their journey. We dragged on in this way from Kiev to Warsaw for ten days. In normal times such a journey would have taken around 24 hours.

The family whose valise I was carrying took very good care of me the whole time. They would often come into my railroad car to see how I was doing, bringing me a piece of bread and some tea. After a time, this attentiveness seemed somehow excessive. When we arrived at Otwock, near Warsaw, I had to leave the train for a moment. The train started to move, and I was unable to jump back on in time. Seeing this, the family became frantic. I shouted at them to wait at the next station, and I would join them with the next train (trains were running frequently from Otwock to Warsaw). I did in fact catch the next train, and there they were, waiting for me at the next station. They thanked me profusely for my help and asked me to please accompany them to the hotel.

We got into a droshky[8] and were on our way.

I was greatly astonished to see they were going to the Hotel Bristol, the most elegant hotel in Warsaw. They checked into a suite of rooms. I went with them. They opened the valises, and I grew dizzy at the sight. The valise they had asked me to carry for them had a false bottom, in which lay gold and jewelry and other expensive luxury items. They offered me several hundred marks for my trouble. I answered that if I were willing to be paid, my due would be half the value of the items I carried, but that I wanted nothing from them. I left their hotel room without a goodbye.

For a long time afterward I could not forgive myself for taking such a dangerous mission so lightly. The inspectors on the trains were then very strict, especially with evacuees from Russia. Had they caught me smuggling such a valise, I would have been in a great deal of trouble.

Notes

1. Skoropadskyi (1873–1945), aristocrat, decorated Russian and Ukrainian general; in 1918 led a coup d'etat, sanctioned by the occupying German army, against the Ukrainian People's Republic, becoming the reactionary, autocratic leader of the Ukraine.—MZ
2. Russian abbreviation for *Ispolnitelniy Komitet*, "Executive Committee," the lead organization consisting of representatives of all the Ukranian labor parties, as well as the illegal, military party cadres.—MZ
3. Vasylyovych Petliura (1879–1926), publicist, writer, journalist, Ukrainian politician, statesman of the Ukrainian People's Republic, and national leader who led Ukraine's

struggle for independence (1918–1921) following the Russian Revolution of 1917. On May 25, 1926, Petliura was slain with five shots from a handgun in broad daylight in the center of Paris by the Jewish-Russian anarchist, Sholem Schwartzbard, to avenge Ukranian pogroms against the Jews.—MZ

4. Emanuel Nowogrodzki (1891–1967): General Secretary of the Polish Bund's Central Committee. In America by chance in 1939 when the war broke out. Founded the Bund Representation and the Bund Coordinating Committee in America. Editor and writer for the Bund's monthly in New York, *Undzer Tsayt*. Author of *The Ghetto Speaks* (Warsaw, 1936?); *Individual, Rank and File, and Leader* (Warsaw, 1934); *Henryk Erlich and Victor Alter* (1951); and *The Jewish Labor Bund in Poland 1915–1939* (2001), later translated into Polish as *Żydowska Partia Robotnica Bund w Polsce 1915–1939* (2005).—MZ

5. Named after Bronislaw Grosser (1883–1912), a Bundist writer and theorist on Jewish nationalism. A lawyer by profession, he was recognized as one of the party's most articulate defenders of Jewish national-cultural autonomy. Defining himself as a Polish-Jewish Socialist whose task it was to defend the interests of the Jewish workers in Poland, he became a Bundist legend, with several cultural, educational, and health institutions established in his name in interwar Poland, including the Bund's renowned Bronislaw Grosser Library in Warsaw.—MZ

6. Borukh Mordkhe Kahan (Virgili), 1883–1936; beloved Bundist activist and labor leader; also active in organizing and supporting the Yiddish secular school movement; 20,000 Jewish workers attended his funeral in Vilnius.—MZ

7. United: A member of the *Fareynikte Yidishe Sotsyalistishe Arbeter Partey* (United Jewish Socialist Workers Party), a unification (*fareynikung*) in 1917 of the Zionist Socialist Workers Party and the Jewish Socialist Workers Party. The Uniteds, like the Bund, believed in fighting for civil rights and cultural autonomy in Poland and the Ukraine, but also, unlike the Bund, in seeking to create a Jewish state in any available territory (not necessarily in Palestine).—MZ

8. *Droshky*: a low, four-wheeled, horse-drawn, open, passenger carriage.—MZ

CHAPTER 2

Back in Warsaw

Upset, I left the hotel and started walking. With my small bundle in my hand, I walked in the direction of Nowolipie 7, the editorial offices of *Lebns-Fragn*, the Bund's daily newspaper. As I walked, I looked around at the streets of Warsaw. They made an awful impression. Warsaw was somehow darker, greyer, the streets neglected, the houses shabby, gloomy. I had not seen her since the prewar years. The city appeared to be terribly neglected.

Now I found myself at the end of Długa Street. I trembled. At this spot was the jail, the so-called "Arsenal." Over four years ago they had led me out of there in chains, when I, together with Yankl Levine and several hundred other political prisoners, were exiled deep into Russia. On this street my wife, Lucia, had waited for me, along with Comrade Mania Majerowicz (now Mania Mayer, in New York), Czilba Krisztal (now in Melbourne, Australia), and others. Here is where we left Medem[1] behind, sick and in the hospital. Now I pass that same "Arsenal," free, unshackled, and without fear. It is different now, Warsaw.

I turned down the little way from the crossing and was already at Nowolipie 7, at the *Lebns-Fragn* building. I went up to the fifth floor, entering the editorial offices. The first one I saw there was Victor Shulman,[2] Secretary of the editorial board. We embraced warmly. We knew each other well from our party work in Warsaw as far back as 1907. The first thing the good-natured Shulman asked me—as he waved his finger in my face—was, how did I know before anyone else about Nokhem? When I was imprisoned in the Arsenal, I had sent out a note to the party that I suspected Nokhem of being a provocateur. Later, after the Russian revolution, when the archives of the Czarist Okhrana were opened, it turned out he was indeed in the service of the Russian police.

Bejnisz Michalewicz[3] smiled when he caught sight of me. He reminded me that he arrived in Warsaw in 1912 in rather shabby attire, and that I then

Figure 11. H. Leivik (Leivik Halpern, 1888–1962), prominent Yiddish poet/playwright, Bundist, in chains, sentenced in 1906 to 4 years' hard labor in Siberia, died in America, 1962. From the Archives of the YIVO Institute for Jewish Research, New York.

"polished him up," accompanying him to buy some new clothes. I exchanged greetings with Medem. The last time we saw each other was in jail, in that very "Arsenal" I had just passed on my way here. Now we met in freedom. Comrade Noyekh[4] approached me with a warm greeting. This was no small thing for me. Up to the time of my arrest, he was angry with me for greeting him on the streets of Warsaw. For a long time he could not forgive me such a breach of conspiratorial principles. He now forgave me that sin and shook my hand warmly.

I felt drawn to the broader mass of Bundists. I exited the editorial offices and sprinted over to Nowolipki Street to Lucia's mother, where she was staying. I greeted them, left my package there, and went off to Karmelicka 29, to the Bund's Grosser Club.

I felt as if I had fallen into a beehive. It was already nightfall, and the Club was full of people. They were all around, in every corner. There were meetings in

Figure 12. Noyekh (sometimes also known as Jozef), Yekusiel Portnoy (1872–1941). From the Archives of the YIVO Institute for Jewish Research, New York.

all the rooms: a choir was practicing, the reading room was packed—you could hardly push your way through the corridors. I recognized old comrades from our former illegal work together, and I also saw new, young, unfamiliar faces. Despite my wearing an old military uniform, and despite my face having changed quite a bit, I was immediately recognized. They started embracing and kissing me. Running up to greet me were Janek Jankliewicz, Mordkhe Feigman, Yoysef Lifszytz (Bosakmakher), Berl Ambaras (Berl Szteper), Menachem Rosenboym, Elje Sztrigler, and many, many others. Our joy was simply indescribable, especially that of my own. It was for just this warmth and intimacy that I had journeyed all the way from faraway Kiev, and I had not deceived myself.

A few days later, Janek Jankliewicz, Secretary of the Bund's Central Trade Union Council, had a talk with me. He suggested I start working for the Council, concentrating my efforts especially in the weaker unions, such as the Food Workers Union, and the Bookbinders and Paper-Workers Union. I agreed and went immediately to work for the Central Council.

One of my first tasks was to help the strike of the staff of the Jewish Kehilla (Community) and of the teachers in their schools. The Kehilla staff and the teachers had long had a union, but they were typical white-collar workers ("*manjet*-proletarians," as we called them, "cuff-proletarians"), and when it came to strikes, they were quite at a loss. To the Executive Board of their union belonged, among others, old, experienced Bundists, such as Comrade Jakub Klepfisz (father of Mikhl Klepfisz, the young hero of the Warsaw Ghetto Uprising) and Dovid Nojsztat (later a Director of the "Joint"[5] in Poland). While leading the strike I was arrested for the first time in independent Poland, but imprisoned for only a couple of days. After a short time, the strike was won.

Next came the attempt to win back the Jewish women workers in the Poliakewicz cigarette factory who had been under the Bund's influence. Before the war, when organizing was illegal, the Bund had had a great influence among the several hundred women workers in the Poliakewicz factory on Bonifraterska Street. During the war, the factory did not operate. After the war the party appointed Janek Jankliewicz, and later me, to reorganize a strong Bundist group in the factory. We had to wage a fierce struggle with the Communists at this time, but not for long: when the Polish government monopolized the tobacco industry, it also took over Poliakewicz's factory, and one of its first "accomplishments" was to fire all the Jewish workers. Now a totally different struggle at the factory began: to retain the Jewish workers' jobs, and if that didn't succeed, to at least win severance pay for the workers who were fired.

A few weeks after that I was co-opted to be a member of the Warsaw Committee of the Bund. I was asked to lead the Bund's work in Praga,[6] and also to perform a parallel function, to lead trade union organizing there. I thus acquired oversight over both the party work and the trade union work in that great Warsaw suburb.

Notes

1. Vladimir Medem (1879–1923), the main theorist of the Bund and its most famous and celebrated leader, revered and beloved.—MZ
2. Shulman, Victor (1876–1951): Noted journalist, leading figure of the Bund, joining in his early youth. Exiled to Siberia; escaped. From 1915, resided in Warsaw where he was managing editor of the *Folkstsaytung*. During Nazi invasion, escaped to Lithuania and, in 1940, among a handful of political refugees permitted to enter the United States.—MZ
3. Michalewicz, Bejnisz (1876–1928): One of the most important Bund theoreticians in the 1920s. Forty thousand Jewish workers marched in his funeral profession. Three hundred and thirty-nine wreaths were laid at his bier on behalf of various labor and social-democratic delegations, both foreign and domestic. The national idea of the Bund, he wrote, was that every nation does not necessarily need a separate state and that every state does not necessarily need to be inhabited by one nation. A state of nations was the way of the Bund—a large, open state, accommodating diverse nationalities.—MZ

4. Noyekh (sometimes also known as Jozef), Yekusiel Portnoy (1872–1941), leader of the Bund in Poland, a charismatic paternal figure with enormous moral authority. —MZ
5. Joint Distribution Committee—a worldwide Jewish relief organization.—MZ
6. A large suburb on the other side of the Vistula River from Warsaw proper.—MZ

CHAPTER 3

Praga

Praga was the largest Warsaw suburb. Although it was separated from Warsaw by only the Vistula—with the Kierbedzia Bridge connecting them—it was an entirely different world.

Life in Praga was provincial, less fast-paced. The streets were broader, interrupted here and there with large empty fields, overgrown with grass. There were many narrow streets with little wooden houses. Here and there around the edges of Praga were small peasant yards in which chickens paraded and hogs fed. There were also built-up city streets, with tall brick buildings, as in Warsaw proper. Praga was a mixture of big city, small town, and village.

Praga was poor; no wealthy people lived there. It was also an important industrial center, with a large working class population and a great many large factories.

Praga contained two important economic activities: transport and slaughter. It had two large train stations, where hundreds of porters and teamsters (drivers of horse-drawn wagons) worked, and among them, many Jews.

During the First World War, the German occupiers established the Central Administration of Provisions in Praga for all of Warsaw and its surrounding area. (A better title for this Administration would have been: Administration for Starving the Population.) Several hundred workers labored at this Administration of Provisions facility, a sizeable number of them Jews. This administrative office continued to exist for many years, even in post-World War I, independent Poland.

The central slaughterhouse was also situated in Praga. The Czarist Russians had begun building this slaughterhouse before the war; the Germans finished it during the occupation. It was a very modern installation. All the previous slaughterhouses (on Powązki, Ochota, Sielce, and Wola) were demolished, and the entire meat-mart was now concentrated around this newly completed Praga slaughterhouse.

The markets for cattle and hogs were situated around the slaughterhouse. Special train tracks connected these markets with the Praga train station. Over a thousand people worked in and around the slaughterhouse, among them around 600–700 Jewish meat workers. These were a separate caste. Entire families had been doing this work for generations.

When I took over the Bundist work in Praga, there was already quite a large group of Bundists there. They had their club on Brzeska 17, with a library and a reading room. Among the active Bundists there, these stood out: Mendl Goldman, nicknamed "Mendl Prager"—active since Czarist times—by trade a quilter; Dovid Lichtenstein, also active before the war (for a time a Board member of the "Literary Society"), by trade a tanner; his wife, Zlatke, who had a stand selling fancy goods in the Praga marketplace—she was called "Zlatke the Cossack"—a sobriquet well deserved, as she displayed enormous energy and initiative, very useful to the Bund later, when she became a passionate Bund activist.

Also active in the Praga Bund were: Tsvi Etkes (from a rich merchant family, now living in Israel); Henyek Szwalbe, a student who later became a doctor; Y. Szafran, a student (later left for Belgium, studying there to become an engineer, very active in the Bundist organization in Brussels, now an active Bundist in Chicago,); Comrade Sarah (who later became the wife of Y. Szafran (she died in Chicago in 1954); the two Laska sisters, who worked in the Bund library (one of them is now the wife of Comrade H. Gestel in Buenos Aires); Shmuel Richter, worked for a business firm, today in Australia; Comrade Blumshteyn, a librarian (now in Paris); and many others.

Figure 13. The Presidium of the Gala Assembly at Opening of the Bund Reading Room, 1930. From the Archives of the YIVO Institute for Jewish Research, New York.

Figure 14. Recruitng poster for the Youth-Bund Tsukunft, 1930. The Yiddish reads: "Into the 'Tsukunft.'" From the Archives of the YIVO Institute for Jewish Research, New York.

There was also a quite lively *Tsukunft* group in Praga then. This was the Bundist youth organization (the full name for the *Tsukunft* group—was *Yugnt-Bund Tsukunft in Poyln:* Youth-Bund Future in Poland). Among the most active young people in the *Tsukunft* group, one stood out: a student, a youngster of about 15–16 years of age, who distinguished himself with his eloquent rhetorical temperament. This youth was Comrade Y. Falk (today in Montreal, Canada). At that time he was already speaking at general meetings. Also active in the *Tsukunft* group were the aforementioned H. Y. Szafran and his wife-to-be.

After we had laid the foundation for our political and party work in Praga, I turned my attention to my second function, organizing the unions. In this arena there was nothing solid to lean on. No prior union organizations had existed in Praga. As a first step, we created a special union Secretariat, consisting of Comrades Shmuel Richter, Kalman Richter, Mendl Prager, and several others.

Conflicts arose almost immediately with the Warsaw unions. The Warsaw unions, especially the large Garment Workers Union, demanded that in Praga there should be an office only for collecting dues, and that all other union activities should be conducted by the union in Warsaw. The Praga comrades, on the other hand, demanded autonomy so that they might conduct the work of the union independently and control the factories located in Praga. In the end, the autonomists won. The Warsaw unions consented to allow the Praga unions to exist as affiliates that would not merely collect dues, but also deal with union issues, such as local strikes, putting forward specific demands to Praga factory owners, etc. In broader actions, however, such as trade-wide strikes or general demands of all factory owners, the Praga affiliated unions would have to submit to the Warsaw office. In other words, every decision made in Warsaw regarding a general action would also have to apply to Praga.

After a short time, such affiliated unions were formed in Praga of garment workers, leather workers, bakers, and later also of transport workers (porters and teamsters). In the course of forming these local unions, I encountered various problems and difficulties.

The first problem came in organizing the Food Workers Union. The problem centered around the Jewish workers who worked in the Central Provisions Administration Office, by then, under the governance of the Warsaw City Council. There were about 200 Jewish workers, mostly former tailors, shoemakers, tanners, carpenters, and others, who couldn't find work in their trade during the war, and so took on this unskilled labor (portering and horse-drawn wagon driving) in order to earn a living.

When we started to organize the local union we encountered workers who were knowledgeable, aware, and who joined the union immediately, even becoming active in it. Others, however, didn't want to hear about a union. It was difficult to even find a common language with them. Their obstinacy soon softened, however, an indirect result of the antisemitic politics of the Warsaw City Council.

When the City Council officially took over the Central Administration of Provisions Office, it immediately began to dismiss the Jewish workers. This was done, not openly, but with the excuse that the Provisions Office was gradually

Figure 15. Executive Committee of the Bundist Garment Workers Union, Warsaw, 1917. Seated, far right, Benyomin Taytlboym, Yiddish novelist (pen name: Demblin). Seated second from right, translator's father, Rubin Zuckerman.

being liquidated. But every insider knew what the truth was. When this became clear to everyone, all the Jewish workers joined the union, which then immediately began fighting against the dismissal of only Jewish workers.

An important part of this fight was winning the support of the Polish workers. In this we received real help from several activists, from both the PPS (*Polska Partia Socjalistyczna*—Polish Socialist Party) and the SDKPiL—by then already Communist—who were active among the workers of the Provisions Office.[1]

Most prominent in this effort was Stanisław Leszczyński. He was the representative of the workers of the Provisions Office to the City Council. Many others supported us in this work: Jan Rutkiewicz, a worker at the Provisions Office, later a representative of the Warsaw Fund for the Sick. My acquaintance with him stretched all the way back to Czarist times when, in 1911–1912, we were both imprisoned in the jail on Daniłowiczowska Street. Another was Cechnowski, the leader of the Praga division of the earlier SDKPiL, with responsibility for their party's work among the workers in the Provisions Office. I also knew him from an earlier time. When the First World War broke out and soup kitchens for the workers were being organized in Warsaw, I met him at the joint Labor Committee that the Polish Socialists and the Bund then created for the purpose of distributing material help among the workers and coordinating agitation against the war.

All of this work helped to weaken the tempo of eliminating Jewish workers. Reductions could not be carried out without coming to some mutual understanding with the union and the workers. When the officers of the Provisions Office posted a list to reduce the labor force, and the union representatives saw that it consisted almost entirely of Jews, they protested and demanded that the list be changed. Having the moral support of the representatives of the Poles, we were better able to wage an open, successful battle against the reduction in force of the Jewish workers.

At the same time, we started organizing local unions for the garment workers, leather workers, bakers, as well as a union for unskilled workers. For every trade a special commission was formed, and then a Central Secretariat was created, covering the entire organizational effort for all the various local unions.

Things got lively in the Praga Bund. Every evening the Bund club—it was also the center of our organizing effort—was full of people. Meetings of the trade-union commissions, meetings of the Secretariat, conferences with the workers of individual factories, and conferences of delegates from several different factories were constantly going on. Party and cultural work also took place at the club. People came to exchange books in the library. The reading room was full. There were often readings, lectures, and discussion evenings. It was like an anthill, seething with life.

We also expanded our Bund work to the outskirts of the great Praga suburb. Connections were made with Grochów, Pelcowizna, and Szumolewizna. In Szumolewizna we organized the workers in the *pasharnyes* (farms where chickens were raised and sent to Warsaw).

The largest of these pasharnyes belonged to a certain Jew named Gotthelf, who supplied half of Warsaw with his chickens. Gotthelf employed about 40 workers, Jews, and Poles alike. The Poles also belonged to our union. The workers were divided according to various "specialties": those who fed the chickens, the guards, and the clean-up men, and the teamsters who distributed the chickens to the wholesalers in Warsaw. It did not take long for a strike to develop at Gotthelf's place. When Gotthelf refused to yield to the demands for a wage hike and better working conditions, we turned to the transport workers in Janusza's yard, a famous marketplace at the ends of Krochmalna and Gnojna, the center of the chicken market and the chicken slaughterhouse. We asked them to prevent the unloading of the chickens by the strikebreakers. The transport workers of Janusza's yard did just that and helped us win the strike.

Note

1. SDKPiL: *Socialdemokracja Krolestwa Polskiego i Litwy* (Social Democracy of the Kingdom of Poland and Lithuania), a Marxist political party founded in 1893. In 1918 it merged with the PPS-Left to form the Polish Communist Workers Party. Its most famous member: Rosa Luxemburg (1871–1919).—MZ

CHAPTER 4

The Seven Lions

Organizing the transport workers in Praga was somewhat harder. But help came from an unexpected source.

Not all the members of the Bund Club on Brzeska were members of the Bund. Some came into the Club to use the library, listen to the readings or lectures, attend a cultural affair, and so on. Among them was one called "Zelig the Carpenter." A comrade pointed him out to me and said he was one of the famous seven brothers called "The Seven Lions" before whom all of Praga trembled. All of them were teamsters, except for Zelig. He was a carpenter. Since I was seeking to connect with the transport workers, I was glad to make the acquaintance of Zelig, and through him connect with his teamster brothers. And that is, in fact, how I became acquainted with this "dynasty" of Praga teamsters.

The family had lived in Praga for generations. I don't remember the family name, but I think hardly anyone ever really knew it. They had been teamsters for generations, and for generations had always been referred to as "The Lions." It was said that before they settled in Praga they had lived somewhere in the Miłosna Woods. Miłosna, a village not far from Warsaw,[1] was in my time well known for its great forest (we often used to have day outings from Warsaw to these woods). In previous times the whole area was wooded and full of thieves who used to fall upon the merchants on the roads passing through the forest. There, in these woods, among peasants and thieves, this family lived. How they occupied themselves is not clear. It was said that they had some connections with the thieves. The family was known in Praga for its giants, its Samsons. Especially famous was one of the grandfathers whom the peasants called "Yankl Lev" (Yankl the Lion). Everyone in the neighborhood trembled before him. It was from him, in fact, that the appellation "Lion" stemmed, a title that stuck with the family from generation to generation.

As already mentioned, one of these "Seven Lions," our sympathizer, Zelig, broke out of the family tradition, and chose for himself a more refined craft—carpentry. He began to interest himself in culture, and started coming to our readings. Because of this, his brothers bestowed upon him nicknames, such as, "the intellectual" and "chump wearing a cap." They made fun of him, saying that he lived on "milk and toast."

The eldest of the seven brothers was Yankl. He was also called "Yankl Szczerba" because he had a deep scar on his face (*szczerba*: Polish for "notch" or "gap"). He probably acquired it in a fight. In his honor people also called all the brothers "Szczerbowie," in addition to their more popular name, "The Lions." One of the other brothers was called Avrom; his nickname was "the brain." And still another brother was called Noyekh. I don't remember the names of the rest of the brothers.

I asked Comrade Zelig, since we were seeking to connect with the transport workers in order to organize them, could he please acquaint me with his brothers, or at least one or two of them? He introduced me to the eldest of his brothers, Yankl "Szczerba." Yankl Szczerba liked me immediately, probably because his youngest brother was connected to our party, and because, even though they made fun of their brother, "the intellectual," in reality, they were proud of him. If his respectable brother had a good opinion of me, then he, Yankl Szczerba, could also trust me. Through Yankl we acquired much easier access to the Praga transport workers.

Yankl Szczerba, because of my friendship with his brother, invited me to a family celebration in his house. His brother Noyekh was getting married. He was marrying into the Shvalbs (swallows).

The Shvalbs were a well-known family of Praga thieves. This family had been in the trade for years. They were called Shvalbs because in their trade they were as quick and light as swallows. So the family of the "Lions" became joined with the family of the "Swallows," and I too was invited to the wedding celebration. I gladly accepted the invitation. First, because I was interested to see what such a wedding celebration was like. And second, because I understood that I would be able to make contact there with many of the teamsters. That would greatly help me in my efforts to organize the transport workers union in Praga.

It is worthwhile to describe this wedding celebration.

First, in the synagogue, as is customary, came the call up to the *bimah* (raised platform) to read from the Torah, and then to partake of cakes and whiskey.

But the real celebration was at Yankl Szczerba's house.

Yankl lived on Zygmuntowska Street in an apartment with two rooms and a kitchen. Practically all the furniture pieces had been removed from the apartment and in their place were set up long tables and benches to make room for the guests. A crowd of about 60 men gathered. Poles were also present at the edges of the crowd. Two hired waiters served the crowd, and there was also a professional singer. The tables were loaded with large plates of *tsholnt*,[2] fish, meat, and flasks of whiskey. Alongside the walls stood barrels of beer. There was a great deal of everything, and the crowd ate, eating so much it was hard to imagine that people could feast so prodigiously. The celebration, that is to say primarily the eating, lasted from about noon until six in the evening. The whole time, Zelig, "the intellectual," stood by my side, eating less than the others. By standing next to me the whole time he wanted to emphasize his differentness from the crowd. There was a great deal of drinking, but despite that, there were no quarrels or fights.

At this celebration I did indeed get acquainted with several slaughterers and teamsters, with whom it turned out I later worked in our trade union movement.

Although our organizational work in Praga had barely begun, it quickly gained broad recognition. Whole groups of workers came on their own, asking to be organized. With Passover around the corner and the beginning of the *matse*[3] season, a group of people came to us who did the unskilled labor connected with baking the matses. They requested that, since the bakers were organized as part of our movement, they should also be organized. They asked to be led in an action to gain better working conditions. Altogether they were about 100 men. We did organize an action for them, and easily won.

Notes

1. Stara Miłosna is now part of Wesoła, a district of Warsaw on the east side of the city.—MR
2. A baked dish of meat, potatoes, and legumes served on the Sabbath, kept warm from the day before because of the prohibition against cooking on the Sabbath.—MZ
3. *Matse* (or *matzoh*): unleavened flat bread for Passover use.—MZ

CHAPTER 5

The First of May Demonstration in Praga, 1920

In the Poland of 1920, the First of May was not just a workers holiday, but also an occasion for a political demonstration.

We had less than a year of organizational work behind us in Praga, but we had already achieved so much, that for the first time, we undertook the organization of an independent First of May demonstration of Jewish workers marching, in close ranks, from Praga to Warsaw.

We discussed it with the Polish labor parties, and it was decided to organize a united Polish-Jewish First of May column. After much negotiating back and forth—mainly about whether the parties should march separately or commingled—it was finally agreed that from Praga to Warsaw we would march together in one column, in the following order: PPS (Polish Socialist Party), Communists, and the Bund, each party with its own banners and slogans. After crossing the bridge at Krakowskie Przedmieście Street, each group would separate and march off to the central gathering point of its own party.

On the First of May we all gathered in the great square near the Greek Orthodox Church. We formed the agreed-upon column. Altogether there were about 5,000 people, with about 2,000 from the Bund, more than a third of the whole column. A huge crowd of Praga residents stood alongside the streets and watched the demonstration. For them it was a great spectacle: such demonstrations had never before taken place in Praga. Pragers normally joined such demonstrations in Warsaw on their own, individually—and now, suddenly, Praga was elevated to having its own demonstration!

The demonstrators marched proudly forward with flags and banners, and with the resounding melodies of Polish and Yiddish labor songs. The mood was

Figure 16. Warsaw, Bund May Day Demonstration. From the Archives of the YIVO Institute for Jewish Research, New York.

extraordinarily festive. At that moment, in 1920, the Polish labor movement was still full of hope, and we Jewish workers were also full of belief in a better tomorrow. True, attacks upon Jews were a frequent occurrence. The "Hallertchikes," soldiers in General Haller's[1] army, were beating up Jews in the streets and cutting off the beards of pious Jews. In the provincial towns it was even worse. But we were deeply convinced that this was a passing phenomenon, and that tomorrow belonged to us.

At the Kraków suburb, just on the Warsaw side of the bridge, our Bundist column separated itself, marching toward the central Bundist assembly point in front of The Iron Gate. From there our Bundist group was to march to the Theatre Square, where the Polish workers were also assembling. Our march was not without risk, because we were passing through residential streets that were strictly Polish, and in 1920, when attacks on Jews in the streets were a daily occurrence, marching with red banners displaying Yiddish slogans and singing Yiddish songs was no small thing. But we marched courageously and resolutely, arriving at the assembly point without incident.

When we had gotten quite close to the square in front of the Iron Gate, a magnificent panorama came into view, a sea of countless heads over which waved a forest of flags and banners. Twenty thousand people filled the square! Medem spoke at the demonstration. A speech of Medem's was in itself a great, festive occasion for us. Soon the columns were being formed in preparation for the march. Suddenly the police, who had the whole time been standing close to the demonstration in the side streets, along with a large band of hooligans, attacked the demonstrators. They began to rain murderous blows upon us. The square was closed off on three sides. There was no place to run. A large number of us were beaten and bloodied.

That was the beginning of a chain of persecutions and harassments against the Jewish labor movement, stretching throughout the whole period of Polish independence. It met with consistent and determined resistance by the Bund.

Note

1. Józef Haller (1873–1960), a Polish general and military hero; member of Polish parliament, 1922–1927. Because of his nationalist views, considered one of those responsible for the antisemitic riots in Czestochowa, 1919.—MZ

CHAPTER 6

Pogrom at the Praga Bund Club

The first large demonstration of the Bund in Praga on May 1, 1920, the march of about 2000 Jewish workers, made us very happy. But this same success also greatly interested certain others—the Polish police and the government. Their assault on our organization came quickly.

Suddenly, one night, when the Bund Club was closed and no one was around, a large contingent of police arrived. People referred to them ironically as "canaries," because of the light yellow stripe on their hats. The police broke into the club and wrecked everything, breaking tables, chairs, filing cabinets—anything it was possible to break. They scattered and tore up all our papers, including the books in the library—and then left a notice that this location was being "requisitioned." The Praga Bund was left out on the street, homeless.

When we found out about the destruction the next morning, we, of course, felt great pain and anger. But on that same day we began working to restore the Club. First we established an office for both the Bund and its affiliated unions on Ząbkowska Street, one of the centrally located streets. Committee meetings took place in the private residences of our Praga activists, and after a short time the Bund's organizational work was reestablished.

We began looking for a new location for the Club. This was no easy task. Many landlords were afraid to rent to the Bund. After much searching, however, we finally found a landlord willing to rent us an apartment at 19 Ząbkowska Street. The house was a dilapidated wreck. The courtyard was overgrown with weeds. Around the courtyard stood old neglected cattle stalls. They were willing to rent us this wreck of a place, where no one wanted to live, except for very poor folk. We rented the whole fourth floor, containing a number of rooms. Here we could even set up a large meeting hall for larger assemblies and readings. But the apartment itself was even more dilapidated than the rest of the house. Its walls had long not seen a living soul.

Nevertheless, we were very happy with this "bargain." We had found a new home for the Bund in Praga. We began to refurbish our new location. We did almost everything ourselves. Our carpenter comrades did the carpentry work and our painter comrades painted the rooms. At the end of 1920, we reopened the new Bund Club on 19 Ząbkowska Street.

It remained the headquarters of the Bund's work in Praga during the whole duration of independent Poland.

CHAPTER 7

Janek Jankelewicz

A misfortune occurred in the course of our tumultuous party work that shook all of us profoundly—the sudden death of Yoysef (Janek) Jankelewicz.

He was one of the chief organizers of our trade union movement. Right from the beginning of the German occupation during World War I, when we were organizing the legal trade unions, he became the Secretary of the Central Congress of Trade Unions. With his energetic and systematic approach to the work, he quickly rose to a leadership position, together with Victor Shulman, Chairman of the Central Congress. Later, in independent Poland, when the trade unions greatly expanded and grew in number, he continued in office as the Secretary of the Central Congress, becoming the central figure in the whole Jewish trade union labor movement in Warsaw.

He was very much loved by the Jewish workers. Everyone in Warsaw knew him from before the war, when the trade unions were more involved with aid and support for the unemployed starving workers than with union struggles. He was a quiet, good man. Thin, not tall, somewhat bent over, weak, he nevertheless displayed great energy and stamina. He also possessed a practical feel for the work.

He and I had been close friends since before the war. We were both from the same generation of Bundists, and during Czarist times it often happened that we worked together on the same party tasks. Janek was a printer by trade, so the party assigned him to run the Bund's illegal printing presses. Because it often also fell to me to help with this task, working together printing illegal literature we became even closer friends. We were also both chosen as delegates from Warsaw to attend the Bund's eighth convention in Vienna, although, because of the outbreak of the First World War, it didn't take place. After the war, when I came back to Warsaw and began working for the Central Committee, we became close again. I felt a strong bond with him.

Around 1920 he traveled back to his hometown in Wolyn to see his family. There he contracted typhus, and as soon as he got back to Warsaw, he fell ill. He was admitted to the Wolski Hospital for infectious diseases, and after a few days, departed this world.

His funeral took place Sunday, the 25th of January, 1920. It turned into a mighty political demonstration by the Jewish workers of Warsaw.

The tradition of funerals as demonstrations had a long tradition in the Bund, stemming from the times of the illegal struggles against Czarism. In those days we often organized funerals for victims who fell in our battles with Czarist power. Such funerals were intrinsically political demonstrations that more than once resulted in new victims. But even in independent Poland, under the circumstances of legal and half-legal work, the funeral processions did not lose their political significance. The marching of thousands of Jewish workers, the stepping out onto the streets in close ranks as an organized mass, proceeding through the streets, including Polish streets and half-Polish streets, carrying red flags with Yiddish writing on them, also had, in the circumstances of the time, a political effect.

We experienced unusual difficulties, however, in arranging such a funeral demonstration for Janek.

A typhus epidemic was raging in the country at the time, and a regulation stated that no corpse that had died of typhus was permitted to be released, nor could anyone be allowed to approach the coffin. Our activist, Julek Shatzkin (since the twenties, in America), succeeded in cutting through the red tape and was able to extricate the corpse, along with permission to arrange a public funeral.

Janek's funeral turned into a gigantic spontaneous demonstration. Young and old—around 20,000 people—came to honor and pay their last respects. The

Figure 17. The funeral of Bundist leader, Yisroel Likhtenshtayn (Lichtenstein), Lodz, 1936. From the Archives of the YIVO Institute for Jewish Research, New York.

Figure 18. Julek Shatzkin. From the Archives of the YIVO Institute for Jewish Research, New York.

funeral took place on a Sunday, a cold and snowy day. Despite that, thousands came to pay their respects. The street in Wola, a working-class suburb in Warsaw where the hospital was located, was black with people.

Right from the start there was a sharp clash with the police. From Wola you could get to the Jewish cemetery on Okopowa Street by way of alleyways and smaller streets on the outskirts of Warsaw. The police wanted to redirect the funeral procession through those thinly inhabited outskirts of the city, so as to circumvent the center of Warsaw. But we did not obey the police. We led the procession the length of Wolska Street to Żelazna Street in Leszno, that is, to the center of the city. The mass of thousands veered to follow the coffin. The police did not dare to shoot or disperse such a mass of people, especially at a funeral. The massive procession was led by the Bund Militia in perfect order, under the leadership of Gershon Zibertin.

Just as the funeral procession was passing through, the Polish populace was at that moment exiting church in great numbers. It was a totally Polish neighborhood. The Poles behaved with respect to the procession, however, and there were absolutely no incidents or antisemitic outbursts.

Leaving the Polish streets, the procession entered the Jewish neighborhood, proceeding through Leszno to Przejazd. Here the procession halted in front of the office of the Bund Central Committee at 9 Przejazd. After that, by way of Dzika, it wound all along the length of Gęsia to Okopowa, where the cemetery was.

With the Jewish authorities, the Kehilla, there was also trouble. The Bund demanded that Yankl be laid to rest next to Peretz's grave. This was distasteful to the lordly officials of the Kehillah. Such a prominent place for a lowly worker-activist? On top of that, there was the large expense—such a spot cost a pretty penny. And just as before when we dealt with the Polish police, we confronted the Jewish Community Council with a fait accompli. The funeral procession proceeded to the row of graves containing Peretz's grave site, and next to it, Janek was buried. Vladimir Medem spoke at the open gravesite.

Janek was now buried, but for me he was not dead. I couldn't forget him. Lucia was pregnant, and we decided between us that our baby, boy or girl, would bear Janek's name. Six months later our only son was born; we called him Janek. And we started a tradition: On the anniversary of Janek's death we went to his grave and placed flowers there. We always took our little Janek along.

CHAPTER 8

The Cracow Convention

In the spring of 1920 a convention for the unification of the Polish and Galician Bunds took place, an important moment in the history of the Bund.

In preparation for the convention, discussions began about what direction the unification should take.

Three factions arose: One, quite strong, held that the Bolshevik revolution in Russia should serve as an example for the kind of politics the Socialist parties should adopt in all countries. A second—the centrist faction—was to a large degree critical of Bolshevik politics, but nevertheless believed, as Socialists all around the world then did, that the Bolshevik experiment was so immensely significant that it could not be ignored, that its mistakes could be corrected, and that

Figure 19. Central Committee of the Galician Bund on the eve of its amalgamation with the Polish Bund, 1920. From the Archives of the YIVO Institute for Jewish Research, New York.

it was possible to have a revolutionary-Socialist oriented International, without its splitting politics, with Socialists and Communists working together. The third faction—the right faction—was under the ideological leadership of Medem—who already then, in 1920, during the honeymoon days of the Bolshevik revolution—had an absolutely negative attitude toward the Bolshevik experiment and to everything the Bolsheviks preached. Medem at that time wrote the astoundingly prophetic words that Bolshevism would proceed on a path of ever greater and greater terror, until the Bolsheviks would in the end begin murdering each other.

The rightist faction under Medem's leadership was in fact not really a faction, because Medem was against any kind of factionalism, and his authority was so great among his followers that his was the deciding word. Right before the voting on which direction to take at the convention, I took it upon myself to call together a small group of people to consult and prepare a resolution for the larger meeting. Included in this small group were Medem, Bejnisz Michalewicz, Zalmen Woyland, Mauricy Orzech, Hershl Himmelfarb, myself, and several other comrades.

Our resolution had no great success in the voting. That came as no great surprise. At that time, 1918–1920, half the world was drunk with the Bolshevik triumph, and the Bundists did not escape this intoxication either. Nevertheless, several delegates from the rightist faction were selected, and I had the honor of being one of them. I was sent as a delegate to the unity convention of the Bund in Cracow.

It was a great experience for me, personally. It was the first time I had ever traveled "abroad." Western Galicia was then a part of Austria; hence, "abroad."

The delegates from the Galician Bund made a rather strange impression on me. I was used to the Socialist conferences in Russia, where dressing simply was customary and one almost made a show of one's simplicity of dress: Russian blouses, dark shirts without ties, long disheveled hair, boots—in Russia this was the revolutionary fashion. The delegates from the Galician Bund, however, belonged largely to the Western European intelligentsia. Many of them were doctors and lawyers. Moreover for them a Socialist convention was a kind of party celebration, to which one came dressed as for a holiday. Many of the Bundist delegates from Galicia did just that. Some of them came dressed in black suits or in long black jackets with elegant ties. Several also wore top hats. I wondered at seeing these leaders of the Galician Bund, whose well-earned fame extended well beyond the borders of Galicia—such figures as Dr. Jankew Bros, Dr. Henryk Schreiber, Dr. Leon Feiner, Dr. Ignacy Aleksandrowicz, and Dr. Sigmund Gliksman—going about so elegantly attired.

I and several other delegates who were in Cracow for the first time, took the opportunity to get acquainted with this beautiful, old Polish-Jewish city. Our guide was the writer Yoyl Dembitser, son of the Chief Rabbi of Cracow, and a brother of the well-known Bundist activist Peysakh Dembitser (who died here in America in 1937). Yoyl Dembister was also a Bundist, and he happily undertook to acquaint us with this old city. He showed us the old Jewish synagogue, the old cemetery with the grave of RM'O;[1] he also showed us Wawel.[2] In Poland I was accustomed to the attire of the Hasidim, but the Cracow Hasidim, with their white stockings, black round hats, and long fur-lined coats, looked strange to me.

In Cracow I became more closely acquainted with Comrade S. Blum, an old activist of the Galician Bund. A bootmaker by trade, he prided himself as being a proletarian among the Galician Bundist leaders, who were, for the most part, intellectuals. His manner of speech was different from that of the other Galician activists. At mass rallies, he was very eloquent, speaking in a folksy manner, with a voice that resonated and was full of temperament.

The convention had a great many dramatic moments. The left and the center factions together constituted a majority. Medem delivered a sharp speech in which he warned against following the Bolshevik model. Although his personal authority was very great, he did not succeed in winning over the convention politically. He remained firm as a rock, however, and would not yield to any compromise. Before the vote on the proposed resolutions, we, the small group

Figure 20. Vladimir Medem, 1920. From the Archives of the YIVO Institute for Jewish Research, New York.

of delegates for the rightist faction, spoke with Medem, arguing that we should vote for the centrist resolution and in this way strengthen the centrist faction as against the leftists. He would not hear of this, and out of loyalty to him, we voted for our own resolution.

When it came to a vote of all the delegates, Medem's declaration that he would not allow himself to be elected to the new Central Committee exploded like a bomb. No one expected anything like that. A Bundist Central Committee without Medem?! He was begged to accept a mandate to the Central Committee, but he remained unmoved as a rock. I went home in a saddened mood. I am sure that many of the delegates had the same thought I did: A Central Committee without Medem? An editorial board without Medem? Continuing our work without Medem? Unthinkable.

Not long after that Medem announced his decision to leave for America. I—like a lot of other Bundists—took this in with a heavy heart. He would not permit any big send-off, but a small gathering at engineer Heller's apartment did take place for a small number of active Bundists. There Medem said that he very much hoped that the political illusions would not last long in the Bund—that soon the Bundists would sober up—but as long as these illusions continued, he could not participate. He gladly undertook, however, to be the representative in America of the Polish Bund and to work in its interest. At the end of 1920, he left Warsaw and went to America.

In America Medem did indeed accomplish a lot for the Polish Bund. He represented TSYSHO[3] there, raising a lot of money for the secular Yiddish schools. In addition, he raised the first large sum of money for building a chil-

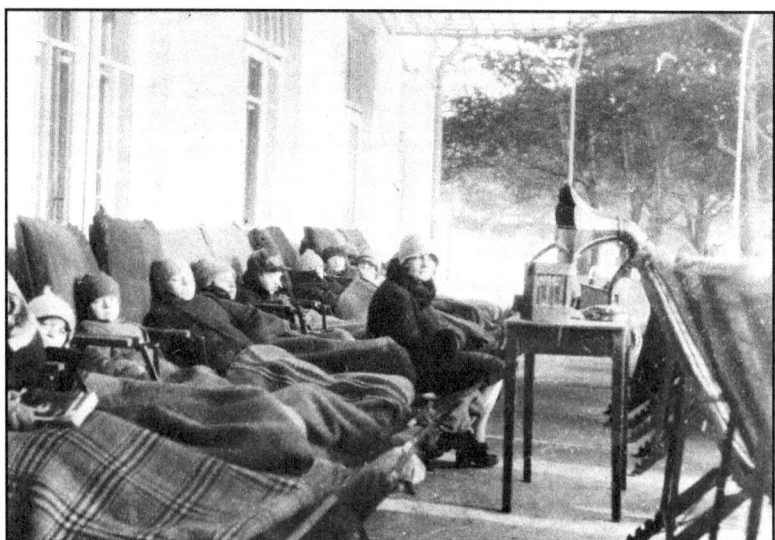

Figure 21. Children listening to the radio in the Medem Sanitarium, 1930s. From the Archives of the YIVO Institute for Jewish Research, New York.

dren's sanitarium outside of Warsaw that was posthumously named after him—and which later became famous as the *Medem Sanitarium* (see chapter 44).

After the convention, a small pro-Communist group from the leftist faction broke away. We were glad to get rid of them. But in the meantime the party underwent a sharp crisis.

Notes

1. Acronymn (pronounced "Ramu") for Rabbi Moses (Moyshe) Isserlis, 1520–1572), Talmudist, famous for his decisions in Jewish law; renowned author of *ha-Mapah*, a commentary on Jewish law.—MZ
2. Castle and cathedral in Cracow, a fortress-like complex overlooking the Vistula River, visually dominating the city; from the reign of Casimir the Restorer (1034–1058), it was the leading political and administrative center for the Polish state and of great historical significance to the Polish people.—MZ
3. Acronym for *Tsentrale Yidishe Shul Organizatsye*—Central Yiddish School Organization—which created and administered a network of secular Yiddish schools under Socialist auspices, led primarily by the Bund and Left Po'ale Tsiyon (Labor Zionists); at is peak in 1920, TSYSHO maintained 219 institutions with 24,000 students spread across 100 locations, including 467 kindergartens, 114 elementary schools, 6 high schools, 52 evening schools, and a pedagogical institute in Vilnius.—MZ

CHAPTER 9

A Hail of Persecutions

In November 1918, about 125 years after Poland had been conquered by its three neighboring great powers, dismembered, and divided among them, Poland finally regained its independence. After only a few days of the Lublin "folk government," led by the famous PPS (Polish Socialist Party) leader Ignacy Daszyński, a liberal government was formed under the leadership of the Galician PPS leader, Jędrzej Moraczewski. But this government quickly lost power and was replaced by a government of right-wing parties.

A wave of nationalistic chauvinism flooded the country. The most popular slogan was: "We don't just want an independent Poland, but a 'Great Poland': Polska Od Morza Do Morza! (A Poland from Sea to Sea, i.e., from the Baltic to the Black Sea). In this atmosphere, the unfortunate "March to Kiev" was born. The Bolsheviks proposed an immediate peace. At first Poland did not want to hear of it—so dazzled were they by their early victories and by the hope they would be able to capture all of the Ukraine. The Bund decided to come out openly against this senseless war craze. Comrade Henryk Erlich[1] delivered an impassioned speech at a session of the Warsaw City Council in which he demanded that the government repudiate its imperialistic plans to capture the Ukraine and create a Poland "from sea to sea," and further demanded that Poland seek an immediate and just peace with Russia. The wrath of the Polish governing circles against this courageous and outspoken peace proposal was enormous. With one stroke, the government delegitimized the Bund, rendering it illegal.

The persecutions inflicted on the Bund had actually begun much earlier. The chauvinistic imperialistic wave which swept over Poland immediately after it had regained its independence brought with it intense antisemitism among significant portions of the Polish population. A "happy" Poland must be a Poland free of "foreigners," that is, without Jews—and there followed a series of insults, degrading acts, and savage daily attacks against Jews.

The wave of hatred also poured itself out onto the Bund. It was, after all, doubly "nonkosher": not only Jewish, but Socialist too.

The police persecutions of the Bund movement began early in 1919. Suddenly the Bund daily, *Lebns-Fragn*, was shut down, and all the staff at the newspaper's offices were arrested. True, the newspaper was reopened a few days later, but the harassment and persecutions did not stop. In the Spring of 1920, *Lebns-Fragn* was again shut down, this time for good. The Bund then began to publish its daily newspaper under a different name, but after a short time the government shut that down too. The Bund changed the name of the newspaper again. This cat-and-mouse game went on for a long time. Sometimes the police not only shut down our newspaper, but also arrested the managing editor, Mauricy Orzech, Manye Eliasz (now in New York), and others.

But after Henryk Erlich's courageous antiwar speech in the Warsaw City Council, the persecutions grew harsher—to such an extent that it became, in fact, an attempt to destroy the entire Bundist movement. All the Bund party premises—first of all, the Grosser Club in Warsaw—were shut down with one blow. Practically all the union halls were shut down. They shut down the organization that managed the Bund schools and nurseries. Absolutely no openly conducted Bund public meetings were permitted, and the Bundist press was completely shut down. The Bund was driven back underground. In the new independent Poland, the Bund had to revert to illegal work, techniques it had excelled in and become famous for during Czarist times.

Figure 22. Bundist activists imprisoned in Modlin Fortress, 1917. Man wearing hat, Khayim Vaser (Chaim Wasser); standing, first on left, Rubin Zuckerman (translator's father); standing next to him, Nathan Frankel. From the private collection of Marvin Zuckerman.

During the time of these repressions against the Bund, the police also arrested quite a number of Bundist activists in Warsaw and all across the country. Some were imprisoned, some were sent off to a kind of concentration camp in Dąbie, near Cracow. Police also came to Erlich's apartment to arrest him, but he happened not to be home. Of course, after he was informed of the police visit, he did not go home to sleep, but went instead to the apartment of his sister, Helena Seidman. But he could not isolate himself entirely. From time to time he

Figure 23. Henryk Erlich. From the Archives of the YIVO Institute for Jewish Research, New York.

had to venture out into the street, and then there was the risk that he might be recognized, especially because of his short, pointed little beard, which so suited his longish face. It was therefore decided by the party that he should shave off his beard so as to make himself less recognizable. I was assigned to talk this over with him.

I had first become acquainted with Erlich in 1907–1908, during his student days. I worked with him in the Warsaw party organization, where he was already then playing a prominent role. He was even for a time Chairman of the *Literary Association*, where the Bund had a great deal of influence. Later I met him in Russia working for the Bund, and was with him at a Bund conference in Kharkhov in 1916, in a school where Raphael Abramovich's[2] sister was the principal. After that I met up with him at the tenth convention of the Bund in Petrograd, March 1917, so that we knew each other quite well for many years. For this reason I tried to carry out my mission in the form of personal advice from a friend, rather than as an official party duty. I knew it would not be an easy task to get him to shave off his beard. He had a strong aversion to disguising himself, to displaying personal fear, even when danger threatened. At first he didn't want to hear of it. Not placing one's head in the lion's maw, hiding from arrest—yes—but hiding behind a disguise—no. He remained cold to all arguments. I had to repeat my visit several times before I could get him to agree to shave off his beard. The arguments that eventually convinced him were first, that the party urgently needed him in the current difficult time. Second, if he were arrested a terrible thing might happen to him—in those days there were many cases where the police killed a prisoner on the way to prison with the excuse that he was shot while "trying to escape." I recount this episode primarily because nineteen years later his aversion to disguising himself and his desire to look the enemy in the face may have cost him his life. I am referring to his arrest in Brest-Litovsk in October 1939, when he found himself in Soviet-occupied territory. There he again refused to follow the advice of comrades to shave off his beard. A Communist wretch recognized him on the Brest-Litovsk railway station and betrayed him to the Soviet NKVD. He was arrested and later died a martyr's death—together with Victor Alter[3]—in the killing cellars of the NKVD.

In 1920, however, he did permit himself to be persuaded. Hiding him at the Seidman's would not have been smart. Too many outsiders visited there. So after a short while he moved to the apartment of Comrade Heller on Leszno 13. Engineer Heller died before the war. His wife, the well-known doctor, Anna Broide-Heller, Director of the Jewish Children's Hospital on Śliska and a Bundist, perished in the Warsaw Ghetto. The police, who were constantly looking for him, finally found out where he was. In September 1920—coming out into the street, he was arrested at the gate of Leszno 13. He was imprisoned in the Mokotów Prison in Warsaw.

His arrest made a great impression in labor circles in Poland, and also in the circles of the Polish Socialist Party (PPS). The leaders of the PPS then still had some influence in the country. Ignacy Daszyński, one of the top leaders of the PPS and then Vice-Premier of the "Government of National Defense," intervened in the arrest and after about eight weeks' imprisonment in Mokotów Prison, Comrade Henryk Erlich was freed.

Notes

1. Henryk Erlich (1882–1942), a lawyer by profession, a beloved leader of the Polish Bund between the wars. He was a member of the 1917 Petrograd Soviet; then later in Poland, a member of the Warsaw City Council and a member of the Executive Committee of the Second International. Perished in Stalinist imprisonment in the 1940s.—MZ
2. Raphael Rein Abramovich (1880–1963), a member of the Bund and a leading member of the Menshevik wing of the Russian Social-Democratic Workers Party (RSDRP).—MZ

3. Viktor (or Wictor) Alter (1890–1943), a beloved Bund leader in the interwar period in Poland. An engineer by profession, active in the Polish Bund starting in 1913, exiled to Siberia, escaped to England where he was a conscientious objector during World War I, went to Russia after the February Revolution, came back to Poland where he served on the Central Committee of the Bund and rose to prominence. Executed by the Stalinist regime in the 1940s.—MZ

CHAPTER 10

Illegal Work—Once Again

Immediately after the Bund was driven underground, we went back to one of the old tried and true battle methods of all underground movements—we made use of illegal presses to publish newspapers and political pamphlets. By then I was working in the Secretariat of the Warsaw Committee of the Bund, along with Emanuel Nowogrodski and Sholem Hertz.[1] It fell to me to work primarily on organizing the printing of our illegal literature. We printed the first illegal proclamation at Dovid Hendler's at Długa 26. After a while I had to find a different printer, because it is never a good idea to stay too long in one place when printing illegal literature.

We had a comrade, a printer, who was imprisoned for his Bundist work back in Czarist times. His name was Shmuel Blumental. He later perished in the Warsaw Ghetto. I approached him and asked him to find us a place to print an illegal proclamation. "No problem," he said. "I will print the proclamation in my father's print shop." I was happy to hear his father owned a print shop. It would now be easier to arrange the printing of our illegal literature, especially since his younger brother, Motl (now in America), was also one of our comrades. In Blumental's print shop (on Solna Street) we printed a large number of proclamations.

But, of course, after a while we had to move from there as well.

We moved to a small press on Nowolipki 7, belonging to a certain Greenberg. He possessed only a small manual pedal machine. We couldn't get much done that way. From there we moved to a brother of his who had a bigger press on Nowolipie 17. But we had a lot of trouble with him. He had no great desire to do illegal printing, and we had to expend a lot of effort getting him to agree to do it. But we did have one effective means: to any printer who did the illegal work for us, we would also give our legal work, for example, placards about meetings, material for the trade unions, etc. I often persuaded this Greenberg from

Nowolipie 17 by arguing that if he didn't do the illegal work for us, we wouldn't give him the legal work. But then, eventually, we had to leave his print shop too.

One time, early in the fall of 1920, we needed to do a really large printing of illegal literature. The Central Committee of the Bund had decided to put out an illegal proclamation against the war between the Poles and the Soviets, and about the critical condition of the country and the necessity for an immediate peace, and to spread it all over the country with the help of couriers, as the proclamations could not be mailed or sent by rail. The proclamation had to be printed in tens of thousands of copies. A small press would not do for such a job; it would take too long, several weeks. But we had no way of getting to the bigger presses.

The well-known Warsaw Yiddish daily, *Der Moment,* had just purchased a new big rotary press that could print tens of thousands of copies in just a few hours. We decided to print the proclamation on *Moment*'s press.

Among the typesetters of *Moment* were the following Bundists: Lozer Klog, Moyshe Szklar, and Pesakh Zuckerman, all three of whom met a heroic death in the Warsaw Ghetto Uprising. With these Bundist typesetters, and a few others, we carried out the following scheme: The night before, when all the other typesetters had left, our comrades would quietly typeset the text of the proclamation, prepare the printing plates, and then hide them in a safe place.

The next day, late at night, when all the typesetters had finished making things ready for printing the following day's copy of *Moment* and had left, we would enter the press.

We were a group of four: Comrade Artur Zygielbojm,[2] who had just arrived in Warsaw and was then the secretary of the Metal Workers Union; Comrade Lerner, a metal worker, and an old Bundist who, back in Czarist times, had served time in prison for his Bundist activities together with Viktor Alter; Comrade Abram (I no longer remember his family name), a metal worker active in the administration of the trade unions; and I. We put Abram outside to stand guard.

We quietly took the printing plates that were prepared for us from their hiding place, and went into the press. We approached the expediter—he was also the manager of the press—and told him why we were there. He raised an outcry. We told him to be quiet. To be safe, we led him into his office, locking him in and scaring him with our revolvers to make him understand we were serious. He asked us if we would just let him print the newspaper, because he must deliver it punctually to the train station, but we were afraid to risk it—what if he didn't let us print our proclamation?—so we kept him locked up.

The operator of the rotary press was also a Bundist—Kalmen was his name. He went right to work. In the course of a few hours, our proclamation was printed.

While the press was fully underway, Comrade Lozer Klog came in. He pretended not to know what was going on. He was the city editor of *Moment*, and he always arrived at this time to lay out the pages of the newspaper. So that no suspicion should fall on him, we shoved him into the office, locking him in with the expediter.

Figure 24. The Yiddish reads: "Labor Congress for the Battle Against Antisemitism," and urges Jewish workers to come to various scheduled meeting places in 1935 to elect delegates to the Bund-sponsored Congress. "Jewish Folk Masses of Warsaw . . . Let No-One Fail to Come and Vote . . . Protest Antisemitism, Fascism, and Reaction . . . For Freedom and Socialism!" The Congress was banned by the authorities and was not allowed to take place. From the Archives of the YIVO Institute for Jewish Research, New York.

When the copies of the proclamation were finished, we packaged them into several large bundles, leaving without any difficulty. We, of course, used *Moment's* paper stock. To *Moment's* credit, they hushed this incident up, and there were no untoward consequences.

Until our legal party press was again being published, more or less regularly, we had to resort to illegal presses for a long time. For proclamations that were published in only a few hundred copies (especially for the *Yugnt-Bund*—Youth Bund) we often simply used the hectograph.

Notes

1. Sholem J. Hertz (1893–1992), journalist and leading historian of the Bund. Since 1929, a member of the Central Committee of the Polish Bund. In 1939, fled to America. From 1941–1948, a member of the Bund's American representatives in Poland. Since 1941, affiliated with several Bundist and non-Bundist publications. Since 1947, a member of the Bund's World Coordination Committee, and from May 1977 to October 1985, its Secretary. Published several books, including *Di Yidishe Sotsyalistishe Bavegung in Amerike, Di Geshikhte Fun Bund in Lodz, Di Geshikhte Fun a Yugnt, Doyres Bundistn, Der Bund in Bilder,* and *Di Yidn in Ukrayine.* Edited *Di Geshikhte Fun Bund.*—MZ
2. Artur (Shmuel) Zygielbojm (1895–1943). Bundist leader, labor organizer, and member of Bund's Central Committee. Joined Warsaw Judenrat in 1940, but refused to carry out Nazi demands, making a speech to Warsaw's Jews exhorting them to refuse to go into the ghetto. Escaped across occupied Europe to England where he served as the Bund's representative to the Polish government in exile. Tried desperately but unsuccessfully to arouse Allies and others to halt the annihilation of the remnant of Poland's 3.3 million Jews. Failing that, he wrote a famous last appeal and, May 12, 1943, committed suicide, hoping thus to draw attention to their plight.—MZ

CHAPTER 11

The Danzig Convention

The persecutions by the police, despite how hard they hit the movement, were put on the back burner when a serious, internal party crisis erupted.

After the congress of the Communist International in 1920 when the infamous "21 Conditions"[1] arrived—whose purpose it was to split the Socialist parties, to declare all Socialist leaders as "traitors to the working class," and to simply wipe out the Socialist movement—a pro-Communist group arose within the Polish Bund which called itself *Kombundishe FRAKtsye* (Kombund Faction), shortened to *Kombund*. This faction demanded that the Bund immediately accept all 21 Conditions. This would, of course, have meant submitting to the Comintern, splitting, getting rid of all the tried and true Bundist leaders, and, in short order, doing away with the Bund.

The leftist majority in the Bund was ready to accept 19 1/2 of the 21 points, but rejecting the remaining 1 1/2 points was enough to prevent the Bund from becoming a part of the Communist International. The centrist faction was willing to agree to 16 of the 21 points. After the Cracow convention, the rightist (Medem) faction no longer existed as a cohesive group. We didn't want to complicate matters in the party by creating another faction, so we allied ourselves with the centrist line.

A sharp internal factional struggle began the likes of which had never before been seen in the history of the Bund. This was no longer a struggle between fraternal comrades of one party, but that of a party with its own internal enemy. Among the leaders of the Kombund faction were quite a number of important activists from the trade union movement: for example, Aba Flug from the Textile Union; Kalman Kamashnmakher, Isaiah Zambrovski, Yekhiel Nayman, and Yoysef Lifszytz (Yoysef Basoff) from the Leather Workers Union (the last three later returned to the Bund); Mendl Skrobek from the Paper Workers Union; and others.

In the midst of the heat of this factional battle, Yankl Levine and Moyshe Rafes, important activists in the Communist Party, came to Warsaw from the Russian Bund (both were later liquidated by Stalin). Actually they had come to help the Kombund faction, or to take over the Bund altogether, or to deepen, as far as possible, the split within the party.

I was well acquainted with Yankl Levine, a carpenter by trade. He was a Bundist professional. In 1912 the Bund's Central Committee had sent him to Warsaw to do some organizational work, and that's when I met him. Later we were both imprisoned in the Warsaw Arsenal, and in 1915 we were both evacuated to the interior of Russia. After some knocking about here and there for a while, we both traveled to Kiev, and there threw ourselves back into the work of the party. We used to meet at Bund conventions and at other kinds of party functions. Now, when he came to Warsaw, he was my guest and spent a day and a night at my place. We talked about the "the good old days," asked each other about old friends, and so on. He was easy to talk to, and we talked at great length. He was a happy young man and a good conversationalist; he could sing well too. It was pleasant spending time with him.

When I asked him why he had come to Warsaw, he answered, "No particular reason—just so." Since he was going to Vilnius to visit a friend, he said, he figured he'd at the same time stop by Warsaw and visit old friends.

I had also known Moyshe Rafes for some years. He had been in Warsaw for a short time, sent by the Bund's Central Committee to conduct the elections for the delegates to the Bund's eighth convention that was to take place in Vienna in 1914. Later I met him again in connection with work for the party in Kiev. He was also staying with me as a guest at my place. But I already knew the nature of his mission. He had already caucused with the Kombund activists, and had also attempted to discuss matters with other comrades. When he came to my place I asked him, in a not very friendly tone, why he had come. He answered that he had not come to visit me, but to visit Lucien. I left the house, leaving him there.

Yankl Levine left quickly to go back to Russia, but Rafes stayed in Warsaw for some time.

It wasn't too long before I succeeded in discovering, by chance and at just the right moment, a key person in the Kombund faction. I was well acquainted with an old activist of the old PPS-Left, Stefan Królikowski.[2] He was for many years a personal friend of mine. Before the war I knew his family and was a frequent guest in his home. He would always declare his love for the Jews. He could even talk a little Yiddish. When he was asked why he loved the Jews so much, he would answer, "It is because of a stone." Why of all things a stone? During the pogrom of 1881 in Warsaw, when he was still a baby, his mother was carrying him, and a stone from a pogromist accidentally hit him and injured him slightly. He therefore thought of himself thereafter as a victim of pogromists.

I was imprisoned in the jail on Daniłowiczowska[3] together with him and his brother Kazik (Kazimierz)—a gasworks worker. Later we were both exiled to Siberia. When I was badly beaten in Siberia by the Czarist police and put in a hospital that happened to be in the very village to which he had been exiled, he hung around me like a brother. Once while in Siberia, we were sent into the forest to chop wood. Suddenly a terrible blizzard started up, tearing at branches and uprooting trees. It was impossible to keep one's footing. We tied ourselves together with a rope and barely made it back to the village. In a word, many shared, harsh experiences had created a strong bond between us. Later in Warsaw, when the PPS-Left became part of the Communist Party and he became a Communist activist, our friendship was nevertheless, not broken off, at least not in the beginning. He would drop by my house, and I at his. After a while he was selected as a delegate to the Polish parliament. Some years later he went to Soviet Russia and was liquidated.

One night during the difficult factionalist struggles with the Kombund, he visited me at my place. We were eating, drinking, talking. Our conversation shifted to the factional fight within our party. A heated discussion flared up between us. He assured me there would be a split in the Bund, and that a part of the Bund would leave the Bund and join them, the Communists. I, on the other hand, argued that no matter how sharp our internal differences, no Bundist would betray his party; there would be no split. In the heat of the discussion, Królikowski let slip that the Communist Party was financing the Kombund faction, and that an important Bund activist was receiving money from them. Hearing this, I began to draw him out, until he revealed that the Bund activist was Alexander in Lodz. Later, in the 1930s, Alexander came back to the Bund and became—and still is—in speech and in print—one of the sharpest opponents of communism. I had to promise Królikowski that I wouldn't tell this to anyone. But this time I did not keep my word. I immediately went to the leading figures of our party, to Henryk Erlich, to Noyekh, the Chair of the party, and to Emanuel Nowogrodzki, the Secretary of the Central Committee, and told them this news.

Alexander was immediately summoned to appear before the Central Committee. Alexander, who was known for his personal honesty, openly admitted that he received money for the Kombund faction from the Communist Party. He was immediately expelled from the party. This news made a tremendous impression on the party membership and drew quite a number of comrades away from the Kombund faction who were, in principle, in agreement with it, but could not stomach such an open betrayal of the party.

Finally, it was decided to have the second convention of the Bund in Poland. In 1921 it took place in the free city of Danzig, which was economically a part of Poland but was politically autonomous, with its own small parliament, its own president, and its own police force. To get into Danzig you had to have a Polish passport. Even though the Polish police no longer had any power in Danzig, we nevertheless arranged the convention in Danzig illegally, underground. There were a lot of Polish police agents in Danzig, and on the return trip they could have had all of us arrested. The Bund convention took place in the Danzig Transport Workers Union Hall.

This particular convention was perhaps the most fateful in the history of the Bund, one in which the very existence of the Bund hung in the balance. The central question before the convention was "the 21 Conditions."

All three factions were represented. The left faction, those in favor of 19 1/2 conditions, was in the majority. The Kombund had only six delegates. In addition to the 21 Conditions, the Comintern sent a special letter to the convention demanding that the party expel its "rightist leaders." When the letter was read to the delegates, it was as if a storm had erupted. Expel Erlich, Alter, Noyekh, and Michalewicz from the party?—the pride and prized ornaments of the party?—such a thing could not be fathomed by even the most leftist among us—except, of course, for the few Kombund delegates, who were already by then in fact slavishly following the dictates of the Communist Party. When it came to a vote, the 21 Conditions were rejected in their entirety.

After the convention, the Kombund faction held a separate meeting at which they decided to leave the party. Not all present, however, were in agreement with this. Several of them did not want to countenance a split and did not leave the party—among them, for example, was Kalmen Kamashnmakher.

The Kombund faction then founded its own party, but after a brief period of independent existence, it merged and disappeared into the Communist Party of Poland. Thereupon the Communists immediately began total warfare against the Bund, a war to annihilate the Bund by any and all means. From that time on, the Bund found itself, out of necessity, at war with them. It had to defend itself against an enemy that recognized absolutely no morality at all and absolutely no decency.

It is worthwhile to tell here about a characteristic fact surrounding the Danzig convention. I was given the job of distributing the money for the train tickets to the delegates. Two delegates from the Kombund, Aba Flug and Yekhiel Nayman, declined to take the money with the excuse that they did not have a passport with which to make the trip. They did not come to the Danzig convention. After the convention they both became very important Communist leaders, although both of them left the Communist camp later. Yekhiel Nayman came back to the Bund, becoming a very prominent activist in the Paris Bund. In the early thirties, Aba Flug became one of the organizers of the rightist opposition within the Communist Party. For that he was shut out of the Communist Party and denounced as a traitor.

Aba Flug was an intelligent, earnest, and responsible labor leader. He was the recognized leader of the Textile Workers Union. But when he was shut out of the Communist Party for "rightist tendencies," all his former comrades boycotted him and poisoned his life. Not long after, he died. The union to which he had devoted his whole life, refused to arrange his funeral. His wife then came to the Bund and begged to have the Bund arrange it. We did not refuse. We arranged a funeral for Aba Flug.

The new leaders of the Textile Workers Union, they who inherited the mantle of Aba Flug's leadership, Abram Rosenfeld (Abram the Peasant) at their head, did not attend the funeral. They were seen observing the funeral at a distance. Ironically, Abram Rosenfeld's end was even bitterer than his predecessor's. When Hitler attacked Poland, Abram the Peasant fled to the Soviet Union, along with a large flood of refugees. There he saw what kind of a "paradise" his dreamt-of "proletarian fatherland" was. He fell into great doubt and depression. He began displaying signs of mental imbalance. He became pious, grew a beard, began to pray, and after a time went totally insane. He could be seen dragging himself through the streets begging. He died on the street of starvation and exhaustion. This is how the fatherland of the proletariat paid homage to the demise of a person who had served it loyally his entire life.

Notes

1. The "21 Conditions," most of them stipulated by Lenin, had to be agreed to in their entirety by any Socialist parties wanting to join the Communist Third International (Comintern).—MZ
2. Stefan Królikowski (1881–1937), Polish Socialist activist in the PPS and PPS-Left and, later, the Polish Communist Party. Arrested by the NKVD in Moscow in 1937, charged and executed as a member of the Polish Military Organization.—MZ
3. An auxiliary unit of the Tenth Pavilion of the Citadel and Pawiak prison for political prisoners; destroyed in 1944 during the Warsaw Uprising.—MR

CHAPTER 12

Coming to the Defense of the Movement

The final splitting off of the Kombund faction and the loss of some of its members did nothing to weaken the Bund internally. On the contrary—they made it stronger. We were rid of an enemy that had wanted to destroy the movement from within. The party grew more unified and better prepared for battle.

But great difficulties arose in the arena of the trade union movement. Many of the activists of the Kombund had played a leading role in several of the Warsaw unions. They were the leading figures in the Warsaw administration of the Textile Workers Union, the Leather Workers Union, the Lumber Workers Union, and the Bakers Union.

On the other hand, the following Warsaw trade unions remained under the aegis of the Bund: the largest of all, the Garment Workers Union; the Leather-Haberdashers Union (saddlers and harness makers, glove makers, sport haberdashers, etc.); the Metal Workers Union; the Food Workers Union (chocolates, candies, and sweet pastries); the Hairdressers Union; the Printers Union; the Paper Workers Union; and others.

In addition, the Bund had a great many followers in the unions the Communists took over. Within those unions were close-knit, Bundist circles. In the unions in which we retained leadership, the Communists also had their followers.

A basic difference in the tactics between the two "oppositional circles" within the unions of our two opposing camps immediately became apparent. The Bundist circles were loyal to the union work of the Communist-dominated unions in which they were members. They did not conspire to tear the union apart from within or disturb its struggle to better the working conditions of the workers. The Communist circles in the Bund-dominated unions, on the other hand, displayed the highest measure of disloyalty, working to undermine any and every activity undertaken by those unions. They tried taking them over, using every disruptive means possible—and if that didn't work, tried to break those unions by insulting and smearing their Socialist leaders, not stopping short of physical attacks.

The Communists also introduced something hitherto unknown in the labor movement—physical violence. Up until then the struggle between the labor parties was an intense one, but it never overstepped the boundaries of a battle of words. Now for the first time, the Communists introduced a new "argument" to the interparty struggles—the fist, the knife, and the revolver.

They were particularly brutal toward the Bund. As a result we came to understand that caring for the safety of our activists and for the security of our members and our labor institutions was now an urgent need.

From quite another direction, it became apparent that the attacks by the antisemitic hooligans and the police provocateurs—police or police agents dressed in civilian clothes—were not going to be a temporary thing, and that we would have to deal with them for a long time to come. The idea began to take hold that we must create a permanent Bundist self-defense unit that would always be ready to protect our party's clubs, libraries, offices, soup kitchens, and schools, safeguarding the physical safety of our comrades and activists against the continual dangers coming from both the left and the right.

Up to this point, organizing the defense of our meetings was sporadic. When a larger event or street demonstration was being organized, and it needed to be guarded against an attack, or needed some way to simply keep order, several suitable comrades were selected from each local of the party based in our various unions. They were given armbands, and before the meeting, were given the necessary instructions. After the meeting, the group would be disbanded until the next time a meeting or demonstration required protection. We would then request each union to again send us a group of volunteers to serve as guards. Naturally, the same comrades would always volunteer.

But after the Communists began attacking our institutions, disturbing and disrupting our closed sessions and open meetings, and physically attacking our activists, and when the attacks of the antisemitic hooligans and police also continued, the Warsaw Central Committee decided to organize a standing defense unit, a Bundist militia, to protect our movement. I was given the task of preparing a set of rules for this new militia, finding recruits for it, and leading it.

CHAPTER 13

Organizing the Bund Militia

When the Warsaw Central Committee of the Bund decided to create a special militia, we remembered very well the bitter experiences of the battle groups that had existed among some of the revolutionary parties in Czarist Russia—among the Socialist Revolutionary Party,[1] Anarchists, and the Polish Socialist Party (PPS), for example—where part of the revolutionary combat groups later devoted themselves to outright banditry. Out of the former "expropriators" for revolutionary ends, there arose thievery for personal gain. We therefore made it one of our goals to guard with all the means at our disposal against the members of our group drifting in that dishonorable direction. We laid down certain rules and principles.

Only members of the Bund were to be accepted into our militia. Also, members of the militia would have to have a regular trade and earn a living by it, so that guarding the party and its institutions would only be a voluntary party duty for them and not incline them to become professional strong-arms.

Every party local—the garment workers, the sales clerks, the leather workers, the metal workers, etc.—would contribute several people to the newly formed militia. They had to be physically fit, able to withstand a blow from a Communist attacker or a Polish hooligan, and able to return a blow, if necessary.

The militia members were to have the same rights and obligations as members of all the other party groups. They were to receive political and organizational reports from the Warsaw Central Committee of the Bund, discuss all questions that were before the party, and adopt resolutions and decisions.

In addition, the militia was not to have any special privileges. In fact, for the militia, party discipline was to be even stricter than for the others. A member had to come to the militia meetings regularly, and if he missed a meeting, he had to have a good reason.

Right at the outset, the militia encountered a very important problem. Facing vicious attacks by the Communists and the savagery of the hooligans and the

Figure 25. First of May Demonstration, Warsaw. Bernard Goldstein is on the right. From the Archives of the YIVO Institute for Jewish Research, New York.

Figure 26. Bundiwt Youth Militia, Warsaw, 1930s. From the Archives of the YIVO Institute for Jewish Research, New York.

police presented the very real possibility of getting seriously hurt. There was the risk that a wounded militiaman would not be able to work for a long period of time, a common occurrence. Who would support the wounded militiaman and his family during the time he was out of work? In order not to create the impression among the militiamen that they were *kest kinder*[2] of the Bund, the militia decided to take on this responsibility itself. The militia created a sick fund, every militiaman contributing a regular amount. When the support for the wounded militiaman and his family went on for too long, and the militia's own fund could no longer afford to continue its support, only then did the party step in and help. But, most important, the principle was established that the militia cares for its own. This had the additional virtue of creating a feeling of solidarity among the militia members, a feeling of being responsible for one another.

We also wanted to make sure not to create the impression among the militiamen that because they were putting their lives on the line for the Bund they were therefore excused from paying their Bund membership dues. They would have to pay the same amount of dues as all other party members did.

More difficult was the problem of the loss of income due to leaving work. Often we had to call up the militia in the middle of the working day in order to repulse an attack or guard against one that was in the offing. In this as well we decided not to treat the militia differently from any other party members who had to absent themselves from work in order to carry out some party duty. We paid no compensation to party members for lost wages due to their having to

Figure 27. A Bundist *zelbst-shuts* (self-defense) unit with three of their slain comrades. Odessa, 1905. From the Archives of the YIVO Institute for Jewish Research, New York.

Figure 28. One of Many Bundist Self-Defense Battalions. Pinsk, 1905. Note that each person is armed with a gun or a knife. From the Archives of the YIVO Institute for Jewish Research, New York.

Figure 29. A *Yugnt-Bund Tsukunft* (Youth-Bund Future) militia group among the ruins of the Warsaw Ghetto, April 19, 1948, in commemoration of the April 19, 1943 Warsaw Ghetto Uprising. From the Archives of the YIVO Institute for Jewish Research, New York.

leave work to carry out some party duty. We never deviated from this principle, even though many of our militiamen were family men, and it was very hard for them to lose any amount of wages.

We were very disciplined, even in smaller matters. For example, after the militia was organized, we were faced with a problem that required great delicacy. Often we would arrange a cultural evening during which we would not usually expect an attack; for example, a theatrical performance, a literary evening, a recitation, or a choral performance. For such an event about a dozen militiamen would suffice. What to do then with the rest of the militia?

At first the militiamen demanded free admission for all of them to all such cultural events. Their argument was that in situations where their lives were at stake, all of them had to be present. Why, therefore, at those events, where one could enjoy some cultural uplifting, should the doors be closed to them? We wanted to avoid creating a privileged cadre out of them, even in such small matters. We knew that even small things could slowly develop to a dangerous point. We arrived at a compromise: militiamen who were not serving at a particular cultural event were entitled to a 50% deduction in the price of admission for themselves, but not for their families. Those militiamen that were serving that particular evening were to have that same 50% deduction for their families. This way both sets of militiamen had a bit of a privilege, but also had to pay something for tickets to party events.

By being cautious to guard against the risk of privilege and personal gain, we avoided the tragic end that many other revolutionary parties fell into with their battle groups.

Notes

1. Socialist Revolutionary Party (the SRs, or "Es'ers"), a major political party in early 20th century Russia and a key player in the Russian Revolution.—MZ
2. *Kest*: The traditional Jewish custom of the parents of the bride supporting a newly-wed couple for several years.—MZ

CHAPTER 14

The Communists and the Underworld

We had not yet quite gotten used to the physical violence that the Communists had introduced into the labor movement, to their reckless exploits and the fights they were continually inciting—when they gave us a fresh blow which shocked and dismayed us at the level of our most fundamental, deeply held, Socialist conceptions of decency and morality.

During the ceaseless attacks on our meetings and offices, we began to see, more and more often, well-known Warsaw underworld characters among their combatants. After a while, we noticed the same underworld characters appearing again and again, till it became clear that this was no coincidence, but rather that the Communists were turning to a new tactic: employing the underworld in their battle against other working-class parties.

This stunned our ranks. Rooted among the organized workers was the belief that the labor movement and the underworld were like fire and water. As far back as 1905, the Warsaw Jewish workers attacked the whorehouses, mercilessly beating up the pimps. For the workers it was clear that the end of oppression and enslavement meant the end of the underworld miasma as well. And here, suddenly, the underworld appeared as a part of the Communist camp, helping the Communists in their battles against other working-class parties.

A large number of these new Communist underworld associates occupied quite a "high position" in the Warsaw Jewish underworld. In the first rank were Hershl "Walczący," Pinie Gadulnik, Mayer Czompl, and Dovid Milner.

Hershl "Walczący" (he got the nickname "Walczący"—fighter—because he used to work as a boxer in the Warsaw circus) was a strong, broad-shouldered, healthy young man. His chief profession was extorting protection money from shopkeepers, threatening them with "damages" if they didn't pay.

Later Hershl was promoted to the status of an "enforcer" on Świętojerska Street, a branch of the Nalewki, which extended the length of the Krasińskich Garden and where there were a lot of Jewish ready-made clothing stores. Every such store employed people to stand outside and persuade customers to come into the shop. Such employees were called "catchers" because they used to latch on to every passerby, pulling him by the sleeve, sometimes pulling him into the store by force. Some underworld characters insinuated themselves among the "catchers," demanding a percentage of the receipts, even though they did not bring in any customers. They would stand outside a shop, once in a while casually grabbing a passerby, but mainly asserting their domination of the street. The shopkeepers had to pay them off weekly, and rather handsomely at that. These thugs were referred to as "The Strong-Arms," an organized group. The money they extorted from the shopkeepers they divided amongst themselves. Hershl "Walczący" was their leader on Świętojerska Street.

Pinye Gadulnik "Plapler" (a reference to his propensity to babble: *plapler*, one who jabbers or babbles) came from Powązki and belonged to the Powązki underworld. For a time he belonged to Piłsudski's Legions, but he was thrown out of their ranks for some underhanded doings. Pinye Gadulnik was another one of the strong-arms on Świętojerska Street.

A third one of these thugs, Maier Czompel, was also from Powązki. His whole family—his father, and several of his brothers—coal haulers—all belonged to the underworld. Maier Czompel looked like a refined young man, but sticking a knife into someone's side was as small a thing to him as eating a slice of bread. Pinie Gadulnik brought Maier Czompel into the gang of strong-arms on Świętojerska Street, but they later dethroned Hershl from his leadership. This created a great impression in the underworld. A song was even composed about this "accomplishment" that became popular in Warsaw beyond the borders of the underworld.[1]

But the wildest and the most dangerous among the Communist goons from the underworld was Dovid Milner. Upon first meeting him, you were favorably impressed. He was of middle height, big-boned, strong, with light brown hair—a good-looking fellow. He had many "trades." He was an enforcer (a kneecap-breaking, bad-debt collector), a shill at auctions, and with many "brides" on the street. On top of all that, he was also "king" of several whorehouses on Ostrowska Street. As a cover for all these criminal activities, he was, ostensibly, a coal hauler. He was one of the biggest thugs and one of the most dangerous strong-arms in the Warsaw underworld. Because of a dispute over bad-debt money, he shot Maier Czompel and ran away to Argentina, returning to Warsaw in the thirties. But up until the time he ran away, he was for many years the terror of our whole movement, leading some of the bloodiest Communist attacks on the Bund.

Also belonging to the standing "staff" of Communist assailants against the Bund was Froyim "Bults." He was a baker by trade and a big shot in the Bakers Union when the Communists took it over, but in fact he never worked at his trade. He lived off "brides," that is, prostitutes—primarily maidservants. He chose his brides so that each one had a different *wychodne* (day off), so that they wouldn't know that others were also working for him. He had these brides in addition to his wife. But brides were not his only trade. He also kept a whorehouse. When the union of housemaids was organized, he immediately became a constant visitor, with the purpose, of course, of finding some new brides for himself. They had to drive him out with sticks.

It was such a gang of underworld characters the Communists enlisted in their battle with the Bund. What's more, they even gave them a cover of legality. The union of retail clerks in Warsaw was then under the influence of the Communists. The criminal strong-arm enforcers pretended to be "catchers." Catchers were generally honest young fellows who really worked very hard, standing on the street in the heat and frost, virtually dragging customers into the shops that employed them. The Communist Union organized the catchers as a separate local of their Retail Clerks Union. They then signed the underworld characters into this local of honest catchers, securing for them the cover of a legal workers organization. It was for this reason that these thugs were so willing to do whatever little job the Communists assigned them. They did these jobs not simply because beating people black-and-blue was their beloved "profession," but also because they were thus able to cover up a large part of their criminal activities under the mantle of a political party and a legal trade union.

Not all of these thugs were left unmoved by this partnership. It stands to reason that in time a part of the underworld toughs that the Communist Party used in its terrorist attacks against the Bund, became . . . convinced Communists. In other words, they now administered their beatings because of "ideology," because of "revolution," because of "communism." To convert a simple thug, empty of any ideas, into a Communist, was not very hard. He needed only to join the party, which in any case preached and justified violence against all its opponents, especially against the party of Socialists, "traitors to the working class," who may be fought with by any and all means. It was a short distance from being a common thug associated with the Communist Party to becoming an "ideological" terrorist. It was thus easy for the Communists to find powerful strong-arms among these underworld characters who bolstered their criminal battle against the Bund. Because of them, our defense against the Communist assailants became much more difficult.

Note

1. The song:

    Harshl iz geven eyner fun di groyse
    Un vemen er hot gezen, hot er geheysn gebm a koyse.
    Haynt geyt Harshl aropgelozt di noz,
    Er hot gekrign "leyges" (klep) un veyst dokh nisht far vos.

Refrain:
Harshl, vu geystu?—Harshl vu shteystu?—
Harshl, vu bistu mit dayne grobe hent?
Du host shoyn nisht keyn hent,
Du host shoyn nisht keyn vent,
Du vest shoyn nisht nemen af Shvyente-yerske keyn protsent.

Harshl iz geven der shenster fun zey ale
Iz gekumen Maier Czompel un hot im tsugenumen di kale,
Haynt geyt Harshl aropgelozt di noz,
Er hot gekrign "leyges" un veyst dokh nisht far vos.
(Refrain)

Harshl hot geshpilt in orde-borde-shorde,
Iz gekumen Maier Shtempl un hot im ongeribm di morde,
Haynt geyt Harshl aropgelozt di noz,
Er hot gekrign "leyges" un veyst dokh nit far vos.
(Refrain)

Unrhymed, more-or-less literal translation:

Harshl [not Hershl] was one of the big shots,
And whomever he saw he demanded of him a drink.
Today Harshl walks around with his head [nose] held down,
He was beaten and doesn't know why.

Refrain:
Harshl, where are you going?—Harshl, where are you standing?
Harshl, where are you with your thick hands?
Now you have no hands,
Now you have no walls,
You won't be taking any percentages anymore on Svyente-Yerske.

Harshl was the handsomest of them all,
Came Maier Czompel and took away his bride.
Today Harshl walks around with his head down,
He was beaten and doesn't know why.
(Refrain)

Harshl played "orde-borde-shorde"
Came Maier Czompel and rubbed his chin,
Today Harsh walks around with his head down,
He was beaten and doesn't know why.
(Refrain)

CHAPTER 15

The 1922 Election Campaign

It was not long before the newly formed Bund Militia was confronted with a fresh task.

The elections for the Polish parliament were approaching, with the campaigning beginning in the fall of 1922. This was the first big election and political campaign in which the Bund could legally participate since the period of its de facto illegality (1920–1922). The police harassment of the Bund had not completely stopped, but in the new general atmosphere of free elections, it wasn't practical for the government to supress the Bund's campaigning.

The party took advantage of this first great possibility of a free campaign to agitate widely in speech and in writing. We campaigned throughout the country; in Warsaw the campaign's scope was especially broad.

I will tell of only one aspect of our multifaceted campaign work, the one in which I was directly involved.

During the campaign, the Bund arranged countless meetings in rented, large, union halls. Our comrades distributed thousands of leaflets in the streets, rousing our people. Our campaign workers distributed campaign literature to thousands of apartments. We glued our election placards to the walls of houses and in their entryways. It was an enormous undertaking.

Our campaign gave the Communists a lot of work. They had to tear down all our placards and posters and rip them up. They already knew how to disrupt our meetings. They screamed, made a racket, created an uproar—all of which gave the police an excuse to disperse the meeting for "disturbing the peace."

They carried out a total war on our entire campaign. They fell upon and beat up the couples who would go through the streets late at night pasting up the Bund's campaign posters. They attacked the trucks that would drive around the streets decorated with our campaign slogans. They beat up our block canvassers.

Figure 30. "There where we live, there is our country! A democratic republic! Full political and national rights for Jews! Ensure that the voice of the Jewish working class is heard at the constituent assembly!" Kiev, ca. 1918. The poster further urges Jews to vote for the Bund candidates, Slate 9, in an election following the Russian Revolution, when non-Bolshevik parties were still being tolerated by the Communist regime. From the Archives of the YIVO Institute for Jewish Research, New York.

Our militiamen had to guard dozens of large and small meetings, ride along on the campaign trucks, and often accompany the Bundist canvassers going from house to house. They were exhausted. But they did their job and were in place wherever they were needed.

Characteristically, the Communists only attacked the Bundist campaign meetings and only beat up the Bundist campaigners. Other political parties, in particular the Polish Socialist Party, they left in peace. Only once did they try to break up a PPS meeting. A big fight erupted, and in the end a Communist lay dead on the floor. They thus saw that such exploits would cost them too dearly, so they gave up trying to disrupt PPS meetings. But at Bundist meetings they continued to have their fun.

On Election Day, the 5th of November 1922, the Communists really lit into our Bundist campaigners. In Poland it was permitted to campaign in the streets on the day of the election, but not within 100 feet of a polling place. One particular attack was so powerful that, by itself, our own militia could not have withstood it. Fortunately for us, some PPS campaigners and their militia were also located at the same polling place. They helped us drive off the Communist attackers.

Although most of the time we were fighting off Communist attackers during the campaign, we also had to deal with attacks by the Endek[1] hooligans, as well as a great deal of additional harassment by the police.

Everywhere our militia had to safeguard the security of the Bund gatherings, protecting them from our enemies of the left and the right. This election campaign was the first great trial of the young Bund Militia, and it emerged from it with honor. It always adhered to the role of defender, and in that role never descended to excess, never lost its self-discipline, its sense of responsibility.

Figure 31. *Tsukunft*ists putting up Bund election posters in Baranowicze, Poland (now Baranavichy, Belarus), ca. 1930. From the Archives of the YIVO Institute for Jewish Research, New York.

This was not, however, the only trouble we had to confront during this election campaign. There was also the "legality" issue, not so easy to deal with.

The police did not openly ban our meetings, but in an underhanded way, they tried to make it difficult for our meetings to take place. The police let the owners of the theatres and movie houses know not to be too hasty to profit by renting to the Bund. Of course, the owners, who were very much dependent on the good will of the police, had to reckon with them and their warnings. There was, fortunately, a simple way to deal with this: pay a really good rental price. For a really good price, the owners were willing to take a chance.

We had in fact foreseen this problem and had, therefore, well ahead of time, signed leases with the owners for the period of the election campaign.

We mainly used the following halls: the Scala Theatre, a Jewish theatre on the corner of Dzielna and Dzika and the Theatre Central[2] on Leszno 1 (these were both in the very center of the Jewish quarter); Kamiński's[3] Theatre on Oboźna, in a strictly Gentile locale, but possessing a very large auditorium; and Theatre Powszechny, on the corner of Leszno and Żelazna—also in a Gentile neighborhood, but not far from the middle of the Jewish quarter at Karmelicka and Smocza.

We paid, as I said, a very dear price for these locations. To sweeten the deal, we also agreed to forfeit the rent money if the police should ban the meeting. We had to agree to this condition, or we would not have been able to rent any halls at all.

Figure 32. Posting Bundist Election Placards. From the Archives of the YIVO Institute for Jewish Research, New York.

In addition to the high rental price, the theatre owners had another good reason for being inclined to rent to the Bund. They suffered great losses from scalpers who bought up large numbers of tickets and then resold them at greatly inflated prices. These scalpers were tied in with the strong-arm thugs I described in the previous chapter. The theatre owners trembled before them. They knew, however, that the Bund and its unions were waging a fierce battle with these thugs. The owners therefore sought for ways to stay on good terms with the Bund and its unions, hoping in this way to be able to turn to them for help against the scalpers and strong-arms if and when the need arose.

But securing a meeting hall was only the beginning.

Having rented a meeting hall did not mean the meeting would take place or that it could proceed peacefully. At every meeting there were a number of police and Political Secret Service agents. For any trifle, they had the right to disperse the meeting with the excuse that we were "disturbing the peace." The Communists were always more than willing to provide this excuse. The police assigned to a meeting could disperse it even for simple Communist heckling and yelling, not to mention violence. Against this danger there was a powerful weapon that softened even the most despotic police detail—bribery. We had to bribe the police assigned to our meetings handsomely, so they would not interpret the law against disturbing the peace too strictly.

In addition to all this, there was yet another trouble. It was also possible to disperse a meeting for "agitating against the government." Our speakers were not sparing in their sharp criticism directed at the Polish government, and rightly so. We again had to make sure that the Polish political experts overseeing the content of the speeches did not take too seriously their duty to protect the honor of the government and not too often be offended in its name. Again, the weapon against this was money.

But the best strategy of all was to lure the police and the secret agents who were ensuring all was "kosher" out of the hall altogether. To this purpose a simple solution was also found. Since the theatre owner was interested in having good relations with the police and the agents of his precinct for his own reasons, we would ask the theatre owner to invite the political and police *mashgiekh* (traditionally, the religious supervisor enforcing the kosher laws) outside the hall for a glass of brandy, at our expense, of course. The police agent, or several of them, who normally had no aversion to the bitter drop, did not have to be asked twice. In this way we often lured the police and political "kosher enforcers" out of the meeting.

In this way, using tricks, bribery, and subterfuges, we were able to see to it that a meeting that had previously been formally legalized by the regime could in fact take place.

I want to tell now about one person who took upon himself a very large share of the whole weight of the Warsaw election campaign: Comrade Abram Stoller (now in New York).

I knew Comrade Abram—as we used to call him—from a much earlier time, since the end of 1915. I had come to Kiev through Moscow, after escaping the police guards in Tver. There, I immediately threw myself into party work. In connection with that work I often happened to come to the Jewish students' soup kitchen for company and to take care of various party matters with the members of the Bundist party group. A few of them, the active ones, I remember well to this day: One of them was Buzi Spivak, a student in the Technological Institute; another was Fayvish Morgnshtern from Kamieniec-Podolski, a medical student in his last semester; a third was Leyb Rozovski, a jurist, from the Caucasus, who could barely speak Yiddish but was very Jewishly nationalistic in his sympathies; a fourth, Zhuk, studied economics. These people remain living in my memory because of their genuine folk-feeling and friendliness. Except for Rozovski, they all spoke a rich, beautiful Yiddish. The positive impression they made on me was particularly pleasant, because, in general, the Jewish Socialist students in Poland,

Figure 33. "For Democracy and Socialism. Vote for the list of the Bund and the Bund federation of trade unions." Warsaw 1930s. From the Archives of the YIVO Institute for Jewish Research, New York.

and especially in Warsaw, held themselves a bit aloof; they were stiff, even a little stuck up and haughty. I was struck by the contrast between the aloofness of the Jewish Socialist students in Poland, and the friendliness and ease of the Jewish Socialist students in the Ukraine.[4]

In this same student kitchen, one student, a medical student, immediately caught my eye. He was always agitated, always running about, always looking rushed, as if he had something urgent and important to take care of. This was in fact Abram Stoller. He was at that time a *Sejmowiec*.[5] We quickly became personally acquainted. Since I had not long ago arrived from Poland, I was asked to give a report to the literary-artistic club, called "Khudoshestvyennyi Klub" (Club for Lovers of Art and Culture)—in reality it was a cover for a general, interparty, Socialist organization consisting mostly of students and intelligentsia, both Jews and non-Jews. Since my Russian was weak, I spoke in Yiddish. A Gentile who knew Yiddish—Semitshke they called him—translated my talk into Russian. After my talk, the student Stoller approached and thanked me profusely for my talk. That is how we first became acquainted. Later, in 1921, Comrade Stoller came to Warsaw and joined the Bund. He immediately threw himself wholeheartedly into its work, and in a short time became one of the most active members of the Warsaw Bund's party secretariat.

From that time forward, until the moment of our great Catastrophe, which parted us for a number of years, we both worked in the closest friendship and harmony in the Secretariat of the Bund's Warsaw organization.

Abram excelled with his extraordinary activity and dynamism. He could work uninterrupted for 16–18 hours a day, "wasting" only five to ten minutes to stop for a meal.

In general, he limited his personal needs to a minimum. When fall came, and it got very cold outside, he didn't "notice," and it didn't occur to him that he needed a winter coat. I dragged him off to a store and bought him (with his money, of course) a cheap but warm one. That's the way he was. And so he remained when he married the young Bundist from Vilnius, the teacher, Libe Andrajewska, and so he was even after Libe gave birth to their only daughter, Rokhl.

Comrade Stoller carried out a huge part of the Bundist election campaign in 1922, and also in the various election campaigns of the Warsaw Bund in later years. He led the work of the Bund's election secretariat in Warsaw, getting election campaign literature delivered to tens of thousands of addresses, sending off hundreds of couples to electioneer among the Warsaw courtyards and apartments and to distribute flyers in the streets. He also administered and managed the activities of the regional election committees in Praga and Krochmalna, and secured speakers for countless small election meetings and neighborhood gatherings.

It is hardly necessary to say that his electioneering campaign work played a huge role in spreading the Bund program among the Jewish folk masses.

Notes

1. Fascist, antisemitic National Democratic Party of Poland ("Endek" from the name of the letter *n,* here standing for the initial letter of the first word of *Narodowa Demokracja* + *-dek* (from the *d* and *k* in *Demokracja*).—MZ
2. *Teatr Centralny*, directed by Ester Rokhl Kamińska.—MR
3. The Abraham Izaak Kamiński Jewish Theatre on Oboźna, Street Number 1–3.—MR
4. Buzi Spivak continued to remain a Bundist under Bolshevik rule. He worked with the illegal social-democracy; was arrested and murdered by the Bolsheviks. Morgnshtern died during the 1918 flu epidemic when he threw himself into the work of saving those who had contracted the illness. Rozovski went back to Kafkaz; I don't know what happened to him there. Zhuk became a Communist.—BG
5. *Sejmowiec*: A member of SERP (the Jewish Socialist Workers Party), which called for the establishment of an extraterritorial Jewish diet for all of Russian Jewry, with national political autonomy.—MZ

CHAPTER 16

Unifying the Trade Union Movement

In that same election year, 1922, an historical event took place that played a very important part in the history of the Jewish labor movement in Poland: the unification of the entire Polish trade union movement.

It was really a double unification: (1) the unification of the Polish Trade Union Movement with the Jewish Trade Union Movement, under one central administration, to be called the Central Committee, and (2) the unification of all the Jewish trade unions in Poland, also under one administration, to be called the *Landrat,* or National Council.

The Bund's position had always been for a unified national trade union movement, with autonomy for each ethnic group's organization.

Right after after World War I when Poland regained its independence, the Bund took the initiative in unifying the Jewish and Polish trade unions. The Bund's Dovid Mayer, then Chair of the Bund's Central Committee, began the discussions, concluded by him and Viktor Alter, who, as the Chair of the Jewish Trade Union National Council (*Landrat*), stood at the very head of the whole Jewish Trade Union Movement in Poland.

The chief negotiator for the Polish trade unions was Zygmunt Żuławski, one of the finest PPS leaders.

The unification did in fact provide cultural autonomy for the Jewish workers, as well as autonomy, largely, in trade union issues.

Cultural autonomy meant that each union in any city with a large Jewish component would be required to form a separate Jewish affiliate. In the larger cities, where there were a large number of unions, all these separate Jewish affiliates would be required to create one central administrative center, to be called Cultural Bureau (*Kultur Amt*). This Bureau was to be responsible for satisfying the cultural needs of the Jewish workers, and also to care for their specific trade

Figure 34. The Presidium at a joint meeting of Jewish and Polish Workers. Among the PPS and Bund leaders, Henryk Erlich, seated second from left, and Artur Ziegleboym, seated first on the right. From the Archives of the YIVO Institute for Jewish Research, New York.

Figure 35. Executive Board of the National Association of Jewish Labor Unions in Poland. Standing, first on left, Yoshke Ofman; Seated, first on left, Lichtenstein; Seated, center, Sarah Shveber; Seated, second from right, Khayim Vaser (Chaim Wasser).

union needs. In some cities, for example Warsaw or Lodz, this central administrative center retained its old name, Central Council.

At the head of the whole Jewish segment of the general united trade union movement was the National Council, chosen at a convention of all the Jewish trade unions. It would also, at the same time, be the official central Cultural Bureau, representing Jewish workers on the new, unified, Polish-Jewish Central Committee.

In this way the Bund, for the first time, successfully realized its principle of a unified Polish Labor Movement, making the Bund an integral part of the broader Polish Trade Union Movement while recognizing and ensuring national-cultural autonomy for its Jewish workers. On this issue, the Bund achieved a principled victory over the Communists who, on the question of national-cultural autonomy, vehemently fought the Bund.

It didn't take long for this Bundist achievement to have a practical outcome. It happened first with the Leather Workers Union.

After the split, the Jewish Communists, as I mentioned earlier, became the leaders of the Shoemaker and Shoe-Leather-Cutters-and-Stitchers Union. To head us off, they quickly came to a unification agreement with the Polish Shoemakers-and-Stitchers Union—without any special conditions, without any special cultural rights for the Jewish members, and without the slightest sign of any kind of autonomy for the Jewish workers.

The Jewish leather workers totaled 6,000 members nationally; the Polish ones, only 2,000. But at the unification convention, the Polish Communists demanded that the Central Committee consist of a majority of "*naszych*" ("ours," that is to say, Poles); the Jewish Communists acceded to this demand.[1] Later the Polish Communists demanded that the regional secretaries and other leading officials should also be "*z naszych*," and here again the Jewish Communists yielded. As for having union proceedings and correspondence carried out in Yiddish as well as Polish, the Polish Communists wouldn't hear of it. The Jewish Communists swallowed this demand as well, without any protest. (There was one single secretary of theirs, let it be said, who persisted in sending his reports in Yiddish.) In the end, the Jewish Communists paid dearly for this policy:

Figure 36. First Convention of the Bundist Leather Workers Union, 1919. Seated, fifth from left, Rubin Zuckerman, translator's father. From the Archives of the YIVO Institute for Jewish Research, New York.

they quickly began to lose their influence over the Jewish shoemakers and shoe leather cutters and stitchers.

The Jewish Shoemaker and Shoe Leather Cutter and Stitchers Union in Warsaw was located on Nowolipki 7; the Polish one, on Żytnia 32. They each remained in their separate offices. But only Polish was spoken when the two affiliates came together at a meeting, even though the Jewish workers were the overwhelming majority. If a Jewish worker stepped up to the platform to say something in Yiddish, the Poles would not tolerate it. They would ridicule the speaker and even shout antisemitic remarks. The result was that the Jewish workers came less and less often to these meetings. The more the Jewish workers cooled toward the Communist Union at Nowolipki 7, the more they warmed to the Bundist Union on Pawia 32 (later moved to Leszno 19). The Bundist Union quickly formed locals for the shoemakers and later, after a time, the Bund acquired a majority of the Jewish leather workers in all the leather trades, except for the shoemakers, who remained with the Communists.

At the unification convention of the Jewish trade unions in 1922, the Bund was the dominant force. Of the 38 delegates from all corners of Poland, the Bund had 28, the Jewish Communists 5, the Labor Zionists 4, and the Uniteds 1. After the convention, the non-Bundist Jewish unions in the various cities joined their local Cultural Bureaus, all of which were under Bundist leadership.

Figure 37. A Conference of Bundists and Trade Union Leaders, Warsaw. Bernard Goldstein standing behind and to the left of central figure seated and holding papers. From the Archives of the YIVO Institute for Jewish Research, New York.

When all the Jewish trade unions in Warsaw joined the Central Committee, I was asked to familiarize myself with a few of the unions that had recently joined, among them (1) the Slaughterers Union and (2) the Transport Workers Union.

In the following two chapters I will describe these two very special unions. Each had its own special character; each added its distinct color to the overall picture of the Jewish Labor Movement in Warsaw.

Note

1. A similar situation occurred in the Garment Workers Union, where the majority of the workers also were Jewish. Appropriately, the Bund had a majority on the Central Committee; it never even occurred to the PPS to demand a Polish majority on the Central Committee.—BG

CHAPTER 17

The Slaughterers Union

It was not difficult for me to acquaint myself with the structure and internal affairs of the Slaughterers Union. I already knew quite a number of the people working in the slaughterhouse or connected with the meat business. Some of them I knew from the time I worked in Praga, and some I knew from a much earlier time: the meat wholesaler, Anshl Kolniczanski, for example, who had a lot of influence both in the slaughterhouse and in the union. It did not take me long to get a clear picture of the whole strange tangle of the meat business and the Slaughterers Union.

If one can speak at all of a political orientation for the Slaughterers Union, it is that it was under the influence of the Uniteds. Back in 1906–1907, the Socialist Zionists[1]—who would later become the largest part of the Uniteds—organized a group of slaughterers in the Warsaw suburb of Powązki, where at the time a large slaughterhouse was located. Yankev Lestchinsky, Shloymke Zusman, and Aaron Singalowski (Aaron Czenstochover) came to speak to these slaughterers. But this organized group of slaughterers didn't last long. During World War I, however, the Socialist-Zionist Party renewed its contact with the Powązki slaughterers, and when the big, new central slaughterhouse was built in Praga and the Slaughterers Union was founded, this party, now called the Uniteds, gained influence over it and began thinking of itself as the union's political boss. The contact between the union and the Uniteds mainly consisted in that the union systematically paid a certain—and a rather large—sum to the party, and also in that the Secretary of the union and several other activists in the union were members of the Uniteds Party.

The Secretary of the union was Betsalel Gelender. They called him Tsalel. He was a Socialist-Zionist adherent even before World War I. He had no particular trade or profession. His wife was the wage earner. She served up "home-style meals" on Nowolipki Street. His only occupation was helping her out a little at times with her business. Their patrons were Socialist-Zionist party members and activists, intelligent workers, and so on. Tselal never had played a part in trade union activity, but during World War I, the Socialist-Zionist Party sent him over to the group of slaughterers on Powązki. When they undertook to found the Slaughterers Union, he helped, and in this way he became their Secretary. He was very handsomely paid, the highest paid of any Secretary of any Jewish union in Warsaw. In addition, he was a representative of the local union of sausage workers, receiving payment for that as well. He didn't really have much to do, because the real leadership of the union was not in his hands but in the hands of others, as I will shortly explain. Some of the Executive Board members called him (behind his back) "the wedding gift from the Uniteds." When I spoke to him about the unhealthy relationships within the union, he would hold up his hands and say that he knows all that, but what can he do?

There was one Bundist who sat on the Executive Board of the union. His name was Yankl Futerman, called Yankl Flaczaz because he worked with tripe.

Yankl Flaczaz was a politically aware worker and had behind him quite a revolutionary past. He had begun as a member of the Polish Socialist Party, "Proletariat." In 1906 he and several Proletarians carried out an assassination attempt on a police precinct behind the central covered marketplace. He was not captured during the shooting, but he was later arrested, receiving a light sentence of four years' hard labor and permanent exile.

During the time of his hard labor, he was jailed with a group of Bundists, and under their influence, he became a Bundist too, remaining one for the rest of his life.

In 1916 I met up with him in Siberia, in Ilansk, Yeniskeyser Province, where a whole set of leading Bundists and Russian revolutionaries (Rachmil Weinstein, Kamenev[2], Boris Nikolayewski, and others) were exiled. After the outbreak of the 1917 Russian revolution, he was for a time Commissar of the small Crimean spa town, Alushta, near Yalta. In 1918 he came to Warsaw. He immediately became active in the Bund and was chosen to be on the Executive Board of the Slaughterers Union. He was also a member of the Polish association of those who had suffered political arrest during Czarist times. In addition, he was the Slaughterers Union liaison to the teamsters. There were also another two members of the Executive Board who considered themselves sympathizers of the Bund. These were Srul (Yisroel) "Zuze" Shvartsnobel and Yosl Langer, both from Praga.

Srul Zuze was a man with a huge, coarse body. He was over six feet tall and very broad shouldered. He loved his grub, and ate with great gusto. When he ordered meat, he told the waiter to bring him a lot of gravy, lapping it up with great pleasure. For that reason he acquired the nickname, "Zuze," Yiddish for "gravy."

He also had a revolutionary past. Before the war, he was an adherent of the PPS and was exiled to Siberia. Although he was a rather uncouth fellow, he cherished and held onto one ideal his entire life: he wanted above all for his son to become a doctor. He committed himself to this goal and persisted in it with great tenacity. He sent his son to *gymnasium*,³ even though that was a very heavy financial burden for a worker in Poland. And when his son finished gymnasium, Srul Zuze began working on realizing his ideal of sending his son to study medicine. This was in the thirties, a time of greatly heightened anti-semitism when for a Jew to gain admittance to a medical school was simply impossible. So he turned to me for help. I went with him to Tomasz Arciszewski, the Chair of the PPS—one of the most highly respected figures in the Polish political world—and to Mieczysław Niedziałkowski, the Editor-in-Chief of *Robotnik*, chief organ of the PPS. Although times were tough and they had other things on their minds, they showed a great interest in him. Finally with their help, permission was granted to allow Srul Zuze's son to be admitted to the veterinary institute, from which one could, after two years, automatically transfer over to the medical school. Srul Zuze eventually achieved his ideal: his son studied medicine. Sadly, Srul Zuze was not fated to enjoy his good fortune for long: the Second World War began. His son now lives somewhere in South America and is a practicing veterinarian.

Another slaughterer, Yosl Langer, also a Bund sympathizer, was still another strong man. Because of his strength, he was very much admired by the Polish workers in Praga, and they got along very well with him. His good comradeship with the Polish workers came to good use for us more than once during the time of the street fights with the antisemites and hooligans.

The union also employed a bookkeeper that worked in the office. He didn't have much to do, so he spent most of his time writing letters or formal requests for union members.

The union was divided into several locals: slaughterhouse workers, kosher butchers, nonkosher butchers, sausage makers, and so on. The chief base of the union was, however, the slaughterhouse workers, both because of their higher rate of pay and their overall importance.

The slaughterhouse workers were, in turn, divided into locals, according to how the work was distributed in the slaughterhouse. The working locals were as follows:

- *Drivers*: These workers drove the cattle and other animals from the trains to the stalls around the slaughterhouse, feeding them till they were led away to be slaughtered.
- *Skinners*: These workers were the essential slaughterhouse workers, doing the most important and most skilled work. They hoisted the carcass onto the overhead bar, skinned it (you had to know just how to do this so as not to cut the fur and so the hide would stay in one piece); they then removed the innards and cut the carcass into halves, then quarters—in a word, they did all the skilled labor.

- *Hide Haulers:* These workers hauled the hides to a special spot where the merchant tanners came to buy them.
- *Writers:* These workers recorded how much and what kind of meat a butcher bought, how much was owed by each butcher, and so on.
- *Meat Haulers:* These hauled the quartered or halved carcasses to the wagons.
- *Teamsters:* These workers drove the horse-drawn wagons and distributed the meat to the butchers throughout the city.
- *Others:* In addition there was a local of tripe workers, and a local of those who worked exclusively with calves.

Every tradesman had his own fenced-off spot in the slaughterhouse where only his cattle were slaughtered. Large tradesmen had several hundred cattle slaughtered a week; smaller tradesmen only slaughtered about twenty or so a week.

The workers in each local worked on a cooperative basis. Everything they earned went into one treasury or pool, as they called it. Each local had its treasurer who kept the pool. At the end of the week each member of the local got his share of the pool, but not according to his work or his qualifications, but according to a formula they themselves had created. There were certain general traditions: for example, an unmarried man—no matter how qualified—received a smaller share from the pool (he was called "the kid," whether he was 30, 40, or even 50 years old). In addition to a treasurer, each local also had a chairman and a secretary, but they had no great say.

The one with the real say in their affairs was someone else. Sometimes it was a member of one of the three slaughterer dynasties (about which I will tell later), and sometimes it was a "tough," the real boss of the local, who would get the largest share of the pool, even if he only worked a few hours a week. He would settle any conflicts that might arise among the members of the local, and had the last word in any dispute.

Every local also had appointed to it a delegate from the Executive of the Slaughterers Union. This delegate had very little say in the affairs of the local, but he got a share of the pool. He also got some money for "expenses" connected with being a delegate. The delegate didn't have to be a person who worked in that local. Sometimes he was a person who worked in a different local. Such a delegate received money from two pools, the one he worked in and the one he was a delegate to. Sometimes such a person didn't work more than a few hours a week—because he was supposedly as busy as a delegate to another local. Nevertheless he received a full share—and often quite a hefty share—from both pools.

The Executive of the union, and therefore their delegates to the locals, were in the pockets of three old slaughterer families, three dynasties, who were the real power over the whole union, over the whole craft, and, as a result, over the whole of the Warsaw slaughterhouse.

Notes

1. Founded in Odessa in 1905 as the Socialist-Zionist Workers Party and committed to territorialism, the idea that Jews should seek to found a state anywhere in the world it might be possible to do so.—MZ
2. Lev Borisovich Kamenev (Rosenfeld), 1883–1936: Joined the Bolshevik faction of the Russian Social-Democratic Workers Party in 1901. Worked closely with Lenin. Married Trotsky's sister. Prominent Soviet leader after Bolshevik takeover; in 1919 member of the Politburo and Moscow party boss. Became opposed to Stalin's leadership and was executed in the Great Purge of 1936.—MZ
3. European secondary school at about the level of the American community college.—MZ

CHAPTER 18

Three Slaughterer Dynasties

The biggest and strongest slaughterer dynasty was the Kolniczanski family. They were originally from the Warsaw suburb of Powązki. The Kolniczanski family had been slaughterers there for generations. When the several small slaughterhouses in the suburbs surrounding Warsaw were liquidated, and the large, new, central slaughterhouse was established in Praga, the Kolniczanski family went to work there too. There they again became the ruling dynasty.

There were four Kolniczanski brothers: Anshl, Itshe, Yoshke, and Motke.

The eldest, and their leader, was Anshl. In his youth he had belonged to the PPS and was a PPS militiaman. He was also for a short while a member of the Socialist-Zionists, in that very same Powązker group I talked about previously. He was one of the best marksmen in the PPS Militia. In 1905, during the big raids by the revolutionaries on the Warsaw brothels and their pimps, Anshl was one of the most active participants on the side of the revolutionaries. He was exiled to Siberia for his revolutionary activities, returning to Warsaw before the First World War, when he married in a quite romantic manner.

The daughter of a ritual slaughterer fell in love with him. The pious and proud ritual slaughterer would not hear of a match for his daughter with a mere slaughterer-youth, and a former convict to boot. Her parents, afraid that their daughter would steal off quietly to meet her beloved, kept her locked up in the house, not letting her out into the street. But the two young lovers behaved according to all the old romantic rules: Anshl stole his beloved out at night through a second story window, ran off, got married, and lived happily ever after.

During the First World War, under German occupation, Anshl and his brothers became big-time smugglers of meat, making a lot of money. By the time the war was over, Anshl was quite rich. In independent Poland following the war, he became a cattle merchant. His PPS past helped him, and in particular the fact that he had been exiled to Siberia. The old fighters for Polish independence, especially those who were tried and exiled to Siberia—the so-called "katorzhnikes," those sentenced by the Czarist regime to hard labor in Siberia—were a privileged group in independent Poland. Anshl was still friends with a lot of his former PPS comrades, many of whom occupied high office in independent Poland. All the doors of the government bureaucracy were open to him, all of which contributed to his becoming one of the richest meat merchants and one of the key players in the cattle and meat market. As a result, his household had become "intelligent"— his two daughters attended the gymnasium, spoke Polish, and behaved the way rich youngsters behave.

Anshl's authority was respected not only by the cattle merchants, but also by the workers and by the entire Slaughterers Union. His word was listened to. He would get involved in the internal union disputes, even though he was not a worker, but an employer, a merchant. The union would give him a break, make concessions for him, discount the price for working a head of cattle, and so on. The union did it simply because Anshl's power was so very great.

His three brothers greatly benefited from their brother's power, and as a result were also very influential in the Slaughterers Union and in the slaughterhouse. All three were members of the Executive of the union, and all three were also, of course, "delegates"—in other words, each received a large share from two pools and didn't have to work very hard. Yoshke was the delegate of the Hide Haulers local; Motke, a delegate of the Kosher Butchers local; and Itshe, a delegate of the Meat Haulers local. There was only one of the brothers, I have forgotten his name, who tore himself away from the family tradition, becoming a milliner, and after a time going off to Paris.

The brothers also set up one of their brothers-in-law in the slaughterhouse, Leyzer Shikhter, their sister's husband. He acquired a monopoly of a large number of the wagons that distributed meat from the slaughterhouse. That was his "dowry."

The Kolniczanskis remained the most powerful influence in the slaughtering business—until the city took it over.

The second slaughterhouse dynasty was the "Khayetshkes." Their real family name was Rosenberg, but nobody called them by that name. They were everywhere known as the "Khayetshkes." They acquired this nickname in honor of their mother, Khaye, who was the head of a very large family—with sons, daughters, daughters-in-law, sons-in-law, grandchildren, and great-grandchildren. Khayetshke herself lived to the ripe old age of 90. She survived three husbands, having children with each of them.

Most of her sons, the "Khayetshkes," had nicknames: Shmuel "Gabay"[1]; Leyb "Philozof"; Yosl "Meshugener," or crazy one; Yankl Srul "Ushek"; Chaim Shloyme "Beyn." Every nickname had a reason: Shmuel "Gabay," becaue he was the eldest son and the leader of the whole dynasty; Leyb "Philozof," because he could read newspapers and books, could write letters, and had some education;

Yosl "Meshugener," because he was a wild kid; Srul " Uszek" because he had big ears that stuck out (in Polish, "ucho" means "ear," "uszko," a little ear); Shloyme "Beyn" (Bone) because he was missing two fingers and a bone stuck out of one of them.

The eldest brother, Shmuel, had three sons and a daughter. His sons were provided for by working in the slaughterhouse; the daughter—the youngest of his children—belonged to our *Yugnt-Bund Tsukunft* (Youth-Bund Future), the Bund's youth organization.

The mother—Khayetshke—had a butcher shop selling giblets (intestines, tripe, lungs, liver, and so on). She did very well, because she paid practically nothing for what she sold. Her sons used to bring her the giblets for next to nothing. During Czarist times she used to hide revolutionaries. She used to cook large kettles of food and feed them generously, often slipping them a little money too. In her later years, when Poland had already achieved independence, she liked to boast, "I still vote for Number 4," the number always given to the Bund's list of candidates to the parliament, city council, or Jewish Community Council.

The Khayetshkes also had a foster child, an orphan, whom they adopted and raised. His name was Yukele, but he was called "Yukele Ganef" or Yukele the Thief. I will tell more about him later.

Shmuel, the oldest brother, was the representative of the slaughterhouse workers, that is to say, of the largest and most skilled local of the Meat Workers Union. Leyb Philozof was the representative of the Writers local (after all, he could read and write Polish, and, because he had spent some time in America, even knew a little English). Yosl and Yankl worked in the slaughterhouse, but in honor of their influential brothers, they got a bigger share of the pool. Srul, "Ushek," was a card player and hung out with the toughs—Shloyme "Beyn" would hang with him, too. When their shady dealings didn't go well, they would come to the slaughterhouse, and their brothers would set them up working among the teamsters. Their brother Chaim was a quiet sort, peaceful. He didn't get involved in community affairs and was not a "representative" of anything, nor a member of the Executive Board of the union.

The third "dynasty" was the family "Berczikes." I don't remember their real family name. This was their nickname because their grandfather was called Ber. They were from Pelcowizna, where, for generations they were employed in the local slaughterhouse. In Pelcowizna there was a small synagogue that had always been called "the little Berczikes synagogue." In my time one of the Berczike brothers was still the warden of that synagogue.

The Berczikes were four brothers: Yosl, Avrum, Beyrish, and I don't remember the name of the fourth one. The Berczikes had seniority in the Calf Local of the Praga slaughterhouse. Beyrish was the representative of that local. The other brothers worked in the local and ruled over it.

A constant struggle was quietly going on between these three dynasties for power in the union and in the slaughterhouse. Each had its sworn loyalists among the workers. According to the number of these loyalists, the Khayetshkes were the strongest, but the Kolniczanskis had more power and controlled more of the key positions, partly because of the great power of their eldest brother Anshl and his connections to the Polish slaughterers, to the leaders of their union, and to the Central Committee, where the Jewish union was also represented, and also, because Anshl was a pal of the General Secretary of the Foodstuffs Union, Edek Morawski. Before World War I they had both belonged to the PPS Militia and were both exiled together to Siberia. Incidentally, this Edek Morawski used to collect regularly, "on the side," a weekly payoff from the Jewish Slaughterers Union, an amount equal to the pay for slaughtering one head of cattle. This amounted to thirty or forty zlotys a week. This payoff was arranged for him by Anshl.

These three dynasties had extended and entrenched their power widely over the union and over the whole slaughterhouse. If one of the families needed to get a job for a relative or one of their own in the slaughterhouse, they got him one. If it happened that at that particular moment no additional workers were needed in the slaughterhouse, some fictitious piece of work was created, thus adding another taker from the pool. The smaller locals of the Slaughterhouse Union—as for example, the hide haulers, the meat haulers, the teamsters—were in fact filled with such fictitious workers, overflowing with unnecessary workers, who for at least half the time, took money for doing absolutely nothing. Such a job was sometimes given out as a dowry for a sister or some other relative. Through such fictitious jobs, the power of the three slaughterer dynasties was strengthened, because their new people received immediately the same say in things as any other worker.

The situation was much the same in the Polish Slaughterers Union. All the Polish workers belonged to the Polish union, both those that worked in the kosher part of the slaughterhouse and those that worked in the part of the slaughterhouse that slaughtered pigs. No Jews worked at slaughtering pigs, but a large number of Poles worked in the kosher part of the slaughterhouse, mainly in the

Figure 38. Executive Board, Meat Cutters Union. From the Archives of the YIVO Institute for Jewish Research, New York.

skilled unit of the slaughtering work. In the other locals—Hide Haulers and Meat Carriers—no Poles were employed. The Polish workers who worked in the kosher local of the slaughterhouse received a single large sum from the pool, which they then distributed among themselves.

Note

1. Literally, the warden of a synagogue.—MZ

CHAPTER 19

The Transport Workers Union: Back Porters

In 1922, in addition to the Slaughterers Union, I was assigned by the Central Committee to work with the Transport Workers Union, a union that then consisted exclusively of porters who carried things on their backs.

As with the Slaughterers Union, this union was also led by the Uniteds, who gained their access to it through their leadership of the Slaughterers Union. There was a close kinship between the slaughterers and the transport workers. They lived in the same neighborhoods, even in the same courtyards, and spent time in the same taverns. They knew each other well.

The Transport Workers Union had its peculiar characteristics, different from those of the Slaughterers Union.

The large numbers of back porters arose after the First World War. Before the war there were only a total of four back porter stations: one behind the large covered market (fish porters); another in the area of the great Warsaw commercial center located on the Nalewki-Gęsia-Franciszkańska Streets; and two more at the freight train station. In those days the teamsters themselves unloaded the goods from the trains.

During World War I, when commerce was greatly reduced, when the large commercial center around the Nalewki Street neighborhood was practically dead and most of the horses were requisitioned by the military, the teamsters were practically put out of business. At that time a large number of the teamsters started to get involved in various shady dealings.

This was for some of them quite an easy transition. Before the war many of them had already been connected to the underworld. Some had a criminal past, and even when they were making a living as teamsters, they supplemented their earnings with various dishonest dealings. From such teamsters a merchant rarely received all the goods being sent him—some of it always remained with the teamster. The teamsters had many different tricks for this sort of thing. If, for example, they were transporting flour, sugar, rice, beans, or other produce, they would fasten a box under the bed of the wagon and puncture the bottoms of the sacks of produce so that flour, sugar, rice, and beans would pour into the box below—all of which would remain, of course, with the teamster.

During World War I, when the smuggling of foodstuffs became a major occupation, some of the teamsters took advantage of the situation. They established stations of back porters over the entire commercial locale of the Nalewki-Gęsia neighborhood. Any wagon that came through with smuggled items had to be unloaded by these porters, even if a merchant didn't want them unloaded, either because he didn't want the porters to know what kind of merchandise he was bringing in, or because he simply wanted the teamster to do it. The merchant had to pay the back porters, whether they unloaded the merchandise or not. If they didn't, if a merchant was stubborn and refused to pay for someone doing nothing, it cost him dearer still. Either the stuff "vanished," or the police requisitioned it. It didn't take long for the merchants to learn that you didn't mess with the back porters: when they wanted to be paid, you didn't discuss it, you just paid!

When the war ended and normal commerce in the two large Warsaw Jewish commercial centers resumed (the first in the neighborhood of Nalewki-Gęsia-Franciszkańska and the second on Grzybowska-Gnojna-Zimna in front of the iron gate to the large covered market), these back porter stations remained. They established the rule that only they, and not the teamsters, must unload the materials from the wagons. There were at that time about 50 such back porter stations, with an average of about ten porters at each station.

The back porters were, even during the war, not used to hard work—quite the opposite, they were used to easy earnings. They had, therefore, even in the more normal postwar times, no desire to work hard. They hired *pomocnikes*—helpers—who mostly did the hard work of hauling crates and packages. The back porters hardly worked at all. These helpers would be grown men, often even family men, who sought a living and were ready to work hard for it. The back porters would normally not accept their assistants into the back porter's association. A *pomocnik* you were and a *pomocnik* you remained for the rest of your life. Leaping ahead and becoming part of the privileged back porters—that almost never happened.

Right after the war, the Uniteds began organizing the back porters. They were given space in the party headquarters at Leszno 49, and they appointed a certain Noyekh Shapiro as the party's point of contact for them. He was an old Socialist-Zionist Workers party member, one of their activists for many years, an energetic man, full of temperament. Not long after, he became a Communist and went off to the Soviet Union. There he shared the fate awaiting so many other foreign Communist activists who went to the Soviet Union—he was shot.

The situation in the Transport Workers Union seemed the same as that in the Meat Workers Union, but only superficially. There were many essential differences between the two unions. In general, the back porters were connected to the underworld; there were few of this sort among the meat workers. Generally, the meat workers were honest people. Many of them even had behind them an honorable revolutionary past. The meat workers were also diverse: there were even among them quite a number of religious Jews, wearing beards, dressing in the pious Jewish manner, and praying every day. There was among them a well-known *Mizrachi*[1] activist (Friedman, now in Israel). Besides, the meat workers trade was an old, established one, whereas the back porters trade was a relatively new one, more or less "invented" by the back porters themselves.

Actually, the Transport Workers Union was not really a union in the true sense of the word, because the back porters had no employers, no bosses. The union was really a loose association of workers working cooperatively. Each station was a cooperative of the workers who manned it. Just as with the different locals of the Meat Workers Union, each station had a pool, a kitty, and one or two officials: a treasurer and a secretary, sometimes both functions being carried out by the same person. As with the meat workers, the "strong-arms" took a larger share of the pool, and the smaller fry got a smaller share. These latter felt they were being taken advantage of, that they were being given a "Turkish account." They made an outcry, protested, but it did them no good—they had to take whatever the strong-arms doled out.

There were some large and good-paying stations in the Nalewki, Gnojna, and in front of the large open market where one could make a good living, and there were second-class stations, where the earnings were worse. The main function of the union was to straighten out the disputes between the stations, which eventually came down to one thing: the desire of the carriers in the poorer stations to get into the better stations, and the determination of those in the good stations not to let them. The porters' lives were consumed by this struggle.

Among the back porters there existed a kind of social security system of their own devising. If a member of a station got sick and couldn't work, he received his usual share from the kitty. If a member died, his vacant spot at the station went to his son or his son-in-law. If there was no son or son-in-law who could or wanted to take his spot, the porters' station paid the widow a weekly pension for a year—not the full share of the deceased, of course, but according to what seemed just—and the amount was, in fact, quite just. If someone in the station had a celebration or married off a child, they bought a gift or a wedding present with money from the kitty. If a condolence call to a family was necessary, the whole station would go at once and bring along a cask of brandy. Each station was autonomous in the way it carried out this mutual aid.

Among the back porters one obligatory good deed was especially popular: the commandment to visit the sick. Every Saturday and Sunday it was their custom to go to the Jewish hospital on Czystem to stand by the bedside of patients to fulfill the religious obligation to visit the sick, either their friends or simply anyone. In the Jewish hospital on Czystem on any given Sunday one could find, at a minimum, one hundred back porters who had come to visit the sick.

They were not particularly pious, the back porters, but during the Days of Awe—between Rosh-Hashone and Yom Kippur—many of them went to the synagogue to pray. Most of them went to the synagogue in the Gęsia cemetery. In this synagogue thieves, pimps, prostitutes, and other underworld characters had the right to pray during the Days of Awe. Back porters who were mixed up with these types came to pray there. One time I had an impulse to see how it was, the praying of this bunch. I went there with a friend. Some of the back porters who knew me approached, saying, sarcastically, with an ironic smile, "Comrade Bernard, whose grave have you come to visit?" meaning, "Have you come to observe us as if we were some sort of curious oddity?"

Notes

1. *Mizrachi* is an acronym for *Merkaz Ruhani* (*Religious Center*), the name of the religious Zionist organization founded in 1902 in Vilnius at a world conference of religious Zionists who believe the Torah should be at the center of Zionism.—MZ

CHAPTER 20

Back Porter Types

As I became better acquainted with the Transport Workers Union (TWU), some of the back porters attracted my particular attention. Among them were several very unusual types. A number of them underwent great changes in their lives under the influence of our movement, later playing an important role in the union.

The first Chairman of the TWU was a certain Alikum, as he was called by Poles and Jews alike. I never had occasion to hear his family name. Stationed behind the covered market, he was an old back porter from before the war. He was in fact the eldest porter. He was not called *Forzitser*, Yiddish for Chairman, but *Prezes*, Polish for Chairman. It had a more ceremonial ring to it. He was very proud of his office. At the demonstrations he alone would carry the union's emblem, beautifully embroidered on a sash worn diagonally over his chest like a field marshal's.

He was a fiercely devoted opera buff. For about 40 years he went to the Warsaw opera several times every week. The opera's Board of Directors grew to know him, and in his later years gave him a permanent free pass to attend the opera daily, which is exactly what he did. Actually he was only *Prezes* of the TWU for a few years. He died in the twenties in his early sixties.

Another interesting character in the union was Hershl Dorfman. They called him Hershke "Kupke"—droppings. He came from a bourgeois family. His father and the whole family were ashamed of him because he wasn't a "somebody," because he had become a mere back porter. As a boy he had studied in a religious school. He could read and write Yiddish, Polish, and Russian, and was, therefore, Secretary of the union, able to compose a motion and write a resolution. Hershl himself had no criminal life, but he was very tight with the toughs among the back porters. As a result he was able to work himself up to a very good station on Gnojna Street. He was the Writer of his station and made good money. He gave his children a proper upbringing, sending them to our Yiddish secular schools. One of his daughters was a *Tsukunftist*. Later he himself joined the Bund.

But the most interesting individual among the back porters was without a doubt Shaye-Yudl. His family name was Zilbershteyn. He was healthy, broad shouldered, and well built. When I made his acquaintance he was in his early thirties. At the union meetings he drew your attention with his quiet demeanor, his relaxed manner, and his refinement. He was a clever man. If he spoke about an issue or proposed something, it was always both sincere and sensible. I began to watch him with great interest. He was quick to notice this and began, on his part, to grow better acquainted with me, but slowly, cautiously, as if he didn't want to put me in a difficult position. In time he began to talk to me more often, discussing various things, till he finally revealed a frightful abyss into which he had fallen in his youth.

He was from a family of teamsters. At 11 years of age he was already hanging out with horses, wagons, and drivers, also becoming acquainted there with the underworld. He took on criminal ways—using a knife was a trifle to him. He spent a lot of time in jails, even back in Czarist times. In the street and even in jail, people trembled before him. During the war he was sought for some criminal activities, so he registered with the Germans for labor under a false name and was sent to somewhere in Lithuania. After a while he escaped from there because, even there, he did something criminal and was going to be arrested. Shortly after that he married a worker in Polakewicz's cigarette factory. The influence of the Bund had been strong for years in this factory, so his wife understood the Bund and workers organizations.

Under the influence of his wife, Shaye-Yudl began to go straight. He shed his criminal ways, became a back porter, and began to earn a living from his work. When the Back Porters Union was organized, he became one of its most active members, and it seems a certain inborn but dormant honesty awakened in him when he encountered issues where you needed to use, not the knife or your fist, but your head. When I came to the union, Shaye-Yudl had already acquired a reputation as a clear-thinking person who could quickly understand an issue without having it spelled out for him. He still had ties, however, to the underworld.

I understood that he wanted to cut himself off completely from the underworld, but that he needed help with this. I began to befriend him, but he held back. He was still not sure if he could burden me with his issues. He seemed to be waiting for a sign from me. Of course, I came to his aid. He changed virtually before my eyes. He became an idealistic person who was prepared to sacrifice himself for his convictions. Many years later he was put to the test, and because of his loyalty to the Bund, lost his livelihood. I'll tell more about that later.

Another back porter was called Abram the Lady. He was crippled—he had a wooden leg. But he was always elegant, keeping himself slim and well dressed. It was because of this elegance that he acquired his nickname. He had a revolutionary past. He had been a member of the PPS's militia. In 1905 he organized a group of wagon drivers in the PPS, all of them strong lads and good marksmen. In the PPS Militia, he belonged to the same secret cell of five as Borukh Shulman, the famous hero who exploded a bomb under the Czarist satrap, Constantinov, and paid for it with his life. Abram was very proud of that, and bragged quite a bit about it. He himself was wounded at a demonstration and was arrested. At that time they amputated his leg and exiled him to Siberia. He didn't get back to Warsaw until 1918, after the Russian revolution. In the PPS he learned the language of party politics and always liked to talk with "big" words. When he took the floor at a back porters meeting, the crowd of back porters would shout at him, "Don't use such big words! Talk with plain words!" He was a member of a station behind the covered market, but since he couldn't work because of his leg, he was the secretary and treasurer of the station and received the same share of earnings as all the others.

Another interesting personality was Zishe Zatorski. I knew his family from before the war. His grandfather had been a ritual slaughterer. His father had not worked, but had studied Talmud right up to the time he got married. After his marriage he became a real estate broker, growing to be quite successful. From being an orthodox Jew he suddenly became an unbeliever, and on top of that, a melomaniac, often running off to the Warsaw opera house. Every Yom Kippur, at *kol-nidre*, the required Yom Kippur-eve prayer, he would run off to the Warsaw opera instead of going to the synagogue, continuing this practice into his old age. He had many children. One son was a tanner and a Bundist. His daughters all married Bundists—one of them, Surele, worked in the soup kitchen for the Bund's Workers Corner on Przejazd 9.

Even as a child, Zishe was not "respectable." He didn't want to study—he was drawn to horses. As a boy he would run to the stables and hang out with the horses and the wagons. Eventually he was apprenticed to a teamster. I lost track of him for a long time. After the war, when I came to the Back Porters Union, I suddenly spotted him, all grown up, strong, well built, with a red neck, now a back porter. He was very happy to see me. He was always boasting to me about the Bundism of his family. Later he, too, became a Bundist.

Itshe Anders, or Itshe "Zbuk," was an entirely different sort of person. He was not liked by his own fellow back porters. In earlier years he had been a teamster, but at the same time a criminal type, a knife wielder, who had already done lots of jail time. He was a big shot among the strong-arm boys. He had had countless wives. Either he had divorced them or they had died. When the back porters would quarrel with him, they would always throw his many wives in his face. Itshe "Zbuk" was the one who later split the Transport Workers Union and led the majority of them away to the *FRACs*.[1] Those days were the highpoint in his criminal activities—he would extort money from the porters and from others—but more about that later.

Shmuel Jakubowicz, a former teamster, was an important activist in the Transport Workers Union. For a time he was chairman of the union. His brothers were all underworld characters, but he himself was an honest man with a respectable household. His wife was both beautiful and a fine woman. The wives of Smocza Street, where the Jakubowiczes lived, used to say that he probably cast a spell over her in order for her, a respectable girl from a fine home, to have married him, a common porter. On Smocza Street they called her "the lady." She did in fact dress beautifully, elegantly. When she would come to the bazaar to shop, the wives would point to her, saying, "That woman, that's Shmuel the porter's wife."

One of the worthiest people among the porters was Moniek Dembski. He also succeeded in extricating himself from the underworld and transforming himself into a socially useful human being. As a youth, Moniek Dembski was a thief, but after the war he became an assistant to the back porters on Gnojna Street. When I became the delegate of the Central Committee to the Transport Workers Union and became better acquainted with the people there, he attracted

Figure 39. Back Porter, Warsaw, ca. 1935–1938. Photograph by Roman Vishniac, © Mara Vishniac Kohn, courtesy International Center of Photography. Print from the Archives of the YIVO Institute for Jewish Research, New York.

my notice. I saw something in him that evoked a feeling of trust in me. He approached me to complain about his hard life as a back porter's helper, working very hard and getting paid very little in comparison with what the porters took for themselves. One time he poured out his bitter heart to me: "At least among the thieves, things were better. There the 'earnings' were fairly divided, whether one did a small task or a big one, everyone got the same share. And if someone tried to cheat, they broke his bones. For such a thing one could kill. And here—what do I get out of all my hard work?"

I became afraid that he would return to the criminal world where he saw more "justice" than among the porters. So I decided to take a chance. I knew some people in an international import-export firm. I asked them to give him a job and I guaranteed his honesty. I then pulled him aside and warned him: "Remember, Moniek, your future is at stake. If you behave honestly, you will be able to achieve much." He shook my hand and promised to be honest. He didn't disappoint me. He became so well liked at the firm that they paid for him to attend a training course for chauffeurs, a well-paid and hard-to-get job in Poland at the time. Later he even became chief buyer for one of the big department stores.

He married a widow with a small child, a little girl. He loved that little girl to distraction. He sent her to high school—very few workers could afford such a thing in the Poland of that time. His gratitude to the party that allowed him to become a respectable person was without limit. There was nothing the party could ask him for that he wouldn't gladly do. He was ready to give his very body and soul for the Bund. I will have occasion to talk more about him later.

Notes

1. The "FRACs," or PPS-Revolutionary Faction (FRACcja), a breakaway party from the PPS, formed in 1906 by Pilsudski, who wanted a more militant nationalism (including a war of liberation against Russia), a position rejected by the 1906 PPS Congress.—MZ

CHAPTER 21

Rope and Handcart Porters

The rope and handcart porters were the pariahs of the transport workers. On Zimna, in front of the covered market, on Mirowski Place, in the Nalewki, and other locations they stood waiting together in groups for work.

Summer and winter one could see the rope porters clothed in the same shabby outfit: heavy boots, cotton-quilted trousers, a cotton jacket, their hips encircled with thick rope as if with a belt—they waited for a box or a package to transport. If a customer on Zimna bought a box of lemons, oranges, or other fruit, he hired a rope porter to carry it for him. The rope porter would throw the box onto his back, tie it with the rope around his chest, and in this way, half bent-over, he would carry the box, sometimes for quite a considerable distance. If a well-off housewife had a large package, she would sometimes hire a rope porter to carry it for her.

The situation for the handcart porters was similar. They also had stations at the marketplaces, and they stood there with their small handcarts, waiting. If a tradesman had to transport several boxes or packages of material that a rope porter could not carry on his back, or if a poor man had to transport his rags, bag, and baggage, from one apartment to another and couldn't afford to hire a wagon, he hired a handcart porter. The porter drew a strong rope over his shoulder—he would simply harness himself to the cart like a horse—and pull the handcart, sometimes for long distances. Wintertime one could often see such a porter pulling a handcart through the snow at the very limit of his strength. Sometimes it happened that the porter did not have enough strength to pull his loaded cart up a hill or pull it out of a deep snowdrift. People would notice, run over, and push the wagon to a spot easier for him to go on from.

When the Transport Workers Union joined the Central Council, only the back porters, who were good wage earners, were members. The Central Council began to demand that the union broaden its membership and admit the other kinds of transport worker also: first of all their own *pomocnik* (helpers), and also the rope porters, the handcart porters, and the *stavnikes*. These last were workers who worked with herring. They were partly porters and partly hired hands. If a shopkeeper came to buy a barrel of herring, for example, a *stavnik* would have to roll out a barrel from the storeroom, open it, and show it to the customer. If the customer didn't buy the barrel of herring, then the *stavnik* had to nail the barrel shut again and roll it back into the storeroom.

The back porters opposed this demand to allow the lowly helpers and stavniks to join their union. The Bund was forced to wage a hard fight to get them to agree to create two new locals within their union, one for the rope porters and one for the handcart porters. These two kinds of porters worked very hard and earned very little. There were no "strong-arms" among them, as there were among the back porters, so there was no monopolizing of the work or enforcing of strong-arm demands. They were poorly paid. They labored very hard, and from the sweat of their brows, earned barely enough for a piece of bread.

The contrast between the back porters and the rope and handcart porters—they often had stations right next to each other—was immediately apparent. The back porters were well-built and broad shouldered, with thick red necks and happy faces. They were loud, optimistic, and smug. Working hard was not to their taste, but if they had to, then it was best to do it with panache. A back porter liked to show that he could carry a heavy iron case down several flights of stairs. But working continually and hard—that wasn't for them. That's what they had their helpers for.

The rope and handcart porters were just the opposite: they were thin, exhausted, and downcast. They were, in general, formerly skilled workers who, out of necessity during the war, became rope or handcart porters. The back porters looked down upon the rope and handcart porters, calling them *tshaptshakes* (low, beggarly). Even when the locals for the rope and handcart porters were formed within the Transport Workers Union, the back porters continued to harbor their antagonism towards them.

We also fought to bring the helpers of the back porters into the union. The helpers were often older people who had to support entire families with their earnings. They had absolutely no way to protect themselves against the back porters, their bosses. Eventually we prevailed in this instance as well: the helpers were brought into the union, gaining some degree of protection.

Among the handcart porters, the union possessed quite a number of important activists. I will describe just a few of the more interesting ones:

Moyshe Venger was one of the most active. Before the First World War he was a metal worker. During the war he was sent off to Germany for forced labor to work in the coalmines. When the German revolution broke out in 1918, he joined "Spartacus" (an organization that split off from the Independent German Social-Democrats and later became the seed of the German Communist

Party). He became acquainted there with Rosa Luxemburg and Karl Liebknecht and was very proud of that: whatever he spoke about, he always dropped their names. When he returned to Warsaw and couldn't find work as a metal worker, he partnered with a handcart porter, and stayed with this occupation. He joined the Bund and became very active in the Transport Workers Union. His attitude toward the back porters was very critical: "Comrade Bernard," he would warn me, "from the 'horses' (by this he meant the handcart porters) you will get much *nakhes* (joy, pleasure, pride); but from the back porters—nothing."

Another was Leybl Oberberg. He was once a tailor in a small town, but during the war he became a handcart porter. He was an intelligent worker and could articulate a complicated thought at a meeting. Every day he read the *Folkstsaytung*[1] aloud to the back porters at his station (in Simons Passage, at the Nalewki). He used to come often to our readings, always in the company of his wife and child. After a while, he was elected chairman of the Transport Workers Union. For the 1936 elections to the Warsaw *Kehilla*, the official Jewish Community Council, the Bund put forward a list of candidates that included a large number of workers and labor activists. Some of them were elected, and among them was Leybl Oberberg. This was the first time in the history of the Warsaw municipality that a worker, and not only that, but a lowly porter, became a councilman, a member of the *Kehilla*. This created a big commotion in Jewish bourgeois circles. They could not tolerate such an unheard of thing. The Bund was, of course, proud of this achievement. Leyble Oberberg used to say of himself: "If one lives on Szczęśliwa Street, among thieves and gangsters, and one doesn't himself become a thief, then he is a real hero."

Another activist of the Transport Workers Union, Yekhiel Maroko, was also once a skilled worker. Before the First World War he was a comb maker. During the war he became a rope porter, remaining one after the war was over. His station was on Zimna Street, where the wholesalers for groceries and spices were located. Among the merchants there were some who had worked themselves up from portering and knew Yekhiel Maroko well. Maroko was not a well man; he suffered from tuberculosis. The merchants of Zimna Street, his former fellow porters, saw to it that he did not overexert himself. For many years the

Figure 40. Executive Board, Bund Union of Transport Workers. From the Archives of the YIVO Institute for Jewish Research, New York.

Bund took care to see that he should be able take off at least once a year to go to a sanitarium. He was extremely devoted to the party. He sent his children to the TSYSHO school at 36 Krochmalna Street (he lived on Krochmalna). Later his children belonged to SKIF and then to *Tsukunft*.[2] When the Second World War broke out, he joined the stream of refugees to the Soviet Union, and there he died. One of his sons is now in America and is an active member of the Bund in New York.

Notes

1. "People's Newspaper," the Bund's daily newspaper.—MZ
2. The Bund created frameworks for younger members. It established the *Sotsyalistisher Kinder Farband* (SKIF; Union of Socialist Children) and *Tsukunft* (the *Future*, for young people), blending scout activities, sports events, and politics. In 1939, membership in Bund youth organizations had reached 12,000, with 200 branches across Poland.—MZ

CHAPTER 22

The Food Workers Union

I now had to begin working closely with the Food Workers Union on Leszno 19. This was a different sort of union from the ones I have previousy described.

It lacked the most important workers in the food industry: the bread bakers. They had their own separate union. This separation of the bread bakers from the general food workers union had a history. The bread bakers had organized in the early, formative years of the Bund in Czarist Russia, and had a rich revolutionary past behind them.

There was also antagonism between the bread bakers and the pastry bakers. The conflict between the two kinds of bakers had to do with the baking of *challahs*[1], and also with, for Passover, the baking of *matses*[2] and macaroons (Passover cookies made of almonds and without leavening).

The pastry bakers—who baked cookies, torts, and "tshastkes" (a kind of small tort)—claimed that since challahs fell into the category of finely baked goods, the baking of challahs rightly belonged to them. The bread bakers, on the other hand, held that the baking of challahs should by rights belong to them, since challah was a kind of bread. This conflict over to whom the right to bake challahs belonged grew especially intense in the first years after the World War I, when unemployment among the food workers was great, and workers were fighting over every scrap of work.

In addition to the pastry bakers, the following other food workers belonged to the General Food Workers Union: chocolate and candy workers, tea packers, egg packers, and hard liquor packers.[3]

Of all these various locals of the general union, the largest local consisted of the candy and chocolate workers. These workers were mostly girls, for the most part from respectable households, and so it was hard for them to adjust to the raw language of some of the bakers. Also the candy workers considered themselves "aristocrats" in relation to the bread bakers. In addition, there was the already described economic conflict between the bread bakers and the pastry bakers. All this was enough for mutual distrust among the three sides. There could thus be no talk about unifying all the food workers into one general union.

About 400–500 members belonged to the General Food Workers Union, most of them, women. It was a poor union. There was great unemployment, because right after the war, chocolate and sugar were scarce. The great poverty of the war years was still being felt many years after the war. The office of the union, on Leszno 19, was the poorest of all our Warsaw union offices. Membership dues were not paid regularly. From time to time a special surtax had to be levied on the membership to pay the rent and avoid eviction. Often they had to borrow money to pay the electric bill. After a while, the Leather and Haberdashers Union moved in and took over the greater part of the office. The Food Workers Union was left with only one small room, just enough space to accommodate the Secretariat. But more space wasn't really needed, since the members of the Food Workers Union did not come to the union office to spend time, as was the custom at other union offices, where the offices also served as workers clubs. The feminine membership of the union, whether married or single, was busy in the evenings with work at home, and had no free time to go to the union office for socializing or otherwise entertaining themselves there.

The secretary of the union, Greenberg (I don't remember his first name), had been a bookkeeper before the war. During the war he couldn't find work, so he began working as a food worker. Since the new union couldn't afford to pay a secretary, and Greenberg was a literate person, he performed the secretarial duties. A little later they began to pay him a little, and in this way he became their official secretary. He was a quiet, peaceful, refined person, but phlegmatic. In addition, he was a fanatic opera buff, more into operas than into union affairs. He showed little initiative; this left its mark on the union's state of affairs.

Among the active members of the Food Workers Union, there were a number of interesting and worthwhile people.

The most remarkable among them was the Mendelsund family: belonging to the union were Benyomin, the father; Golde, a daughter; and a son. A brother of Benyomin's also belonged to the union. Benyomin was a middle-aged man with a beard, a long coat, and a Hasidic-style hat, altogether looking quite respectable. He was very active in all aspects of the life of the union. The union activists were usually young, secular people. For an orthodox Jew like Benyomin to be a professional union activist was a rarity.

Benyomin came from a respected family of Gerer Hasidim.[4] His father was reputed a great Talmudic scholar. Only a few specially selected wealthy Hasidic youths (among them, Avigdor Mendelson, a brother of Shloyme[5] and Mayer Mendelson) were chosen to study with him.

With time, however, Benyomin found himself attracted to our social movement. One time he heard Medem speak, and he was captivated. He began being sympathetic to the Bund, and after a time became a party member. Of his piety he left much behind: he smoked a cigarette on the Sabbath, but he kept his beard and long gabardine for a long time, well into his thirties. Slowly he shifted from his union activities to becoming active in our secular Yiddish school system for children—not only in our school on Karmelicka 29 that his two children attended, but also in our Warsaw Central School Board. He became a friend and admirer of Shloyme Mendelson. He was an energetic person, idealistic, and a sober, practical, and effective activist.

Benyomin's daughter Golde was also active in the union. Along with her father, she was a member of the Executive Board for the Chocolate Candy Workers local. More than once it would happen that father and daughter would have intense discussions between themselves about various union issues. Golde was a modest girl, tactful in her relations with people, and very good-natured. As a result of her initiative, the local of chocolate candy makers decided to share their earnings with their unemployed comrades.

If there was a scarcity of work, those who were fully employed would not work an entire week, but give up some of their week's work to their unemployed comrades. Although she was an excellent and skilled worker, she could not get the kind of work she was qualified for. The most skilled positions were given to the men; women were only assigned positions as assistants, even if they were more qualified than the men. She was very devoted to the union. Her quiet modesty was in sharp contrast to the energy and dynamism displayed by all the other Mendelsunds.

The younger Mendelsund children added greatly to the family's popularity. Henokh was one of the most talented of the students in the TSYSHO School on Karmelicka 29. When SKIF was established he was one of its first members and immediately became one of its most active.[6] Also, their youngest daughter,

Figure 41. *SKIF* Youngsters engaged in an athletic exhibition, Warsaw, 1930s. From the Archives of the YIVO Institute for Jewish Research, New York.

Figure 42. Orthodox, middle-class Jew, Elijah Alebard, who from his earliest years participated in revolutionary activities of the Bund among Czarist soldiers and in the Illegal Transportation of people and literture over the border. Perished during the 1944 Polish uprising in Warsaw (from *The Jewish Labor Bund: A Pictorial History: 1897- 1957*). From the Archives of the YIVO Institute for Jewish Research, New York.

Rokhele, distinguished herself in the Yiddish secular school, in SKIF, and in the Medem Sanitarium.

Benyomin's brother—tall, thin, with black eyes and a black beard, quiet and withdrawn—was not active in the union. He was very pious, dressed in orthodox garb, the tassels of his fringed garment dangling over his trousers. I remember a particular incident involving him. I was present one time when there was a meeting of the union of the workers of Minkov's candy factory, where he worked. The meeting started after work, just before nightfall. Suddenly a sharp bang on the table rang out, and Benyomin's brother cried out that the meeting must be interrupted because the evening prayer must be said. It was explained to him that a meeting could not be interrupted at the whim of one person. He answered that there were present more than the required quorum of males and that therefore the meeting must be interrupted so that all could rise and recite the evening prayer. Of course he did not prevail. He went off angrily to a corner and recited the evening prayer all by himself, then left.

The chairman of the union was Yitsrok Greenberg. He had been a Bundist since before the war, a schooled and reliable activist. A very skilled worker, he later became an instructor in the ORT[7] trade school, training students to work in the candy industry.

Another member of the Executive Board was Fishl Tsukerlekhmakher.[8] He was active in the Bund since before the war. During the protest-strike conducted by the Bund during the Mendel Beilis trial,[9] he went to shut down the newspapers and was arrested. In Czarist times, Fishl was the leader of the Bund's illegal food workers union. He was also at that time an active member of Warsaw's Yiddish literary establishment, as well as a member of *Hazomir*,[10] where he was often in attendance.

Avrom Floymenboym was chairman of the candy makers local and a prominent member of the Executive Board of the union. He too was an active member of the Bund since before the war. Now he was not only active in the union but also on the Board of our TSYSHO schools. His two daughters were active in the Bund's youth organization, *Tsukunft*.

The two brothers Studnia, active in the union, were from a well-known baker family. Three of their brothers were businessmen and owned a large bakery and several fine pastry shops in the Jewish neighborhood. The two younger brothers worked in their older brothers' bakeries, but were nevertheless devoted members of the union. They often led strikes, even at times, when necessary, at their own brothers' bakeries.

Figure 43. Demonstration by members of the Bund's Barbers Union, Czestochowa, Poland, 1930s. From the Archives of the YIVO Institute for Jewish Research, New York.

Feyge, a Bundist (I don't remember her family name), was a member of the Executive for the chocolate candy makers and a delegate from Warszawski's factory. She was an older girl and devoted to the union body and soul. One time when the union was about to be evicted from its office space for a half-year's nonpayment of rent, Feyge brought her saved up dowry money and lent it to the union. She would also do the same thing if the union couldn't pay its electric bill. Feyge would often complain to the union: Why doesn't the union create a fund to help its sick members? And when she could not get her way in this with the Executive Board, she created her own kind of "sick fund." If a member got sick, she would go to him and help him in any way she could.

The intellectual of the union was Comrade Bigelmayer. She was a member of the Chocolate Workers Executive. She sang beautifully and spoke perfect Polish. At joint meetings with the Polish food workers, she would always step forward and speak in Polish in the name of the Jewish food workers.

The Food Workers Union did not play a large role in Warsaw's trade union movement, but among its members and activists were many quiet, refined, and congenial people. It was gratifying to work with them.

Notes

1. Braided holiday bread.—MZ
2. Also transliterated as *matzoh*, the flat unleavened bread eaten during Passover, to the exclusion of ordinary bread with leavening.—MZ
3. The hard liquor packers section of the union lasted only a couple of years after the First World War, when the liquor manufactures in Poland had not yet been reopened. All hard liquors were at that time imported into Warsaw in large barrels from the region of Posen and Galicia; in Warsaw they were poured into separate bottles and packed into crates.—BG
4. Hasidism is a branch of Orthodox Judaism that promotes spirituality through the popularization and internalization of Jewish mysticism as the fundamental aspect of the faith, along with song, dance, and festive celebration. The central feature of Hasidism is allegiance to a holy master (rebbe [Hasidic rabbi] or *tsadik* [saintly man]). The place where the rebbe resides defines where his "court" is located and the name of his brand of Hasidism. In pre-Holocaust times, for example, the Belzer rebbe resided in Bełz in Galicia and the Gerer rebbe in Góra Kalwaria in Poland (called Gur in Yiddish, but referred to as Ger by the Hasidim).—MZ
5. Shloyme Mendelson (1896–1948): Prominent Bundist leader, writer, speaker, public intellectual, member of the Polish Bund's Central Committee, and starting in 1926, president of TSYSHO. "A kind of spiritual leader inside the movement. . . . elected to the Warsaw City Council in 1938; . . . considered by his colleagues an inspiring orator and prolific writer; . . . a giant in the movement. . . . thousands attended his funeral in New York City, demonstrating how popular and influential a figure he was" (David Slucki, p.180.)—MZ
6. Now in New York, a member of the Bund, and an official of the ILGWU.—BG
7. *Obshchestvo Remeslennago i Zemledelecheskago Truda Sredi Evreev v Rossii* (The Society for Handicraft and Agricultural Work among the Jews of Russia: ORT). Es-

tablished in 1880 in Russia to support craft education in schools and workshops to encourage Jews to become artisans and agriculturalists. Branches were active in almost every Russian city having a substantial Jewish population. After World War I, ORT began to work outside of Russia.—MZ
8. Oddly enough, this second name means "candymaker."—MZ
9. Blood libel case, referred to as the Beilis Affair; a Jew, Mendel Beilis (1874–1934), was accused of murdering a 12-year-old Christian boy in Kiev in 1911 for ritual purposes; the trial received official protests from both Jewish and non-Jewish intellectuals, politicians, clergy, and dignitaries throughout Western Europe and North America; Beilis acquitted, 1913.—MZ
10. *Hazomir* was founded by the classic Yiddish writer, I. L. Peretz, to replace the Yiddish Literary Society banned by the Czarist government. Chaired by Peretz, it became an important cultural center in Warsaw, featuring his readings, speeches, and his famous "question-and-answer-box" evenings.—MZ

CHAPTER 23

The Bakers Union

The Bakers Union had a long history with the Bund. In 1902–1903 the Bund had illegally organized the bakers union. Since then the Bund had always stayed in close contact with it. Several outstanding Bund activists had emerged from their ranks. In Czarist times the bakers had established a custom of sharing their *fayranter*[1] with their unemployed baker comrades; they continued that practice.

By the twenties, almost all the bakers were older men. Only a handful were young and were called *pomocniki* (assistants) or "third hands." A *pomocnik* had to work many years, six or eight, before he was allowed to "approach the box," that is, to make the dough. It was one of the reasons so few young people entered the trade. Another reason certainly was the occupation's bad reputation among the Jews. The old saying with which parents used to threaten their children was still current: "If you don't behave, you'll be apprenticed to a baker." If there were some few young people who did become bakers, they were almost always provincials. A young man would come from a provincial *shtetl* to Warsaw seeking work. If he couldn't find it and had no roof over his head, he would apprentice himself to a baker. That way he would at least have a piece of bread, and perhaps also a place to sleep.

But perhaps the chief reason for the small stream of young people to the baker trade was the difficult and unhygienic working conditions. The bakeries in the Jewish quarter of Warsaw were located in small, narrow, dark, often dank cellars. These were small bakeries, with at most only two or three bakers working. If a baker had a free half-hour in the middle of his shift, he would lie down on the steps of the cellar, or on a sack of flour, or on the lid of the "box," or even on the plank bed on top of the tile stove. In the morning one could see the bakers returning home from work with packages of bread or rolls under their arms (it was traditional to bring baked goods home), tired, sleepy, downcast, their faces coated with a pale white matte. Seldom did you see a baker happy or smiling. The bakers loved to sing Rosenfeld's famous song, *Mayn Yingele*.[2] But they sang it with a variation: instead of the verse, *The coming of* day *drives me early from the house*, they sang *The coming of* night *drives me early from the house*.

Most of the bakers were from the provinces. One could encounter among them pious Jews with beards and long gabardines, as well as enlightened workers who participated in the socialist movement. There were also, however, bakers who were connected to the underworld, even those who had "brides" (prostitutes) on the streets, mostly servant girls who had been led astray. The bakers were always embroiled with servant girls and "brokers" of servant girls. Their acquaintance with the servant girls stems from, of all things—*tsholnt*.[3] In the wealthy homes that kept servant girls, the girls would be sent Friday night before sunset to the bakers to have their *tsholents* placed in the bakers' ovens to keep them warm. The girls were then sent back Saturday evening, after prayers, to pick them up and bring them back to the houses for dinner. In the process, acquaintanceships would be struck up between the bakers and the servant girls. Sometimes legitimate matches and respectable families grew out of these acquaintanceships, and sometimes tragedies and misfortune.

When I returned to Warsaw, the Bakers Union was located at Pawia 8. There I met old comrades from our prewar, illegal work together in the Bund, for example, Elye (Eliyohu—Elijah) Sztrigler, or "Elik the Philospher," as he was called. Before the war he used to send dispatches to the St. Petersburg Bundist newspaper, *Tsayt* (*Time*). He was a quiet, restrained person and an abject pauper. Because of his poverty and family troubles, he had become unkempt, apathetic, and withdrawn. He was, nevertheless, a member of the Executive Committee and quietly did his work. Elye Sztrigler died in 1929. His son left for Paris that same year.

Meylekh Ciglman was a veteran Bundist and our leading organizer among the bakers. He was tall and broad shouldered, with an angular, striking, and expressive face. His appearance reminded one of the "ideal proletarian" then being pictured on socialist posters. He was quiet and reticent. When he spoke, it was quietly, slowly. No coarse language ever came out of his mouth. He hated it when bakers used profanity. In the work of our movement he was judicious, thoughtful, strong in character, consistent, loyal, and devoted. He later became a member of the Warsaw Executive Committee of the Bund, and when the Bund regained its influence over the Bakers Union, he became its Chairman. He had nine children. The youngest attended our Yiddish secular schools. The older ones were members of our SKIF and the *Yugnt-Bund Tsukunft*. One of his sons is now in America and a member of the Bund.

Yankl Frimerman was also a veteran activist, schooled in the Bund. Though he was not well—asthmatic, he was nevertheless very active in the union's Executive Board. He was also a member of the Warsaw School Board and participated energetically in the work of our Yiddish secular school system.

When the Bakers Union was under the aegis of the Bund, Israel Bass, another veteran Bundist, was always the one to carry the union's banner. His only son, Alter Bass, belongs among the immortal heroes of the Warsaw Ghetto. In the ghetto, he was the distributor of the illegal underground press of the Bund and the Youth-Bund, *Tsukunft*. If he had been caught, he would have suffered horrific torture and death. During the Nazi occupation, secret, illegal meetings of the Bund would take place in his family's apartment. Alter would stand guard on the street below. He was arrested while carrying out one of his underground tasks for the Bund, and in the Gestapo prison was horribly tortured to reveal who the others were who worked with him in the underground movement. He withstood the worst possible torture, but would not betray his comrades. He didn't survive, never again to return to us.

Khayim Itskovitch mostly occupied himself in the union with Bundist issues. The bakers called him the "virgin," because he would not permit obscenities to be uttered in his presence, and in general devoted himself to the "higher things," with books and culture.

The union also had its nonpartisan members. These were of two types: True nonpartisans not wanting to get themselves too involved with the party work of the Bund, but loyal members of the union. And then there were those who wanted to avoid union discipline. Among the latter were also those who were involved in dirty dealings. In order to evade responsibility for these illicit activities, they tried to get themselves off the hook by saying they were in the "opposition" and were "nonpartisan." It took a lot of work before we could rid the union leadership of this latter kind of "nonpartisan."

The most prominent among the truly nonpartisan union members was Yankl der Shvartser (Jacob with the Black Hair). With his slow-paced, sedate manner, he was particularly suited to negotiate with the bosses. He was the "diplomat" of the Executive Board and performed this task till he left for America.

A typical example of the other kind of "nonpartisan" was Yirmiyohu who was also a member of the Executive. He hardly worked much at all as a baker, but he had lots of money from his "side businesses." He was a representative of the Executive to the *fayrant* committee whose job it was to secure unemployed bakers with a night's work in accordance with the old tradition of the union. Instead Yirmiyohu made a deal with some of the bosses and bakers: he would not send any unemployed bakers to their shop to pick up the overtime hours, and the full-time bakers would kick back to him some of the money they earned by not giving up any of their overtime to an unemployed baker. At Passover, during the *matse* season, he made quite a lot of money through such deals with the "oven men." When we tried to raise the question about

Yirmiyohu's shady dealings, he screamed bloody murder, saying the Bund was persecuting a "nonpartisan." There were also underworld thugs among these so-called "nonpartisans."

Among the activists in the union belonged one called Shmay Beker. Before the war he had been a Bundist, and distinguished himself in our fights with the strikebreakers. After the war, he connected up with the goons and occupied a prominent place among them. He was one of the first to leave and join the Communists, creating a great deal of trouble for the bakers in the Bakers Union. Later he left for Russia.

The normal, year-in-year-out activities of the Bakers Union were divided into two periods. Almost all year it was quiet at the union—there was little work and many members didn't pay their dues. But during matse week (which in fact lasted four weeks), the union came alive. The bakers earned well, bought clothes for their wives and children, and prepared for a beautiful holiday. They even were able to set aside a little money for the slow time to come. The members paid off their backlog of owed membership dues (deducted from their salaries), and the union could also set aside a little money for the between-the-busy-season times.

When the Kombund split off from the Bund, the Communists, together with the Kombundists and the strong-arm thugs, captured the Bakers Union. (The Polish Bakers Union also fell under Communist domination.) The Jewish Bakers Union seceded from the Central Council of the Jewish Trade Unions. The Bundist bakers, however, did not leave the Bakers Union. They remained as an internal opposition, and in the thirties the Bund finally won the union back.

Figure 44. Executive Board, Bakers Union. From the Archives of the YIVO Institute for Jewish Research, New York.

Notes

1. *Fayranter* is what they called overtime hours at that time in Poland. In several trades the established custom was that the fully employed workers would give up their overtime hours to their unemployed comrades; it was an especially old tradition among the bakers.—BG
2. This popular Yiddish song is a sweatshop father's lament that his son doesn't know him because he can never see him during the little boy's waking hours—his work drives him out early in the morning and he only sees the boy when he comes home late at night, when his beloved little boy is asleep; it is a poem by Morris Rosenfeld (1862–1923), one of the NY Yiddish "sweatshop poets."—MZ
3. A special dish (meat, potatoes, and legumes) for the Sabbath meal, prepared the day before and stored Friday night in bakers' ovens so it could be picked up and served warm on the Sabbath, when no cooking is allowed.—MZ

CHAPTER 24

Bagel Bakers and Peddlers

Within the Bakers Union, the bagel bakers were almost entirely autonomous. They remained on the sidelines, not involving themselves in the general struggle of the Bakers Union. But because of their members' constant conflicts with the "bosses" of the bagel bakeries, ample paupers themselves—not much better off than their workers—they caused the Bakers Union plenty of trouble. If most Warsaw Jewish bakeries were poor, unhygienic, dark, and close, they were palaces compared to the bagel bakeries, located in tiny cellars where you could hardly turn around.

Usually the "boss" in these bagel bakeries was the only worker, except for his wife, and often their children. Some bagel bakeries also employed one hired hand, or at the most, two. Continual conflicts took place, both with the bosses that worked alone—of whom the union demanded that they hire at least one worker, and with the bosses who did employ a worker or two—the union demanding that they improve their workers' intolerable working conditions.

The most important organizer and leader of this local union of bagel bakers was Hershl "Filozof" (Philosopher), a likeable, enlightened worker and a Bundist. He left for America while still in his twenties. Here, in America, a machine at work cut off one of his hands. He lives in New York.

Bagels were a favorite and beloved baked good among Jews. The peddling of bagels in the streets burgeoned in Warsaw—especially in the evening. In the Jewish neighborhoods you could see the bagel peddlers late into the night with their great big baskets of bagels singing out, "Fresh, hot, steaming bagels, two for a three-er, or five for a six-er." Even around one o'clock in the morning one could still see children of 8–10 years old, or elderly women, with baskets of bagels, leaning against a wall, calling to the passersby to buy the "hot, steaming" bagels. They stood in the cold, in the rain, in a frost or in a blizzard, standing with their baskets of bagels late into the night. Theatergoers would buy a hot bagel and eat it right there in the street on their way home. The bagel peddlers would stay on the street till the theater crowds were gone.

There was one other group of bagel customers: the poorest and the unemployed that did not have enough to eat to make it through the day and stuffed their stomachs with a few hot bagels for a three-er or a five-er that they had somehow, somewhere, managed to scrape together. How many provincial youths coming to Warsaw seeking work became unemployed, having in Warsaw no home and no relations; how many such unemployed youths made it through the day with a few dry bagels, sometimes accompanied with a hot glass of tea they bought at the union buffet? It was better to make it through the day with bagels than with dry bread—they were tastier, as well as warm and fresh.

The bagel peddlers had one sworn enemy: the police. The bagel peddlers had of course no license to peddle—where would they get the money to buy a license?—so the police harassed and chased them with the nastiest kind of malice. When a policeman caught one, he would drag him to the police station. There they would confiscate his basket of bagels, put him in a jail cell for the night, and, more often than not, beat him badly. The worst blow—worse than the vicious blows to his body—was the loss of his basket and his bagels, for they were his entire "capital."

As a result the bagel peddlers created a "security system." A mother stood with a basket of bagels. Next to her stood a younger son, switching from time to time the peddling of the bagels with his mother. The father stood somewhat apart, at some distance, standing guard and looking in all directions to see whether the police were coming. If one appeared, the son would snatch the basket from his mother's hands and start to "pull" (run away). Bystanders would also help. If one of them saw a policeman approaching, he would call out "Six, six!"[1] or "Pull," and everyone would run in every direction and hide themselves wherever they could find a good hiding place.

Walking down the street, one would often see the following kind of scene: A crowd of bagel and other peddlers are running down the street with all their might, breathless, trying to escape the police in hot pursuit. Suddenly from the opposite direction comes another policeman. Between these two fires, the peddlers have no place to run. In the next moment the two policemen are leading the peddlers off to the police station, the bystanders on the sidewalks sadly looking on at the procession.

Once in a while, however, there would be a policeman with a heart. When such a policeman came upon a bagel peddler, he had to arrest him, because "that's what the law demanded." With a show of anger, he would drive away the "funeral procession" that was tailing them. When there was no longer anyone around to see, he would say to the boy "Uciekaj"—"Run!"—and the boy would make tracks.

But despite all these troubles, the bagel peddling business continued strong. More than a little Jewish poverty drew some kind of sustenance from it, or at least a supplementary pittance to some other kind of bitter pursuit.

Figure 45. Child vendors in Warsaw's Jewish slums. Frame enlargement from Bund's movie *Mir Kumen On* (We Are On Our Way) documentary about their Medem Sanitarium. Directed by Aleksander Ford, filmed in Poland, 1935. Courtesy of J. Hoberman.

Notes

1. "Six" was the accepted warning that "a policeman is approaching." This probably stemmed from the fact that the Warsaw police were in the sixth district of the governmental police force (the police in Poland were organized nationally, rather than municipally), and every Warsaw policeman wore the number 6 on his collar.—BG

CHAPTER 25

A Day in a Slaughterhouse

But let's get back to the Meat Workers Union.

This union interested me because of its variegated membership, its great number of different types. A few close friends of mine, a couple of old Bundists, and others that I had known for many years, provided me with a connection to this union. They agreed to take me into the slaughterhouse for an entire working day, from early morning until noon, when work stopped.

Very early in the morning, on the agreed upon day, I went off to the slaughterhouse. The street that takes you to the Praga slaughterhouse is wide. Among the shops on both sides of the street, one kind is most evident: restaurants and taverns—Gentile and Jewish, kosher and nonkosher. The street comes to life as early as five in the morning, when it is packed with wagons waiting to distribute meat to the city, and with meat merchants, butchers, teamsters, and slaughterhouse workers, all of them heading toward a long, red brick building at the end of Namiestnikowska Street,[1] the Praga slaughterhouse.

When you first enter the slaughterhouse, you are met with a huge, cavernous hall filled with large separate enclosures made of iron railings. Inside each enclosure, quarters of cow and calf meat are hung up for display. Each of these enclosures belongs to a meat merchant. Butchers come to these enclosures to buy meat for their shops. There are a couple of hundred butcher shops in Warsaw, both kosher and nonkosher. Around this huge, cavernous hall, people in white smocks are running about: these are veterinarians inspecting the animals before they are slaughtered, and checking and stamping the meat afterwards. The clamor in the hall reaches to the high heavens. The butchers bargain with the merchants at the tops of their voices. After they have already bought the meat, the shouting then begins anew: "Yosl, get my meat! Yankl, haul it down! Khatskl, take my quarter first!" And to make it more emphatic, they throw in a "the devil take your father's father," or some other such curse, just out of habit.

Mixed with the cries of people, one hears from a distance the rumblings and bleating of the cattle, pigs, cows, and calves that are penned up in the nearby stables. Closer by, in a neighboring hall, one hears the loud bellowing of the bulls that are resisting being led to slaughter. The bull doesn't want to go. He is pushed and pulled from all sides. Those pushing and pulling are also crying out wildly. But even all this is drowned out by the bellowing of many more bulls as they are being slaughtered, a dreadful bleating of approximately 50 cattle that are being slaughtered at the same time in various corners of the hall. All these cries blend together in a frightful, hellish din that throws a horrific fear over anyone who steps for the first time across the threshold of the slaughterhouse.

And an even greater fear overcomes one stepping into the slaughtering arena itself. The bellowing of the bulls being tied for slaughter, or in the process of being slaughtered, becomes here even more frightful. Streams of blood flow in the canals going from the slaughtering corners of the hall and running together into a central canal. The blood is then collected and sold for various purposes. The slaughterhouse workers, in tall rubber or leather boots and in wide leather aprons, stand in water with large knives and steel blades in their hands. They are totally spattered with blood. Sweat pours down their faces. With long, shining knives, they flay the bulls that are yanked up onto hooks, and with large axes split them into halves, and then into quarters.

The sight of the freshly slaughtered bull throws one into a panic. The animal trembles, kicks. You think he will jump right up into your face at any moment. All the work around him goes on in a frightful din, including the shouting. One worker cannot simply talk to another; he must shout at the top of his voice to be heard over the wild cacophony.

After several hours of such extremely exhausting work a person is totally drained. His nerves are so strained and taut that he *must* run out and grab a drink in order to regain his courage and warm his blood. Drinking is regarded by the meat workers as a necessity for maintaining their strength and skill. In this way they free themselves a little bit from the atmosphere of blood and bedlam.

Around eight o'clock in the morning, my friends say, "Time to go eat breakfast." They grab a couple of large chunks of raw meat, wash them, and take me along to "Rokhl's" restaurant.

Rokheleh welcomed us and greeted all of us as if we were old friends. She was a short, broad woman, middle aged, blond, and pale faced. Her restaurant consisted of two large rooms with large, long, plain tables. A fire burned in the fireplace. Upon entering, they gave her the pieces of meat. She speared them onto skewers and stuck them in the fire to roast. She then quickly put a tablecloth on one of the tables, set out a large plate at each place, along with bottles of whiskey, fresh bagels, and other baked goods. Our small crowd took their places around the table. Then Rokhl came over and asked, "Who's paying?" Somebody answered that he was paying. She noted this down in a notebook. After a week, everybody paid his bill according to Rokhele's "bookkeeping." She brought over the roasted meat right then, and everyone started on the feast. Of course Rokhl would not serve up all the meat she had just been given to roast, but nobody held it against her—that's the way it had always been. At table everyone spurred the others on and piqued their appetites, especially for the drinking: "We have to drink the tea!" The brandy was served in tea glasses. "Drink a little corn water!" (an allusion to the whiskey, distilled from corn).

This was only the first "lunch." It was called, modestly, "grabbing a bite." After work, between one and two o'clock in the afternoon is when one then went for a proper "lunch." The same scene as in the morning repeated itself, except this time, no one is in a hurry. One eats more relaxedly, more slowly. After everyone is now warmed up, the tables of several groups are pushed together; meat merchants come in and seat themselves at the table and eat together with the slaughterhouse workers. It becomes one big eating and drinking fest.

At this point the beggars come into the restaurant. They know when to come—not at the beginning of the meal, but afterwards, when the crowd has eaten its fill and is warmed up. These beggars aren't penny grubbers. These are "honorable" beggars. They come to ask for "a dowry for a poor bride," for "medicines for someone sick," for "orphans and widows." The crowd opens its purses and gives money. Everyone gives something.

It occurs to me to compare the meat workers and the bakers.

Their working hours are almost the same. Bakers work all night and go home in the morning. The meat workers begin their workday early, before dawn, and end their workday around noon. But what a difference between the two! The baker is dejected, weak, pale, sickly; the meat worker is full blooded, healthy, broad shouldered, with a ruddy, healthy-looking face. They both usually live in the same neighborhoods: Smocza, Niska, Wołyńska, Krochmalna—they are often seen together. But what a contrast in appearance, mood, and bearing!

Materially, the meat workers also live better. The bakers are mostly depressed, without ambition. The meat workers, on the other hand, have a drive for something better. They raise their children differently, sending them to school, some dreaming of higher education for them. They live on the street and around the slaughterhouses, but for their children they want a better life.

Slowly my circle of friends among the meat workers widened, and they began to think of me as one of their own. This happened first because of a couple of good, old friends such as Yankl Flatshazh, who was much loved by the meat workers, and Anshl Kolnitshanski. Through Anshl I was drawn closer to the whole Kolnitshanski "dynasty": the "Khayetshkes" and the "Bertshikes."[2] Certainly it was partly because I did not exploit my friendship with them for material gain that I quickly won the confidence of the whole meat worker clan. They began to invite me to parties at their homes, asked me for advice about family matters, told me their troubles at home, and poured out their hearts to me as if I were a close friend. They even suggested a permanent stipend for me from their union. When I refused to accept, they tried to persuade me. When that wasn't working, they tried suggesting loans and presents. When they convinced themselves that I would not accept any gain from my office in any form whatsoever, they were impressed.

Notes

1. Now, Sierakowskiego Street is in the Old Praga area.—MR
2. See Chapter 18 for these two branches of the meat workers "dynasty."—MZ

CHAPTER 26

Jewish and Polish Meat Workers

The Polish workers working in both sections of the slaughterhouse—kosher slaughtering and nonkosher pig slaughtering—had their own union, a local of the General Polish Union of Food Workers. The Polish union was perhaps numerically larger, but the Jewish union was better organized.

The secretary of the Polish union was Geniek (Eugeniusz) Gajewski, a member of the PPS. He was an intelligent worker-activist—he had even written a book on the economy of the Polish meat market and about the place Poland occupied economically in the international meat market. After he became secretary of the union, he continued to work in the slaughterhouse and would not accept a paid position in the union, serving unpaid as secretary. He would, however, be excused from work if union matters required his attendance. And if not excused with pay, the union would compensate him for the unpaid hours he missed.

The Polish workers had a number of unusual personalities.

Władek Matraszek was an older worker. He was tall, crude, broad, with a gait as lumbering and ungainly as an ox. On his face and his whole body you could not find a smooth piece of skin, so beat and cut up was he from the fights, reckless escapades, and stabbings in which he was continually engaged. Because of these fights and wild adventures, he spent many a year in jail. He was also a terrific glutton and drinker. His son also worked in the slaughterhouse. As a young man his son had attended gymnasium and, I think, finished six classes. Externally, his son was thin, not tall like his father, rather weak, and with a chronic cough, the opposite of his father. He would not drink whiskey, only French cognac, and excused himself to his friends for this by saying that because of his poor health he could not drink any coarse drinks, only "refined" ones. He was a member of the PPS.

Nowak (I don't remember his first name) was also an older worker, but quite a different type from Władek. He was tall and well built, with a large wen on the nape of his neck. He spoke a Yiddish that was as good as that of the Jewish workers. More than once he would even correct the Yiddish of a Jewish worker. There was no Yiddish curse he didn't know. He even understood "the *goy* (Gentile) is coming." He loved talking Yiddish while having a drink. Once he said to me, pointing to the Jewish workers, "I can be a better Jew than they."

His two sons, Felek and Staszek, also worked in the slaughterhouse. They both belonged to the PPS and were both good socialists. In the thirties, when we were street fighting with the Polish antisemites and Fascists, the Nowaks often came and fought on our side.

In general, the relations between the Polish and Jewish workers in the slaughterhouse were not bad. But, as everywhere, when economic interests came into play, one group would think it was being taken advantage of, and on that basis, conflicts would often arise. One such conflict went on for some time.

The slaughtering in the slaughterhouse was generally done for private merchants. In addition, however, some slaughtering was for the municipal and the national government, for governmental hospitals, or for the military, etc. The Polish workers held that for governmental work they should get a larger share of the work. Around this issue, there were often disputes between the Jewish and Polish workers, and with time they became more and more vehement. Once the members of the Executive Committee of the Jewish Slaughterers Union told me the conflict was getting quite heated and that I should be ready—that they might need me.

It did not take long, in fact, and I got a phone call to come to the slaughterhouse right away. When I arrived, a big fight was about to erupt. The work had halted. The workers with their steel blades and knives in their hands stood in groups opposite each other and were swearing at each other. The cries grew louder and louder until one couldn't make out the words, but only a wild shouting. Their rage and agitation was such that some of them were even foaming at the mouth. At any moment one of them might have thrown himself on the other with his gleaming knife, and a wild slaughter would have broken out. Looking around, I saw Geniek Gajewski standing to one side. He stood there quietly, looking on at the uproar. I ran over to him and tried to persuade him we should do something, or blood would soon be flowing. At first he remained indifferent, and I had the impression I would not move him. But eventually I convinced him.

We both went into their midst, between the two sides circling each other. Geniek shouted that everyone should shut up, and it did in fact become quiet. I then began to talk to the workers. I told them that in such an agitated state this dispute could not be settled other than by slaughtering each other. I appealed to both sides that they should first of all calm down. This dispute could not be settled here—after all, we have our unions for that. Gajewski spoke next and said I was right. The workers listened to us quietly, but they were far from happy. Out of anger they threw their knives and blades to the ground with such force that they bounced up from the asphalt floor into the air, but they listened. In the end their discipline and loyalty to the union won out. One by one they picked up their blades and knives and returned to work.

How much was drunk "in honor of this 'reconciliation,'" is not difficult to imagine.

The dispute was in fact later settled between the two unions, and both sides were satisfied.

CHAPTER 27

At Parties and Celebrations

After a time I grew close to many of the meat workers, and they began to invite me to their family parties and festivities. I will describe one such celebration.

Once, in the summer of 1924, around the time of *Shvues*,[1] Shmuel Rosenberg (the one they called Shmuel "Gabai"[2]), the eldest of the "Khayetshkes," invited me to a family celebration. What was this celebration about? Shmuel's grandchild, one he had raised, a child of one of his daughters who had died, had been very sick and had, fortunately, regained its health. To celebrate that, Shmuel threw a grand party. It was like one I had never seen before.

It took place on a Sunday afternoon in Otwock, where Shmulik and his family lived in the summer. Not in the elegant part of Otwock, but in the neighborhood of the *kolejka* (little train). It was more sparsely populated, with simple wooden buildings.

Long tables and benches were set out in a large, thinly wooded pine forest. Around the table were seated around 150 people: family members, meat workers, and some Poles too. The tables were laden with all kinds of good things: fish, meats, baked goods, herring, cakes, compotes, and so on. To the side were field kitchens with large steaming kettles of soup and meat. Nearby were large tubs of ice upon which were heaped bottles of whiskey and barrels of beer. A little farther off were tables loaded with stores of food. From these steaming kettles and tubs of ice, and from the tables with the stores of food, servers and family members of the "Khayetshke" clan continually served the guests more and more food and drink, the crowd continually consuming the abundance of food noisily and with happy chatter. Grandma Khayetshke herself, small, a little fat, in her orthodox married woman's wig, also busied herself. She circulated among the tables continually urging the crowd: "Eat, children! . . . Children, are you full yet?" "We're eating, Granny," they answered her from all sides.

Shmuel had also brought the union's brass band to the celebration, about 30–40 men, who the whole time played Jewish and Polish labor songs, such as *Di Shvue*,[3] the *Czerwony Sztandar* (Polish labor hymn), and others. The members of the brass band also participated in the feast, of course, eating their fill. The guests sang labor songs, folk songs, and marches.

After a little while the hosts, seeing they were running out of food, sent someone into the city. Back came a wagon loaded with various meats, sausages, baked goods, whiskey, and beer—and the eating and drinking began anew.

From the surrounding neighborhoods hundreds of people came running to look on at the banquet. Suddenly the Commander of the Otwock police and a bunch of his policemen appeared on the scene and began to harass the celebrants, stating that this was an illegal gathering, that for such a large gathering one had to have a permit from the police. The Commander threatened to call the authorities in Warsaw right away. It became abundantly apparent to all, however, what was really going on, so they invited the police and their Commander to join them. They were given food and drink, and into their palms a little something more, some cash; they promptly forgot about phoning Warsaw.

The feasting lasted from two in the afternoon until dark, and although people had eaten and drunk a great deal, and quite a number of people were quite drunk, there was, nevertheless, no brawling at all the whole time.

The whole Executive Board of the Meat Workers Union came, except for the Kolnitshanskys; the "Bertshikes" did come. It was right after the elections for a new Executive Board. The "Khayetshkes" had defeated the Kolnitshanskys, and Shmuel "Gabai" was elected the Chairman of the union. I suspected that Shmuel had really arranged the whole party to celebrate his election as chairman, the recovered health of his grandchild being just an excuse.

The Kolnitshanskys held it against me that I went to the celebration. But they couldn't say this openly, so instead they complained that I had allowed the union band to play at a private party.

Notes

1. In Sephardic Hebrew, *Shavuot*, a Jewish holiday celebrated seven weeks after Passover, to commemorate the giving of the Torah at Mt. Sinai.—MZ
2. Title of the administrative manager of a synagogue; overseer; trustee.—MZ
3. *Di Shvue* (The Oath), the Bund's anthem (see Glossary), written by S. Anski (Shloyme Rapoport, 1863– 1920), also author of the famous Yiddish play, *The Dybbuk*.—MZ

CHAPTER 28

Resistance: The First of May Demonstration, 1923

I have previously mentioned that in 1920 the Polish government declared the Bund illegal. Bund clubs, Bund union offices, and our Yiddish secular schools were closed. Our daily newspapers, and the Bundist press generally, were consistently confiscated or shut down. Bundists were imprisoned. The Bundist First of May demonstrations were dispersed.

It all started on May 1, 1920, when the police and Polish hooligans attacked the Bundist demonstration on the square in front of the Iron Tower, beating and dispersing the demonstrators.

Despite this attack, at the next First of May, in 1921, we came to an agreement with the PPS, and we gathered at the Theatre Square (*Plac Teatralny*) where the PPS also held its demonstration. The police, with the help of plainclothes agents and hooligans, again attacked the Bund demonstration and dispersed it.

We would not allow ourselves to be intimidated. In 1922 we came once again to demonstrate on the First of May and, yes, in the same Theatre Square, together with the Polish workers. The police again repeated their game, and again dispersed the Bund demonstration.

We decided this could no longer go on. Until now we had been satisfied with passive resistance, coming annually—despite the attacks—to demonstrate, and, especially doing so in the prominent, symbolic Theatre Square. But after the First of May demonstration had been dispersed three times in a row, we felt we could no longer tolerate it, that we must actively resist the attackers. We began to prepare.

A few days before the First of May 1923, the government suddenly shut down the *Folkstsaytung* (People's Newspaper) on the basis of a court order. The judicial process leading up to the court order had been dragging on for a long

Figure 46. Henryk Erlich and some of the leading staffers of the Bund's daily Warsaw newspaper, *Di Folkstsaytung*. From the Archives of the YIVO Institute for Jewish Research, New York.

time, but just before the first of May, the judge suddenly remembered to issue an injunction to shut down the newspaper. This was, of course, no coincidence.

The Polish judges were mostly reactionary, antisemitic and, "acting according to their own consciences," issued cruel and unjust judgments against Jewish socialists. Besides, they served the administration. In this case the Polish administration must have let the judge know that at this particular moment it would be convenient to have an injunction shutting down the Bund's *Folkstsaytung*—and the judge obliged. Shutting down the Bund's newspaper right before the First of May was calculated to intimidate us just as we were preparing for the workers holiday. But our newspaper did not shut down. The very next morning it appeared under a new masthead, *Di Naye Tsayt* (The New Times), and preparations for the First of May proceeded as before.

We organized a large First-of-May Militia, in addition to our regular party militia. Each party unit had to contribute a larger number of people to the special militia. We also enlisted in this special militia the separate militia units of the Bund unions. All together we mustered about 1000 men for the First of May 1923 demonstration. This enlarged militia was divided into separate sections, and each section had its own commander.

On the day of the first of May 1923, the central gathering point was in the Nalewki 34 courtyard, where the Metal Workers Union office (and later the Garment Workers Union office) was located. Each union came to its own preappointed spot at the central gathering point.

Resistance: The First of May Demonstration, 1923

A crowd of more than a thousand gathered. The demonstration started to move forward. In front was the large flag of the Bund, surrounded by a strong guard of militiamen. Behind the flag marched the Central Committee of the Bund. After them came the unions, again in the same order: In front, their flag surrounded by a group of militiamen, behind the flag the Executive Committee of the union, and behind them, the mass of union members. In the middle of the marchers came the Youth Bund, *Tsukunft* (Future), and behind them, several more unions. At the very end, the train of marchers was secured and anchored by a strong group of militiamen who were there to guard against an attack from the rear. Along the whole length of the parade, the marchers, in addition to the red flag, carried aloft banners in Yiddish and Polish with various slogans and political demands.

The long train of marchers, proceeding in this way through the Nalewki, Długa, and Bielanska, marched into Theatre Square, occupying the place near the Bielańska and Senatorska that had been reserved for the Bund according to a prior arrangement with the PPS, which was also observing its First of May celebration in Theatre Square. When the head of our train of marchers marched into the Square, its end was still deep in the Nalewki.

When we arrived at the agreed upon spot in Theatre Square, we immediately saw that the entire space that the Bund was supposed to occupy was completely surrounded by hooligans and plainclothesmen. In addition there were, of course, many uniformed police. We erected an improvised platform, placed upon it the large flag of the Bund, and surrounded it with a strong guard of mi-

Figure 47. First of May demonstration, ca. 1930s, Warsaw. From the Archives of the YIVO Institute for Jewish Research, New York.

Figure 48. Bund Demonstration, Warsaw. Bernard Goldstein in black overcoat behind the flag bearer. From the Archives of the YIVO Institute for Jewish Research, New York.

litiamen. We also surrounded all the other flags with a strengthened guard. We anticipated that the hooligans and police would attack our flags first.

The first one to speak from our platform was Comrade Henryk Erlich. After him Emanuel Nowogrodski began to speak. In the middle of his speech a loud disturbance could be heard from the other side of Theatre Square, on the Trębacka Street side of the square, where the Communists had gathered—they had also come to Theatre Square. The fighting started there. Soon the battle carried over to us. And just as we expected, the attackers went first for our flags. A furious struggle soon was on between our milita guards and the hooligans and plainclothesmen over the flag of the Central Committee. At a certain moment I saw that it did not look good for the flag. I threw myself on top of the flag, tore it off its heavy pole, and hid it under my coat, quickly merging into the crowd. Old, grey Michalewicz, not so old as he was grey—he was then not quite yet 50— could not contain himself, and struck left and right with his walking stick till the stick broke in this duel. Similar battles took place at just about each of our flags in the whole area of our demonstration. Our guards, armed with sticks, fought back, and also our demonstrators fought back. After a while the uniformed police stepped in with the argument that *we* (!) were "disturbing the peace," and dispersed our demonstration. People were wounded, beaten, and bloodied on both sides. Many of our people had to be taken to first aid centers to have their wounds bandaged. This was how we conducted our first big and open active resistance in independent Poland.

In the afternoon, after the demonstration, we had our traditional May First commemorative gathering, as usual, in the theatre "Nowości" on Bielańska Street (one of the largest theatres in Warsaw). The auditorium was packed to overflowing with people. Among them was many a bandaged head.

At a meeting of the Bund militiamen after the First of May battle, we discussed what had happened. It was decided to accept Bejnisz Michalewicz as an honorary member of the militia and to present him with the gift of a walking stick with a silver handle—to compensate him for the walking stick he had broken in the resistance at Theatre Square. Comrade Michalewicz carried this walking stick with pride for the next five years—until in 1928 a serious illness brought him down and took him from the world.

CHAPTER 29

Struggles over the Saturday Edition of the *Folkstsaytung*

In 1922 the editorial staff of our daily newspaper, the *Folkstsaytung*, decided to publish on the Jewish Sabbath, on Saturday.

No other Jewish daily newspaper published on Saturday. Since there were not many buyers in the Jewish neighborhoods for Polish newspapers, no newspaper peddlers in the Jewish neighborhoods kept their kiosks open on Saturday. We were forced, therefore, to send out our own hawkers to distribute the Saturday edition of the *Folkstsaytung*. For the most part these were our *Tsukunfistn*, our young Bundists, who, with their usual enthusiasm, went zealously to work.

On the Jewish streets something new happened. Every Saturday morning, when most Jews, who didn't go to work or to their places of business, were still sleeping, one could now hear in the courtyards the singing out of young voices, announcing they had the *Folkstsaytung* for sale. Their cries echoed through the empty, sleepy streets. Many of these young people displayed their "creative talents": they invented their own rhymes or amusing little jingles to get people to buy and read the Saturday *Folkstsaytung*.

But the religious Jews—the Sabbath observers—had a very different view of things. They raised a hue and a cry against the *Folkstsaytung* and began attacking our youthful distributors of the Saturday edition on the street. Most of the time this happened when the pious emerged after prayers from the synagogues and the small *Hasidic* houses of prayer. They threw themselves on the youthful hawkers of our newspaper, tore the bundles of newspaper out their hands, and ripped them to pieces on the spot (apparently it was all right to tear paper on the Sabbath!), at the same time beating up our young people.

This continued for some time, and our young comrades would show up more and more frequently at the administrative offices of the newspaper, beaten, with torn fragments of the newspaper, to complain about the *Hasidic* terror. We had to mount a resistance, so we sent out our Bund militiamen to defend our young comrades. This battle reached its highest point when the Warsaw Rabbinate issued a writ of excommunication (!) against the newspaper, its staff, and its hawkers. The religious zealots now attacked our distributors with even more zeal, but the attempt to intimidate us with a writ of excommunication evoked a storm of protest throughout the country. Now it was no longer just about a Saturday edition, but about free speech. After some time, when the attackers saw they could not intimidate us, they grew quiet and stopped attacking our young hawkers.

Figure 49. "Worker, Your Newspaper Is the *Folkstsaytung*." Warsaw, 1936. From the Archives of the YIVO Institute for Jewish Research, New York.

After a few years, the *Folkstsaytung* stopped the publication of its Saturday edition—not because of the attacks of the pious zealots, but to lower the deficit it accrued after each edition, including the Saturday one.

In 1931 the First of May fell on a Friday. All over the country, our First of May demonstrations were being held jointly with the PPS. This cooperation had enormous political significance. The party, therefore, didn't want to wait two days to publish reports of these joint demonstrations, so on May 2, 1931, a Saturday, a special edition of the *Folkstsaytung* was published, dedicated to the reporting of these joint First of May demonstrations throughout Poland. This edition sold out very quickly. The financial situation of the newspaper improved. It was decided to publish the Saturday edition permanently.

From that time on the *Folkstsaytung* was published regularly every Saturday, up to and until our great Catastrophe. The Saturday edition sold well. Throughout the Warsaw courtyards on Saturday mornings, the ringing singsong of our SKIFISTs and *Tsukunft*ists was once again to be heard: "A new edition of the *Folkstsaytung!*"

CHAPTER 30

Commissar Cechnowski

One event in the twenties, although it had little to do with our movement, made such a deep impression on me that I could not forget it for a long time after.

On a certain evening in 1924, as I sat in the Central Committee offices, I suddenly received an alarming telephone call. Police had descended on the offices of the Garment Workers Union on 17 Graniczna Street and were conducting a search.

When I arrived there I introduced myself to the police as a representative of the Central Committee. I identified myself and declared that I wanted to be present during the search. I demanded this because the police could plant illegal literature, as they so often did, and use this as an excuse to shut down the union offices. The policemen told me to wait—they would ask their superior officer seated in the main office supervising the search. They did not let me enter. After a few moments, they showed me into the anteroom to the main office. I saw that they had already set apart a group of union members for arrest. They indicated I should go into the main office where the commanding police officials were seated.

When I entered the main office, I was absolutely dumbstruck. There I saw Cechnowski—the same Cechnowski who had led the Communist movement in Praga around 1920, about which I have already told in the first few chapters. In a brief moment a whole span of time passed before my eyes: 1914, the year he was the representative of the SDKPiL and we were active together in the interparty labor committee; his leadership of the Communist *Dzielnica* (district) in Praga; his activities among the workers in the provisions department; his work when he and I organized and led the First of May demonstration in Praga in 1920—and now suddenly I see him leading a police search of a union office!

My head was spinning. Is this really Cechnowski, the leader of the Praga Communists? Apparently I grew quite pale, because this Cechnowski ordered a glass of water to be brought. He handed it to me. I drank and slowly regained my senses. Then he whispered: "Bernard, calm yourself, I will explain everything. But I can't do it here." He asked me to come into his office. Then he added quickly, "I am not the only one." This meant, apparently, that he was not the only Communist to leave and join the police. He gave me his phone number and asked me to call him today, or at the latest, tomorrow, and he would explain everything. He ordered a halt to the search and arrested a couple of people, ordering the release of the ones he had previously set aside for arrest.

I did not telephone him, and I never saw him again.

That was the first time that a former Communist activist revealed himself before my very own eyes as a police agent. In later years the Communist movement teemed with provocateurs and police-agents, and one got used to such things. But at that time, in 1924, it was a new phenomenon.

Some time later his name was linked to sensational news: He was shot dead in Lemberg[1] by a Communist youth, Naftoli Botwin. In Lemberg an illegal Communist conference had been uncovered by the police in the cellars of the cloister of the Holy Yuri. This illegal conference was discovered by the police, probably with the help of a spy, and all those in attendance were arrested. Commissar Cechnowski was a witness during the trial of the accused. In revenge, Botwin assassinated him. All this happened in the summer of 1925. Botwin was convicted, given the death penalty, and executed by firing squad.

Note

1. Polish, Lwów; now in the Ukraine, Lviv.—MR

CHAPTER 31

Kalmen the Bootmaker's Death

In the midst of the seething life of our movement, a tragic event once again occurred: Kalmen the Bootmaker died.

On a certain day in the spring of 1926, I was informed that Kalmen the Bootmaker was ill. I went to see him right away. He lived in the very poorest Jewish section of Warsaw, on Niska Street. He rented some space from a bakery worker, a religious Jew with a beard and a long kaftan. The whole apartment consisted of one room and a kitchen. Kalmen lived in the kitchen—that is to say, he had a bed there. Actually not a bed, but a sleeping bench, a bench that served for sitting in the daytime and for sleeping at night. Kalmen had a fever. I immediately called a doctor. The doctor said it was typhus and ordered him admitted to a hospital without delay.

When I dressed Kalmen (he could no longer dress himself), I grew frightened. He was emaciated, hunched over, greatly diminished, hardly a body at all—just a sack of bones with a skin stretched over it. He was full of lice. When I dressed him, he could no longer stand on his own. I took him to the hospital in a droshky. In the droshky I had to hold on to him because he could not even sit up without help.

I came to visit Kalmen in the hospital several times. They wouldn't let you near a typhus patient, so I could only see him from a distance, through a glass door. His exhausted body could not overcome the illness, and after a few days, he died. The Bund gave him a big funeral and buried him in a prominent place, near Janek Jankliewicz.[1] He was only some thirty-odd years old.

Kalmen was one of the most interesting working class types in our movement. I first got to know him in 1911 at an illegal Bund meeting in Warsaw. He was active among the leather workers. He was intelligent, read much, loved to discuss things, and could do so beautifully. He was a kind of "beautiful proletarian spirit." Besides appearing at the Bund's illegal meeting place, he was also often a guest at the Yiddish Literary Club. The Literary Club met at the Golkowa Allee in the Saxon Garden (*Ogród Saski*). It was called the "Literary Allee" because the great I. L. Peretz[2] loved to stroll there. Also many Bundists used to come there, especially on Saturdays: Bundists, litterateurs, cultural activists, and the like. Kalmen, as was the fashion then, wore a broad brimmed black cap and a tie in the form of a black bow. In 1912, after Peretz had published his famous article, "Back to the Synagogue," on a Saturday (Sabbath) morning a group of Bundists approached Peretz—in that very Golkowa Allee—among them, Kalmen, and presented Peretz with a traditional Hebrew prayer book, saying, "You shouldn't be here today; you should be in the synagogue." Peretz darkened, but didn't answer. He published a second article, defending himself for his slogan, "Back to the Synagogue."

After the First World War, when the Bund's political wrangling with the Kombund began, Kalmen also belonged to the Kombund Faction, but when it split off from the Bund, he did not follow it, staying loyal to the Bund. He was a member of the Bund's Warsaw Committee and was appointed Representative of the Union of Domestic Workers.

Figure 50. I. L. Peretz, 1892. From the Archives of the YIVO Institute for Jewish Research, New York.

In the practical, day-to-day work of the Bund, Kalmen did not really participate very much. He loved literature, art, and intellectual discussions. He was a yearning sort of person who was drawn to beauty and to higher things. Though he was talkative and loved to be around people, he was a loner, locked up within himself. He cared little about his material well-being, seldom complained, and never talked to anyone about his troubles.

Kalmen often went to the Literary Club at Tłomackie 13.[3] The Yiddish writers there loved to discuss things with him. They treated him with respect and listened to his word, because Kalmen was a person who thought, and what he said was the result of his independent thinking.

Notes

1. Janek Jankliewicz (1887–1920): Typesetter. Led illegal typesetting, printing, distributing of Bund underground press. Member of the Central Committee. Selected as delegate to Bund's planned 8th convention in Vienna in 1914. Executive Secretary of the Central Bureau of the 20-Craft Association of Trade Unions (1915). Arrested by Germans in 1916. 20,000 Jewish workers attended his Warsaw funeral.—MZ
2. I. L. Peretz (1852–1915): Called the father of modern Yiddish literature, considered one of the three great founding authors of modern Yiddish literature; born in Zamość, Poland, then under Russian rule; lived most of his life, till his death, in Warsaw, his home there being visited by aspiring young Yiddish writers seeking his encouragement and approval. Sympathetic to the Bund.—MZ
3. Literary Club (1916–1939): *Fareyn fun Yidishe Literatn un Zhurnalistn in Varshe*: Association of Yiddish Writers and Journalists in Warsaw, an advocacy group and social meeting venue for writers. Its initial location was at 13 Tłomackie Street, an address associated with the Yiddish secular cultural movement. The premises functioned as a social meeting place not only for members, but also for actors, artists, teachers, guests from abroad, and others who were interested in Yiddish secular culture. In addition, the Association offered a large variety of literary and other activities, both for its members and for the general public. See Z. Segalowicz's *Tlomatske 13*, Buenos Aires, 1946.—MZ

CHAPTER 32

The Piłsudski Coup, the PPS, and the FRACs

In May of 1926, Józef Piłsudski, the Commander of the Polish Legion in the First World War, and the first president of independent Poland, organized a military coup against the reigning right-wing government of peasant leader Wincenty Witos. After a few days of battle the government fell and President Stanisław Wojciechowski (second president of independent Poland) tendered his resignation. Piłsudski, supported by the military, became the de facto ruler of Poland.

One of the deciding factors in Piłsudski's rapid victory was the general strike of the railway workers under the leadership of the PPS. The strike made it impossible to bring the loyalist military from other parts of the country into the city. At the time of the coup, and for a time after, the Polish workers, the PPS at their head, were entirely on the side of Pilsudski. In the beginning, the Communists also supported Piłsudski.

The coup was strictly military. But I remember as if it were today how fervently we were in sympathy with the events. We were caught up in a sort of feeling of freedom, although we Bundists were somewhat more sober than the others because we never had any real trust in Pilsudski. On the evening of the first day of the coup, May 12th, I could no longer contain myself. I thought to myself: "A revolutionary upheaval, there is shooting in the fortress of reaction and oppression, and I am not there, taking part in it?" So three of us, a triad— Bejnisz Michalewicz, Viktor Shulman, and I—went off to the neighborhood where the shooting was taking place: Theatre Square, Cracow Suburb, Old Town, around the Royal Palace, where the residence of the president was located. On the viaduct of the Kierbedzia Bridge, opposite the palace, we saw a dead soldier lying, and next to him—his rifle. Instinctively I went to grab the rifle, but Shulman shouted at me, "Are you crazy! What are you doing? You don't have a permit to carry a weapon!" Late that night we came home, overcome with hope and fear over what this upheaval might bring.

Piłsudski carried out the coup in the name of a "moral cleansing," that is, to make the country healthy, set aside corruption, redress injustices, put an end to all those things that in the course of the last few years had made the rightist regime hated by the workers and by all who were yearning for a little more justice. Piłsudski's revolutionary past, his long years of leadership and activism in the PPS, the large number of prominent socialists in the ranks of his Legion, and finally, his soaring rhetoric all created an illusion that what we had here was a liberal coup and that the working masses would finally have a say under his new rule, cleansing the land.

In the early stages this illusion was very strong among the PPSers. After all, Piłsudski came from their ranks; he was for many years one of its chief activists and the leader of its armed organization in the epoch of struggle against the Czar. He was a legendary figure in the PPS. Many of them hoped, therefore, that his sympathy to his old comrades and his ties to the old program still held. But it didn't take long for all these hopes to be dashed. The majority of the PPS began to see that Piłsudski was now very far from them. He displayed terrible dictatorial tendencies. He began to connect himself more and more closely with reactionary elements. One needed, therefore, to judge him by his deeds.

Some of the PPS leadership, however, still blindly believed in Piłsudski. On the basis of this difference of opinion, a deep division developed within the PPS. Internal struggles began which eventually led, in the fall of 1928, to a split. Of the most prominent PPS leaders, the following left: Moraczewski (a former premier-minister), Jaworowski (the recognized leader of the greater organization of the Warsaw PPS), and several others. They founded a new party under the name "PPS-Former Revolutionary Faction."[1] This newly formed party quickly became popularly known as the "FRAC," and that's what I will call them here.

In the provincial towns, the split was not so deep, but in Warsaw, practically the whole PPS organization joined the FRAC, as well as its entire militia, under the leadership of Dr. Łokietek and Tasiemka, a city councilman (real name, Siemiątkowski). The FRAC also took over the premises of the PPS Warsaw organization on Allee Jerozolimskie. Warsaw locals of the Polish national unions also joined the FRAC. On the other hand, the Executive Boards of the national unions all remained loyal to the PPS. The Central Committee of the whole Polish trade union movement also remained in the hands of the PPS.

At the old PPS in Warsaw, only a small group of comrades remained, but all of them were proven veterans of the movement. In addition, what remained were the youth, the students, professionals and intelligentsia, and practically all the old activists. The FRAC began to attack the meetings of the old PPS, disrupting them. In defense the PPS created a new militia that did in fact also consist mainly of youths, students, and the intelligentsia. At the head of the new militia stood Tomasz, the old, respected veteran and chairman of the PPS, and also Dzięgielewski, the new secretary of the Warsaw organization. There was a great fear that the FRAC would try to seize the building that housed *Robotnik*, the PPS newspaper and central organ of the party. So Arciszewski himself, along with a group of the new militiamen, guarded the building day and night. They even slept there for many long weeks, guarding the building 24 hours a day until the danger was past.

Note

1. "Revolutionary Faction" was an historical name within the PPS: in the time of the struggle against Czarism, a sharp ideological struggle took place within the PPS around the question of how to achieve the independence of Poland: the rightists and more nationalistic of those in this struggle called themselves "The Revolutionary Faction."—BG

CHAPTER 33

The FRAC Militia

As I previously mentioned, the whole PPS Militia, under the command of Dr. Łokietek and Tasiemka, joined the FRAC. I must pause now to tell at greater length the history of this FRAC Militia, not because we had to deal with them often, but because, from their history, it becomes clear how great the dangers are that threaten the morality of such an organized battle group, and how low, morally, they were, in fact, to sink.

    Dr. Łokietek, the commander-in-chief of the FRAC Militia, was a Jewish convert to Christianity. He had been a chemist, with a position as chemist at the public free clinic. But after he and his militia went over to the FRAC, he devoted himself more and more to FRAC fights. He began to drink more and more, until he became a deranged alcoholic. One time, before dawn, he entered, drunk, into the Warsaw revue theatre, *Kwi Pro Kwo* (Quid Pro Quo), and demanded that the servers, who were at that moment cleaning the theatre, perform for him. The servers explained that the performers were long gone and there was no one present to perform. He shouted that he didn't want to hear any such excuses. They must perform for him immediately! When he saw no one was obeying him, he pulled out his revolver and started shooting.

    Łokietek tied himself ever more closely to the underworld, sinking ever deeper into their morass, until he simply became one of them, a partner in criminal acts of terror and extortion.

    The other leading commander of the FRAC's fighting group was Tasiemka. He was an old fighter for the PPS, as far back as Czarist times. He was raw but cunning.

    Because of his old battle exploits and triumphs, the PPS had made him a councilman in the Warsaw City Council; he remained a councilman for the FRAC as well. His path to the underworld was far easier than Dr. Łokietek's.

While Dr. Łokietek, in his deepest decadence, never himself directly engaged in any criminal act, remaining a quiet partner to theft, Tasiemka organized his own gang, known as "Tasiemka's Band," participating often in terrorizing merchants and shopkeepers in the marketplace, enforcing protection money, and extorting money in other ways.

A third man in charge of the FRAC Militia was a certain Szeczka. He was deported to America for his gangsterism. When he returned to Warsaw from America he was quickly able to insert himself back into the FRAC fighting militia, and with their help, was able to transfer his gangsterism to the streets of Warsaw. The FRAC made him the secretary of a small union of Polish bakery workers, as well as secretary of the Jewish Porters Union the FRACs had taken over and separated from our Transport Workers Union. Later he became a police agent, and since his former comrades in the FRAC Militia were now very much afraid of him because he knew too much, they killed him.

This criminal behavior was strengthened from another direction. In Poland, even before the Piłsudski coup, there was an organization consisting mainly of former members of Piłsudski's Legions, called *Strzelec* (Marksman). When Piłsudski came to power, this organization was now in great favor. It became a semiofficial military organization. Its members wore a sort of military uniform and paraded around the streets, generally acting as if they owned the place. In the FRAC Militia there were also quite a number of former Legion soldiers. Tasiemka, for example, once belonged to Pilsudki's personal guard. There was also a close relationship between the FRAC Militia and the *Strzelec*. The FRAC militiamen, dressed as *Strzelec*, paraded in their uniforms whenever they felt like it. This made it easier for them to terrorize the street, especially since the police looked the other way when they carried out their acts of terror, even helping them quietly, since the FRAC was an important supporter of the Pilsudski regime. The Strzelec-FRAC mafia extorted money from merchants and shopkeepers, terrorized workers, and got into other criminal activities. Whoever stood up to them or refused to quickly give in, paid for it dearly.

Having such power, the FRACs now turned on the Jewish labor movement; mainly, the Bund. They started taking over whole Bund unions or splitting off sections of them. Because of this there were often sharp conflicts between the FRAC and us. But more about that later.

The end of the FRAC was rather tragic. After a while, they began having internal strife. Moraczewski left them and created his own organization, a would-be syndicalist one, "Z. Z. Z." (*Związek Związkow Zawodowych*, i.e., union of unions). The broad working masses grew sick of the terror, the criminality, and the immorality of the FRAC and their fighting units. The workers started turning from them en masse and returning to the old PPS. The FRAC was left a small group, actually little more than a well-organized terrorist band. This was certainly not the goal of Jaworoski, who was himself an upright and honest man, though a strong opportunist and a fanatic follower of Piłsudski.

But I have gotten ahead of myself. Let me get back to telling things in their chronological order.

CHAPTER 34

A New Gang of Communist Strong-Arms

The physical attacks against us Socialists, the harassing and disrupting of our meetings, the insults and the taunting, the falling upon and the beating of our comrades that the Communist Party had been practicing, did not stop. But although these kinds of struggles had been going on for years, we could still not get used to the idea that the Communists were doing this in a cold-blooded, purposeful, calculated way. When the Bund's Central Committee appealed with an open letter to the Central Committee of the Communist Party, asking that they order their followers to stop these continual assaults, the Communist Central Committee answered with a letter that completely justified these assaults and, what's more, accused the Bund of being, no more nor less, "agents of the police." After this the Communists broadened and increased their assaults on us. They then went so far as to enlist a new group of well-known underworld characters to help them in their attacks. It is worthwhile to acquaint ourselves with these new members of the Communist assault gangs.

First place among them goes to a certain Simkhe Macz—thin, blond, of medium height, with light, almost white, cross-eyes. He was then about 26–28 years old. At first glance you would not think he was a strong-arm. He distinguished himself first of all with the "lofty status" of his family background. His father, called "Macz," was in his youth a thief. Later he switched "professions" and became a pimp. In time he worked himself up in this field and became the proprietor of a whorehouse. The whole family helped in this enterprise: his wife, his daughter, and his son, Simkhe. Simkhe had an important job in the business. He had to protect the family whorehouse from the competition of other pimps. Simkhe, like a lot of underworld characters, also had a nominal trade. He was, to all intents and purposes, a coal carrier. Although he hardly ever had a basket of coal on his back, that didn't stop him from taking for himself some of the earnings of the real coal carriers station, of which he was a nominal member.

Another infamous goon was "Rifke the Cow" (*Rifke,* Yiddish for *Rebecca*). Rifke the Cow was not—God forbid—a woman, but a male, but everyone called him that in deference to the equally high status of his mother, the real Rifke the Cow, who owned a whorehouse on Wolińska Street. His job in his mother's business was the same as Simkhe Macz's: to protect it from the competition. His appearance was awkward: tall, fat—blubbery—his eyes deep in fat, a large horsy head full of blond hair, a dull face—it was awful to look at him. He too was a faux coal hauler; in fact, he—just like Simkhe Macz—occupied himself exclusively with the Communist beatings and with the family "business," his mother's whorehouse.

A third one of these goons, perhaps the wildest of them all, was Leybenyu, small, of medium height, thin, with dark hair and shifty little eyes. Looking at him, no one would imagine that he was one of the wildest thugs. He was extraordinarily quick with a knife or a revolver. He stemmed from a respectable but financially ruined bourgeois family—his grandfather was now a partner in a whorehouse. He was apprenticed to a hat maker at a very young age. He was even for a time a member of the Garment Workers Union, but he didn't stay with this trade long, and quite rapidly descended to underworld activities. He lived off protection money from gambling houses, illegal nightclubs, houses of prostitution, and the like. His family consisted on the whole of respectable people who were terribly ashamed of him. Before the war he had paid a large sum of money to become a meat-hauling teamster in order to have a cover for his criminal activities.

In addition to these "aristocrats" of the Communist assault gangs, there were several other well-known thugs: Moyshe Czompel, a brother of Mayer Czompel from Powązki (see chapter 14). When Mayer Czompel was shot to death, his brother quit the gang of thugs. There was a coal carrier who was mixed up with the shooting of Mayer Czompel, along with the two brothers "Pojces"—one a coal carrier, the other a teamster on Gęsia Street—and Borukh "Tsaban," a teamster in Praga who once killed someone from the underworld and was therefore considered by his comrades to be a great hero. In addition to this bunch, quite a number of coal carriers and cobblers also belonged to the Communist assault gangs.

Simkhe Macz and Leybenyu could be thought of as the "political" leaders of this Communist band of thugs. They and sometimes others of their gang could often be seen with Communist party activists or with known young Communist women—rich daughters dressed in "proletarian" leather jackets. The Communist Central Committee, in its announcements of meetings and other pronouncements, took under its wing this gang of thugs and defended them against any and all criticism.

In truth it must be said that along with these gangs of criminal thugs, honest workers also participated in the attacks who were in no way connected to the underworld. The criminal types also helped the Communist Party in its illegal political work. They guarded the Communist youth as they festooned the overhead tramway wires with their little red flags, or when they distributed illegal flyers, or held demonstrations. For these criminal types it was convenient to have political activities as a cover for their criminal underworld activities. This partnership between the Polish Communist movement and the underworld continued for many long years.

It is more than likely that a certain number of these criminal thugs were secretly in collusion with the police. For one thing, the police never arrested them. Not at fights, harassments, shootings, or other sorts of attacks they conducted, and also not at illegal Communist public appearances, during which many others were often arrested, but never one of these underworld thugs. And since they knew quite well they were "untouchable," this gave them more chutzpah in their assaults on us. If it happened that a private citizen complained to the authorities about some criminal act they had suffered at the hands of the Communist thugs, and if there were other private citizens who were witness to it, and there was then no alternative but for the court to convict them, they would be convicted, but then, generally, would not serve out their full sentences.

I will tell of one typical instance. At the end of Summer 1930, during a Communist wildcat strike of the tailors working in the men's clothing department stores, they assaulted the workers in a factory producing goods for dressmaking and sewing for men's clothing, and beat some of them severely. Two of these workers, Dovid Gelbras and Elle Grossman, who were among those severely beaten, did not want to let this brutal act go unpunished and brought a complaint to the authorities. There were sufficient witnesses, and the court convicted Simkhe Macz and a couple of others in his gang to several months' jail time. But in the end they never served any time at all. In a quiet way, the whole incident was glossed over.

CHAPTER 35

Communists Shoot at a Workers Convention

Shockingly different from their earlier assaults was the armed raid by the Communists on the Transport Workers Union National Convention.

It happened in June of 1927, when the Jewish section of the Transport Workers Union called a national convention in Warsaw. The convention took place in the hall of the Union of Newspaper Distributors on Nalewki 17. In addition to the Warsaw delegates, delegates came from Lodz, Grodno, Białystok, Siedlce, and several other large cities.

During one of the first sessions of the convention, an urgent call from the convention came to the editorial offices of the *Folkstsaytung*. The Communists had attacked the convention and had shot at people. Promptly informed, I rushed over immediately.

A gang of the Communist Union of Coal Carriers, not part of the general Union of Transport Workers and therefore not entitled to participate in the convention, tried to force their way into the convention hall. They were prevented from doing so by the guards. They then—with Dovid Milner and Simkhe Macz in the lead—shoved the guards aside. Tearing open the doors to the hall and forcing their way in, they entered the meeting hall, shooting. They weren't just shooting into the air. They aimed at the Presidium. The Chair of the convention at that moment was Zalmen Białostocki from Białystok. In addition, with the Presidium were sitting Mordkhe Faygman, as a representative of the National Council, Shaye-Yudl from the Warsaw union, Hershl Dorfman, and several others. One bullet struck Shaye-Yudl in the foot, wounding him severely.

When I arrived at the convention, the Communists had already gone. Seeing Shaye-Yudl wounded, I tore off a piece of my shirt and quickly bandaged his bleeding foot. In the meantime Emergency Aid came and drove him off to the hospital.

The Presidium of the Warsaw Committee quickly held counsel. We came to the conclusion that if we did not react quickly and boldly, on the spot, we were lost. Whoever knew the character and the tactics of the Communists knew full well that if we did not give them a strong, prompt answer, there would be more shooting. The Communists had aimed at Shaye-Yudl intentionally. They had wanted to show the Transport Workers that they could do as they pleased and were not afraid of anyone, not even the Bund. We had to show the Communists they could not shoot at people with impunity.

I then went off to our porter stations and took several volunteers from each one. The outrage at this bloody Communist assault was great. In addition, Shaye-Yudl was much loved, and every one of them felt as if they themselves had been hit by that bullet. The honor of the porters was at stake. In a short time I had assembled quite a number of them. We went to places where we knew we would find the shooters, and we taught them a good lesson. They probably did not count on such a swift and strong answer and were not prepared to offer resistance.

In the meantime the news of the assault on a workers convention had spread all over to all workers institutions and among the broad working masses. The outrage everywhere was enormous. That night we gathered the Transport Workers Militia in the meeting hall of the Garment Workers Union, so as to have everyone in one safe place. There were grounds to fear that there would be an organized Communist assault on our Transport Workers Union premises. Our Bundist comrades quickly found out about the call to gather, and the hall was soon full to overflowing with Bundists and workers who wanted to find out exactly what had happened and to offer their help. Since the audience was eager to hear the particulars, we quickly improvised and turned the gathering into a formal meeting. I spoke to the crowd. I emphasized that the Communists wanted to drive us off the street with terror, but in this they would not succeed. The Bund would not allow it.

In the press of the crowd I was approached by Henoch Mendelsund,[1] then still a young boy, a gymnasist, in short pants. He asked me quietly whether there was some way he could help me. It immediately occurred to me that he could actually be of use to me. I asked him to carry my revolvers for me. He accepted this assignment with great pride. When it got late I told him to go home and go to sleep, but come back promptly early the next morning. He refused; he wanted to spend the night here in the hall with the whole group. In the morning we went back to the coal carrier stations: I divided our force into several groups, each group going off to a different neighborhood where the Communist coal carriers were concentrated. Henoch not only carried the revolvers for me, but also served as a runner, carrying instructions to the different groups and bringing back reports.

These battles lasted four days. On our side, only porters participated. In this battle, I did not enlist any members of our general Bund Militia who were not also porters. More than once in these battles we resorted to guns, but only to frighten, never aiming at anybody. I explicitly warned every member of every battle group about this. The couple of weeks that Shaye-Yudl lay in the hospital, we visited him as if making pilgrimage to a holy rabbi. He was the hero of the day. Bund organizations and delegates from unions and other institutions adopted protest resolutions, sending him sympathy telegrams and expressions of solidarity. Delegations and several friends brought flowers, food, and other gifts to him in the hospital. Normally visitors were allowed only twice a week, but this rule did not apply to the transport workers! They came when they wanted to; for them there were no locked doors; they knew ways to get around them.

Shaye-Yudl had seen who had shot him: the infamous Simkhe Macz. When he emerged from the hospital, Shaye-Yudl wanted revenge. The Bund forbade this: we didn't want to ignite another battle. Shaye-Yudl obeyed, although he could not at all understand why he should be forbidden to take just revenge against someone who had shot at him and had wanted to kill him. But he obeyed. This was perhaps the first time when, in the milieu of the porters, the primal law of vengeance did not prevail—rather, a higher social discipline did.

Figure 51. Central Committee of the Warsaw Transport Workers Union. From the Archives of the YIVO Institute for Jewish Research, New York.

Note

1. Henoch Mendelsund (1911–1994): Worked as a mechanic and attended Warsaw University. Arrived in the US in 1941 as one of 1,500 Bundist labor leaders and intellectuals rescued from the Nazis through the efforts of the ILGWU and the Jewish Labor Committee. Joined the ILGWU as a sewing machine operator. While working in the shop during the day, attended the New School for Social Research at night, earning a master's degree in economics and sociology. Served as a member of the National Coat and Suit Recovery Board staff, and in 1949, became secretary of Cloak Finishers' Local 9. In 1953 became assistant general manager of the ILGWU New York Cloak Joint Board, and then general manager in September 1959, a post he held until 1973. Also served as ILGWU vice president and director of its International Relations Department from 1968–1980.

CHAPTER 36

Morgnshtern

The Bund sports movement in Warsaw began in the twenties in a modest way with a gymnastics group that met at the TOZ[1] building on Gęsia 43. Formally, this gymnastic group was nonpartisan, but in fact it was organized by the Bund and consisted exclusively of Bundist youth and members of the youth divisions of our unions. The directors of TOZ knew this quite well, but they were dedicated to the cause of physical education for the Jewish population and, therefore, helped anyone who did something toward that goal. They were glad to give us a suitable hall for our gymnastic group, and they generously even paid some of our expenses. Dr. Leon Woolman, the long-time Chief Secretary of TOZ (today in America), had excellent relations with our gymnasts.

Figure 52. Gymnasts of the Warsaw *Morgnshtern*. From the Archives of the YIVO Institute for Jewish Research, New York.

The negotiations with him to establish the group were initiated by Comrade Dovid Meyer right before he left for America. The first Secretary of the gymnastic group was Comrade Bergheuer, who emigrated to Paris in the twenties and continues there now an active Bundist. After him the office of Secretary for the gymnastic groups was assumed by Morris (Borukh) Gelbron, a *Tsukunft* activist who threw himself into the sports work (he died on May 16, 1956, in Melbourne, Australia). I was asked to assume the Chairmanship of the Board of Directors of this athletic group.

The athletic group soon added members and grew too large for the space the TOZ gave us. Also, under the aegis of TOZ, we could not build up the athletic group and enlarge it as we would have liked to do. We started thinking about organizing an independent workers sports organization that would be openly associated with the Bund movement. We began taking the necessary steps to found such an organization. We decided to call it *Morgnshtern* (Morningstar) and said goodbye to the hospitable, friendly TOZ and its sympathetic leaders.[2]

Oh, I almost forgot. We also said a warm goodbye to Wolski, the Polish janitor. Between him and our young sports enthusiasts there was constant warfare. The crowd of young people, when they gathered together in the courtyard, or when they were saying goodbye late at night (the sport groups lasted until eleven o'clock at night), made a racket, and they took a long time leaving. Wolski would drive them away, and not very politely. He could speak perfect Yiddish, and he knew many Yiddish curses with which he dispersed the young people. The fact was, he thought well of the Jewish people and even sent his daughter to

Figure 53. *Morgnshtern* gymnastics team, Lublin, 1929. From the Archives of the YIVO Institute for Jewish Research, New York.

Figure 54. "Worker Athlete: A Monthly Publicaton of the Labor Sport Federation. Comrade, Prepare Yourself for The Vienna 1931 Olympiad. We Must Demonstrate There the Strength of Our Movement." 1930. From the Archives of the YIVO Institute for Jewish Research, New York.

Figure 55. A *Morgnshtern* group on an outing in Skalka, Poland. Late 1920s. From the Archives of the YIVO Institute for Jewish Research, New York.

Figure 56. A *Morgnshtern* gymnast performing at the annual *Morgnshtern* meet in Warsaw, 1930s. From the Archives of the YIVO Institute for Jewish Research, New York.

the TSYSHO Yiddish secular school on Karmelicka 29. He did not believe in the *powszechna* (state) school; he said he wanted his child to have a good upbringing.

After obtaining the proper legal permits for *Morgnshtern,* we rented a spacious hall in the well-known *Pasaż Simonsa* (Simon's Arcade) at Nalewki 2, and the new worker sport organization quickly became popular. After a short time, our *Morgnshtern* counted over 1,000 members and became the largest Jewish sports organization, not simply in size, but also in the breadth of its activities.

Morgnshtern was sharply distinct from other sports organizations in Poland or anywhere else. It placed its primary emphasis on group sports, like gymnastics, rhythmic movement, light athletics, touring, cycling, hiking, and nature study—all aspects of sport that did not require long and difficult practice and did not rely on "stars" or "champions." In other sports organizations (including Jewish ones), much greater emphasis was placed on soccer, boxing, and other sports that were more about individual professionalism, rather than about the average young worker who had very little time to practice. In the group sports and in the lighter athletic sports, *Morgnshtern* quickly emerged in first place, and even had a few champions. Comrade Lazar Eikhl, for example, a young printer and *Tsukunftist*, became one of the fastest short distance sprinters in all of Poland (he died in Russia during the war; his wife Sheva and daughter are now in New York).

In the thirties *Morgnshtern* also organized a soccer team, and after that—following a long, heated discussion regarding Socialist principles—boxing was also introduced. But these two sports did not play a large role in *Morgnshtern*, which remained to the end a sports organization devoted to sports that deemphasized the individual in favor of the team. In this arena *Morgnshtern* acquired an excellent reputation.[3]

Warsaw's *Morgnshtern* also instituted its own holiday, an annual sports festival that took place around the time of Passover in the *Cirk*, the largest hall in Warsaw, drawing over 4,000 attendees. Hundreds of athletes, children, and young people, performed at this festival of gymnastics, light athletics, rhythmic movement, and other presentations of group sports.

The culmination of this festival was a parade of all the athletic groups in the *Cirk* arena. At the head marched the lead instructor, M. Golfayl (a professional athlete); behind him came the red flag of *Morgnshtern*, and behind the flag marched, to the rhythm of labor songs played by the brass band, the various sports groups, from the eldest to the children's groups, each group dressed in its own colors. When all the different groups had filled the arena it looked like a meadow in spring, covered with hundreds of colorful flowers. Looking at this wonderful picture of youth, freshness, strength, rhythm, and color, one's heart filled with pride, and everyone had the thought that our Bund movement

Figure 57. Warsaw *Morgnshtern* Executive Committee, 1937. From the Archives of the YIVO Institute for Jewish Research, New York.

had come a long way from the small, secret circles, hiding in attics or cellars in Vilnius or Minsk—to this open, colorful, massive sports festival in the largest Warsaw hall, packed to overflowing.

Soon after *Morgnshtern* was organized in Warsaw, similar Bund sports organizations began to appear in other cities. The first was in Łódź. A national convention of these various sports organizations was called, and a Central Committee was created. Dr. Khayim Pieszyce was named Chairman of the Central Committee, and he remained at this post till the end. He was an extraordinarily fine person, a devoted Bundist with a great deal of initiative, energy, and vitality. He perished in a Soviet prison. When Soviet Russia marched into Lithuania, where he had fled after September 1939, he was in Riga, and there he fell into the paws of the NKVD. After his arrest, every trace of him disappeared.

Figure 58. A group of *Morgnshtern* athletes, 1937. From the Archives of the YIVO Institute for Jewish Research, New York.

Figure 59. Exhibition by Warsaw *Morgnshtern* atheletes, 1937. From the Archives of the YIVO Institute for Jewish Research, New York.

Also selected to serve on the Central Committee were Dr. Leon Feiner (later the Chairman of the Central Committee of the Underground Bund resistance in Nazi-occupied Poland); Morris Gelbron; Leybl Friedman (the leader of the Łódź *Morgnshtern*); Shloyme Notkowski; Pinkhas Schwartz; and I. Morris Gelbron became Secretary of the Central Committee, a position he held until 1936. After that this office was occupied by Zalmen Frydrich, later the heroic "Comrade Zygmunt" of the Warsaw Ghetto Uprising.[4]

For several years I continued as Chairman of the Warsaw *Morgnshtern*, but in name only. I could not participate in the practical work of the organization. In the thirties Shloyme Notkowski—an engineer and a *Tsukunft* activist who was for a time Secretary of *Tsukunft*—took over the chairmanship. Notkowski was a quiet, courteous man. Somewhat taller than medium height, he was slender, olive skinned, with black hair and a long face. With his constant smile and good-natured humor, he gained everyone's trust and sympathy. He was very systematic and industrious. He threw himself with all his heart and soul into the work of the Warsaw *Morgnshtern*, and under his leadership the organization blossomed. He, his wife Stasia, and their child were killed during the first days of the war.

As soon as *Morgnshtern* became a national organization, discussions were held with the Polish workers sports movement about unification—but only unification if in accord with the Bundist principle that in every country a united labor movement must consist of autonomous, national/ethnic organizations. The head of the Polish sports organization, under the direction of the PPS, was Dr. Jerzy Michałowicz, a young doctor and son of Professor Michalowicz, one of the greatest medical authorities in Poland. Professor Michałowicz was an ardent liberal and one of the few Polish professors who openly and courageously defended

Figure 60. Members of the Bundist youth organization, *Tsukunft*, and members of *Morgnshtern* gathered for an event on the TOZ sports field, Lublin, Poland, 1928. From the Archives of the YIVO Institute for Jewish Research, New York.

the Jewish students during the infamous battle over the "ghetto-benches."[5] We couldn't quite agree on everything, and the discussions did not end with a formal unification, but instead with a joint Coordinating Commission that publically represented the entire labor sports movement in Poland, including *Morgnshtern*. At the Labor Sports Internationale, however, which had its seat in Prague, *Morgnshtern* was represented independently, and in all sporting events participated under its own name.

Figure 61. *Morgnshtern* members on a foot race in a city street during a gathering of *Tsukunft*, Warsaw, 1932. From the Archives of the YIVO Institute for Jewish Research, New York.

Notes

1. TOZ (*Towarzystwo Ochrony Zdrowia Ludności Żydowskiej*: Society for Safeguarding the Health of the Jewish Population): Established in Warsaw in 1921; by 1939 in charge of 368 clinics and institutes in 72 towns, employing 1,000 physicians, nurses, and residents.—MZ
2. In Cracow there had existed much earlier a Bundist sports organization called *Jutrzenka* (Morningstar). Dr.Leon Feiner was its last chairman. When the Executive Board of the Warsaw *Morgnstern* was established, the Cracow *Jutrzenka* united with *Morgnshtern*, their Dr. Feiner joining the united Executive Board. We chose the name *Morgenshtern* because of Cracow's *Jutrzenka*.—BG
3. For more insight into the role the philosophy of the Bund as a socialist party played in the athletics of *Morgnshtern*, see Roni Gechtman, "Socialist Mass Politics through Sport: The Bund's Morgnshtern in Poland, 1926–1939," *Journal of Sport History* 26, no. 2 (Summer 1999): 326–52.—MZ
4. Zalmen Frydrich (1911–1943): Served in the Polish army, fought the Germans, and was taken prisoner. Released, he returned to Warsaw and joined the underground.

In early August 1942, during the mass deportations, he was sent by the Bund to Treblinka to find out exactly what was happening there and report back. On September 20, 1942, the Bund's underground newspaper, *Oyf Der Vakh* (On Watch), published, "The Jews of Warsaw Are Being Murdered in Treblinka," based on Friedrich's report. During the Warsaw ghetto uprising, Friedrich was courier between the fighters and ZOB Headquarters. On April 30, 1943, he escaped the burning ghetto via the sewers. In May, while accompanying a group of fighters to a village hiding place, he fell in combat.—MZ

5. Forcing the Jewish university students to sit on separate benches on the left side of the classroom, apart from the other students; see Chapter 58.—MZ

CHAPTER 37

The Labor Sports Olympiad in Prague

In the beginning of July 1927, the Czechoslovakian Labor Sports Organization mounted an Olympiad in Prague that evolved into an international Labor Sports Olympiad. It drew countless delegations of labor sports organizations from almost every country in Europe. Our *Morgnshtern* also decided to participate. A few dozen of us traveled to Prague, mostly our athletes, of course, but also including some of our Central Committee members: Dr. Pizhits, Pinkhes Schwartz, and I, and, in addition, the correspondent for the *Folkstsaytung*, Sholem Hertz.

This was my first trip to a foreign country. It felt like a holiday for me. But it was the Olympiad itself that made the greatest impression: the beautiful parades and demonstrations, the colorful delegations from the various countries, the massive competitions, and the happy folk festival atmosphere. It was at a time of the ascendancy of the European labor movement, and the Olympiad reflected that power and glory. All of this warmed the heart of every socialist present, strengthening our belief in our cause.

The president of Czechoslovakia, Professor Thomas Masaryk, hosted a reception for the delegates from all the countries. For us, we socialists from Poland, who were used to a government which showed us only a fist and the policeman's knout, the friendly reception by the humane, liberal President Masaryk was a wonderful surprise.

All of us members of the foreign delegations were given free train passes to travel anywhere in Czechoslovakia to acquaint ourselves with the country. Pizhits and Schwartz had to get back to Poland immediately, but Hertz and I embarked on a journey all around the country. Since we didn't have much money, to save on hotel expenses we traveled on the trains at night and visited the cities during the day. We spent several days in Kladno, a large center of the iron and coal industry, and other places. In Kladno we visited the buildings housing the

Czech Socialist Party, and also that of the Communist Party. In general, the freedom enjoyed by the labor movement in a truly democratic country made a deep impression on us.

After that we traveled to Marienbad. We arrived at dawn. Although I was by then a little tired, and probably Sholem was too, we took off to visit the city and the surrounding mountains. As we were hiking up a narrow trail in the quiet morning outside the city, we suddenly heard singing. There were no people or houses nearby. But from a distance somewhere the sound reached us of a sort of prayerful singing that bounded off the mountains in the early morning stillness. When we made it through the thick woods to the top of the mountain, we could see a house from there in which a Jewish family was living. We saw a Jew with a beard, dressed like a Hasid, several boys with long side-curls, and a woman wearing the wig required of orthodox married women. It was these Jews, singing out their prayers on the top of this mountain, whose voices echoed over the whole mountainside.

Coming back down the mountain to the city, we found out from the morning newspapers that workers had set fire to the Palace of Justice in Vienna. This fired up the journalist in Sholem's blood. He jumped up, ran right to the train station, and caught a train to Vienna to report to the *Folkstsaytung* from on the spot. In the meantime I realized I was left all alone without any money. I went off to Carlsbad. Since there were quite a number of Jews there visiting from elsewhere, including guests from Poland coming for the cure, I might meet someone I knew there that I could borrow a little money from so I could get back home.

As soon as I got back to Carlsbad, I went immediately to where they drink the mineral waters and where the foreign guests stroll about. I got there quite early. I wandered around, hungry, stressed, swallowing my saliva, and drinking the salty and bitter mineral water. I looked around for a familiar face, but found none. I wandered around for several hours. Suddenly, I brightened. I spotted a familiar Warsaw rich man, a certain Aaronson, who had a big silk business on Nalewki and was also a partner in the Simon Arcade. I knew him because, from time-to-time, I had to intervene at his place of business about various union conflicts with the retail clerks who worked for him. I approached him. He recognized me immediately and was happy to see me. We strolled around for about a half hour. I told him why I was in the country, but could not yet bring myself to ask him to lend me some money.

Suddenly he had a golden idea: "Perhaps you would like to come with me and have a coffee?" he asked. I answered in a friendly way, but with pretended indifference: "Why not?" but inside me all my hungry organs were practically jumping for joy. I had not eaten for almost 24 hours. We went into a café and sat down at a table. We were served coffee with delicious, small rolls. I could have eaten whole trays of such rolls, but I was ashamed to. I told him some more about my trip, about my impressions, but still held off asking him for money, till finally I mustered some courage, telling him I was left without a penny, and asking him to lend me a little money so I could get home. He responded to my request in a friendly way. "Please," he said, "I can lend you as much as you need, but how much do you want?" "A few hundred crowns," I said (this was actually just about twenty *złotych*). He asked me again, with a touch of irony in his tone, "More than that you don't need?" "No," I said, "I just need enough to get me from the Czech border to Zakopane." He took out the two hundred crowns and handed them to me. I thanked him heartily, said goodbye, and went off to the train station.

From Carlsbad I traveled to Franzisbad, from Franzisbad to Asch, from Asch to the elegant, beautiful little spa, Szczibskie on the lake with the same name at the foot of the Czech side of the Tatra Mountains. Without stopping to rest, I continued over Mt. Risi to the Polish side of the Tatras. More than once I had hiked on this wondrously beautiful, somewhat difficult climb, from the Polish side, from which you can see the most beautiful panorama in the whole chain of Tatra Mountains. But this time I was traveling all by myself, hurrying to get to Zakopane as quickly as possible, barely paying attention to the beautiful countryside around me, focusing on getting to my destination. I didn't arrive until dusk at Morskie Oko, the famous lake on the Polish side of the Tatras. There I found a nice tourist inn. I had barely enough money left to have a bite to eat and pay for a night's lodging, but did not have enough money to get to Zakopane, around 18 miles away. I set out on foot the next morning on the road that goes from Morskie Oko to Zakopane and cuts through a large part of the Polish Tatras. I was not paying the slightest attention to the surrounding natural beauty, just hurrying to get to my destination.

I arrived at Zakopane at dusk, dead tired, covered with the dust of the road. I looked around for my Zakopane comrades, who I knew were there. Luckily I soon ran into Comrade Leyvik Hodess on the street (died in New York in 1957), and borrowed some money from him. I stayed in Zakopane a few days to rest, then took off for Warsaw. As soon as I arrived home, I wired Comrade Hodess the money I owed him, or he would not have had enough money to get home either.

A few days later I went to the merchant Aaronson and gave him back his money. He received me with a warm welcome, and when I told him why I had come, he called his whole staff together, told them the story, laughing with them at my beggarly ways.

This first foreign journey was refreshing to me. I witnessed with my own eyes a part of the mighty, West European, Socialist labor movement.

CHAPTER 38

Ominous Dark Clouds on All Sides

The armed attack on the Transport Workers convention was something completely new that at first left us entirely perplexed. We had grown used to the usual wild Communist methods: the beatings, the splitting of heads, the knifings, the jeers and raucous shouting of insults to disrupt meetings. But attacking a workers convention by shooting guns aimed at workers and their leaders? This was something totally unexpected, even under the circumstances of the existing antagonisms and conflicts. It soon became apparent that this presaged the beginnings of a new, intense Communist war against the Socialist, unionized, non-Communist labor force.

This became even clearer to us in 1928, when the Comintern (Communist International), at its Sixth Congress, adopted explicit resolutions against the social-democratic movement and the unions under their leadership. Socialists were labeled by the Comintern as "Social Fascists" and "Enemy Number One" that must be fought against and destroyed by any and all means.

This new, intensified, anti-Socialist tactic resulted in tragic struggles—in Berlin, Paris, Vienna, Prague, and so on—terribly weakening the whole labor movement. The Communists also pursued this tactic on the Jewish streets of Poland. It was particularly intense in the small Polish-Jewish towns, and also in the Warsaw Jewish quarter, on Karmelicka, Smocza, Pawia, and Gęsia.

The Communists also stepped up their efforts to split the unions. Their first target was the large Warsaw Garment Workers Union, their efforts being accompanied by the incessant harassment of union meetings, assaults on individual organizers, and unending streams of invective. They succeeded only in splitting off a small part of the large Men's Garment Workers Union, and parts of two-or-three other small craft unions. They then immediately called a strike of the men's garment workers (against the will of the garment workers themselves,

80% of whom stuck by the Bund's Garment Workers Union) and proceeded to enforce this strike with savage terror. Every day for a week they fell upon our union members in the street, beating and knifing dozens of them.

They also tried to split other unions with the same tactic of harassments, beatings, and attacks on individuals. Among others, they attacked and beat up Berl Ambaras, the Secretary of the Leather Workers Union (now in New York); Shmayen, another activist of this union; Issar Goldberg, the Secretary of the Metal Workers Union (now in New York); Comrade Wawer, an activist in the Metal Workers Union (now in Australia); and countless others. The unions thus became an arena of intensified and unceasing beatings and assaults.

These increased attacks didn't limit themselves to the unions. On the May 22, 1927—the day of the elections to the City Council—the Communists attacked our campaigners on the streets, beating up large numbers of them. The assaults grew even more intense during the year of the elections to the *Sejm* (Polish parliament) in 1928. On the day of the elections, March 4, it culminated in an intense confrontation in the Warsaw suburb of Ochota, where the Jewish Communists, with the help of the Polish Communists, tried to drive our campaign workers off the street. I rushed there with a large group of our Militia, and with the help of the Polish Socialists (PPSers) of that district, we succeeded in fighting back the attack of the Polish and Jewish Communists, reclaiming the right of our campaigners to remain on the streets.

In the provincial towns, the Communist attacks were even worse than in the big cities. In Kaluszyn, for example, they established such terror that for many weeks a Bundist risked his life by showing himself on the street. The Communists shot at targets in all directions. In Falenica they assaulted and beat up an innocent excursion to the countryside by our *Tsukunft*ists. In Mszczonów they destroyed our library, tearing the books into pieces. In Ciechanow they assaulted a district gathering of Youth-Bund *Tsukunft* on the street, tearing up their flag. This course of intensified hooliganism and terror lasted till the early thirties.

It wasn't long before a second serious onslaught against our entire union movement came from quite another direction—this time from the FRACs.

Initially the FRACs succeeded in taking over the Meat Workers Union. The meat workers joined the FRACs with a heavy heart. "We had no choice," they would say. The Praga slaughterhouse belonged to the city, and since the Polish Meat Workers Union split off and joined the FRACs, they "had no alternative" but to join them.

The FRACs also found it easy to split the Transport Workers Union. The TWU porters worked in the streets and had to deal with all kinds of police and city regulations. To help the FRACs take over the whole transport industry, the police established a new regulation requiring all transport workers to possess a certificate from the police stating they were honest people. Only if a worker had such a certificate could he get a "number" from the city permitting him to continue working as a porter. The police rationale for this regulation? They said they simply wanted to cleanse the Transport industry of criminal elements. In truth what they really wanted was to institute a system of corruption and "protection" that would force the porters to come to the pro-Piłsudski unions to ask for the favor of a certificate. The pro-Piłsudski union would then assure them they would get it for them "under the table."

When this new regulation was promulgated, there was great consternation among the transport workers. And many of them did in fact have reason to worry. Both the left-wing and right-wing Labor Zionists took advantage of this situation, promising the transport workers the moon and the stars, saying they would intervene and get them the certificates. A stampede began among the transport workers. Some of the coal carriers affiliated with the Communists ran to join up with the right-wing and some with the left-wing Labor Zionists. The largest part of the back porters went off to join the FRACs, who had earlier organized their own little Back Porters Union. Some of the porters did, nevertheless, remain with our union—mostly the hard-working handcart porters and rope porters, who had the least to fear from a police investigation of their moral character. All this resulted in the whole transport industry being broken apart and dispersed among the many large and small parties.

When we became aware of this new regulation requiring a "moral certification," a delegation of our Central Committee went to the authorities and protested, saying it could only bring harm to the industry. The authorities assumed a pious demeanor. "What is it we want, really? We want a good thing, an innocent thing, nothing more than to cleanse the transport industry of criminal elements." In reality the whole "cleansing" became a farce. If they were paid, or if the FRACs told them to, the police gave certificates to all kinds of malefactors, miscreants, pimps, and underworld characters testifying to their morality. A group of newspaper peddlers (under the leadership of a certain Mannes Marmurek) joined the FRACs, because they too were dependent on municipal concessions. The FRACs also organized the "Dzondtses" (those who kept the police-regulated records of ads for vacancies in the apartment buildings), because these were also dependent on the police. In addition, the FRACS took over the Sausage Merchants Association; they too were dependent on the city's health authorities.

In a word, all those industries that were dependent on city regulations or concessions were easy prey for the FRACs. The FRACs also tried their luck with the garment workers, but there their efforts failed.

The FRACs split away all these unions and groups from the unions under the leadership of the Bund. This caused frequent conflicts between us and the FRACs, sometimes very intense ones. There were times we came close to open warfare. Although they had the authorities on their side, we never wavered, meeting their threats with energetic resistance. And thanks to our resoluteness, we accomplished a great deal.

Shortly after all this, an even heavier blow fell—an attack by the government on the democratic rights of the whole Polish population.

The elections to the Sejm in 1928 did not give Marshal Piłsudki's party a majority. When Piłsudski became convinced that no kind of backroom dealings would allow him to overcome the opposition, he decided to pursue the path of an open dictatorship. He dissolved parliament and set up new elections, organizing them in such a way that his party would be absolutely assured of receiving a majority. On the night of September 10, 1930, two months before the new election, in order to terrorize the country and create panic in the opposition—especially the left opposition—he had the following well known Socialist representatives arrested: Herman Lieberman, N. Barlicki, A. Prager, S. Dubois, and Adam Ciołkosz; the leader of the Peasants' Party who had several times already been Premier, Wincent Witos; the two liberal Peasant representatives, Piątek and K. Bagiński; and others. He had them imprisoned in the Brisk (Brest-Litovsk) Fortress, appointing as their prison commandant a well-known sadist, Colonel Kostek-Biernacki. The arrested leaders of the opposition were beaten, insulted, forced to do filthy labor, kept on bread and water, and tortured. Despite all this, the government, as a result of the elections of November 14, 1930, was forced to descend to outright election fraud in order to gain a majority in the new Sejm.

After reaching a "majority" in the Sejm in this way, Pilsudski instituted a de facto dictatorship, papered over with the appearance of a democracy. He did not liquidate the opposition political parties, but through all kinds of harassments, he stymied their activities. He did not outright ban the oppositional press, but through constant confiscation and other means, he strove to ruin, or at least limit, their ability to be effective. In this he was much harder on the opposition from the left than he was on the rightist opposition of the extremely antisemitic Endek Party.

This dictatorial regime, which in the early thirties had already taken on a more-or-less Fascist character, threw itself with greatest savagery on the Jew-

Figure 62. Bundist press in Poland between the wars. From the Archives of the YIVO Institute for Jewish Research, New York.

ish population, and most especially on the Jewish labor movement. The Bund's activities became very difficult to carry out. We were met at every step with ever more intense police harassments. The *Folkstsaytung*, the *Yugnt-Veker* [Youth Awakener], and other Bund publications were very often confiscated. Meetings were banned with the phony excuse, for example, that the hall was not safe ("the ceiling might collapse").

In short, a deep change occurred in the sociopolitical life of Poland, and also in the life and struggle of our movement.

We were simultaneously subjected to heightened attacks from three sides: from the Communist side, from the FRAC side, and from the government side, with its increasingly dictatorial course.

A couple of years later was added still a fourth kind of attack: greatly worsened antisemitism.

On all sides, dark clouds.

CHAPTER 39

Concerns about Self-Defense

With our political insight and our long experience of revolutionary struggle, it was clear to us early on that extremely difficult times lay ahead. We understood we needed to be prepared for the worst, and that soon we might have to defend our very physical existence. In such times we could not be satisfied with the few miserable revolvers we then possessed. We began to look for means to strengthen the ability of the Bund to defend itself more effectively.

We knew that first we had to acquire more weapons. We contacted a former Polish Legionnaire Officer and paid him in advance for 20 revolvers. It took him a long time to deliver the weapons, and when he did, he supplied us with only 12 instead of the 20 we had paid for and were promised. But at least it was a start.

Another source was much more important. Through the PPS we were connected with someone who worked in a gun shop. Normally each revolver arriving in a store is registered by number. That number is then used to record to whom the revolver was sold. This particular shop received its gun shipments from a factory in Danzig. We got our contact in the gun shop to agree (for good money, of course) that he would order one case of revolvers more than the shop needed, and that this extra case of revolvers would then be ours.

But how would we obtain this case of revolvers? As soon as the cases of weapons are delivered to the train station, they are immediately registered. This meant we had to remove the case of revolvers from the train before it arrived at the station. This was relatively easy for us to arrange through our comrade Moniek Dembski, who worked for a large, international, export-import company. Every day he was at the train station picking up or sending goods to or from foreign countries. He undertook to accomplish the removal of the case of revolvers for us with the help of friends of his who worked at the train station. When the train arrived from Danzig with the weapons, Moniek Dembski removed the case of revolvers before the train arrived at the main terminal, mixing them together with the cases of delicatessen that arrived for his company. Our case of revolvers would thus vanish from the car containing all the numerous other cases of weapons, and we then, with luck, would have our weapons.

But then another difficulty arose: Where to store such a large cache of weapons? Where could we stash them? They must be stored in a dry place to prevent rusting, and we must be able to access them easily. We solved this problem as well. We distributed the guns in various places. We hid several revolvers at Renia Jarecka's (later Renia Pieszyce) place—she was a rich man's daughter who had her own room in her family's wealthy residence. Other revolvers were hidden at Hela Wojdisławska, another wealthy daughter and also one of our Bund TSYSHO students and, of course, a Bundist. Others were hidden at my place. A lot of them were hidden at Henoch Mendelsund's, and so on.

This solved the problem of where to store the guns, but also caused some unpleasant moments.

Figure 63. *Tuskunft* militia in Wolkowysk, Poland. From the Archives of the YIVO Institute for Jewish Research, New York.

One evening when I was sitting with some comrades at Tabachinsky's, a coffee house on Przejazd 9, in the same building that housed our Workers Corner, where Bundists often used to come, my son Janek suddenly came running, pale, agitated, and quietly told me he had taken one of the revolvers to play with (it was impossible to keep the revolvers hidden from him) and it had gone off and shot Simkhe Krisztal in the leg. We were then sharing an apartment with Tsluve Krishtal and her brother Simkhe. I quickly ran home. Simkhe was lying there, half dead. I first looked at his leg to see if the bullet was still there. Luckily it was not. I found it lying next to the stove. I was afraid to call the Emergency Medics, so I ran off to the pharmacy and bought gauze, bandages, and iodine, and bandaged him up. The bullet had struck him in the soft flesh of his leg. In the morning we called our Bundist comrade, Dr. Anna Brojde-Heller. She told us it was a light wound and nothing to worry about. The wound did in fact heal quickly.

After that I removed all the revolvers from my apartment and stashed them elsewhere.

CHAPTER 40

A Wave of Wildcat Strikes

Around 1929–1930 the Communists started calling countless strikes solely for political purposes, without any economic justification, and explicitly against the will and interests of the workers.

They called these strikes with the help of the splinter unions they had founded from the split-off segments of the larger, recognized labor unions. Their justification was that these strikes "revolutionize" the masses and prepare them for the final struggle that would come in the end when these small, local "revolutionary" demonstrations would come together into one great "revolutionary" uprising that would bring the working class (i.e., the Communist Party) to power.

The Communists enforced every strike with violence, even when it became obvious the strike would fail. Several years later, when the Communists again changed their tactics to that of a "united front" and a "folk front," they themselves characterized their previous tactics as totally mistaken.

Such strikes—we called them "wildcat strikes"—the Communists particularly liked to call in the very trades that had originally been organized by Bund unions, so that, with these strikes—even if they were doomed to failure—they might wipe out the existence of the corresponding Bund-dominated union.

The Communists tried to impose their new "revolutionary" tactic on the workers by force, with terror, assaults, and beatings. And the avant-garde of these Communist waves of terror was again their familiar underworld characters: Simkhe Matsh, Leybenyu, Dovid Milner, and others. Our party militia had to fight off these attacks more than once.

I will describe only some of the more telling cases to give some idea of the poisonous atmosphere of terror the Communists created.

Figure 64. Executive Board, Bundist Leather Workers Union. From the Archives of the YIVO Institute for Jewish Research, New York.

As I have mentioned earlier, there were two leather worker unions in Warsaw: the Bundist one at Leszno 19, and the Communist one with its meeting place in a large cellar on Stawki Lane.

Our union on Leszno 19 had a large majority of the workers, about 80% of the shoe leather cutters and stitchers. The Communist union consisted mostly of cobblers, with only a small number of cutters and stitchers. The Communists decided to call a strike in this craft without the knowledge of our union leadership, who, naturally, did not want to impose a strike called by outsiders, especially when there was no possible chance of prevailing. As soon as the Communists proclaimed the strike, they demanded of the workers that they support the strike "over the heads of their leaders." When the workers refused, the Communists began terrorizing them, attacking the shops, beating the workers, and forcing them to leave work.

The union personnel at 19 Leszno could not, on their own, fight off the Communist thugs, so they turned to the Bund Militia for help. Berl Ambaras, the Secretary of the union; Hershl Ramet, the Chairman; and Elye Kleinboym, one of their foremost activists, all spoke to me, arguing that since the Communists were using their "aggrieved" cobblers, their coal carriers, and all their underworld goons to drive the cutters and stitchers from their shops, the union had no other choice but to appeal to us for help. Rationally, I knew they were right, but because of my aversion to these brawls and my desire to avoid them, I refused their request. They appealed to the Presidium of the Warsaw Bund Central Committee, who decided that because the Bund union on Leszno could not deal with the attackers without our help, and because the Communists were using outside forces in their attacks—coal carriers and underworld thugs—their request was justified. The Presidium decided that the Bund Militia was obligated to beat off the attacks of the Communist terror bands.

At that time, on my own, without asking anyone and without telling anyone, I thought perhaps—as I then believed—there was something that could be done to help avoid a new series of battles between worker and worker. I imagined that if one could reason with the Communists, they would see that these wildcat strikes were useless and brought great harm to both sides. Since I knew the Communists were calling a general meeting in the morning of all their members from all crafts to mobilize a concerted assault, without letting anyone know, I decided to attend that meeting and to appeal to their sense of justice to stop this battle between brothers. I chose three healthy young men to accompany me: a meat worker (they called him Foysz); a back porter, Yosl Karpkes (now in America); and a third, Yitsrok Shuster. They were to help fight off any attackers who might want to assault me at the meeting.

I went off to the meeting. I entered the great cellar hall where the meeting was taking place. It was packed with people. The air was blue and heavy with sweat and smoke. I placed two of my escorts in front of the door and one in the doorway to hold it open just in case I had to escape. With a firm step, I proceeded to the platform. When the crowd caught sight of me, there was a hushed silence. All were stunned, astonished to see me, parting to make way for me. I got up on the platform and immediately started talking. I spoke for about five minutes. I said to them: "This has been going on far too long—forcing workers to strike against their will and against the will of their unions. Workers are being beaten bloody if they refuse to leave work without a strike call from their unions. I appeal to you to avoid further bloodshed. Stop the beatings. Let the unions come to an understanding with each other and work things out—union to union. If not, if you continue to force the workers to strike against their will and against the will of their unions, we will defend ourselves and you will meet with strong resistance."

I got down off the platform and, again with a firm step, went to the door. The hall was as still as death. The crowd parted, letting me through, and I left.

It did not take long for the news of my unauthorized attempt to make peace to spread among our party circles. They were very angry with me about it. That I came out of it alive and in one piece was considered an incomprehensible miracle. My friends considered it a terrible piece of thoughtless recklessness that I risked such a thing. I myself could not understand later how it had occurred to me to do it, and also how it happened that I emerged in one piece from such a large Communist gathering. Perhaps it was because after seeing me, their confusion was so great, they were stunned into immobility.

My illusions were quickly shattered. In two to three hours I saw that my appeal had had no effect whatsoever. News was brought that the Communists had come to a shop on Pawia 48, demanding that the workers stop work immediately. The workers refused, knowing the Communists would return with their goons and try to force them off their jobs.

I quickly assembled a group of men and went to Pawia Street. At the end of Smocza, I saw beaten and bloodied workers the Communists had already succeeded in forcing from other shops. When we neared Pawia 48, I saw the street full of Communist strong-arms—shoemakers, coal carriers, and others. I feared that if my small party of men remained on the street, a fight would start. I told one group of our men to occupy the courtyard where the shop was located, at Pawia 48, and the other group to wait in a nearby coffee house.

It didn't take long for the Communists to attack the shop. When we got to the courtyard, fighting and shooting had already broken out. The police arrived. When I spotted them I handed my gun to Shepsl Mosek, one of our Militiamen, a garment worker. The police arrested me and a coal carrier on the Communist side who had exchanged shots with me. We were both taken to police headquarters and from there to the political police. On the way I said to the Communist fellow, "Now that we are both arrested, let it be that I don't know you and you don't know me." He agreed. At the interrogation they found a revolver on me, a second one that I hadn't used, and a revolver on him.

In the morning, as he was writing the report, the police captain asked me, "Who shot at you?" "I don't know," I answered. He started to laugh. Holding the report, he read to me that the other fellow, the coal carrier, told them who I was and that I had shot at him. I didn't believe the police captain because I knew they often "read" things out to you that are not written in the report. I requested a confrontation with the other man. They brought him right in and he declared right in front of me that he knew me, that I am Bernard Goldstein, and that I had shot at him. Then I demanded an examination of both revolvers, his and mine. Of course, the examination showed that my revolver hadn't been shot and that his had. I was let go under "police surveillance" until the trial should take place. He was imprisoned for 9–10 months before the trial.

While he was in jail, his mother and father, his sisters and brothers, came to me, asking me to not give evidence against him, even though he had betrayed me. I felt I should now tell the truth in court, but the Bund decided otherwise. The party then—and also later—held to the principle that conflicts within the labor movement are an issue for the labor movement itself, and that one must not make use of any kind of direct or indirect help from an outside, third party. The party leadership therefore decided that I must not give evidence against the Communist gunman and that I should stick to the version that I didn't see who shot at me. I submitted to the decision of the party.

In court my defense attorney was Comrade Ludwig Honigwilll. We were both, the coal carrier and I, seated on the bench for the accused. I again repeated that I didn't know this fellow and that I didn't know who shot at me. The prosecuting attorney was Grabowski, later Minister of Justice. During recess, he approached Comrade Honigwilll and said that the Communist should be freed, and I should, at the least, get five years, because he, Grabowski, knew quite well from the confidential police report everything that had happened. "We know the whole truth, that he is covering up for a Communist that had shot at him." The court freed us both due to lack of evidence.

After the trial the coal carrier approached me, thanking me profusely. After this he left the Communist movement.

A similar situation occurred among the food workers. The strongest element in their union was the pastry workers local (spiced honey cakes, tarts, pastries, etc.). The pastry workers were 100% organized in our union, and the local had strong control over the whole industry. The Communists had only one follower in this whole labor force. He did everything in his power to disrupt the unity of the union. He would refuse to carry out the decisions of the union. He even refused to contribute his share of a day's work for the unemployed, which was a point of honor among the food workers.

The union committee decided to transfer him to another bakery where he would earn no less than what he was earning at his current workplace. He would not consent to this move. The committee decided they would have to physically remove him from his current job location and transfer him to his new one. He apparently was expecting that and prepared a large Communist squad to wait nearby, ready to come to his aid. When the union committee, Chairman Avrom Flamenboym at their head, came to the bakery on Karmelicka 24 or 26 to remove him from his place of work, the Communist band, along with their familiar "strong-arms," immediately appeared and began an unequal battle: the Communists were not only armed, but also more numerous than just the two union people.

The union immediately telephoned the offices of the Bund about the danger threatening our people, and I and several others of the Bakers Union went off to the place of battle. We drove off the group of Communists that had attacked the union committee, drove them out of the courtyard, and closed the gate. We stayed there, however, because we understood that the Communists would not so easily surrender, that they would bring reenforcements. In a short time the Communists did in fact return with a large group. They began to storm the locked gate. To avoid a great deal of bloodshed, I divided our group this way: I sent some into the bakery, posting them by the windows to keep watch (the bakery was located in a cellar with the upper half of the windows looking out into the courtyard). Others I placed at various other gates to the courtyard. The Communists broke open the gate, entering with wild cries and shots. Hidden in the various entrances to the courtyard, we shot back. When they heard shots coming from all sides and couldn't see where they were coming from, they were frightened and ran off in a great panic. There was almost no fighting. Only Comrade Shloyme Finkelstein, a militiaman and a garment worker, came out of it with his head split open.

Again we were confronted with a riddle: no police were anywhere to be seen. Karmelicka was a lively street, a commercial street. During the day it was crowded with people. Streetcars were constantly moving through this street. A police station was located just a few blocks from where the shooting took place. The battle lasted more than a couple of hours—and no police came to the scene. Only after it was all over a police sergeant from the third precinct, the convert Torn, came with a group of policemen. He asked what had happened here and began blaming us.

Again our suspicions that the police had a hand in these fights were confirmed. They provoked or assisted the Communists in carrying out their armed attacks so as to weaken the labor movement by these continual internal battles.

The Communists did not limit themselves only to wildcat strikes. They also exploited other opportunities for escapades and attacks. They did not, for example, spare the Bundist elements existing in the unions where the Communists were in charge. A typical case took place with the Bundists in the Communist Shoemakers Union.

In line with the Bund policy in those unions controlled by our political opponents (e.g., the Communists), the Bund cobblers did not leave the Communist-controlled union. They remained loyal, carrying out all the duties of a member, but at the same time created an organized, internal Bund group.

Incidentally, in those unions under the aegis of the Bund that were not, on average, larger than the Communist-controlled unions, the Communists, even though they were a small minority of the membership, also organized their own Communist faction. But they enjoyed more rights with us than the Bundists did in the Communist-controlled unions.

The Bundist faction in the shoemakers union was lively, resolute, and let its oppositional voice be heard often at the meetings of the union, despite harassments and interference. Once, on a Saturday morning at the Workers Corner on Przejazd 9, a meeting took place of the Bundist members of the Shoemakers Union. An important issue had come up that had to be dealt with. The Bundist leaders and Comrades Noyekh and Emanuel Nowogrodzki[1] came to the meeting. Suddenly a group of Communists broke into our party offices and began shouting and raising an alarm, cursing and insulting Comrades Noyekh and Emanuel, and carrying on in such a way that the meeting could not continue. Several of the Communists grabbed "Black Khatskl," a shoemaker belonging to the Bundist faction in the Communist-led Shoemakers Union. They pushed him to the wall, held his arms, and then one of them burned a hole in his lip with a burning cigarette. They then ran off.

I was not in Warsaw that Saturday. When I got back in the evening, I was informed of the incident. Our shoemaker comrades and our Militiamen were extremely provoked by it. Burning a hole in someone's living flesh? We decided to get even with the fellow who did it. The next day, Sunday, was not a workday. We knew that the Communist shoemakers were to be found at their exchange on Gęsia Street, between Smocza and the Jewish cemetery. Around one o'clock in the afternoon I went there with Yankl Placzaz and Yankl Rosenberg (both of them militiamen from the Meat Workers Union). At the exchange there was a large crowd of them, also the secretary of their union, a certain Edward. We sought out "Mendele Parkh," the person who burned the hole in Khatskl's lip, and gave him a good beating in front of all his comrades—and left before the Communists could grasp what had happened. When we reached Smocza Street, they caught up to us and started a fight. In the middle of the fight Marian Romanowski, the secretary of the Polish Construction Workers Union, happened by. He immediately grasped what was happening and joined us. He was a healthy youngster and helped us drive off the Communists.

Note

1. Influential Secretary of the Bund's Central Committee and one of three members of the Presidium of the Central Committee (Noyekh and Chaim Wasser, the other two); author, *The Jewish Labor Bund in Poland (1915–1939)*, Rockville, MD, Shengold 2001. See chapter 2, footnote, for more about him.—MZ

CHAPTER 41

An Attempted Murderous Assault on Me

It happened in the summer of 1929. A group of us Bundists had traveled to a summerhouse in the village of Marianka, about four miles from Mińsk-Mazowiecki. This was a prosperous little village founded by German settlers. The houses were comfortable and the natural surroundings beautiful. Also, it was not very far from Warsaw. Someone recommended this comfortable little spot, and several Bundist families went there: Leybetshke Berman and his family, the Perensons, Misza and Karola Scher (they were also relatives of Lucia's), the teacher Poliak, and my family and I. The women and children stayed there the whole summer; the men, who worked during the week, came out on the weekends. My vacation was in July, so we decided to spend it there. Several Bundist comrades arrived from Warsaw on Friday, as usual. Toward evening we took a stroll: Leybetshke, Perenson, and I. We strolled the paths through the fields and the forest trails, talking about various things, and when twilight came, each of us went our separate ways, back to his own cottage.

It was already rather dark when I arrived at my cottage. Lucia told me that a young man had just been there asking for me, saying that when I got back, I should be told to go to Moyshe's store, that someone was waiting for me there. The store was a typical village general store where you could buy almost anything. In addition, it was a sort of summer club for the young people. They congregated there in the evenings, drank seltzer mixed with fruit juice, cracked sunflower seeds, and rendezvoused. Sometimes older people, who had come to buy something, also stayed a while and joined in the conversation. Since I was a little tired, I didn't feel like going there. If someone needed to see me, I thought he would probably come here.

It didn't take long, perhaps about twenty minutes, and someone knocked at the door and an unfamiliar young man entered, thin, of medium height. He told me that at Moyshe's store there were several people who would like to see me. They had been waiting a long time, and so would I mind going there with him? The store was a little distance away and I still didn't feel like going there, so I said, "Since my place is quite comfortable, it would be better for them to come here." The young man would not agree to this and insisted I go there with him. I again refused, and he began to argue with me and wouldn't leave. He began to reproach me, saying it isn't right to let comrades wait so long.

I held to my argument—why does it have to be in the store? Why not here in my cabin? We continued arguing thus, and I continued to refuse for the tenth time. He then suddenly said to me with *chutzpah,* "You must come!" Now suddenly I grew very suspicious—what does he mean, "I *must* come!"? Now I categorically refused to go with him and got up to accompany the boy to the outer fence. When we stepped down from the verandah, he made a suspicious gesture with his hand and turned his flashlight on. In that moment there appeared before me a tall Pole. I immediately realized what was going on here. With one leap I was behind a tree. The Pole shot at me but did not hit me. Still behind the tree, I grabbed my revolver and shot back at him. Both of these intruders then disappeared into the darkness.

I went back into the cabin. The peasant who was the landlord came running to ask what had taken place here. I told him everything. He said he had a permit to carry a rifle and he in fact had one—just let someone else dare to come here again!

About an hour later I could hear voices from the forest, which was not far from our cottage—three or four drunken voices talking Polish, saying, "It's that window." "No, it's that other window." I went over to the landlord and told him about it. He immediately went out with his rifle and shouted: "Whoever dares to cross my fence will not come out alive!" At this you could hear the bunch in the forest, with curses and invective, moving farther away.

I went back into the cabin, fastened the shutters, and lay down to sleep, but Lucia and I couldn't sleep that night.

In the morning Leybetshke Berman and Perenson came. They had only this morning found out the whole story. They stayed with me just in case it might be necessary to help defend me. Around ten o'clock in the morning, Khayim Kirschenzweig arrived on his bicycle, out of breath. He was one of the most energetic *Tsukunft* activists, a member of the Warsaw Committee of *Tsukunft*, and Vice-Commander of the Bund's *Tsukunft* Militia (he died in Melbourne, Australia, in 1953). His parents and his whole family also were staying in a summerhouse in the region, but much closer to the town of Mińsk-Mazowiecki.

That morning he had overheard talk that the Communists were preparing a demonstration against me. He had rushed over on his bicycle, he said, to warn me of the danger and to tell me I should immediately go back to Warsaw. I calmed him, telling him I had no intention of running away.

In a few hours there did indeed appear on the path in the field a band of about 100 young people. They stayed at a distance and began to shout in unison: "Down with Bernard!" "Down with the Social Fascists!" They shouted like that for a while and then withdrew.

Khayim Kirschenzweig, when he saw I would not leave, telephoned the party in Warsaw, telling them all that had happened. The next morning a group of our militiamen came to protect me (among them, Leyzer Levine, Shaye-Yudl, and Monyek Dembski).

Monday morning I received a phone call from Noyekh saying I was urgently needed in Warsaw and that I should come immediately. When I arrived and went to him he informed me, with his familiar mild severity, that he forbade me to go back to Marianka.

I could enjoy the rest of my vacation wherever I wanted, but not there. I decided to go to Zakopane. I took my Janek with me. Lucia decided to stay in Warsaw.

Figure 65. Standing, right to left: Henryk Erlich, Sophia-Dubnow Erlich, Berta Kastalansky, and Victor Alter. Seated, right to left: Noyekh, N. Chanin, and Abraham Kastalansky. From the Archives of the YIVO Institute for Jewish Research, New York.

CHAPTER 42

In Zakopane

Zakopane is a town in the very heart of the Polish Tatra Mountains. It is the central jumping-off point for excursions into various parts of the mountains, as well as a well-known and popular summer and winter resort. In Zakopane I stayed at the camp belonging to the *Kultur-Lige* (Culture League).

Although the *Kultur-Lige* was a Bund organization, no one was asked his party affiliation; everyone was accepted. Even Communists enjoyed the entertainments and organized activities of the *Kultur-Lige*. It was the TSYSHO teacher and school board member, S. Abramson (now in Montreal, Canada), who first developed the Warsaw *Kultur-Lige*. He was not a Bundist, but he worked loyally for the Bund. In his leadership of the *Kultur-Lige* he displayed a great deal of initiative, enterprise, and vision. In the thirties the Bundist cultural activist Herman Kruk took over the leadership of the *Kultur-Lige*. During World War II, Kruk was one of the most active members of the underground Bund in Nazi-occupied Vilnius. He was murdered by the Nazis in 1944.[1]

The activities of the *Kultur-Lige* were multifaceted. It conducted a folk university with language and other evening courses, cycles of readings, concerts, and dramatic performances. It also offered discount tickets to Yiddish and Polish theatrical productions. Its most popular activities, however, were centered on its summer camp and the hikes in the country, including trips to other countries. In its summer camps, set in the most beautiful regions of Poland, workers and worker-intelligentsia could, for a reasonable price, enjoy their vacations in a region they could not otherwise have afforded. Besides providing a typical camping experience, the *Kultur-Lige* also sought to maintain a high level of culture in its camps.

In 1929 the *Kultur-Lige* had organized such a camp in Zakopane, and after the incident in Marianka, I went there for my vacation. The leader of this camp was Grisza Jaszunski, a law student at the University of Warsaw. His assistant was

Figure 66. *Kultur Lige* choral group, Warsaw, 1932. From the Archives of the YIVO Institute for Jewish Research, New York.

Luba Szabrinsky, also a student, a Zionist belonging to *Hashomer Hatzair*[2] and for many years a teacher in our *Tsukunft* evening school.

After a couple of days there, the famous writers John Galsworthy and Ernst Toller came as guests to the camp. They were brought by Dr. Leon Feiner,[3] a lawyer and Bundist leader from Cracow. At that time the International Congress of the PEN Club was meeting in Cracow. Dr. Feiner brought several socialist writers from there as guests to visit our camp and get to know Jewish workers. I had a long talk with Ernst Toller. He understood my Yiddish perfectly—I avoided using Hebraisms. He was greatly interested in all I told him—about the living conditions of the Jewish workers, their cultural life, the secular Yiddish schools, the Yiddish theatre, our political struggles, antisemitism, and much more.

I led short hikes into the valleys and mountains surrounding Zakopane. One time we had to negotiate a narrow trail beside a deep gorge. At that moment, a young Communist was walking next to me, who, I was told, had said about me as soon as I arrived at the camp, "The murderer is here." So I said to him, "You can see that you could easily disappear into this gorge and no one would ever know—but let us go on." A moment later he approached me somewhat shamefacedly and said that since he has been with me here at the camp he sees that he was misled about me, and that the poisonous party conflicts are to blame.

Anna Rosenthal was also in the camp at this same time. She stood out, as always, with her proud and aristocratic, but friendly, manner. She gained the respect of all. However she had great personal anguish due to one thing: Grisza Jaszunski was carrying on a flirtation with a Communist girl in the camp from

Figure 67. Bundists in Vienna. Seated, from right: Dr. Leon Feiner (later to play a key role in Bund underground movement in Warsaw, leading to the Warsaw Ghetto Uprising), Yitsrok Blind (veteran of Jewish Socialist movement in Galicia), and Dr. Lippe Rosenman. Standing, from right: Dr. Chaim Pizhits (perished in a Soviet prison during World War II), Avrom Yitsrok Chaikin. From the Archives of the YIVO Institute for Jewish Research, New York.

Częstochowa, and she, Anna, couldn't stand it. With Anna in this case it was not a matter of mixing into things that were not her affair. Years ago in Vilnius, the Jaszunskis were neighbors of Anna's. The sons of Jaszunski, Grisza and Misza, were still small children then, and they used to come into the Rosenthal home so often that the Rosenthals thought of them as their own children (they had no children of their own). That was why Anna was so upset about Grisza's flirtation. It was as if it were a stain on the honor of her own family.

Shortly thereafter Grisza's parents came to the camp. Anna immediately told Grisza's mother, regretfully, about this grave misfortune. "One shouldn't take this sort of thing too seriously," said Mrs. Rosenthal, calming Comrade Anna.

Grisza's father, Engineer Yoysef Jaszunski, showed himself to be quite another person in the camp, altogether different from the one we ordinarily knew.

His external appearance had always impressed me as strict and rigid, a hard kind of person. He also created that impression at work—he was the Chief Director of ORT in Poland. But here in the camp he revealed himself as talkative and approachable, a friendly man. Jaszunski had very poor vision. He could barely see. Nevertheless he wanted to go on hikes in the surrounding hills and valleys. Taking him along with a group of hikers was out of the question. He would have held everyone up—he actually had to be led by the hand. For that reason, just he and I went on hikes together. During these hikes he talked freely, telling me much about his youth, his student years in St. Petersburg, about his social life then, and so on. These hikes were a great pleasure for me. No matter what interesting and unusual thing in nature we happened to come across, Jaszunski would launch into a lengthy lecture about it, in a popular, captivating way, as only he could do. His "Shmuesn vegn Naturvisnshaft un Tekhnik" (Discourses on Natural History and Technology), published every week in our *Folktsaytung*, were much beloved by our readership. Once in a while, the gentle and pleasant Mrs. Jaszunski would also come along on our hike. And once in a while, but not so often, Comrade Anna would also join us.

Also coming to the camp from *Białystok* were Benyomin Tabaczinski[4] and his wife, Krayndl, and their only son, Shmuel. They both died in the *Białystok* Ghetto. Comrade Tabaczinski did not hold with hiking in the mountains. Mounting barricades, that he understood, but risking your life mountain climbing? For a short hike in a valley one could drag him out, but he wouldn't let himself be led off for a hike in the high mountains, or even in the smaller ones. But he brought a great deal of merriment and pleasantness into the camp. At table he was a masterful conversationalist, a terrific singer, and always full of sparkling humor—it was a great pleasure to spend time with him.

His Shmulik, on the other hand—he was then about 6–7 years old—wanted very much to go hiking in the mountains. And not so much hike as run. He had to be restrained. He soaked up the wonders of the surrounding nature with a sharp eye and with the keenness of an intelligent and alert child. During the hikes he would constantly jump at me with exciting news. "Bernard, did you see, there's a doe!" "Bernard, did you see, that rock over there looks like a bird!" Also his fantasy came into play and he saw imaginary things: "Bernard, did you see, a lion just ran by!" He simply came to life in the mountains.

My son, Janek, was also deeply moved by the mountains. He had been to Zakopane before, but this time I took him along on the longer hikes into the not-too-high surrounding mountains. I also took him along on a bigger hike for the first time into the actual Tatras, into the popular *zawrat*,[5] on the ridge of the mountain where there were at that time glaciers in several places. When Janek saw snow in the middle of summer, he was almost wild with astonishment. I could hardly restrain him. I hiked quite a number of times with him in the mountains. He could not contain himself, running ahead, wanting to see more. No warnings or dangerous spots could hold him back.

One time I played a trick on him. We were hiking the Nossl, a not very high or difficult mountain, near Zakopane. There was however a deep gorge in a certain place. Janek, as always, ran ahead. I pretended to have fallen down into the gorge and called out to him to come back and help me grope my way out. Apparently hanging over the abyss, I instructed him how to save me. I told him to take everything out of his backpack, and, holding fast to the leather straps, lower the backpack down to me and in this way slowly pull me up.

For many years after he firmly believed he had saved me, and he used to relate this story many times, with great pride. When he grew up, he became a great lover of the mountains. He would hike on quite dangerous mountain trails, mostly in the company of Mayus Nowogrodski (today in New York) and

Rueben Lifszytz, who was, at 25, taken from the world so young in the crash of a Polish military airplane in 1945. He was a pilot in the Free Polish armed forces in England.

Notes

1. Kruk, Herman (1897–1944): Director of the library in the Vilnius Ghetto; chronicler, author *The Last Days of the Jerusalem of Lithuania: Chronicles from the Vilnius Ghetto and the Camps, 1939–1944* (New Haven, 2002). He buried his journal on September 17, 1944, a day before he and almost all the other prisoners in a Nazi concentration camp in Estonia were forced to carry logs to a pile, spread them in a layer, and lie down naked on them so they could be executed and burned in a massive pyre.—MZ
2. Hebrew for "The Youth Guard," a Socialist-Zionist, secular Jewish youth movement founded in 1913 in Austro-Hungary. By 1939, it had 70,000 members worldwide, its membership base in Eastern Europe. In contradistinction to the Bund, *Hashomer Hatzair* believed the liberation of Jewish youth could be accomplished by immigration to Palestine and living in kibbutzim.—MZ
3. Leon Feiner (1885–1945): While living as a Pole on the "Aryan" side of Warsaw under the assumed name "Berezowski," he was a leading figure in the Jewish underground, meeting with couriers, distributing funds, acquiring arms for the uprising, finding hiding places for Jews on the "Aryan" side, etc. He was the author of most of the communiqués of the Bund from Poland to the Western allies, in which he described the Nazi terror, brutality, and genocide. Served as a guide for the Polish courier Jan Karski inside the Warsaw Ghetto (they both crossed into the ghetto through the Warsaw sewers). Survived the war and the uprising, dying of throat cancer in Lublin in 1945.—MZ
4. Benyomin Tabaczinski (1896–1967): Active Bundist in *Białystok*. Emigrated to America in 1938 where he became Executive Secretary of the Jewish Labor Committee, and a leading figure in the World Yiddish Culture Congress, YIVO, and Workmen's Circle; also a member of the Bund's Representation to Poland and the World Coordinating Committee of the Bund.—MZ
5. A narrow mountain pass located on the eastern ridge of Świnica in the High Tatras at an altitude of 2,159 meters above sea level.—MR

CHAPTER 43

Attacks on a Night School

According to the Communist way of thinking, not only should Socialist Party offices and unions be attacked, but anything that had anything to do with them, even a night school for young working-class people.

From the early twenties on in Warsaw, the *Yugnt-Bund Tsukunft* had been sponsoring night schools for young workers. Up until 1926, there were five such night schools, with several hundred students attending. To prevent the schools from being harassed by the police, *Tsukunft* created a special Educational Association called *Veker* (Awakener) as the legal body in charge of the schools. Pedagogically these night schools were associated with TSYSHO and even met in their schoolrooms. The two largest and most stable *Tsukunft* night schools were on Nowolipki 68 and Miła 51. These two night schools were very popular among the Warsaw Jewish young working people. These Jewish working class youths, who had never attended any kind of elementary school—they had to go to work as children—not only benefited from the general education being presented, but also from the broader cultural activities offered. And most importantly, they found a warm, comradely atmosphere. Two important cultural institutions developed from these night schools: The *Tsukunft* Chorus, under the direction of Yoysef Glatshteyn (killed by the Nazis), and the Dramatic Group, under the direction of M. Perenson (now in New York). The night schools were open to any Jewish young person and were also an important source of new recruits for *Tsukunft*. Hundreds of young people came to the Bund youth organization because of the night schools. The Communists couldn't tolerate this. They began to harass our night schools.

They had started the harassments before, but in the beginning of the school year of 1929–1930 they put particular pressure on the night school on Miła 15, which lay in the very heart of Warsaw's Jewish poverty. They would stand at the

Figure 68. First school in Yiddish in Poland. Warsaw 1919. Leading class discussion, Shloyme Gilinski, founder and head of the school (later, Director of the Bund's Medem Sanitarium. Notice children barefooted, too poor to own a pair of shoes and with heads shaved to rid them of lice. From the Archives of the YIVO Institute for Jewish Research, New York.

gate of the school and grab the students as they entered. They would break into the school facility itself, coming into the classrooms in the middle of a lesson and shouting, catcalling, etc. It went so far as throwing rocks at ten in the evening at the teachers and the students, who were going home. It became frightening for the young people to go home alone after class. Even the instructors had to be accompanied home by our militia. Mothers and fathers, older brothers and sisters, used to come in the evening to accompany the children home. Many students, although they were already working during the day, were still children of only 12–13 years of age. We had to call up our militia more and more often to drive the Communists away. The Communists began bringing their goons; there was hardly a night there wasn't a fight at the night school.

Once, at the beginning of winter 1930, when the youngsters were already sitting at their desks and quietly doing their lessons, rocks started flying into the classrooms through the windows—the school at 51 Miła was on the ground floor, so the windows faced the street. In a few moments the classrooms were full of rocks and broken glass. A few dozen windows were broken and several students hurt. There was panic in the school. The lessons were interrupted. The party Secretariat was called immediately and a group of Militiamen came, but met with no one. The Communists had already fled. From then on things were peaceful at the school. The Communists understood what kind of retribution awaited them for such a piece of work, and they no longer appeared at the school.

But the attack on the night school on Miła 51 was but child's play compared to what the Communists did next.

Figure 69. A class in a TSYSHO school, c. 1930. From the Archives of the YIVO Institute for Jewish Research, New York.

Figure 70. Students of the Michalewicz School in Bialystok, named after Beynish Michalewicz, Bundist leader and writer. From the Archives of the YIVO Institute for Jewish Research, New York.

Figure 71. *Children of the World,* a Yiddish literary anthology, published by TSYSHO, Vilna, 1940. From the Archives of the YIVO Institute for Jewish Research, New York.

CHAPTER 44

The Medem Sanitarium Attacked

The Medem Sanitarium for children with tubercular-weakened lungs was the crown jewel of the Bundist movement. We surrounded it with motherly warmth and tenderness. We basked in its success as a mother and father would in the success of a gifted child.

Whoever knew the condition of the Jewish workers in Poland, and then saw what it was that the Medem Sanitarium represented, could easily understand our enthusiasm. The poverty, the narrowness, the need, the malnourishment of the Jewish workers in Poland, the suffocating air of the overpopulated quarter in which they lived—all of this was well known. The Medem Sanitarium was in shining contrast to all that. Located on the famous Otwock Railway Line between Miedzeszyn and Falenica, it stood in an open field, surrounded by meadows and woods. The wooden, sparklingly white, painted buildings were enveloped in green, surrounded by trees. On the campus of the Sanitarium were playgrounds, paths adorned with large beds of flowers, a hothouse for plants, chicken coops, a large dovecote (a favorite of the children), facilities for teaching the children natural history right in the lap of nature itself, and a multifaceted, self-governing board, consisting of representatives elected by the children.

As soon as you passed through the gates of the Sanitarium, you were moved by the festive atmosphere. Your eyes were dazzled by the ideal cleanliness, the exemplary planning of the entire surroundings. You had the feeling that you stood in a temple of beauty and continual festivity. And in the center of the beauty and upliftedness—the children themselves, who filled the entire place with life and joy.

Tuberculosis threatened the health of the Jewish children in Poland, just as it did all children. Establishments existed in Poland that were occupied with healing those sick with tuberculosis, but they all had the character of hospitals. Sanatoria existed, but everyone there knew that he or she was sick and had to behave like someone who was sick. In the Medem Sanitarium quite another atmosphere prevailed. The children were brought there to heal their weak lungs, but for them, for the children themselves, the sanitarium was no hospital, and their whole stay at the sanitarium was a great holiday of joy, uplifting, and happy learning.

All this was achieved thanks to the fact that the sanitarium was established as a Yiddish, secular, modern, pedagogical healing facility.

It would be wrong not to mention at least some of the people who threw their hearts and souls into making the Medem Sanitarium what it became: Noyekh (Chair of the Board of the Medem Sanitarium); Shloyme Mendelson; Shloyme Gilinsky (Director); Yoysef Brumberg (Board Member; both he and Gilinsky now in America); the two teachers, Mordkhe Gilinski (known affectionately as "Batke") and Yankl Trupianksi; Dr. Anna Brojde-Heller (all three of the foregoing murdered by the Nazis); and many, many others.

For a Jewish worker, sending his or her child to the Medem Sanitarium was a great joy. Once a child came for just one time to the sanitarium, for them it was an experience never to be forgotten. And yet . . .

The Communists attacked this island of joy, beauty, and innocent, childlike happiness.

Figure 72. Medem Sanitarium, ca. 1930. From the Archives of the YIVO Institute for Jewish Research, New York.

Figure 73. Medem Sanitarium, ca. 1930. From the Archives of the YIVO Institute for Jewish Research, New York.

Figure 74. Medem Sanitarium, ca. 1930. From the Archives of the YIVO Institute for Jewish Research, New York.

Figure 75 Medem Sanitarium, ca. 1930. From the Archives of the YIVO Institute for Jewish Research, New York.

How did it come to that?

The sanitarium had a large staff—medical, pedagogical, and technical (kitchen staff, janitors, orderlies, etc.). Part of the technical staff belonged to the Union of Housemaids in Warsaw, which was a member of the Central Council, and part of the technical staff belonged to the union of workers for the resorts along the Otwock railway line. The latter had a union office in Otwock and was under the leadership of the Communist Party.

At the end of 1930 some staff members put forward various absurd demands of the institution. For example: On one occasion the person in charge of the kitchen had words with one of the staff members, as sometimes happens in a work situation. Thereupon, the Communist union called on the parents of the children to remove their children from the sanitarium. To the children themselves, they put out a call that they should declare ... a hunger strike! In those days of "Social Fascists" (as the Communists then referred to the social democrats) and Communist-inspired wildcat strikes, we were used to all kinds of Communist wild tricks, and consequently no great attention was paid to this nonsense.

Shortly thereafter, the Communist union put forward economic demands to the managing committee of the Medem Sanitarium—outlandish demands, impossible to grant. They did this, it was clear, only to have an excuse to foment trouble at the sanitarium. The staff at the sanitarium had long had better, much better, working conditions, not only in pay but in other particulars as well, than the workers at all the other resorts along the Otwock railway line. Nevertheless the management committee of the Medem Sanitarium did not refuse the demands; instead they proposed to the union that the dispute be turned over to arbitration by a higher labor instance; for example, to the Central Council, the Regional Council, or even to the Central Commission of the Labor Federation, the highest instance of all the labor unions in Poland—to which the Otwock Communist union also belonged. But the Otwock union would not hear of it: all their demands must be met immediately without any discussion. And without waiting for any further negotiations, they immediately called a strike, calling on that portion of the staff that belonged to their union to walk out, and then calling for the rest of the technical staff to join the strike and declare a work stoppage. They then called for the entire sanitarium staff, not just the technical personnel, but also the medical and pedagogical, to join the strike. Of course, the rest of the personnel would not even consider such a thing.

At this point, the Communists began actions to undermine the sanitarium. They went to the baker in Falenica, who supplied the sanitarium with its baked goods, and prevented him from supplying the sanitarium. They spread the news to the parents of the children that in the sanitarium a "dreadful exploitation of personnel" was being perpetrated and that, therefore, they should, as a protest, remove their children from the sanitarium. They threatened further to blockade the whole sanitarium and prevent any products at all from entering. When all this came to nothing—they fell back on their old proven method—an armed attack.

Thursday, February 12, 1931, around two o'clock in the afternoon, a band of 150 men, Jews and Poles, attacked the Medem Sanitarium and carried out a pogrom. They broke into the electrical station and ruined it; they entered the kitchen and broke dishes and utensils; they attacked the medical and technical personnel; the teacher Mordkhe Gilinski (Batke) was struck on the head with an iron bar; they didn't even spare the women and beat up Dr. Cibulski; they broke the window panes in all the buildings and even in the isolation ward (a small building that housed the children confined to bed with a high fever). But all this was still nothing for them: they also started a wild spree of shooting, and a large number of bullets landed in some of the rooms, including the children's clubroom. Fortunately, the children had already been led out of it and none were struck by a bullet.

One can easily imagine the panic that gripped the children. When the sanitarium personnel regained their composure, some of the teachers and nurses grabbed the children and took them off to far corners of the sanitarium; others began to fight back. The board member Brumberg fought very bravely against the Communist band of pogromchiks. When the personnel tried to telephone Warsaw to let us know about the attack, it turned out the attackers had cut the phone wires. Brumberg sent one of the personnel out a back way to get to a phone and telephone us in Warsaw to let us know what the Communists had done.

Figure 76. Medem Sanitarium: Children reading the *Folkstsaytung*, the Bund's daily newspaper. From the Archives of the YIVO Institute for Jewish Research, New York.

As soon as I got the news, I immediately went to the sanitarium, together with a group of our militia and some parents that we were able to quickly round up. In less than an hour we were on the spot. The Communists had already left. We conferred about what to do and decided that for a time a small patrol should remain at the sanitarium. First, there remained the danger that the Communists would repeat their attacks and even escalate them. Secondly, we needed to help the technical staff, because some of them, the Communist ones, were, in fact, on strike. We figured we needed a few dozen of us to remain. We divided them up thus: One group of our militia guarded the sanitarium from external attack, to protect against another Communist assault; a second group helped with the work in the kitchen and with other technical work; a third group guarded the sanitarium from an internal attack, because the Communists might make their way into the sanitarium through one of the back ways. Keeping the patrols busy in the kitchen and in cleaning up, etc., had another purpose: we didn't want the patrols to wander about with nothing to do, but that they keep busy all day doing something. The hardest thing was the night watch. It was then the coldest part of winter—February. All night we had to keep watch at the entrance and over the whole area of the sanitarium. The watch changed every two hours. When it was a particularly cold night, we changed the guard every hour.

Besides guarding the sanitarium and helping with the technical work, the patrols also brought all the produce from the town of Falenica to the sanitarium. When one of the technical staff had to go to the town, we sent a small guard of our Militia to accompany him. But if one of us had to arrive at the sanitarium from

Figure 77. Medem Sanitarium, 1930s. From the Archives of the YIVO Institute for Jewish Research, New York.

Figure 78. Medem Sanitarium, 1930s. From the Archives of the YIVO Institute for Jewish Research, New York.

Figure 79. Medem Sanitarium, 1930s. The metereological station. From the Archives of the YIVO Institute for Jewish Research, New York.

Warsaw, we got off the train at Falenica, not at Miedzeszyn (where the sanitarium was located), walking through the town on our way to the sanitarium. This we did to demonstrate to the Communists that we were unafraid to pass through their "fortress" (Falenica). Only once did they shoot at Brumberg, but they missed. We did not make a fuss about it, as we did not want to inflame the conflict anew.

The Communists for their part also did not remain silent. They organized demonstrations against the sanitarium. They appeared in front of the sanitarium, made noise, catcalled, shouted invective, but kept their distance—no longer did they approach the sanitarium.

The news of the attack and shooting at the Medem Sanitarium deeply shocked the broad Jewish working masses: Attack a *children's* sanitarium and shoot at it? Threaten the lives of innocent *children*—or even just frighten them to death? Hundreds of workers from Warsaw wanted to go to Falenica and simply tear the Communists to pieces. The Bund Central Committee would not allow it. We wanted to avoid the sharpening of the conflict and a renewal of the shooting.

Our Militia remained at the sanitarium for more than two weeks. After the first few days, when the situation around the sanitarium had grown calmer, I left the sanitarium, but returned every day for a few hours. In the beginning our militia consisted of about twenty, but we slowly diminished the number, until everything around the sanitarium had returned to calm.

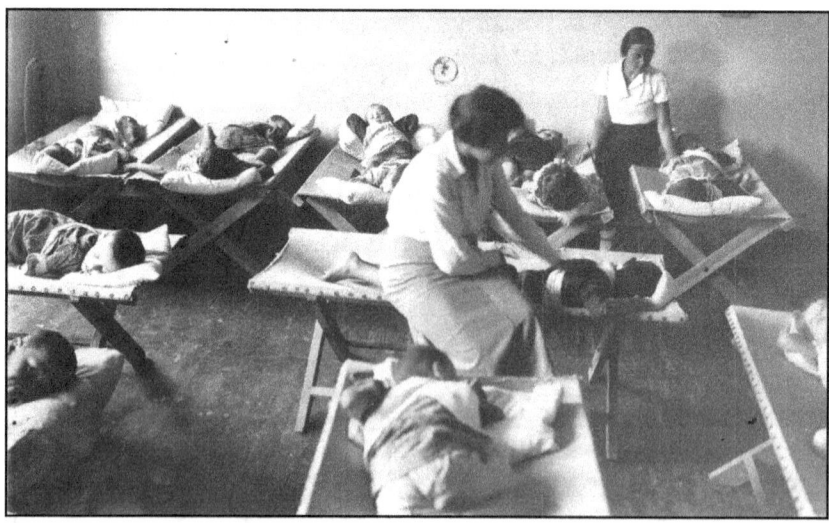

Figure 80. Naptime: Litvak Day Care Center, run by YAF (*Yidishe Arbeter Froy*: Jewish Working Woman). Vilna, 1934. Caption by Jack Jacobs, *Bundist Countercuture in Interwar Poland*. From the Archives of the YIVO Institute for Jewish Research, New York.

CHAPTER 45

Another Attempt on My Life

Spring 1931. I arrived home at my apartment at Karmelicka 6 late one night, at about one o'clock in the morning. As was the custom then in Warsaw, the gate to the building was locked. I rang and waited for the caretaker, who took his time coming. Gazing into the empty street, I noticed a car emerging from Nowolipki Street and heading in my direction. The car stopped, two figures jumped out and began sidling along the opposite wall. A shot rang out. I got down on one knee behind a stone column at the end of the gate and, grabbing my revolver, shot back. They quickly scrambled back into the waiting car and sped off.

During the shooting the neighbors in the surrounding houses opened their windows and began shouting, "Shots! Someone's shooting!" The noise drew the police. Spotting me, the police came over; we went through the gate together. Taking advantage of the dark, I tossed my revolver into a dark corner of the house. The police wrote an incident report. Later they found some blood on the spot where the Communist shooters had been standing. Apparently I had wounded one of them; that was why they had retreated so abruptly.

For many weeks after that our comrades guarded me every step of the way. I shouted at them to go away, but they just changed their tactics, keeping at a distance so I wouldn't spot them. One time I came home late at night and suddenly encountered one of our young militiamen, Yukele, standing at the gate. "Yukele, what are you doing here at this time of night?" "Just strolling around, no particular reason," he said. I walked with him around the block a couple of times and finally got out of him that he had been following me for over the last three hours—wherever I had gone, he had followed, at a distance. Many other comrades did the same. This had all been organized and orchestrated by the Bund Militia.

Not long after that our Comrade Ludwig Honigwill, the lawyer, was defending a Communist in court. It was a principle among the Socialist lawyers that, despite the anti-Socialist assaults, invective, and murderousness on the part of the Communists, they should nevertheless be defended in court. The Socialist lawyers, and even some liberal ones, used to do this pro bono or for a minimal honorarium. While looking through the files of this case, Comrade Honigwill found a military intelligence report stating that the Communist party had issued a death sentence against Bernard and that efforts were already underway to carry it out. This information was investigated through other sources and confirmed.

When our people heard about this, the Communists were warned from every side that if anything happened to Bernard, heads would roll.

The party issued an open warning to the Communists that was printed in large letters in the *Folkstsaytung* on May 19, 1931:

> WARNING! In the course of the last few days we have received continual reports that the Communists have decided to kill our Comrade Bernard Goldstein. These reports reach us from circles that conduct the work of the Jewish Communists. We are informed not only about this decision, but also regarding the particulars of how it is to be carried out. We are not interested at this point in making any political or moral judgments regarding this scandolous decision. We simply want to warn, with total seriousness, that for the

Figure 81. Right to left: The author, Bernard Goldstein; his wife, Lucia; his friend and prominent Bund leader and public intellectual, Shloyme Mendelson; Dr. Chaim Pizhits and his wife, Renye Yaretski. From the Archives of the YIVO Institute for Jewish Research, New York.

slightest effort to carry out this criminal act, we will hold every leader of the Communist movement in Poland responsible.

Let them remember this and think twice.
—The Warsaw Committee of the BUND

Apparently this warning was effective—from that time on, the Communists made no further organized attempts to assassinate me.

CHAPTER 46

Krochmalna Street

Krochmalna Street was for a long time a Communist stronghold. In those days the street was called "Little Moscow" and "The Kremlin." If a well-known Bundist walked through the street, they would yell after him "Bundist Krupnik" (Bundist Barley Soup). This was the Communist epithet for the Bund. It was supposed to mean that the Bund was concerned only about the material needs of the workers, and not for "higher" things, for the "revolution." Communist terror ran rampant on the street. Bundist members handing out or posting flyers were beaten and driven from Krochmalna. Bundist posters were immediately torn down or not permitted to be posted at all.

Krochmalna was also long known as a stronghold of the underworld; this also prevented the spread of a Bundist influence in the area.

Krochmalna had a reputation in Warsaw as—for as long as I can remember—one of the poorest, most densely populated, and dirtiest streets in Warsaw. The walls of the houses (the houses were, in fact, large, with large courtyards) were deteriorating and dank. The street was narrow, and in many corners the sun never reached, the mud there never drying from one year to the next. The whole street, with its decaying, dark walls, with its mud, and gloomy people, was like a kind of black hole.

Krochmalna was encircled by large marketplaces: the "Gościnny Dwór" (later this marketplace was called "Welopole"); Gnojna Street, where Janusz's market courtyard was located (a large marketplace at the end of Gnojna and Krochmalna), with many wholesalers of foodstuffs; and Mirowski Square, the center of fruit commerce. As a result, Krochmalna did not have many skilled workers, but mostly poor tradesmen at the surrounding marketplaces, and porters and teamsters, with stations there.

In addition, various people with uncertain means of livelihood lived on Krochmalna, along with criminal elements. What percentage of the residents were criminal types it is hard to say, but they ruled the street—especially the infamous "*pletsl*" ("little place" or square), a four-cornered square at Krochmalna 7 and 9. That was their "kingdom," their chief exchange.

Another street of poverty was Smocza Street, but how great was the difference between Krochmalna and Smocza! Smocza was a lot cleaner, mostly inhabited by skilled workers who belonged to unions and to the Bund. Many of the children from Smocza were students in our secular Yiddish schools that were concentrated in that neighborhood. They belonged to SKIF, to *Tsukunft*, or to other progressive youth organizations. The Smocza neighborhood was a center of Jewish organized labor. Despite its poverty, the street was lively and happy.

Two centers of Warsaw Jewish poverty—but how different!

The Bund did not give up on Krochmalna Street. After the parliamentary elections of 1922, we made a concerted effort to lift the street out of its social and moral abyss. The Bund created a special commission for the Krochmalna region whose job it was to broaden the Bund's influence there. A secular Yiddish school was opened at Krochmalna 36. It was an immediate success. The children who attended the new secular Yiddish TSYSHO school began bringing home new cultural outlooks and manners that slowly began influencing their homes, not least of which, it should be mentioned, was washing your hands before eating, something they brought home from school. Through the children, the school became a cultural factor in the homes of Krochmalna. The schools also had an influence on the homes directly, through parental meetings and teacher visits to the students' homes. A large number of the children were recruited by SKIF, and these new SKIFists brought home new songs, quite different from the ones that used to be sung on Krochmalna. They dragged their parents to cultural evenings the Bund or the *Kultur-Lige* organized. In short, *dos redele hot zikh ibergedreyt* (literally, "the little wheel had turned over," i.e., "things changed") and the children were teaching their parents and becoming the bearers of culture in their homes.

The party also worked through the unions. A number of the members of the Meat Workers Union and of the Transport Workers Union, as well as of other of our unions, lived in the neighborhood of Krochmalna. Through them we started spreading Bundist literature and recruiting readers for the *Folkstsaytung*. At special party meetings of Bundists from the neighborhood, the difficulties surrounding our work on Krochmalna Street were continually discussed. Also our youth group, *Tsukunft*, organized several circles of Krochmalna young people and created a special Krochmalna section.

When the work of the Bund, *Tsukunft*, and SKIF had taken root, the Bund rented an office at 14 Grzybowska Street, very close to Krochmalna, and established a club there for the SKIFists, *Tsukinft*ists, and adult Bundists of the neighborhood. The Warsaw Committee of the Bund appointed a special delegate for the activities of this new region, Comrade Abrasza Blum, one of the leaders of the wartime underground Bund and later hero of the Warsaw Ghetto Uprising.[1] *Tsukunft* delegated a person who was one of the rarest and finest individuals— Yankele Mendelson. Khayim Ejno led the SKIF work. A group of our women comrades decorated the club, making it more attractive and remaining on duty in the evenings. Especially active in this work were the comrades and students Dina Berman (the daughter of Leybetshke Berman, now Dina Mlotek, living in New York), and the *Tsukunft*ist Yentl Bergman (active in the Warsaw Ghetto; she perished there), and many others.

In time Krochmalna became a Bundist stronghold. We overcame the dominance and terror of the Communists. The power of the underworld was broken, and in the end the Bund was the main force in the whole neighborhood. In the municipal elections of 1938 the Bund won two out of the three seats from this neighborhood. Also the whole surrounding region, like the other electoral regions in Jewish Warsaw, became, in its majority, Bundist.

The Krochmalna neighborhood was exceptional with its unique types. It is worthwhile telling about some of them.

Figure 82. Abrashe Blum, Bund hero of the Warsaw Ghetto Uprising, shot dead by Gestapo, summer of 1943. From the Archives of the YIVO Institute for Jewish Research, New York.

Figure 83. Warsaw *Tsukunft*ists on a hike to a Bund camp in Gabin, Poland, 1938. From the Archives of the YIVO Institute for Jewish Research, New York.

Note

1. Blum, Abrasza (1905–1943): By profession, a structural engineer. Beginning in 1930, a director of the *Folkstsaytung*. In September 1939, participated in the defense of Warsaw, helping to organize all-Jewish detachments. When Warsaw fell, most of the Bund's senior leadership evacuated the city: they were too well-known; the leadership of the party fell to the Youth-Bund *Tsukunft*ists. Abrasza worked in the ghetto brush factory, 1942–1943. He was Bund representative to the Jewish Fighting Organization (ZOB). Escaped the burning ghetto through the sewers, hiding in the apartment of the Bund courier, Władka. The janitor reported him to the Gestapo. Abrasza escaped through the window on a rope made from bedsheets, but broke his legs in the fall from the third story; captured and murdered by the Gestapo in 1943.—MZ

CHAPTER 47

Fat Yosl

Fat Yosl had a restaurant (it was called a "Piwiarnia," i.e., a beer hall) on Gnojna Street. But really he and his beer hall belonged to the world of Krochmalna Street. He was called by various names: "Yosl Betchke" (i.e., Yosl beer barrel), "Gruby Yosl" (Polish for Fat Yosl), but most often, just Fat Yosl. He really was fat as a barrel. He was observant, and on the Sabbath and on Jewish holy days, he wore a velvet hat and the long silk kaftan worn by pious Jews.

Gnojna Street, where his tavern was located, was a short street, between Grzybowska and Krochmalna, but it was an important commercial center, containing wholesalers of spices, herring, imported dried fruit, and the like. The street ended at Janusz's courtyard, hard by Krochmalna Street. It was a courtyard market for fish, poultry, dairy foods, plates, etc. It also contained a slaughterhouse for poultry. Several back porters, handcart porters, and teamsters were also stationed on this street. The street was always full of wagons and droshkies,[1] echoing with the noise and shouting of tradesmen, customers, porters, and teamsters.

Fat Yosl had his beer hall through the gate and inside the courtyard of Gnojna 7. It was a typical apartment, consisting of an entry hall, two large rooms for eating, and a kitchen. At around six in the morning, this restaurant and beer hall started filling up with porters and teamsters who came for breakfast: usually herring, a large plate of hot groats and meat, a bagel or a roll, and a flask of whiskey. Later, around ten, the same crowd would return to warm up with a glass of tea, a glass of beer, and a bite to eat. This went on until about six in the evening, when the crowd headed home from work. Between ten and eleven o'clock at night the restaurant began to fill up with people again, but now of an entirely different sort: droshky drivers, prostitutes, pimps, and thieves. The rooms were packed with people, and the air was hot and thick. When the outer door was opened, it emitted a blast of steam as from a locomotive. It continued this way until late into the night.

In all of this, there was nothing out of the ordinary. Practically all the taverns on Krochmalna and its neighborhood were this way. But Fat Yosl did have something out of the ordinary. Nobody knew why it was, but his tavern was a beloved place for Warsaw's rich—they were regulars—and for Polish high officials, government people, and military officers. Very often, between three and four in the morning, into Fat Yosl's tavern would storm the well-known Colonel Weniawa-Długoszowski, Marshal Piłsudski's personal adjutant and notorious Warsaw drunk; the government Commissar Jaroszewicz; Colonel Jurek of the police; former governmental Commissar Janusz; the actor Grabowski, a brother of the District Attorney and Minister of Justice; the famous actor Jaracz; and many others from Warsaw's high society. They came here from the most beautiful and elegant Warsaw nightspots. Around three and four in the morning when the elegant nightspots closed, someone in the tipsy crowd would shout out: "Jedźmy do grubego Joska!" ("Let's go to Fat Yosl's!"). Droshkies were hired and off they went to Fat Yosl's. Entering stormily, they drove everyone out. Once in a while they would call some of them back and demand they serve them food and drink, and sing for them! To Fat Yosl they said: "Yosl, zapisz!" (Yosl, write it down!)—and they paid! They would stay a half hour, sometimes an hour. As they were leaving, one of the high officials would demand a "loan" from Yosl ("Josek dawaj paręset złotych," that is, hand over a few hundred zlotys.).

Because of his highly placed regulars, people were afraid of Fat Yosl. The police were afraid of him; if not for that they would have shut him down more than once for unsanitary conditions. The police hated him because he would not bribe them, and if a policeman suddenly got it into his head to report him for unsanitary conditions, the police commissioner would next morning receive a phone call from some high government official, and that would be the end of that report. His competitor tavern owners were also afraid of him because of his highly placed guests. Once in a while he would do a tradesman a favor, get someone who had been arrested released, get someone a break on their taxes, and the like. From time to time he would go to one of his highly placed officials, his frequent guests, and ask for a favor. But he was no *shtadlan* (traditionally, a public intercessor for the Jews with the authorities, but the term has acquired pejorative implications).

As already mentioned, Fat Yosl was pious. He liked to do a favor for a *Hasid* he knew and give to charity. He closed his tavern on the Sabbath (Friday night) and wouldn't open it again on Saturday night until the requisite three stars appeared in the night sky after sundown and the prayer ending the Sabbath was recited.

Several times I called on him about getting his help for our Comrade Calka, who was his wife's brother. He and his wife answered all my requests angrily: "We wanted to make a proper person out of him, did everything for him, wanted to take him into the business—but he wanted the Bund. He doesn't see fit to come in here to our place. Okay then, so let the Bund help him," and they refused me.

Once I was able to drag out of them a little money to pay a few month's rent for Calka when he was about to be evicted.

Quite another type in the Krochmalna brood was the ill-famed Itshele Isaacson. Itshele Isaacson came from a rich family and was himself rich. He owned the big house at Krochmalna 5–7. He also carried on all sorts of businesses, semilegal or totally illegal. He was also—what we used to call—a community busybody, one of the founders in the Krochmalna neighborhood of "Khesed Shel Emes" ("True Grace"), of a society called "Beys Lekhem" ("House of Bread"), and of cheap kitchens for poor folk. He was also a big shot among the "Good Sabbath Jews."[2]

But there was talk that from all these associations Itshele was skimming money for himself on the sly. He also lent money at interest, and was one of the original "percenters," charging interest by the day. Thieves, swindlers, and card sharks borrowed from him. He was in general embroiled with thieves and swindlers, and with the police. In his youth he himself had been a con artist. They would come to him with *"din toyres"* (literally, lawsuits brought before a rabbinic court; used here ironically), to receive stolen goods with his help, pawn pledges, etc. His "place of business" was the café at Krochmalna 14, belonging to a certain "Godl *pijak*" (i.e., Godl the Drunk).

From time to time we would get into conflict with Itchele Isaacson regarding the activities of the Bund's representatives on the Warsaw City Council. Several of his renters, members of our unions, complained to the Bund's Warsaw City Councilmen that Isaacson was threatening eviction for not paying their rent regularly. I went to Isaacson and warned him that we would write in the *Folkstsaytung* that he is throwing poor workers out into the street. He shouted bloody murder—we were going to ruin his "reputation!" But then he softened a bit—he trembled at the thought of being written up in our newspaper. Finally we agreed that the renters would pay him what they owed in installments, and that from now on, they would pay their rent regularly.

Later, a sharper conflict arose. The Warsaw municipal government issued an ordinance that a certain building in a poor Jewish neighborhood must be repaired because it was about to collapse; if not, it would be torn down. The renters, who were being threatened with eviction, collected some money amongst themselves to repair the building. Itchele Isaacson said he would undertake the repair of the building. The first thing he did, of course, was take the money the renters had collected. After some time, the renters got a notice of eviction from the municipality because the building was about to be torn down. The neighbors then came running to our councilmen with an outcry that Isaacson had tricked them: he took their money and did not even begin to repair the building. Comrade Esther Alter-Ivinska, a councilwoman in the Warsaw City Council and by profession a lawyer—she mostly concentrated on juridical issues raised by the Bundist Councilmen—demanded of Isaacson that he perform the long-delayed building repair. He didn't. She then took him to court for swindling the renters. In court, no pleas or arguments helped him. Comrade Ivinsky, not to be deterred, demanded he immediately perform the repairs or immediately return their money to the renters. He returned the money.

We had one more conflict with Itchele Isaacson. This was while we were making the well-known film about the Medem Sanitarium, *Mir Kumen On* ("We're on Our Way").[3] The movie starts with a portrait of Warsaw Jewish poverty. For this portrait, Aleksander Ford, the well-known Polish-Jewish director, wanted to film life on Krochmalna Street. He happened to pick just the very courtyard that belonged to Isaacson. On a certain day, when Ford came with his personnel and his equipment to shoot the film, Isaacson came running to forbid filming on "his territory." I was immediately called to the scene to deal with the problem. I tried reasoning with him. He would not hear of allowing his courtyard to be filmed: "My buildings and courtyards are all clean, there's nothing dirty!" he shouted. "And besides, you're not even paying me!" The old argument I used before worked again: If he didn't permit the shooting of this film, we would write him up in the newspapers. Of this, he was terribly frightened. He gave permission to shoot the film.

No actors played in the film, just workers and ordinary people, adults and children of Jewish poverty. One of these Krochmalna Street "artists" was our comrade, Khaskele. More about him in the next chapter.

Figure 84. Aleksander Ford, Director of *Mir Kumen On*. Youthful doyen of Poland's politically committed cineasts, mid-1930s. Caption from *Bridge of Light* by J. Hoberman. Courtesy J. Hoberman.

Figure 85. Frame enlargement from *Mir Kumen On*. Courtesy of J. Hoberman.

Figure 86. Jewish children dance under the sky in the last shot of *Mir Kumen On*. Caption from *Bridge of Light* by J. Hoberman. Frame enlargement. Courtesy of J. Hoberman.

Notes

1. *Droshky*: a low, four-wheeled, horse-drawn, open, passenger carriage.—MZ
2. Active for many years in Warsaw, "Good Sabbath Jews" was a Jewish society that gathered food from the general Jewish population to deliver to poor, sick Jewish patients in the hospitals. After prayers on the Sabbath, they would go in groups of three from courtyard to courtyard with large baskets, crying out, "Good Sabbath, Jews! Throw something down! Bring some bread down, *challahs!*" Then they would recite a long list of food items that could be thrown down. Windows would open on all floors of the building and little packages wrapped in paper would begin flying down. If a housewife wanted to give something that couldn't be thrown down from her window, for example, fish or meat, she would send down a child with it. After a while the "Good Sabbath Jews" created a tune with which they sang out their cry. They were very popular in Warsaw. It was a society of ordinary Jews. Social activists, party activists, did not participate in this work.—BG
3. Documentary directed by Aleksander Ford, one of Poland's leading young directors in the thirties, with a script by the well-known Polish novelist, Wanda Wasilewska, produced in 1935 by the Bund and the Medem Sanitarium. Banned by the Polish government and not permitted to be shown in Poland, it was screened in Paris, Brussels, and New York. It is now available in DVD format with the title *Children Must Laugh* from the National Center for Jewish Film, Brandeis University, Waltham, MA.—MZ

CHAPTER 48

Khaskele

Khaskele was an assistant militiaman. He was not a regular member of the militia, but when the militia had to perform a particular task, he would always voluntarily come to help.

We called him "Khaskele Hunchback," although he was not really a hunchback. His back was just a little higher on one side, and he tilted his head at an angle. That was enough for his "fatherland," Krochmalna Street, to dub him "Khaskele Hunchback," and that nickname stuck with him for the rest of his life.

When he first showed up at the Bund, he was in his early thirties, but he looked a lot younger. He was of medium height and broad shouldered, with a sharp, angular face. He was missing his front teeth, which skewed his mouth a bit, especially when he spoke. He was a baker, what was called a "fourth hand," but even as a "fourth hand," he was not particularly good. He was often unemployed. His wife was a cook who cooked for rich weddings and large parties. She earned decent money. She would bring home all kinds of tasty leftovers from the weddings and parties. As a result, though he didn't work much, he had plenty of good food to eat. They had no children. He couldn't write, but he could read a little. He bought the *Folkstsaytung* every day. Some of it he'd read on his own, but for the rest, he would go to his friends and ask them to read it to him.

The work he loved best was recruiting children for our SKIF. The children of Krochmalna thought the world of him—and there was no lack of children on Krochmalna Street. When Khaskele took his place at the center of the "*pletsl*" (little square) on Krochmalna, put his two fingers in his mouth, and whistled sharply several times, the children knew that Khaskl was calling them. In no time, he was surrounded by a throng of children, sometimes as many as 100–150. He would line them up in columns, put himself at the head, and—especially in the summertime—march them off for a hike into the woods outside the city. One would often see Khaskl marching, radiant, on Krochmalna, his head, as always, tilted a bit to one side, and following him—a throng of children, marching in columns (with him there always had to be columns!). For this good deed, the Krochmalna women wished him eternal life. He took their little "bastards" off their hands for a whole summer's day (sometimes even on a weekday). The children wouldn't have to hang around the Krochmalna gutters with its overflowing garbage cans, and they wouldn't be the death of their mothers. Khaskele would bring the children back before nightfall, suntanned and happy. The mothers couldn't have wished for anything better. Khaskele was a true angel in the dismal and gloomy children's world of Krochmalna Street.

Khaskele also helped *Tsukunft* organize youth clubs in the Krochmalna area. He would come every day to the offices of the party Secretariat, always with new ideas on how to broaden the Bund's work on Krochmalna. The plan closest to his heart was to open a Bund club in the Krochmalna area. And this dream of his did actually come to pass. Party offices were opened on Grzybowska. Whole days and nights he devoted to the new Bund offices, and he took upon his own broad shoulders the hardest of the work.

He wasn't satisfied just to recruit new members for SKIF and *Tsukunft,* he also undertook all kinds of other projects: collecting funds, running lotteries, and the like. With the funds he raised, he had blue blouses made with red cravats

Figure 87. Anna Heller Rozental, a leading member of the Bund, addressing children and youth at a SKIF-sponsored summer camp, 1937. "No Passaran" (They Shall Not Pass), a Republican slogan during the Spanish Civil War, was adopted by the Warsaw SKIFists attending this gathering as the name for their portion of the encampment. Caption by Jack Jacobs, *Bundist Counterculture in Interwar Poland.* From the Archives of the YIVO Institute for Jewish Research, New York.

for the Krochmalna SKIFists. He also had a plan he carried around in his head to open a cheap soup kitchen on Krochmalna in the winter.

Whenever Khaskele heard the Militia was gathering someplace to perform a difficult task, he came with a group of his cronies from Krochmalna. "Khaskele, what are you doing here?" I would ask him, and he would always answer: "Comrade Bernard, wherever the Bund fights—I am there!" His energy, his enthusiasm, his devotion to the Bund, was truly boundless.

In the Warsaw Ghetto, when I had to go underground, I lost contact with him. Once, walking in the street, I saw him, and he recognized me as well. For many long minutes he ran in front of me, then behind me. Every time our eyes met, his eyes lit up, as if to say: "Comrade Bernard, I am here, near you, I am with you once more." I never saw him again.

Some time later Comrade Katz, a nurse (she was at one time on the staff of the YIVO[1] in Vilnius), told me that when she was working in the ghetto hospital, Khaskele was brought in sick with typhus. She recognized him and would often visit him to see how he was doing. When he lay unconscious with a high fever, he would constantly be singing labor songs, the Bund anthem, and others. He died with those songs on his lips.

Note

1. Founded in 1925, YIVO (*Yidisher Visnshaftlekher Institut*, or Yiddish Scientific Institute) became the leading institution for scholarship in Yiddish and the history and culture of East European Jews and their emigrant communities. Now in New York, renamed the YIVO Institute for Jewish Research.—MZ

CHAPTER 49

"Malematke"

Another individual, representative of the countless numbers of people the Bund lifted out of the morass of Krochmalna, was called "Malematke."

He was a meat worker in the slaughterhouse, one of three brothers. All three were of medium height, broad shouldered, and very strong; and all three were called "Malematke." This nickname came from their mother's being very short. When the three brothers were children, they lived in Shilets, an old Polish quarter in Warsaw at the edge of the Vistula. The Polish boys they played with called them "*Male Matke,*" Polish for "little mother." From then on, this nickname stuck.

The eldest brother, Hershl, the one I am going to tell you about, was a Bundist and a member of our Militia. His two brothers were sympathizers.

One time an unfortunate thing happened to Malematke. He was caught carrying out a bag of meat from the slaughterhouse. Taking a little meat home from the slaughterhouse was considered an acceptable thing to do. All the slaughterhouse workers did it. It was a sort of semilegal privilege of the slaughterhouse workers to take home a little meat for the household as they left work for home, and it was always more or less tolerated. But after the city took over the slaughterhouse and began its policy of driving out the Jewish workers—quietly, slowly, but systematically—it enforced the various regulations much more stringently against the Jews than against the Polish workers. It is, of course, possible that on that day Malematke had taken more meat than is usually tolerated. In any case, the administration took the opportunity to not only fire Malematke, but to also have him arrested for theft. He was jailed and awaiting trial and sentencing.

From jail he sent me a note asking me to visit him. I did. He asked me to have mercy on him and to save him. He admitted that he had made a big mistake, and he wanted to make it right. He didn't want to be imprisoned as a thief. He asked me with tears in his eyes to do all I could to get him out of jail.

As I was leaving the jail, I decided we really should help him. If he were tried, convicted, and sentenced, and had to serve a long sentence in prison with real thieves, he might very well be corrupted and lost to us forever. I decided to do something for him, and collected a few hundred zlotys to get him out on bail.

I will never forget the moment when I came with the lawyer and the receipt for the bail and he was immediately released from jail. He was beaming with joy, not so much because he was free, but because the Bund cared about him and the Bund freed him—he thought of this as absolution for his sins. He would not, then, be thrown out of the Bund! I did, however, preach to him a little, and he promised he would never do such a thing again. At the trial he was sentenced to a couple of months in jail, but, as there was just then a general amnesty, he did not have to serve the sentence.

At the slaughterhouse they wouldn't take him back. We couldn't just let him wander the streets unemployed, so I went off to the fruit merchants behind the covered market and got him a job there, for which he earned a good salary. Right after that he got married, and quickly thereafter a child was born, a little girl, and he was overjoyed.

One time he had a party and invited me. He lived on Krochmalna, on the aforementioned "pletsl." When I entered the courtyard, it was black with women and children. The windows of Malematke's apartment were wide open, and one could hear the noise from the great number of party guests. In the courtyard, the crowd of women and children followed everything that was going on in the apartment. When the partygoers spotted me from the window, they struck up the "Oath," the Bund anthem.

When I entered the apartment, this is what I saw: The furniture had been removed from the apartment; in their place were long tables and benches, laden with all kinds of good things to eat and drink: fish, meat, roasted goose, bottles of whiskey and a keg of beer against the wall. Among the guests were several members of the Drucker orchestra, along with their instruments (Malematke played in the Drucker orchestra). When I entered, in my honor, they played the Bund anthem again. I looked around the room: the walls were black with grime, the floor was not washed, his wife walked around in threadbare clothes, unkempt; in her arms was their child in a filthy shirt. He himself, Malematke, was happily bustling about among the guests. My entering was supposed to be the signal to sit down at table. I was angered, however, by the slovenliness and dirt I observed around me in the middle of a party that cost a lot more than it would have cost to clean up their filthy apartment. I felt I must react in a manner that would draw the attention of the whole crowd to the issue of their slovenly housekeeping. I quietly stole out of the apartment.

The next morning, a Sunday, a delegation of our militiamen came to see me. They complained vehemently that I had publicly shamed Malematke by the manner in which I left his party. "All Krochmalna street is talking about how the representative of the Bund left the party, that the Bund shamed Malematke—and who?—he, Malematke, one of the most loyal and devoted Bundists. He is afraid to show his face to the neighbors for shame." They spoke to me in this way, in anger. I answered them that at the next meeting of the militia I would explain why I had left Malematke's party.

Every member of the militia came to the next meeting. The tension was palpable. Malematke wasn't present. When the meeting came to order, someone—to make the issue more dramatic—put forward the question: "Why did the representative of the Warsaw Committee of the Bund behave in such a way? If he was busy, he shouldn't have gone. If he had to leave, he should have said so, not stolen away, without a word, so that the whole street would know he ran off from a comrade's celebration!"

I answered quickly. I described the appearance of the apartment where the party took place: filthy walls full of spider webs; the floor black, with layers of mud; the housewife slovenly, carrying their child around in a filthy shirt, unwashed. At the same time, tables laden with all kinds of good things to feast on, geese and bottles of whiskey. I grew heated as I spoke and began to shout: this is demoralizing; one should eat bread and salt but live in cleanliness. First comes cleanliness—then one may give parties!

All this made an impression on the meeting; one could see it in their eyes. I went on: I came to the party because I wanted to join in their happiness, but when I saw the kind of home the wife and child lived in, I thought I must react to this so as to send a strong message. Even if we were to lose one of our best comrades, we in the Bund will always react to such things. When I finished, no one said a word.

Malematke stayed angry for several weeks' time and did not attend the militia meetings. The meetings took place once a week, and attendance was required—if someone did not attend three times in a row without a good reason, they were excluded from the militia. I asked the president of the group not to apply this rule to Malematke, because I knew he needed time to cool off and get over his offended feelings.

In a few weeks time, Malematke invited me again to a party at his place. Other militia members already had informed me that he had put his apartment in order. When I came to the party, I simply didn't recognize the place. The walls were clean, freshly whitewashed, and the floor was scrubbed clean—even the foyer was sprinkled with clean yellow sand. His wife's hair was beautifully combed, and she was wearing a clean, pretty dress. The child, a little girl, had been bathed and dressed in a little white jacket, with a red ribbon in her hair. The party was as before: the same long tables laden with all kinds of good things, the same guests, and even the same members of the Drucker orchestra. I made a toast with the head of the household. We made up, and I celebrated with them into the early morning.

This second party was more talked about on Krochmalna than the first. Blessings for the Bund and for me were not lacking on the part of the Krochmalna housewives.

Probably after both these parties, more than one member of the Militia tidied and cleaned up their homes.

Figure 88. Leather workshop cooperative. Warsaw, late 1920s. From the Archives of the YIVO Institute for Jewish Research, New York.

CHAPTER 50

Yukele

Another interesting type was Yukele. I have mentioned him previously in passing. He used to be called "Yukele the Thief from the Slaughterhouse," not because he really was a thief. We called someone a "thief" (*ganef*) if he was quick, agile, and brimming with ideas. He was a blond boy, medium height, thin, and very quick. Everything about him was quick: he talked fast, walked fast, and worked fast. He was a skinner. In his big boots, in his long leather apron that trailed behind him on the ground, he looked even smaller and thinner than he was. But he worked like an arrow shot from a bow, and he always smiled as he worked. At the same time, sticking a knife in someone's side during an argument was nothing to him. And as for smuggling a piece of meat out of the slaughterhouse, there was nobody better at it. He was a wild youth, reckless and afraid of no one.

This same Yukele came to me one time asking to be enrolled in the Bund. "Comrade Bernard," he complained, "Why won't you let me join the Bund? Ephraim is in the Bund and Dziobek is in the Bund," (these were two of the "Khayetshkes," i.e., the Rosenbergs; see chapter 18), "so why can't I also be in the Bund? Don't I stand up for the Bund, just as they do?" It was true: he would show up unasked at every one of our big demonstrations, and whenever he heard we were going to fight the "Narovtses,"[1] fascist and antisemitic hooligans, he was among the first to show up. But he didn't know, he said, that you had to be registered to be a member of the Militia. He often accompanied the "Khayetshkes" to Bund meetings, and more than once he had come to a meeting of the militia, but they wouldn't let him in. "You have to be a registered member," he was told. So then, in that case, he wanted to be registered, just like the others.

Who was Yukele? He was born to deaf and dumb parents. His father was a teamster at the Powązki slaughterhouse. As a child, his father always took him along to work. He grew up around the slaughterhouse. When he was around five years old, his parents died of typhus, both in one week, and Yukele was suddenly orphaned. Out of habit, he continued coming to the slaughterhouse, hanging around there without any supervision. Taking pity on him, the Rosenbergs (the "Khayetshkes") took him into their home. At first Grandma Khaye herself took care of him; after that, the eldest son, Shmuel, took over, taking care of him as if he were his own son. When Yukele grew up, Shmuel got him a job at the slaughterhouse as a skinner, the most highly skilled and best paying job there.

Since he lived with the Rosenbergs, he would almost always go with the brothers, who were all Bundists and members of the Militia, till he discovered there was one place they went where they wouldn't let him in because you had to be a registered member. So he has come to me to demand that he be given the same rights as all the "Khayetshkes."

Figure 89. *Tsukunft* self defense unit flag bearers, carrying the banner of the worldwide Socialist movement. Warsaw 1930s. From the Archives of the YIVO Institute for Jewish Research, New York.

I explained to him that it is not such an easy thing to be a registered member of the militia. You are given orders that have to be precisely carried out. You have to behave differently than you ordinarily do. He knew all that already from the "Khayetshkes," he said, and accepted it. So we accepted him into the Bund Militia. He became a disciplined member: he was extremely devoted, carrying out assigned tasks precisely as directed.

One time he said he had something important to discuss with me and asked me to set aside a specific time. At the agreed upon time, he came all dressed up. We went off to a café. Greatly moved, almost in tears, he told me what was bothering him.

"Comrade Bernard, I have a secret. I am in love with a girl—Shmuel Jakubowicz's adopted daughter." (I have told about Jakubowicz in a previous chapter.) "I love her very much, and she loves me too. The Jakubowiczes want me to marry her; she wants to marry me; and I of course want to marry her. Oh, Comrade Bernard, she is as pretty as the whole world." "So then, what's the problem?" At this point he starts telling me his life story, all of which I already knew: That when he was five years old he became an orphan, that his mother and father were both deaf and dumb, that his school was the slaughterhouse and the street, but now he had the Bund. "You, Comrade Bernard, are everything to me—my comrade, my advocate, my father, everything. So I ask you, may I get married? Will my children be deaf and dumb? Should I tell Khayele, my bride, about it? Jakubowicz knows all about me, yet he wants us to get married. What do you say, Comrade Bernard, may I get married?"

I assured him not to be afraid. "You don't have to fear that your children will be deaf and dumb. You can see for yourself that you can talk and hear, even though both your parents were deaf and dumb." I persuaded him that he should get married and that everything would be all right. "When you have a child, it will be able to hear and speak," I said with assurance, even though I wasn't really so sure about it.

Yukele got married. I was at the wedding. A child was born to them, a boy, and I was at the circumcision ceremony. He approached me somewhat shyly and said he wanted to name it Bernard. I told him not to. He should name it after a close relative, as is customary. At nine months of age, the child already began speaking. Yukele's joy knew no bounds.

Yukele and his young family later met the same fate that met millions of Polish Jews . . .

Note

1. Members of the virulently antisemitic, fascistic party, the *ONR (Obóz Narodowo-Radykalny* or National Radical Camp).—MZ

CHAPTER 51

Troubles with Cultural Awakening

Attracting raw, uneducated workers into the movement was accompanied by complicated personal problems and issues. Ignorant workers—found largely among the porters, butchers, street peddlers, and other unskilled or semiskilled workers—encountered a world of new ideas and concepts in our unions and in our party, a new culture, a new way of thinking and talking, and new and broader interests. In short, they became aware of general social problems and a different way of life, things they were never before concerned with or had even thought about.

They listened to speeches and lectures at our meetings and acquired there a veritable ocean of new words. Even at the regular union meetings, the secretary spoke about their ordinary, daily work issues in a totally different language than they were used to hearing on Krochmalna, on Gnojna, or behind the large, enclosed, food halls. They began to read newspapers and even books. They started to attend cultural events and the Yiddish art theatre. In short, their cultural world underwent a tremendous enrichment.

But this cultural enrichment often gave rise to difficult personal problems, primarily family problems, and not infrequently, even family tragedies.

Wives did not normally accompany their husbands to these meetings and cultural affairs, so, even in the best cases, they remained vastly backward in comparison to their men. They remained with the old way of life and the old ideas and beliefs, while he, the husband, was now living in a world of new comrades and new ideas. After a time an emotional gulf would sometimes develop between husband and wife, or between a father and his household.

There were also in our circle all types of men: those that made an effort to include their wives, taking them along to meetings, relating to them all that had occurred at the organizations and the meetings, and in this way drawing them into their new cultural and discussion circles. But there were also those who grew more and more estranged from their homes as they themselves were drawn into their new cultural environment. These men found their homes less and less interesting. There were even some men who developed an antagonism to their homes and began looking askance at their old-fashioned wives, becoming infrequent "visitors" in their own homes.

On the part of the women, their reaction to this new situation was varied. Some women suffered in silence and said nothing; others, quite the reverse, made a scene with their men about their new way of conducting themselves. Still others came to the Bund with their complaints: "Why are you taking our men away from us? Why are you causing trouble in our homes?"

We understood the importance of this issue. Our Bundist women, especially, displayed a great interest in it. This was one of the things that led to the founding of YAF (*Yidishe Arbeter Froy*: Jewish Working Woman),[1] an organization founded not only to conduct Bundist political agitation among women, but also to lift the cultural level of the Jewish working woman, to bridge the chasm between the organized working men and their women, and in general to guard these very families against an unhealthy rupture. YAF not only conducted Socialist agitation, but also paid a lot of attention to the personal and domestic problems of its women. A group of women doctors served at a counseling center for women. YAF's department, "Informed Motherhood," had a particularly great success.

We did not turn aside from individual troubles and concerns in a Bundist family. The Bund never viewed its task as simply Socialist mass struggle; we concerned ourselves with the personal problems of the workers' lives as well. To illustrate, I want to tell here of several typical examples of the kinds of family problems which it fell to me to deal with in connection with my party work.

One time a young woman came to see me, the wife of a young Bundist, a member of the committee of the Porters Union and by trade a "*khesedl*"[2] (the name given to those street vendors who sold fruit and other produce from handcarts—mostly things they had bought from "bankrupts"—at low cost). She told me she got married when she was 17 years old. The groom, our comrade, had no steady work, so her brother had given him a handcart as a wedding present. They bought a few wares, and he thus became, "knock on wood," a "khesedl." At first she helped him and stood with him in the street, both summer and winter. But when the first child arrived, she could no longer help him with his peddling. A second child arrived soon thereafter, and she became totally immersed in her housekeeping. They lived together happily, with great joy. Slowly he became an activist in the Bund (in truth he was a leader in the Porters Union only, but the general Jewish public did not differentiate between the Bund and the unions or other institutions which were organized by the Bund; to them it was all Bund).

"I let him," she said. "Why not? They are very fine, respectable people, the Bundists. We continued to live together contentedly and happily. He always came home after peddling. It was a home, a household. But it has been some time now

Figure 90. May Day demonstration in Lublin, 1936. Speaker, Bella Shapiro, leader of the Bund in Lublin and a deputy to the Lublin City Council. From the Archives of the YIVO Institute for Jewish Research, New York.

that he doesn't get home until twelve or one o'clock at night. I cook up a bit of food and it remains standing cold in the kitchen. I used to ask him why he comes home so late. He always had excuses: that he was busy with the Bund, always having sessions, meetings. In the beginning, I believed him. But neighbors came and told me he was running around with girls. So now I don't know if he is deceiving me or not. So I beg you, *Panie* (Polish for "Mr.") Bernard, she appealed, do something about this. I sit whole days and nights alone, and my heart is dying!"—and she started to cry.

I told her that she could, after all, read a newspaper in the evening. She answered that she could not read. I asked her again whether she wasn't perhaps neglecting the household—perhaps the home was repellant to him. She assured me that she kept a neat and clean house. In the end I promised her I would talk things over with her husband and see whether something could be done.

It was easy for me to *talk* to him—apparently just so, by chance—about his home, and his wife and children. I asked him why he didn't bring his wife along to our affairs. He answered that when he comes home he has nothing to talk to his wife about: "About our things," she understands nothing, and other than about small household things and family matters, he has nothing to talk to her about. So I reminded him of his children: "After all, you have two small children; you must give them a Socialist upbringing, prepare them for the Yiddish secular school!" He promised he would pay more attention to his wife and children.

Figure 91. *Tsukunft*ists. Middle row, right, Rachel Fligl, who later married Alexander Erlich, a son of Henryk Erlich. Warsaw, 1931. From the Archives of the YIVO Institute for Jewish Research, New York.

Some time passed. One morning there was a knock at my door. A young woman entered, all dressed up, with a pretty hat and a pretty dress. At first I did not recognize her, but then she quickly reminded me who she was. She was, in fact, the same young woman. She took a seat and told me that she had taken my suggestion to heart and had hired a man for two zlotys a week to teach her to read and write. Since she has now taught herself to read, now she wants to enlist as a member of the Bund—and she asked me to please see that she was admitted. I asked her how she would be able to get away in the evenings—after all, she had two small children. She answered, with some heat, "Let him sometimes sit home at night with the children—what, is it only I that must stay at home with the children? And if he should refuse, I will ask a neighbor once in a while to watch the children."

We talked some more. When she saw that I showed an interest in her, at a certain point she burst out with a cry: "Tell me, Panie Bernard, why does he, my husband run around with other women. Am I so ugly that he must run away from me? "—and she burst out crying. I calmed her and promised her that I would see to it that she be admitted to the Bund's YAF.

Now the husband came to me with a complaint: his wife goes out several times a week and he must sit at home, and he knows this is my doing. I rebuked him: "What do you mean? Is she not also a person? We Socialists are, after all, for full equal rights for women—this equality for women must also apply in the home! You should be happy that your wife has learned how to read and write—

Figure 92. Young Bundst women from Minsk, Belarus, ca. 1910. From the Archives of the YIVO Institute for Jewish Research, New York.

she can already read the *Folkstsaytung* (*People's Newspaper*—Bund's daily newspaper) and can take part in our work. He remained silent the whole time, but I had the impression I had not persuaded him. Somehow these two things could not coexist in his mind: the Socialist program about equality for women and the fact that his wife leaves the house several times a week to attend meetings of the YAF, and that he must sit at home and watch the children.

The relations between this couple grew worse and worse. I thought I must involve myself more in making peace between them, but the husband must not suspect that some external hand was at play. One day I looked her up at the YAF meeting hall and suggested that she invite some guests to her home for a Saturday night get-together. I told her whom I thought she should invite: Shloyme Finkelshteyn (an active member of the honor guard group and a father of eight children who kept a decent home; Arl, the secretary of the group; Zishe Zatorsky; and several other comrades who had families; and finally also me). When I ran into the husband I said to him: "Listen, your wife has invited me to your home for a *bibke* (that was what we in Warsaw called such a small, homey entertainment). She told me that she has invited several others besides me. I will be coming." I wanted to make sure he would be at home. All the invitees came.

At table, after a drink and some good snacks, people started to talk. Since there were two children in the household, the conversation turned naturally to the topic of children. Everyone told how fabulous their little ones were. I introduced such questions into their conversation that would get them to tell how they conducted themselves properly as fathers and as husbands, and how fine their homes were. The wife, who understood what was going on, beamed. Her husband did not speak much and felt a little ashamed and lost. From time to time I would throw in disguised barbs, which would serve as a kind of lesson for him . . .

After this evening the relations between husband and wife greatly improved, chiefly with regard to the care of the children.

A second instance.

The wife of a prominent leader of the Porters Union, an active party member and a member of our Militia, came to me with a fervent complaint: "What have you done with my husband? He is no longer the same man. When he comes home, he sits down and reads the paper, and for hours on end he doesn't speak a word to me. Even when he is physically in the house, he is not really there."

I calmed her and assured her that we don't want to take her husband away; quite the opposite, we want our comrades to be good husbands and good fathers. I promised her we would do something about this issue. I then had a talk with her husband. I told him that with such behavior he brings harm to the Bund. I reminded him: you live on Krochmalna Street, and if you don't send your children to our secular Yiddish school, you will raise Krochmalna street toughs you will be ashamed of. He was an enlightened worker, and he understood the issue well enough.

He followed my advice and enrolled his children in the TSYSHO school on Krochmalna Street, and the relations in his home improved markedly. When their children started attending our school, their mother became a totally different person: She began to learn from her children how to read and write; she began to read their schoolbooks and do their homework together with them. She quickly became active in the school's mothers' committee and was active in recruiting students for the school. And, by the way, she also helped greatly the previously mentioned Khaskele to found a SKIF (*Sotsyalistishe Kinder Farband*: Socialist Children's Union) group in the Krochmalna district.

Many times we had to deal with situations quite different from the ones just described.

Often people joined our movement who, in their daily lives and at home, remained just as unregenerate as they were before. But now the wives had a new weapon against their unfaithful men: the Bund. They threatened their men they would "tell all" to the Bund, and this really frightened many of them. Sometimes simply the threat would suffice. And sometimes the wives would come directly to us (or to the union, which was all the same to them) asking that we influence their husbands to behave properly. In such cases we did not refuse to play a part. I will tell now of one such case—it was one of many.

The husband was a porter who carried loads on his back at a station on Franciszkańska Street. His name was Shaye Shtern, but they called him "Shaye Eye" because his fellow porters considered that he had a "good eye," i.e, he could quickly see what needed to be done. Shaye Eye used to drag himself over the streets all night, playing cards and the horses, and losing all his earnings. He was no Bundist, just a member of the Bundist Porters Union (later he went off to the pro-Piłsudski PPS Factionalists (FRACs) in reaction to a theft from a leather store, about which I will tell later).

One time his wife, Sore-Feyge, a Cossack of a woman, sought me out at the union and poured out her bitter heart: Her husband doesn't give a penny to their household and there is simply no means to live. Talking in this way, she suddenly flew into a rage and shouted, "Comrade Bernard! I tell you I could beat him up good, I am not afraid of him, to me he is not so tough. But then go ahead and make myself a laughing stock! I have a grown daughter to marry off, I have a grown son, I am ashamed in front of the neighbors—why should people know my business. If my sister, the baker (Henye the baker's wife—his bakery was well-known in the Jewish neighborhood) didn't help me, we would die of hunger. I beg you, therefore, Comrade Bernard, do something for me." I told her that the Bund cannot mix into people's private affairs. To this she answered, "Comrade Bernard, to whom can I go? Who can help me? I beg of you, if you wanted to, you could do something. He would listen to you." I asked her what I should demand of him. She answered, "Let him at least give the household something to live on."

She started to leave. When she got to the door, she stopped for a moment. I noticed her hesitating. She then turned back to approach me again, came closer, and in a voice that was quiet now, said, "I have a grown daughter. She must have a dress, a pair of shoes, and a hat. We have to be thinking of a match for her, and there is not a penny in the house to be had. I am afraid . . . " Here she interrupted herself and ended more quietly still, "I am afraid she might go out into the street . . . " With that, she left.

Those last words affected me. I went to work. Shaye-Eye had three brothers who were also porters. On the street, among the porters, they were a force to be reckoned with. I summoned them, meeting with them in a bar at the end of Dzielna, in Dzika (Zamenhof). I told them the whole story about their brother Shaye-Eye. I addressed myself to their pride: "What will become of your family if your brother's daughter should become a streetwalker and his son a thief? You yourselves also have grown children—this would also hurt them. I am not family so I don't want to mix in, but you are, after all, brothers and uncles; how could you let such a thing happen?" I also suggested that they warn him that if he didn't change his behavior, he would be removed from his station and his son would be put in his place. I added that I could get the union to not give him his weekly earnings from the pool, but to give it directly to his wife, but I would rather the family work it out among themselves. The brothers promised to talk with Shaye in no uncertain terms and see to it that the problem was taken care of.

Soon after, they called me and brought their brother, Shaye-Eye. He must look me in the eye and promise, shaking hands on it, that he would give enough money to his wife to support his family, and that he would do what was necessary for the welfare of his children. After that the brothers said to me, "Comrade Bernard, if he doesn't keep his word, you may do with him what you will."

Shaye-Eye kept his word. He gave his wife money to support the household, and peace was restored to the home. Sore-Feyge was very happy. She later became a passionate election campaigner for the Bund ticket. Whenever there were elections to the Kehilla (Jewish Community Council), the City Council, or the Sejm (Polish parliament), she ran to her neighbors, dragging them out to vote for "Number 4" (the traditional number for the Bund candidates' list in all elections).

They also soon married off their daughter to a member of the Leather Workers Union. I was invited to the wedding, joining them in their happy celebration.

Sometimes we had to deal with issues that were much more complicated. One such case almost developed into a war with the underworld.

One morning I was sitting in the Bund Secretariat offices on Długa 26 discussing various issues with Shoshke (Shoshke-Rokhl-Erlich,[3] now in America), a coworker in the Secretariat. Shoshke was privy to many of my confidential matters. She was well informed about my work, and the members of our militia had full confidence in her and called her "our very own child." We were sitting and talking things over. There was nobody in the office at the time. Suddenly the door opened and a young woman entered, elegantly dressed and heavily perfumed.

Figure 93. A family gathering. From left: Victor Erlich; Henryk Erlich; Shoshke Rukhl Erlich; housekeeper; Alexander Erlich; Sophia Dubnow-Erlich; Simon Dubnow. Late 1930s. Henryk Erlich was the son-in-law of Simon Dubnow. From the Archives of the YIVO Institute for Jewish Research, New York.

She turned to Shoshke and said in Polish that she would like to talk to "Pan" (Polish for "Mr.") Bernard. Shoshke pointed to me and said, "This is 'Pan Bernard.'"

I ask her what she wanted. She answered, not so boldly, that she wanted to talk to me alone, privately. I invited her into another room, closed the door, asked her to please be seated, and sat myself down opposite her. For a moment there was only silence. I waited for her to say what she wanted, but she remained silent. I broke the silence, asking her again what it is she wanted. At this she burst into loud and uncontrollable weeping. She had been a prostitute. Some time ago she became acquainted with a young man—someone I knew well, a Bundist (let's call him "A"; he is still alive, has a wife and children, and leads a respectable life). They fell in love and he promised to marry her. But she was afraid that her "groom," that is, the pimp to whom she "belonged," would not only refuse to let her go, but if he fell into a rage, might even kill "A." She didn't know what to do. She said she wavered for a while, but she finally worked up the courage and told her pimp all about it. She wept and pleaded, saying there was someone who wanted to "cover her head" (i.e., marry her); he was not one of theirs, a stranger, a "chump," but a fine person; she believed with all her heart that he really meant it, so she's asking her "groom" to let her go. At first the pimp didn't even want to hear of it, but she was always after him, begging and tormenting him, complaining to him, until— after a couple of weeks—he agreed to free her, but on condition that he meet this chump first. If he likes him and he sees that he really means the thing seriously, he will permit her to marry him and won't do anything to the fellow.

They met. The "chump" appealed to the "groom." He served him a glass of whisky, shook hands on it, told him he was giving him his "bride," and that he was also giving him something more: an apartment as a wedding present. To the girl he said, "We don't know each other anymore" (that meant he was giving up his authority over her, and she was free).

The two got married. "A" lived with her for quite a while. She was very happy. Then, after a while he started coming home very late, and sometimes not at all. This was happening more and more often. Finally she asked him: What's the story, why are you so often not coming home? He answered that it was all over between them, and that he wanted a divorce. She now spoke more softly: Where will you leave me? After all, you "covered my head" (married me). What will I do now, go back on the street? She spoke sweetly, she talked angrily—nothing helped. He stuck with his wanting a divorce. So now she asked him to at least give her some money so she could at least turn to peddling of some kind; buy herself a stall in the marketplace so she wouldn't have to "go back on the street." At this he got mad and threatened that if she didn't leave him alone, it would end badly for her because he had friends who would teach her what for.

Having heard her whole story, I asked, "How can I help you? After all, I cannot force him to live with you. Call him to appear before a rabbi, or get other people to mix in. We are a political party; we cannot mix into the private affairs of individuals."

To this she answered, "Panie Bernard, he is threatening me with Bundist strong-arms; people have told me you can do anything, that you he must obey."

No matter how much I protested that we cannot do anything in this case, she just kept on repeating that she had been told that I could help her and that I should have pity on her: "I beg you Panie Bernard, do something," she implored me with tears in her eyes. "God will help you if you do."

I then asked her what concrete demand she had of him. She answered that she wanted him to give her 1500 zlotys so she could buy herself a stall in back of the food hall; she wanted to do some kind of business; she didn't want to "go back on the street." I promised her I would see what I could do and told her to come back in a couple of days for an answer. She left, her eyes swollen, not having once stopped crying, and on her way out, crying still.

I went back out to Shoshke and told her the whole story. At the time I was listening to her story, I was quite unmoved by it, but when I retold it to Shoshke, I felt that her story had indeed moved me. "A's" behavior was a great shock to me. He was from a prosperous Hasidic family, was quite knowledgeable in social matters, and held a good job with a transport firm.

I summoned "A" to the Bund Secretariat. I told him the story about his wife's visit and began to remonstrate with him. He answered me coldly and calmly: "It is all true, but this is my personal matter. You have no right to mix in; don't drag the party into it." He spoke all this to me with a devil-may-care attitude. I lost my patience and demanded that he hand over his party membership card to me. He answered again, calmly and coldly: "Only the Presidium of the Warsaw Party Committee can take back my party membership card, not you." I answered that I was a member of the Presidium and had the right to do it, and that he could appeal to the President of the Presidium to reinstate him. To this he answered that no one member of the Presidium had the right to rescind his membership, that this must be a decision of the whole Presidium. His tone really angered me; I shouted, "Get out!"

That same evening, quite late, as I was sitting with some people in Tabachnik's Coffee House on Przejazd (in the same house our Workingman's Corner was located), a half-drunk fellow staggered in, ran over to me, and agitatedly began talking to me, saying he had been threatened—that the "Bundist strong-arms" were going to kill him. "What have I done to deserve this?" he cried. From his fragmented words I understood that the threat he was talking about must be coming from "A," and I suddenly realized also that this must probably be the girl's old "groom," the girl's pimp. "What have I done to deserve this?" he kept shouting.

I didn't want to draw the attention of the others to this scene, so I went outside with him. Here on the street he pulled out a long shiny knife and cried, "With this knife I will stab him, and myself too! Why did he deceive her?" he shouted desperately. "Why did he shame her? I believed him. I gave him a furnished apartment, and he shamed her!" These words, "Why did he shame her!"

he repeated over and over. I didn't answer him, just told him to go home and sleep it off. I determined to look into this whole affair.

I was skeptical of his story that the Bundist strong-arms were threatening him, but the next morning I found out that "A" had gone to a group of Bundist porters who worked behind the food hall (whom he knew very well because they and he belonged to the same Bundist militia). He had invited them for a drink, and told them that the pimps wanted to kill him because he had married one of their "brides" and that they were trying to extort money from him. He begged his comrades to protect him, to take his side. From the way he told it, they, of course, assumed he was in the right, and vehemently promised to protect him and teach the pimps a lesson they would not soon forget. They lost no time in letting the pimp know they would settle scores with him if he so much as touched "A."

I assembled the group of comrades that "A" had organized for his "protection." I told them the truth of the whole story, and told them they were forbidden to take part in any kind of fighting with the pimps, and that if they did we would take their Bund party cards away and ban them from the party altogether. They took a strong stand and argued with me heatedly: "What do you mean?" they argued. "On account of one of their 'brides,' pimps want to blackmail one of our comrades and squeeze money out of him, and we should let them? Why does the party have to mix into such matters? It's a private matter of one of our comrades, and we just want to help him out in a comradely fashion when he's threatened. What's the deal?"—they continued—"We want to teach some underworld characters a lesson, pimps, and you're saying it isn't allowed?"

I knew what such a fight could lead to, so I told them again, sternly, that they must not engage in any fighting whatsoever in this matter.

They left disgruntled, but I knew they would obey, because, more than anything in the world they trembled at the thought of losing their party card. Their membership in the party was their greatest pride.

Apparently they had let "A" know immediately about the ban on fighting with the pimps, because that same day, toward evening, he came to the Workers Corner, approached me, and—now in a greatly softened tone—said he wanted to talk to me. "Hand over your party card," I said. He took it out of his breast pocket and, without saying a word, handed it over quietly. Then I asked him what he wanted. He answered that the "groom" had let him know he was going to kill him. Practically in tears now, he said, "Comrade Bernard, can you let that happen?" I said, "I will not talk to you unless and until you do what your wife is asking of you. She wants you to buy her a stall at the food hall so she can make a living and not have to go back on the street. This you are obligated to do, whether it costs one penny or 2000 zlotys." (I knew he made lots of money and the money didn't mean anything to him.) I also took him to task for threatening the pimp with the Bund and trying to draw Bundists into his personal affairs. He promised to do it all. And so it was. Several days later the woman came and told me all was in order. He had given her the money she asked for. I then summoned the "groom" and warned him not to dare to hurt "A" or any other Bundist.

Things quieted down. No more was heard about the matter, and after some time had passed, "A" got back his party card.

This incident, like the others I have told about—and various other similar incidents that I haven't—became quickly known among the women in the Smocza and Krochmalna neighborhoods. They saw in them a clear proof that the Bund defends all those who are wronged and aggrieved.

I also gained somewhat personally from this. Whenever I passed through the Smocza or the surrounding neighborhoods, the women would greet me in a friendly way. Once a group of Communist thugs attacked me suddenly on Smocza Street in the middle of the day. The women threw themselves on them with brooms and rags and would have torn them to pieces.

Figure 94. Bundist activists in Warsaw, ca. 1930. From left: The author, Bernard Goldstein, Victor Shulman, Hershl Himmelfarb, Abraham Kastelanski, and Emanuel Nowogrodzki. Photographer: Menakhem Kipnis. From the Archives of the YIVO Institute for Jewish Research, New York.

Notes

1. YAF aimed to organize not only working Jewish women, but also "Jewish working-class women and, in particular, the wives of Jewish working men" (from Jack Jacobs, *Bundist Counterculture in Interwar Poland*, 89; for a full discussion of YAF, see pp. 89–96 in Jacobs' book).
2. *khesedl*, diminutive of *khesed*, literally means, "favor, mercy, clemency, grace;" the idiomatic Yiddish expression *mit khesed* means, ironically, "it could be worse." —MZ
3. Shoshke married Alexander Erlich, a son of Henryk Erlich and Sophia Dubnow-Erlich, the daughter of Jewish historian Simon Dubnow.—MZ

CHAPTER 52

The Militia Comes to the Aid of Bundist Members on the Warsaw City Council

The work of the Bund's representatives on the Warsaw City Council gained a great deal of popularity for the Bund with the Jews of Warsaw and with Jewish organized labor.

Before our huge victory in the Warsaw municipal elections of 1938 (see chapter 81), we had had seven councilmen on the Warsaw City Council. The Bundist council members used the City Council as a forum from which to carry on the Bund's resolute fight against antisemitism, against discrimination of the Jewish population—especially regarding its right to work—and against the whole Polish reactionary politics in all its forms and manifestations. I am not going to discuss at this point the political activity of the Bund caucus in the Warsaw City Council. I want to limit myself instead to my own experience, and I will, therefore, describe only that part of the activity of the Bund City Council caucus that had to do with easing the poverty of Warsaw's Jewish masses and with shielding them from the wrongs that were daily being perpetrated against them by the Council. The Bund Militia was closely involved in that part of their work.

To help the Jewish population of Warsaw in its daily struggle with poverty, the Bund caucus in the City Council created a special bureau. Anybody could go to it and get help with issues that were under municipal jurisdiction. The bureau was open every evening, every day. The Bund City Council members were there daily to take up appeals by Warsaw's Jewish residents needing help or suffering wrongs or having complaints against the Warsaw City Council.

Workers, toilers, and also poor shopkeepers came. Their appeals were of various kinds: about getting a sick relative into a city hospital or sanitarium; about sending a child to a city summer camp; settling a homeless person into

Figure 95. Presidium of a national conference of Bundist city councilors from all of Poland and the Jewish communal organizations. From right: Bella Shapiro (Lublin), Noah, Henryk Erlich, Dr. Isaac Rafes (Wilno), and Israel Lichtenstein (Lodz). The banner reads: "The Bund in Poland: Proletarians of All Lands, Unite!" From the Archives of the YIVO Institute for Jewish Research, New York.

the city residential barracks; the too heavy tax burden the city had imposed on a tradesman or craftsman; about the threat of the city auctioning off a tradesman's small amount of possessions to pay back-taxes; about evictions for unpaid rent; and so on and on. People also came to the Bund City Councilmen for private matters; for example, to arbitrate between a poor renter who couldn't come to an agreement with his landlord about rent owed, asking them to act as arbiter to get the landlord not to be so harsh. The Bundist Councilmen served the Jewish working population of Warsaw in all these different kinds of cases.

The Bund City Council members had their offices near the National Labor-Emigration Office (first on Przejazd 13, then on Leszno 3). The Bund Council members employed a Comrade Tsalke whose special job it was to act as a receptionist, listen to the problem to understand what it was about, and than send that person to the appropriate Bundist Councilman. If the issue was not a complicated one, he simply wrote it up, giving it to the Councilman for his intervention. In time he oriented himself so well to the issues that he was able to resolve some of them himself by submitting them to the offices of the City Council, where they already knew him well as the one working with the Bundist Councilmen.

Tsalke was an unusual type. Raised in an orthodox family, he was learned in Jewish subjects, but also had a certain amount of general knowledge. He made his chief living from his position as an employee of the National Labor Emigration Office. The work he did in the evening for the special bureau created by the Bund City Council representatives was an extra job for him, but he barely made a living from both of these employments because he had to support a large family with many children. He lived in poverty, in a dank, dark cellar. But he was proud. If I offered to help him out a little once in a while, he wouldn't accept it. He would accept clothes sometimes because he thought of that as a gift, not as charity. "Grober Yosl" (see chapter 47) from Gnojna Street was his brother-in-law. I didn't know this for a long time because he was ashamed of it.

The Bund City Council members did not limit the work of helping Warsaw's Jewish poor to just the evening office hours of the Bureau. More than once it would happen, for example, that, all of a sudden, in the middle of the day, a Jewish worker, a Jewish craftsman, or a poor market stall keeper, would drop in to the office of Comrade Viktor Alter, the Bundist Commissioner in the Warsaw City government (he had offices in the *Labor Credit Union* and in the *National Council of Polish Trade Unions*), with a hue and cry that the police or the debt collector had just come to take away their little bit of possessions for not paying a tax.

Comrade Alter would immediately drop everything, catch a droshky or a taxi, and ride off with the petitioner to City Hall to put a stop to the order. In exactly the same way it would happen that a worker or some poor person would come rushing in while Comrade Erlich was sitting in the editorial offices of the *Folkstsaytung* working on an editorial. The person would be shouting that Comrade Erlich should save him and go with him to City Hall to rescind some order or to stop some harassment. If the matter was pressing, Comrade Erlich would get right up from his desk and go off with the injured party. Viktor Shulman (Editor-in-Chief of the *Folkstsaytung*) or Szmul Adler (manager of the print shop) would come running with a shout that the current issue of the *Folkstsaytung* was going to be delayed because Erlich's editorial was not in yet. Nevertheless, Erlich never denied anyone who came to him with an urgent request to intervene at some City office.

For the most part, however, this work was done by Comrade Esther Iwinska (Viktor Alter's sister). A lawyer, she would often go to court or to the city offices to get harassments, unjust edicts, and vexatious orders stopped or rescinded. When she undertook to pursue an issue she would first scold Tsalke and the concerned individual for having acted foolishly, but she did this out of her good nature and because of her blazing temperament. After that, she would get to work on the matter with all her energy and stubbornness, and wouldn't let up until she had accomplished something for the Jewish worker in need of our help. Now Comrade Iwinska lives in Brussels where she has settled permanently, and now as before, she is occupied with helping people, intervening on behalf of refugees passing through, securing assistance for them, visas, public assistance, and the like. Now, as before, she devotes entire days in the Brussels municipal and governmental offices for those suffering or in need. I hope her interventions are easier to achieve in Brussels than they were in the offices of Warsaw's municipal government, full of antisemites and reactionaries.

In the course of its years of work, the Bund representatives to the City Council intervened in thousands, perhaps tens of thousands, of cases in the lives of the individuals, mirroring the overall injustices and wrongs inflicted by the ruling reactionary capitalists and antisemites. Tens of thousands of Jewish workers benefited as a result of this Bund activity. Typically, the interventions tended to be about renter issues, the defense of women and children, labor rights, tax harassment, and all kinds of antisemitic decrees. Often the interventions were successful and rescued people who were being persecuted and were in need of help.

Now I would like to tell about an intervention that was not typical; rather it was exceptional in the day-to-day activities of the Bundist Councilmen. But I want to tell about it because it illustrates in many ways something estimable about Viktor Alter and the Bund in general.

It had to do with a *shtibl* (a small Hasidic place of prayer, often an apartment in a building) on Nowolipki Street from which the worshippers were about to be evicted with the excuse that the building had to be rebuilt. Efforts by the Hasidim to rescind the eviction had failed, and they were about to be thrown out of their place of worship. Somebody advised them to go to Viktor Alter—maybe he would help them. The Hasidim said, "But Viktor Alter is an unbeliever, a Bundist; would he want to help Hasidim?" The answer came: "He helps everyone; he will likely want to help you too." The Hasidim went off to Alter, and he did in fact undertake to rescind the eviction. He prevailed, and the Hasidim were allowed to remain in their little house of prayer. Their enthusiasm was immense. One of the *shtibl* elders went off to Alter and thanked him profusely for what he had done. He then asked, "Please explain: How does it happen that you, an unbeliever, helped Hasidim, keeping them from being evicted from their *shtibl*?" Viktor Alter answered: "I myself do not believe in your prayers, but I will fight with all my strength for you to have the right to pray." This story spread all over Jewish Warsaw, especially among the Hasidim.

Often it happened that the Bund Militia had to help the Bundist councilmen in their efforts to ease the poverty of the Jewish working people. This usually occurred with evictions, that is, throwing poor people or the unemployed out of their apartments and into the street.

As previously mentioned, the Jewish workers and poor people came to the Bundist councilmen not only with issues concerning city regulations, but also with a lot of other concerns. But when an unemployed worker came to a Bundist councilman to tell him he was about to be evicted from his apartment, for example, nothing could be done at the city council level. It was strictly a private matter between the renter and the landlord. The Bundist councilman would then contact me and ask me to try to settle the matter amicably. I would go off to the landlord, and often we would settle things between us. The landlord would put aside the old debt, for example, and from then on the renter would pay the rent regularly; or the renter would pay off the old debt in small installments and after that pay the rent regularly. If the landlord would not yield, I would appeal to his conscience, to his sense of justice. I tried everything to avoid eviction.

But I couldn't get anywhere with some landlords. They dug in their heels: the tenant would have to be thrown out of the apartment. At this point we would call on the Bund Militia. On the day the eviction was to take place, a group of our militiamen would gather in the courtyard of the building. They would quietly lose themselves in the crowd of tenants that were looking on in silence at the sad procedure, as the police and the superintendent, under the eye of the bailiff (an official of the court authorized to carry out "evictions, auctions, and actions" and other such court orders) carried the few poor possessions of the tenant out onto the street. As soon as the bailiff and the police were gone, our Militiamen went to work: If the apartment was on the ground floor, they tore open a window and put the tenant's things back into the apartment; if it was on an upper floor, they broke the bailiff's seal, opened the door, and put back the tenant's few poor possessions. For breaking the bailiff's seal the penalty was several months in jail, but how could those who broke the seal—strangers who came and went—be caught?

After such an episode the landlord would have to bring the tenant to court again. He again would have to get the court to issue an eviction notice, and then again execute the eviction with the help of the bailiff. Then our militia would again return the tenant's possessions to the apartment. Often enough, the landlord would then see that this battle wasn't worth it and agree to work out some compromise arrangement with the tenant.

In most cases, by the way, we were dealing with evictions carried out by Jewish landlords against Jewish tenants.

About one such eviction—typical of many—I would like to tell in a little more detail. The tenant was a tailor, dumb (he could not speak), and a member of our Garment Workers Union. He lived on Niska Street near the garbage dumpster (many Warsaw buildings had one large garbage receptacle in the courtyard for all the tenants). He lived there in a small dark room with his wife and children. The eviction was scheduled to take place in the late fall, when it was already quite cold outside. I went to the landlord and assured him that as soon as the busy season started up again his tenant would start paying his rent regularly. The landlord would have none of it. Even if the tenant would pay him all that he owed him, all at once, he still didn't want him living there. He told me that the dumb tailor had attacked him with an iron bar and wanted to beat him black and blue. He was even willing to pay him something to be rid of him. And if that wouldn't work, he was willing to do whatever it would take to evict him. No matter how much I talked and no matter what I said, I couldn't budge him. He stuck with no, no, and no! So I left him, and we waited for the eviction.

On the day of the eviction, a group of Bund militiamen was, as usual, already in the courtyard. When the bailiff and the police saw the apartment, the poverty of the hole that was supposed to be an apartment, and the poverty of its residents, they themselves felt pity. You could see it in the reluctance with which they carried out their official duties. The bailiff recognized us (he knew our faces from other places) and he let me know this time that he knows what we are preparing to do here. He asks only that we wait until he and the police are on the other side of the gate so that he would not have to come back and intervene. As soon as they left the courtyard, we began putting the things back into the apartment. The landlord started shouting and screaming. We closed the front gate to the building so the noise would not carry out into the street. He screamed, and we continued to carry the things back into the apartment. After that I warned the landlord not to take the tenant to court because it would just cause him greater expense. We would simply come every time and put the things back in the apartment, so it would be better for him to work out some arrangement with the tenant. He finally did.

In this way the Bund—in addition to its general political and economic battles, and in addition to its cultural activities—also helped the Jewish working people in its daily troubles and needs. And in a few years time, the Jewish people, in Warsaw and in Poland generally, properly recognized the work of the Bund, first in the *Kehilla* (Jewish Community Council) elections in 1936, and then again later in the Warsaw City Council elections in 1938. In that year, out of 20 Jewish City Councilmen, 17 candidates from the Bund list of trade unions and Bund members were elected—and only 3 from all other Jewish parties combined. Similar results were obtained in the years 1936–1938 in other large and mid-sized Polish cities—for example in Łódź, Wilno, Lublin, Białystok, Grodno, Piotrków, Tarnow, etc.

It also fell to our militia to serve our Bund City Council members in quite another way—by protecting them from attacks by antisemitic hooligans. To the extent that our Bund City Council members were beloved by the Jewish population, to that same extent were they hated by the antisemites and reactionaries. They viewed their public stance as "an insolent expression of Jewish impudence."

The Warsaw City Council was supposed to deal primarily with matters of city administration. But our councilmen took every opportunity to speak out about political issues—speeches against the ruling regime, against capitalism, against antisemitism, against the antilabor politics of the government and its "city fathers," etc. Our councilmen also spoke out often about the attacks on Jews in the streets of Warsaw and against the excesses of the antisemites in all of Poland, branding the homegrown Polish Fascists as Hitlerites. The reactionary Polish press would publish tendentious reports on these public stands by our councilmen and did not spare inflammatory antisemitic statements against Jews in general and against the Bund in particular. As a result, more and more frequently young Polish hooligans, students, and street gangs began appearing in the public galleries of the City Council shouting out antisemitic tirades during the speeches of our councilmen. When this repeated itself many times over, our comrades began coming to the public gallery and making counterdemon-

Figure 96. Youth Bundists marching under red banners, Warsaw. From the Archives of the YIVO Institute for Jewish Research, New York.

strations. The outbursts of the antisemites grew louder and more impudent, and we saw that the security of our councilmen was in danger, that the hooligans might attack them as they exited City Hall. We started guarding our councilmen. Whenever there was a session of the City Council, we sent several of our people to the gallery to observe carefully what was going on around them and to immediately let us know at the *Arbeter Vinkl* (Workers Corner) of anything that seemed suspicious. The Workers Corner was located not far from *Plac Teatralny* (Theatre Square), the location of City Hall where the City Council sessions took place. We kept a large group of militiamen ready there so they could quickly get to City Hall if there were any kind of threat.

One time, in the spring of 1937, during one of the sessions of the Warsaw City Council, our observers warned that something didn't look right. There were many more hooligans in the public gallery than usual, behaving more aggressively than usual, and quite a bit more of their type could be seen hanging around at the front entrance of City Hall. In short, there was a strong suspicion that an attack on our council members was imminent. I went off to City Hall with a large group of militiamen. Some of us went up into the public gallery, already packed with hooligans. I told our men to stay close to the gallery door so that they could quickly come downstairs if necessary. Another group of us stayed on the street, close to the front entrance of City Hall. I myself went into a room next to the meeting room. Next to this room was a buffet room reserved for the councilmen. When there was a break in the session, I signaled to a PPS councilman I knew to come out. When I told him I needed to talk to him about something, he led me into the buffet room. I purposely did not call out one of our Bund councilmen so as not to arouse any suspicions that we were preparing anything. After that I led two or three more of our militiamen into the buffet room. I did not approach our Bund councilmen, but our eyes met and they understood.

When the session was over, and the doors of the room were opened, the few of us in the buffet room stood right next to our council members. At the same time the gang of hooligans began running down from the public gallery with shouts, but our men were able to get down before them, quickly forming a protective ring around our councilmen. On the street, at the entrance to City Hall, a similar situation occurred. A group of our militiamen were right by the entrance and the hooligans quickly oriented themselves to who we were, and their desire to attack our councilmen quickly faded. They made do with anti-semitic shouts against the Jews and especially against the Bund. We remained cautious, however, accompanying each of our councilmen home.

CHAPTER 53

The First of May Demonstrations Under the Piłsudski Regime

Over the years, the First of May demonstrations in many countries had changed their character. From a day of political struggle containing in its history chapters of great heroism, often paid for with bloody sacrifices, it had slowly changed into a joyful folk celebration, especially among the Socialists in the West European countries. But in Poland, even after the First World War, and especially for the Bund, the First of May was still a day of difficult trials, struggle, and resistance. In this sense the situation of the Bund was worse than the situation of the Polish Socialist Party (PPS). The PPS had earned some standing in the fight for an independent Poland. Many Polish government officials, especially during the Piłsudski era, came out of its ranks, and their sentiments favoring the PPS remained with them for a long time, to some extent lingering even after the Piłsudski coup. So no one dared bother the PPS, in any case at least not until the Piłsudski regime became openly Fascist.

For the Bund things were entirely different. Along with the deep-seated antisemitism in Poland, especially among the upper social levels and the ruling classes, the Bund was hated both as a Jewish and as a Socialist party. In addition, the Bund was hated still more because of its notion that Jews should be equal citizens of Poland, equal to other Poles. With the Zionists, we had much less trouble. They agreed with the reactionary Poles on at least one point: Both the antisemites and the Zionists believed—although for different reasons—that the home of the Jews, including the Polish Jews, was *not* Poland, that the Jews should and must leave Poland. The Bund believed that the Jews not only had a right to be in Poland, but that Poland must be a land where both Poles and Jews had equal rights. The Bund also demanded and fought for the idea that the Jews in Poland should hold onto and develop their own specific national character, their Yiddish

Figure 97. May Day demonstration, late 1930s, Warsaw. From left: Victor Alter, Henryk Erlich, Noyekh, and Emanuel Nowogrodzki. From the Archives of the YIVO Institute for Jewish Research, New York.

language and their Yiddish culture. Such an "insolent" position the ruling classes of Poland and the Polish government officials could not abide. And for them the symbol of this Bundist "insolence" was—the First of May.

The Warsaw Bund in the first few years after the war used to gather in *Plac Teatralny*, as I have previously mentioned. This square was one of the central points in the non-Jewish, Polish sector of the capital. The Bund would also demonstrate on the First of May in other prominent Polish boulevards and squares where "high society" lived and where the governmental ministries and the old aristocratic mansions were located. The Jewish workers marched in these places under red flags, inscribed with Yiddish slogans, and singing Yiddish songs. For this reason, and others, the Polish reactionaries poured out their greatest wrath on the Bund. It aimed to drive the Bund from the streets, or at least take away its desire to come and demonstrate in the "Polish" streets. For the Bund, however, it was a matter of honor and a basic civil right to be able to hold its mass demonstration in the so-called Polish streets as well.

Right after the Piłsudski coup (May 1926) there was a certain amount of governmental easing toward the Bund's First of May demonstrations. This happened just at the moment the Bund movement had begun its rapid growth. SKIF (*Sotsyalistisher Kinder Farband*—Socialist Children's Union) was established in 1926.

The Youth-Bund *Tsukunft* also broadened its activities at this time. Both of them began to incorporate modern, Western European methods in their pedagogical work: elements of scouting, uniforms for their members (for the SKIF, dark blue shirts and blouses with red neckerchiefs; for the *Tsukunft*, light blue shirts and blouses with red neckerchiefs and trim). A certain amount of color and luster was being introduced. Also our sports organization, *Morgnshtern*, was then being developed, bringing something new into our whole movement. In

The First of May Demonstrations Under the Piłsudski Regime

Figure 98. May Day, 1933, Warsaw. Henryk Erlich speaking at a demonstration in front of the Bundist club on Przejazd Street. From the Archives of the YIVO Institute for Jewish Research, New York.

Figure 99. Members of *Tsukunft*, Przemysl, Poland, 1920. The sign held by the pair in the first row reads: "With united energies we will build the future." From the Archives of the YIVO Institute for Jewish Research, New York.

other fields Bund activities were strengthened and broadened as well: the *Sotsyalistisher Hantverker Union* (Socialist Artisans Union), *Yidishe Arbeter Froy*—Jewish Working Woman—(YAF), and the struggle for equal right to work for Jews, for Yiddish secular schools, and for cultural activities. This new mood and growth was also reflected in our celebration of the First of May. We introduced more color and more elements of a folk holiday. The First of May became not only a day of struggle, but also a day of joy and celebration.

The preparations for the First of May created a holiday spirit, a feeling of elation. For many weeks, the coming holiday was the center of all we did and thought about. A couple of months before the First of May, a large May Day Committee was formed. Several representatives of the Warsaw Bund's Central Committee were on it, a representative of each union—a representative from YAF, from *Tsukunft*, SKIF, and all the organizations and institutions that were under the aegis of the Bund. This broad May Day Committee appointed an executive that carried out the practical details in preparation for the First of May demonstration. May Day committees were also active within each separate organization, especially in the unions, in *Tsukunft*, and in many others.

The Bund wanted to conduct a joint demonstration with all the labor parties. But this was impossible to achieve. We therefore concentrated our efforts toward something that seemed practical and possible: a joint demonstration by the Bund and the PPS. But even with this limited goal, various difficulties arose

Figure 100. Presidium of the first countrywide SKIF Conference, Warsaw, October 1936. From the *Naye Folkstsaytung*, November 19, 1937. From the Archives of the YIVO Institute for Jewish Research, New York.

that could not always be overcome. Nevertheless, even if it wasn't possible to have a joint demonstration with the PPS, we always found a way to manifest a certain solidarity between our two organizations. The two separate demonstrations would often end together at Theater Square, one next to the other, merging as one demonstration, and sharing speakers. We would also frequently exchange speakers at the May Day athenaeums of the Bund and the PPS that took place in the large assembly halls after the marches.

Dr. Emanuel Sherer, Artur Zieglboym (before he settled in Łódź), and I would represent the Bund in discussions with the Warsaw PPS prior to the First of May demonstration. I always took part in the discussions, because one of the most important problems we had to discuss in connection with the First of May demonstration was security.

Meanwhile lively internal preparations for the First of May were starting up in every branch of the movement. First, every organization inspected and prepared its flags. Not only did the Bund have flags, but also *Tsukunft* and YAF had their flags. And not only every union, but also every larger party group, and even separate locals of a union, had their own special flags. In honor of the holiday, sometimes a group that had previously not had a flag, now made one. After seeing to the flags, they next turned to the making of the banners, inscribed with political slogans and demands, usually painted on a long piece of linen cloth attached to two sticks at either end. In addition to its main flag, the flags of the youthful union locals and the *Tsukunft* factions of the youth locals also had dozens of fiery flags that were a true adornment.

Several weeks before the First of May, in all our locations, the "meetings to prepare" took place, the so-called "First of May *Masuvkes*," or pre-First of May meetings. These took place in Warsaw every year by the score, if not by the hundreds. Every local of a union, every youth local, every party group, every organization that was in any way connected to the Bund movement, held its own pre-First of May meeting. On the last Saturday before the First of May, the Warsaw Bund's Central Committee organized a central, pre-First of May final meeting in a large public hall.

All these preparatory meetings had a political character. The current political situation in Poland and the world was discussed. The political slogans that were being put forward were underscored in order to give the imminent demonstration a more militant, political character. A secondary purpose—or perhaps even the first task—of these meetings was of course to move the Jewish workers—despite the enemies' threats, with nobody knowing if they would emerge from the demonstration in one piece—to participate en masse in the Bund's First of May demonstration. All these countless pre-First of May meetings achieved their goal: even in the worst of times, when attacks by the police or hooligans were almost certain to occur, many thousands participated in the Bund's First of May demonstrations.

Figure 101. Bundist youth marching under red flags. From the Archives of the YIVO Institute for Jewish Research, New York.

At the same time, we were vigorously preparing to protect the demonstration from hostile provocations and attacks. Our demonstration was threatened from three directions: from the police, who waited for the slightest excuse to disperse us, in the process delivering vicious blows; from the organized and extremely antisemitic groupings, who wanted to settle accounts with the Bund; and finally, from the Communists, who would try to insert themselves into our demonstration to create a disturbance and in this way destroy and bring to naught a Socialist demonstration. To protect the demonstration from all attacks on open streets was a difficult task. Our militia had to be well prepared for this, and a much larger force than usual was necessary. For every First of May demonstration, therefore, we mobilized a large number of party members and *Tsukunft*ists, also recruiting some of the militiamen from the various unions. By the end of the 1930s, when the Warsaw Bund's demonstrations had reached 20,000 participants, we were deploying a 2,000-man militia.

We divided the entire militia into several groups. One group, the largest, formed a line on both sides along the whole length of the procession—a militiaman at every tenth rank. A second group marched at the head of the procession, and a third at the end. A fourth group was mobile, marching at some distance from the head of the procession, taking up a position at an approaching intersection, where there was the danger of an attack from a side street. In addition we had a "motorized" group of Militiamen, riding mostly on bicycles, with a smaller group on motorcycles, and sometimes in automobiles as well.

They rode on the street at some distance ahead, farther ahead than the mobile group. They studied the surrounding streets to see if a large cluster of police wasn't hiding there, or to see if perhaps hooligans weren't gathering in

The First of May Demonstrations Under the Piłsudski Regime 279

Figure 102. Bundist youth marching under red flags, Warsaw. From the Archives of the YIVO Institute for Jewish Research, New York.

Figure 103. National Convention of Bundist youth, June 10–11, 1932, Warsaw. From the Archives of the YIVO Institute for Jewish Research, New York.

Figure 104. National Convention of Bundist youth, June 10–11, 1932, Warsaw. From the Archives of the YIVO Institute for Jewish Research, New York.

a suspicious manner, or whether or not the Communists hadn't gathered in a certain spot and were getting ready to tear into the procession. They continually reported back what was going on in the surrounding neighborhoods.

We also had a special group of scouts who mixed with the crowd on the "Polish" streets, eavesdroping on their talk, especially among the little circles standing on the streets and corners. For this we had to use people who looked "Polish" and who spoke Polish well. The most important among these were Renia Jarecka (later Pizhic, about whom I have already spoken); Ruta Rutman (later Perenson), a rich girl and student; Sarah Joelson (the daughter of the Bundist activist Jona Joelson), then a medical student and active in *Morgenshtern*, now a doctor in London, her father now in New York; and Josef Gutgold, who could pass as a Polish youth, and others.

Josef Gutgold one time even took over the leadership of a group of antisemitic students as they were waiting at the gate to the University of Warsaw to attack the Bund demonstration about to march by, tricking them into running down a side street.

The night before the First of May the Jewish slums were nervous and tense, but at the same time festive and in a holiday mood. There was hardly a Jewish worker's home where at least one son or daughter wasn't marching tomorrow, not to mention the homes where the father, his sons and daughters, and sometimes also the mother weren't preparing for tomorrow's demonstration. There were more people than usual milling about on the streets. There was lots of commotion around the offices of the unions and the party. Every room and cubbyhole

Figure 105. National Convention of Bundist youth, June 10–11, 1932, Warsaw. From the Archives of the YIVO Institute for Jewish Research, New York.

was occupied, even in the corners and corridors one could sometimes see small groups of people seated in a circle, bending toward each other, with their backs to the crowds around them—engrossed in the final stages of the preparations for the First of May. The militia groups were getting their final instructions. Many of the flag bearers took the flags home with them that night for fear the police might break into the offices and confiscate them or rip them up. With great reverence, they would hide the flags under their coats and quickly run home with them.

The offices emptied early that night. People would run home as soon as the last minute preparations were complete—any later, and they ran the chance of being arrested. On the night before the First of May, the police would carry out many arrests on the streets seeking "Communists"—and which poorly clad worker didn't look to the police like a "Communist?" One would of course be set free after a few days, but in the meantime, one would lose the opportunity to take part in the great, festive workers holiday—so people hurried home and waited eagerly for the morning to come.

By six o'clock in the morning on the First of May, the celebratory atmosphere was already evident on the street. The streetcars and buses were not running because the union of the workers who ran them was on strike (they began running again around two o'clock in the afternoon, when the demonstrations were over). Quite early in the morning one could see boys and girls dressed in blue shirts or blouses and red neckerchiefs—these were our young Bundists, *Tsukunft*ists, hurrying to their assembly points. A little later adults would start to appear, sometimes families, or groups of friends or coworkers.

The festive appearance of the street was heightened by the fact that in practically all the workshops there was no work being done and there were no clerks in the shops. For an organized worker to work on the First of May was not only a breach of discipline, but also a disgrace, a dishonor. For such a breach a Bundist or a *Tsukunftist* would be immediately expelled. A member of a union was also disciplined for such a breach, unless he confirmed beforehand that he worked in a nonunion shop and could lose his job if he took the day off—in that case he was granted permission to work on the First of May. Every union sent inspection groups to check the workshops and make sure no one was working.

A little later large groups of workers would begin filling the streets. By ten in the morning the various unions and organizations had already gathered at their various assembly points. They organized themselves into columns, lifting their flags and banners, and marching to the central assembly point. Some of the unions marched to the assembly point with their marching bands (the Printers Union, the Bakers Union, and the Meat Workers Union). After a short mass meeting, the Bund May Day procession began its march.

I don't know if I have the power to describe even to a small degree how imposing, how beautiful, how festive the great Warsaw Bund's May Day parade was and what energy and happiness radiated from it. In the very front marched a strong contingent of militiamen, youths especially selected for their strength, wearing red armbands, the word "Bund" emblazoned on them. Behind them was the flag of the Bund's Central Committee—a huge flag that shimmered and shone in the May sun with its red satin and red braid and golden embroidered letters: "General Jewish Labor Bund in Poland, Central Committee." Behind this flag marched the members of the Central Committee, prominent among them the proud figures of Comrades Noyekh, Erlich, and Alter. All three were tall, slim, and majestic: Noyekh with his grey head of hair and his grey moustache; Erlich with his good-natured face and small, pointy beard; Alter with his vitality and energy.

Also Michalewicz, the shortest of the group (1928 was his last time in the May Day demonstration), was particularly impressive with his silvery-grey head of hair and his proud bearing. Everyone's notice was drawn to them. Following the Polish Bund's Central Committee, marched the members of the Bund's Warsaw Central Committee; and following them came the unions, each union carrying its flag aloft, some of them, as I already mentioned, with their own marching band.

The Youth-Bund *Tsukunft* occupied the middle of the procession. It was the most eye-catching, colorful part of the demonstration. Besides the usual red flags, the *Tsukunft* also had dozens of militant pennants, each group of *Tsunkft*-ists with its own pennant. These "fighting pennants" were made with red linen, without any inscription, stretched onto a light bamboo pole. In even the slightest breeze, these pennants fluttered and waved. These fighting pennants were all carried behind the main *Tsukunft* flag, four in a row, across the entire width of the street, scattered thinly and separated one row from the other by several long paces. In the late thirties, when the Warsaw *Tsukunft* numbered about one hundred separate groups of youngsters, this forest of 100 fighting pennants made an exhilarating sight. Right behind the *Tsukunft* pennants came several dozen little flags carried by the SKIF circles, held aloft by the older children: little, tri-cornered red flags embroidered with the names of each group. The very youngest children were not taken along to the demonstration—no one knew what might happen. Following the display of flags came the *Tsukunft* chorus, considered one of the best Jewish choruses in all of Poland. Its rhythmic song echoed in the streets. In the middle of the young people's procession marched *Morgnshtern*, some of their units in sports outfits. The Bundist academic, university students group, *Ringen* ("Links," as in a chain), also marched with the young people. In the thirties, the various youth groups in the procession numbered about 4,000 young people: *Tsukunft*ists, *Morgnshtern*ers, young trade union members, and the others.

The whole Bundist May Day procession stretched for miles and occupied many streets at a time. The streets were lined with people. At least 100,000 people watched the Bund's parade.

The Pilsudski regime trod with quick strides to its dictatorial destiny. As early as 1928 the relations between the labor movement and the Pilsudski camp were strained. The Warsaw PPS was on the brink of a split.

In that year—1928—during the First of May celebration at Warsaw's *Plac Teatralny*, a fierce battle took place between the Communists and the PPS. The Communists wanted to force their way into the PPS procession and carry out one of their familiar "joining in brotherhood with the working masses over the heads of their leaders." The PPS put up a strong resistance. Terrible fighting broke out, with gunfire. Dozens of wounded fell, and also several dead. Police immediately interfered, but instead of halting the fighting, they beat people left and right, further inflaming the riot. The Bund procession stood at the opposite corner of the gigantic square at the farthest remove from the battle, but the police could not resist the temptation: people are being beaten, and the kikes should not receive any blows? So they took the opportunity to get back over to the Bund columns and honor them with a goodly number of blows.

But this was not enough. Later, the police fell upon our demonstrators a second time. The Bundist demonstration, following the plan, marched out of *Plac Teatralny* to Przejazd Square where the Bund's Workers Corner was located, and there the Bund ended its demonstration. The marchers quietly began to disperse. In the house on Przejazd 9, the Warsaw Bund had two locales: At the entrance, on the first floor, was the Bund Club (the *Arbeter Vinkl*—Workers Corner) and the Party Secretariat; on the ground floor, with windows facing the courtyard, was the Bund's women's organization, YAF. After the demonstration was over we usually stored all the flags, pennants, and banners temporarily in these two locations. The courtyard was still full of people—flag bearers, banner carriers, militiamen, and others—who were tarrying in the courtyard. Suddenly the police burst into the courtyard, closed the gate, entered the YAF locale where the flags and banners were placed, and began murderously beating whomever they came upon. They badly beat Herman Kruk—who was at that time Secretary of the Culture Department for the Central Committee of *Tsukunft*—as well as Benyomin Kijewsky, one of our most active militiamen, splitting his skull—he had to spend a long time in the hospital. Operated on several times, he remained crippled for the rest of his life, and to this day is virtually incapacitated for work (he now lives in Rio de Janeiro, Brazil).

I quickly came running with Victor Alter. We had been at the editorial offices of the *Folkstsaytung*, only a few minutes away from Przejazd 9. We complained vehemently to the police. They answered that it was a "mistake." Since they saw a large crowd in the courtyard of Przejazd 9, they thought it was an illegal meeting, because there had been no permit issued for a meeting in the courtyard. This was, of course, a cynical excuse. In the morning Comrades Erlich and Alter lodged a strong protest against the government.

A police attack on the Bund's May Day demonstration occurred again in 1929, a year later. Our First of May demonstration set out as usual from its central assembly point on Nalewki 34. At first, the demonstration went on without any disturbance at all. It proceeded through a series of streets, passed part of Senatorska, onto Plac Teatralny, bordered on two sides by Senatorska and Bielańska, marched into Bielańska, and continued onto Tłomackie and Leszno. Suddenly as the tip of the procession had reached the beginning of Leszno, still at Plac Teatralny, mounted police tore into the middle of the procession with a wild gallop. At the same moment, police on foot and civilian hooligans attacked our procession and cut off the part of the procession that was still in Plac Teatralny. This stormy attack came so unexpectedly that near the church next to City Hall, people were falling over each other. Also on Bielańska Street a heap of people lay who had fallen on top of each other.

After a moment, Pinchas Schwartz and I both sprang out into the middle of the street and began shouting at the police:

"What are you doing?"

"Who are you?" they asked angrily.

So we identified ourselves: Schwartz as the correspondent for the *Folkst-saytung* and I as the person responsible for the procession. This stopped the police; they no longer were chasing people, and the ranks of our processions reformed themselves. At that moment another group of mounted police galloped into the crowd. We again stopped them, arguing with them. In the meantime the procession reformed and began with quick steps to catch up with the first part of the procession. Our procession was so long that the front part of the procession did not know what was happening in the middle.

A little farther, on Leszno Street, another incident occurred, this time it was the Communists. A group of Communists, concentrated on the sidewalk, began

Figure 106. Bund May Day demonstration, Nowy Dwor, Poland, ca. 1930. From the Archives of the YIVO Institute for Jewish Research, New York.

shouting, "Down with the Social Fascists." Among some of our demonstrators, especially among those who had just been so brutally scattered and trampled upon by the police, this evoked tremendous rage. Normally our Militiamen were disciplined people. They had been warned not to let themselves be provoked, and normally they strictly observed this instruction. But this time the patience of one of the Militiamen, indeed one of those who had just been attacked by the police, exploded. He broke ranks and with his stick threw himself on the Communist abusers. I ran and pulled him back into his column.

This was perhaps the only time a Bundist in a demonstration allowed himself to be provoked by a Communist. Usually during our demonstrations we did not react to Communist verbal abuse so as not to give the police an excuse to break up our demonstration. Our strategy in such a situation was quite clear: as long as the Communists just shout and raise a racket, but do not tear into our procession, we would not react!

CHAPTER 54

A Joint First of May Demonstration with the PPS

In 1931 the Bund was, for the first time, able to conduct a joint First of May demonstration with the PPS, including a march together through the streets of Warsaw. In other Polish cities, such joint demonstrations with the PPS occurred more often.

It was at the moment the ruling Piłsudski camp had finally and decisively stepped onto the path leading to a dictatorial regime. It was after the great "Brisk (Brest-Litovsk) arrest" of a series of prominent, leading activists and parliamentary deputies from the PPS and the Peasants Party, who were imprisoned and tortured in the Brisk fortress. It was also after the fraudulent parliamentary elections in which the results were clearly falsified. In short, it was after the regime had dealt heavy blows to the PPS and the democratic opposition in general. In reaction, the PPS's oppositional spirit grew stronger. They stopped reckoning with all kinds of "howevers" as before, and decided to demonstrate together with the Bund in Warsaw and throughout all of Poland—in defiance of the ruling clique.

This decision was happily received by the Bund. In the Bund the spirit of internationalism had always been strong. Every concrete expression of internationalism always brought us joy. With great enthusiasm, we began to prepare for a joint First of May demonstration with the PPS.

During meetings with the PPS, we worked through and concurred on all the various political, organizational, and technical problems, and everything was mutually agreed upon. But after these basic problems were solved, came the question of how to protect the demonstration from attack.

The demonstration was going to march through the aristocratic Polish (non-Jewish) streets, and there were grounds for fearing that hooligans and police in civilian clothes would attack the Jewish part of the march. The comrades of the PPS suggested that the Bund march intermingled with the PPS. We would in this way be protected on all sides. We rejected this idea. We wanted to march in the joint demonstration as a unified, independent party: the PPS, followed by the Bund. In the end we arrived at a compromise: We would march as a separate unit in the joint demonstration, but behind us, at the end of our column would march a contingent of the PPS Militia. In addition our Polish comrades suggested we exchange our militias—that we protect their marchers and they, ours. Although the intentions behind this suggestion were tactful and comradely, we rejected this suggestion as well. We did not want to march through the "Polish" streets under the protection of our gentile comrades. We wanted to march openly, without fear, and if it became necessary, to defend ourselves. In any case, it was clear that if there were a heavy attack on our part of the march, they would quickly come to our aid anyway. The PPS agreed: the Bund's part of the joint May First demonstration would be protected by our own expanded militia.

The entire march route of the joint demonstration proceeded without incident. But our spotters informed us that at Warsaw University's gate in the Cracow suburb, a large group of students and hooligans had gathered who were shouting antisemitic slogans and who were probably waiting to attack the Bund part of the demonstration. We had, of course, anticipated this and had previously prepared a strong group of our militia to deal with it. About ten minutes before the Bund segment of the procession was to march past the university, this special group of militiamen marched out of our column and arrayed themselves in two rows right next to the sidewalk in front of the university, with their backs to the marching demonstrators, facing the students and the hooligans gathered there. They stood quietly, tense, but decisively, like an iron wall. The students and hooligans saw this wasn't some sort of fun game and lost their courage. The militiamen stood thus a whole hour until the entire Bund's marching demonstrators had passed.

The joint demonstration went off without incident. Some small incidents came only later, on Warecka Street in front of the entrance to the PPS's daily newspaper, *Robotnik*, after the demonstration had dispersed. Hooligans in the side streets attacked groups of our comrades who were heading home, and here and there fights broke out with our Militia. The hooligans especially fell upon our *Tsukunft*ists—their blue shirts, blouses, and red neckerchiefs made them easy targets.

CHAPTER 55

In Red Vienna

A second opportunity arose to forget for a while the difficult times in Warsaw and to connect once more, in person, with the mighty international labor movement. In Vienna, at the end of July 1931, an international sports Olympiad, organized by the Labor Sports Internationale, was taking place, and following that, a Congress of the Socialist Internationale.

A delegation of about 100 from our *Morgnshtern* athletes traveled to the Olympiad. I gladly took this opportunity to go with them. It put me in a holiday mood, although the feeling wasn't as strong as it had been during my first foreign trip in 1927 to the Sports Olympiad in Prague (see chapter 37). The harsh economic crisis, with millions unemployed; the rise of Hitlerism in Germany, as well as the Fascist tendencies in other countries; and, of course, most importantly, the rise of our own homegrown fascism, all depressed my mood.

But the international labor movement was still mighty, especially in Austria. So we took joy in the coming holiday organized by the Austrian Social Democrats, the pride of European socialism between the two World Wars, and, of all places, exactly where? In famous "Red Vienna."

The trip went well. In addition to our group, there was also a large delegation from the PPS's labor sports association, SKRA (*Robotniczy Klub Sportowy*—Workers Sports Club). Altogether we were several hundred strong, and we occupied several cars. As for sleeping at night, forget it, especially since we were traveling in coach cars, not sleeping cars. There was singing and dancing. Things were lively.

As the train approached Vienna, one could begin to see signs we were in a country where socialism was a real power. Several miles before the city, the houses along the train tracks were decorated with red flags. The Vienna train station was completely decorated in red. A Socialist Party delegation welcomed

Figure 107. *Tsukunft* contingent at the second Labor Olympic games in Vienna, 1931. From the Archives of the YIVO Institute for Jewish Research, New York.

us. Also greeting us at the station were the Viennese comrades who had come to take each of us to his assigned lodgings.

I was the guest of a railroad worker. They were a family of three, two parents and a son, also a railroad worker. All three were Socialists and members of the Austrian Socialist Party. When I entered the apartment, I was immediately struck by a kind of cleanliness that is rarely seen, even in wealthy homes. I took a bath and lay down to rest; my host served me hot milk and chocolate in bed. They treated me like a prince, feeding me all kinds of good things. In the morning I found all my things laundered and pressed. My hostess had taken all my things that night, after I had gone to sleep, and washed them, and then had probably risen before dawn to press them. This was repeated the next morning. I felt very uncomfortable to have my hostess do my laundry every day. I was somewhat embarrassed to say anything about it, so I ran off to the communal house where part of our group was staying (actually it was more fun there), saying nothing to my hosts.

After a couple of days I was summoned to the local Secretariat of the party. I went. It turned out they had been looking for me. My host had come to the party Secretariat raising an alarm—his guest had disappeared! They started looking for me. Of course it was not hard to "catch" me. At the party Secretariat, they asked me why I had run off from the railroad worker. I told them the truth. They laughed. "What do you mean?" they said. "You are after all, our guest, a comrade, so we want to be as good hosts as possible." But I stuck with my point: I didn't want my hostess doing my laundry. At this point they called my host, waiting in a nearby room, to come in. When he heard what it was about, he accepted my condition, just so he could get his guest back.

How Vienna looked then is beyond my power to describe. The whole city was drenched in red. The streets were filled with people in a festive, jubilant mood. Masses of young people and children from the Socialist youth movement and from the "Red Falcons"[1] flooded the streets, shimmering in the hot July sun with their blue shirts and blouses and their red neckerchiefs. Whenever they spotted a foreigner (easy to recognize), they would call out to him at the top of their voices *Freundschaft* (friendship), said with a tone of genuine friendliness that echoed in the streets of Vienna.

And now, about the Olympiad itself! The huge sports competitions! Our *Morgnshtern* group competed in the gymnastic events and did exceptionally well. And the folk entertainments! The stage performances of the various national delegations! The folk parade that took place after a great celebratory competition in the largest sports stadium in Vienna! The folk parade was so grand that the eye was not capable of taking it all in, of comprehending it all. Hundreds of thousands of people participated—a huge, colorful, joyous, and enthusiastic mass of people. The parade was awash in red flags, fighting pennants, national flags, and colorful banners. The delegations from the various countries in their national costumes and in various athletic outfits added color. The famous Austrian *Schutzbund* (Socialist paramilsitary defense force) in its dark grey military style uniforms added weight and seriousness to the demonstration and reminded everyone that this was not just about play, but also about struggle. The huge crowds on the sidewalks were in as festive a mood as the marchers in the parade. They threw flowers and chocolate treats, constantly greeting the marchers. The dense columns of marchers took hours to pass. "Red Falconers" continuously ran up and down the length of the parade with pitchers of water to quench the thirst of the marchers.[2]

Following this was the Congress of the Socialist Internationale. The Bund's delegation to the Congress, ten representatives, actively participated in the debates, in the commissions, and in the plenary sessions of the Congress. The main speech on behalf of the Bund was delivered by Comrade Henryk Erlich on "The International Political Situation." He criticized the politics of a number of Socialist parties that he said were not sufficiently energetic in the struggle against the great dangers approaching. Specifically, he criticized the politics of the German Social-Democratic Party, which in its battles with the growing Hitlerite threat, displayed too little independent militancy and relied too much on assistance from German bourgeois democratic elements. In his speech, Wells, the leader of the German Social-Democratic Party, defended the politics of his party. He spoke with great self-assurance: "Berlin is not Rome," he said, and then continued ironically, "When the time comes for a fight, we will gladly welcome the battalions the Bund will send to help us." Many delegates resented Wells for this tactless remark. Sadly, his self-assurance, as we now know, turned out to be groundless. . . .

I went to the sessions of the Internationale quite often. I had been given a guest pass to the gallery. One time Comrade Raphael Abramowich[3] spotted me there, came upstairs, and took me down into the meeting hall below, among the delegates. Later he introduced me to Karl Kautsky. This old, world-famous Socialist theoretician made a great impression on me. He spoke to me for a few minutes, inquiring about the comrades in Poland in a lively, friendly manner. It was no small thing for me to meet face-to-face with Karl Kautsky, from whose writings in the form of pamphlets and books in the course of decades we, veritably trembling with awe, learned about the ideas of socialism and about the struggle for the liberation of humanity.

Maurycy Orzech[4] was with us then in Vienna, and together we explored Vienna. One time he took me on an excursion to Semmering, where the Tyrolean Alps begin. We climbed up the mountain and were dazzled by the enchantment of the sight. I ran about and could not have enough of looking at the broad, beautiful panorama one could view from many different vantage points.

When the Congress and the Olympiad were over, I stayed on an additional ten days in Vienna to acquaint myself better with the work of the District 10 *Schutzbund*. I familiarized myself with their organization and their methods. I accompanied them on their military exercises and maneuvers and on their marches. I learned a great deal from them, even though many of their practices did not apply to our particular circumstances.

I left Vienna in a cheerful mood. Like so many others, I had no idea how close for Europe and for European socialism the approaching catastrophe was. A

Figure 108. Bund delegation at the Socialist International, Vienna, 1931. In the front, from right: J. Peskin (Paris), A. L. Zelmanowitch, Noah (J. Portney), Anna Rosenthal, H. Erlich, and I. Lichtenstein. Second row: Dr. E. Sherer, Dr. Ch. Pizhitz, V. Alter, and G. Zybert. Above: M. Orzech, E. Nowogrodzki, and J. S. Hertz. From the Archives of the YIVO Institute for Jewish Research, New York.

year-and-a-half later Hitler came to power in Germany. Almost three years later, the *Schutzbund* raised its flag in armed resistance to Austrian fascism. Heroically and with glory, it fell in battle. Misfortune after misfortune fell upon Socialist and democratic Europe. Many at this time lost hope and admitted defeat. But it is clear now that those who did not lose hope and continued the fight finally smashed the black power of fascism to bits.

Notes

1. The name of various Socialist children's organizations, popular in Europe and the United States, emerging during the First and Second World Wars; the first such group was founded by Anton Tesarek, an Austrian Socialist educator.—MZ
2. David Dubinsky, president of the ILGWU (1932–1966), witnessed this Olympiad and said: "[the] highlight [of the international Socialist congress in Vienna] was a mass spectacle, a pageant in which thousands upon thousands of Austrian [and other] trade unionists took part. It was staged in a huge stadium, with at least a quarter million people watching.... I could not get it out of my mind." It inspired him, he said, to establish a Department of Recreational Activities for the ILGWU, a large part of its "social unionism." (Dubinsky and Raskin, *A Life with Labor*, New York: Simon and Schuster, 1977, 189.)
3. Raphael Abramowitch (1880–1963), revolutionary and publicist; born in Latvia, studied at Riga Polytechnic University and in 1901 joined the Bund. Began publishing in the revolutionary press in Yiddish. Arrested in 1904, 1910, and 1918. Menshevik representative to the All-Russian Central Executive Committee; a leader of the 2 ½ Internationale. After the split in the Bund in April 1920, at its Twelfth Conference, he became a founding member of the Social-Democratic Bund, basing itself on Menshevik principles. Published short works about Soviet Russia and the Bolshevik terror, as well as his memoirs, *In tsvey revolutsyes* (In Two Revolutions; 1944).—MZ
4. Maurycy Orzech (1891–1943): Polish-Jewish economist, journalist, politician, and leader of the Bund in interwar Poland; one of the commanders of the Bund during the Warsaw Ghetto Uprising.—MZ

CHAPTER 56

Street Fights with the Polish Hitlerites

The fall of 1931 was a hard one for us in Poland. On "the Jewish street," the intensified anti-Socialist battle of the Communists reached the point of planned, organized murder (e.g., the murder of baker-worker Avrom Neuerman; see chapter 60). The police harassments and the confiscation of our presses, as well as other persecutions, mounted. The terror of the pro-Pilsudski FRAC bands increased. And on top of all that, still another affliction: in the fall of 1931 the Polish antisemitic camp organized attacks on Jews in the streets throughout the country, and especially—on Jewish university students.

What caused this new outbreak of organized attacks on Jews?

A radical change came about among the Polish antisemitic groups after Hitler's great victory in the German parliamentary elections of 1930.[1] Hitler's great success in the election awakened a hope in the Polish antisemitic groups that they could also strengthen their power in Poland by pursuing a wilder, a more demagogic antisemitism than they had pursued up to now. They therefore adopted the Hitlerite methods against Jews.

For many of these young gangs, the "old-fashioned" antisemitic methods of the Endek Party were by now too mild. New, antisemitic organizations began to arise, mainly among the Polish student youth, who took the new, "modern" Hitlerite antisemitism as a model. There arose the ONR[2] (*Obóz Narodowo-Radykalny* or National-Radical Camp), the Falanga, and several more parties of this type. The differences between them were small. One of these organizations might lean more toward the oppositional Endek Party, another toward the ruling Sanacja Party. But a wild antisemitism of the Hitlerite kind united them all. They all wanted to take all civil rights from the Jews, and push the Jews out of all occupations, out of trade, out of industry, and out of Poland itself. These gangs were not satisfied to simply propagandize; they also began organizing a wild boycott of Jewish businesses, systematically terrorizing Jews, attacking them on the streets, individually and through organized mass attacks, and embittering the lives of Jewish students at the universities—all in the Hitlerite manner. It didn't take long before the whole Endek camp—the old, "classical," erstwhile "milder," antisemitic party—adopted a large part of the anti-Jewish program of the new, young, Polish Hitlerites.

The situation of the Jews worsened. The Piłsudski regime got worried that by using the new Hitlerite methods of antisemitism, the Endek faction might grow its numbers. To hold on to power, the Piłsudski camp began to compete with the Endeks in displays of antisemitism. The Jews in Poland were now more and more confronted on two sides by an escalated antisemitism. The government had from time to time to keep up appearances as the official "guardian of law and order," but, nevertheless, it did not react against the wild acts of the Hitlerite antisemites. They were afraid they would be accused of defending the Jews, and were thus happy when elements loyal to the government participated in the antisemitic incitements and acts of terror.

In the beginning of November 1931, right after the Polish universities opened, there was an outpouring of street attacks and massive assaults on Jews. In this particular wave of attacks, Polish students played a major role, with a large admixture of street thugs. The attacks broke out almost simultaneously in various university towns: Vilnius, Warsaw, Cracow, and so on. There was no doubt whatsoever that behind these coordinated attacks lay an organizing hand. The assaults resulted in scores of severely wounded and hundreds of slightly wounded Jews. In Vilnius, for example, it reached the proportions of an actual pogrom. Dr. Weinreich, renowned Yiddish philologist and Director of YIVO, was severely wounded in a street attack there.[3]

The Central Committee of the Bund immediately sent out a call to the Jewish population for an organized self-defense against the anti-Jewish attacks from the Polish antisemitic camp. The Bund immediately set about establishing a self-defense force and organizing resistance against the pogromchiks.

In Warsaw the Bund immediately organized special resistance units against the thuggish antisemitic bands. Our resistance continued for years, and did not cease until the war, the Nazi occupation, and, finally, until our great Catastrophe, when it took on totally new forms. . . .

It was a heavy responsibility organizing physical resistance against the newly arisen Polish-Hitlerite, antisemitic movement. In this respect, the attitude of the broad Bundist masses gave us much courage. At the party gatherings, our members received with great joy the news that we would go out into the streets and offer physical resistance.

The chief strength of this resistance initiative was once again the Bundist Militia. But we now reorganized and greatly expanded it. We formed larger groups consisting of Bund Militia members, along with those who were simply members of our unions. In each such group, the militia members were the core:

they kept the group together and were the first into battle. The groups were sent out to the Saxon Gardens; to Traugutta Park (mostly on Saturdays and Sundays, when Jews went there in large numbers to rest, unless we were alerted in the middle of the week that an attack was taking place); to Paderewski Park in Praga; and to the so-called "wild swim spot" on the shores of the Vistula (again only on Saturdays and Sundays, when the Jewish youth of the neighborhood would come to swim and sunbathe). Our groups would pace about and keep an eye out for what was going on all around. As soon as any of the antisemitic hooligans would start to bother Jews, they would meet with resistance from our battle groups. Sometimes these confrontations would escalate into major fights with sticks and iron gloves. Our people were under a strict prohibition against using guns, unless ordered to do so. The volunteers in the resistance groups were not always the same people, but the regular members of our militia always participated in every battle.

We encountered certain difficulties in protecting the Jewish mothers who would come to the Saxon Gardens with their little children. The antisemitic hooligans would come to the gardens during the day and fall upon the young Jewish mothers, insulting them, and even beating them, driving them and their babes and little children out of the Garden.

It was not so easy to organize resistance groups during the day, since the workers were in their factories then; taking them away from their work too often wasn't possible. To fill this void, we recruited the porters who worked in front of the "Iron Gate" (Żelazna Brama) as well as in the large covered market in Mirowski Square—in other words, from places in the vicinity of the Saxon Gardens. As soon as word reached us that antisemitic hooligans were attacking Jewish mothers and children in the Saxon Gardens, the porters ran there and defended them.

Often large scale battles would erupt in which, on our side, hundreds of workers took part. It also sometimes happened that we would find out beforehand (usually from our Polish Socialist comrades), that the "Narovtses" (members of the aforementioned ONR), were preparing a large-scale attack. We would then organize a large group of defenders and send them to the spot where the attack was expected.

I will describe a few such large-scale battles with the antisemitic hooligans.

One time news reached us that the "Narovtses" were preparing to pogromize Jews in the Saxon Garden on a certain date. Their plan was to occupy every gate of the Garden, and then when the Jews exited, they would not allow a single Jew to leave without broken bones. So we began to ready ourselves for an appropriate resistance. We didn't want it to appear, however, that this was a battle between Poles and Jews, but rather between Fascists and anti-Fascists. So we drew to our side some organized Polish workers. I went off to the slaughterhouse and mobilized a group of Jewish and Polish workers to help us in the resistance. (Among the Polish slaughterers who joined us then were Geniek Matraszek, both of the young Nowaks, and others. Among the Jewish slaughterers were Yankl Flatshazsh, several of the Kolnitshanskis, and also others.) Also accompanying us was Yoysef Gutgold, who was at that time secretary of the Jewish Slaughterers Union. Most of the group, however, were our party militiamen. Altogether, we organized a group of about 100 men. We went off to the Saxon Garden early, before the "Narovtses" were supposed to arrive, and occupied all six gates of the Garden. We took over the most important positions close to the gates, so that just in case the battle should break out and the police should come and close the gates, our people would be able, with one bound, to be on the outside.

Things happened as we expected. Around ten o'clock in the evening, the Jews started leaving to go home. The antisemitic hooligans started to attack them, at which point we emerged as if from out of the earth and gave them some of their own back, driving them off. They were not expecting such resistance. They became confused and began to run away in a panic. One of them became so frightened that, as he ran, he fell into the water in the fountain in the middle of the Garden. A large group of the hooligans ran away through the gate to Piłsudski Square, where the exit led to the wealthy Polish neighborhood. But there our Polish comrades awaited them who gave them what was coming to them. Then the hooligans ran to another gate, but there too they received blows. That evening they had something to remember for a long time to come.

The police arrived. They closed the gates and began arresting people. But very few of our people were arrested. Because we had positioned ourselves close to the exits, most of us succeeded in running off as soon as the police showed up.

Some time after this, we received notice that the Narovtses were preparing a big attack, this time not just in the Saxon Garden, but also in the streets surrounding it. We again prepared a large contingent of resistors who concentrated themselves in and around the square in front of the Iron Gate to the Garden. Our plan was to lure the hooligans into the square enclosed on three sides, block their path on the fourth side, and, as soon as we had them thus trapped, to engage them in battle and give them a lesson they would not soon forget.

Before nightfall, when we expected them, we sent out some of us to wander about the streets that led to the Garden. We figured that when the hooligans would see some Jews walking about unhurriedly, they would not be able to contain themselves and would attack them. We instructed these "wanderers" not to offer any resistance, but to flee to the square in front of the Iron Gate. We were certain that the hooligans would pursue them. Sure enough, when we had a goodly number of the ONR hooligans inside the square, and they went into the Garden, we emerged from the surrounding hiding places, surrounded them on all sides, and in the subsequent fight, wounded quite a number of them, enough so that we had to call out emergency first aid for them. Again we demonstrated that Jewish courage is not nonexistent and that we can offer the antisemites an effective resistance.

A few days after the big fight with the ONR hooligans, I was arrested. I was charged by the investigating commissar with "terrorizing Warsaw" and told they would be sending me to Bereza Kartuska (the Polish concentration camp that was established according to the Hitlerite model, and where the arrestees were tortured, similar to the Nazi camps). I succeeded in sending out a note to the Party about the danger that was hanging over me. The Party immediately secured interventions by prominent lawyers and influential personages. These interventions eventually succeeded, and I was freed after a few days.

I must add here that the resistance did not limit itself to the members of our organized groups. Jewish working people from the surrounding neighborhoods always joined our ranks and helped drive off the antisemitic hooligans. Some of these people had become quite well known to us because they were always coming to our aid. A sort of "united front" formed between the Bundist Militia and the simple, ordinary Jewish working people from the neighborhoods who helped us fight off the antisemitic hooligans.

Things did not go so well in the other big park where the Warsaw Jewish population went to get some fresh air—the Traugutta Park. The park was situated not far from the Yiddish quarter of Muranowska, Miła, Stawki, and Smocza, but lay hard by a purely Polish neighborhood. On one side was the Vistula, on the other side, Żoliborz, a purely Polish quarter, and on a third side, the neighborhood of Mostowa and Rybaki, a part of Old Town that was also heavily populated by Poles. On the fourth side was Muranów, where the already mentioned Jewish quarter began.

In Traugutta Park the antisemitic hooligans could easily and quickly get reinforcements from the nearby Polish streets, from which they themselves probably came. On the Sabbaths, when the Park was filled with the Jewish poor from the Muranowsla-Mila-Smocza neighborhood, the hooligans would come into the Park and fall upon the Jews. Big fights broke out between us and them, but more than once they were stronger than us, and we had to retreat, because, as I said, they could easily get reinforcements from the nearby Polish streets. Often Polish workers would accompany us and help us put up a resistance, covering our retreat when it was necessary. But we never gave up the fight there. We used to show up every Saturday and Sunday, and from the time we organized ourselves to fight back; there was never a time that the antisemitic hooligans did not encounter our resistance whenever and wherever they began beating Jews.

The police? They did not protect those being attacked. Most of the time, the police were not on the spot when the beatings took place. If they did happen to be present at a time when a beating was taking place, they were more likely to arrest those being beaten than those doing the beating.

And so it stretched on for months and years until deep into the summer of 1939, when Hitler had already assembled his troops hard by the Polish border.

Notes

1. The elections of 1930 in Germany made the Nazi Party the second largest party in Germany, with 18.3% of the vote (the Social-Democratic Party was the largest party, with 24.5% of the vote). In elections prior to that, the Nazis had never polled more than 2.6% of the vote.—MZ
2. A virulently antisemitic, fascist party, its members referred to as *Narovtses* or as *Oenerowcy*.—MZ
3. Max Weinreich (1894–1969): Born in Kuldiga, Latvia, then part of Russia; completed his doctorate in linguistics in 1923 at Marburg University; Yiddish linguist, literary scholar, public intellectual, the driving force behind YIVO; the impetus behind an impressive series of academic publications in Yiddish by himself and others; author of a monumental *History of the Yiddish Language*; member of the Bund.—MZ

CHAPTER 57

The Battles Over the Boycotting of Jewish Businesses

Along with the constant street attacks on Jews, the Hitlerized Polish antisemites began an active boycott of Jewish businesses.

The call for an economic boycott of Jews was nothing new in Poland. With the slogan, "Swój do Swego" ("Our Own to Our Own"), that is, "Poles Should Buy Only from Poles," as revenge against Jews for voting for the Socialist candidate Jagiełło and unseating the nationalist, antisemitic candidate, Kucharzewski, the call for an anti-Jewish economic boycott never left the pages of the right-wing Polish press. But now the Polish Hitlerites began to conduct an organized boycott in an entirely different way. They terrorized Polish customers and prevented them physically from entering and shopping in Jewish businesses. They especially pursued this tactic against the Jewish businesses in the strictly Polish neighborhoods of the city.

As is well known, the great Warsaw commercial center of Nalewki-Gęsia-Franciszkańska Streets (also the largest commercial center in all of Poland) was entirely Jewish. In addition, however, there were many Jewish businesses in the Polish neighborhoods, especially in the prominent, central, Polish commercial street, Marszałkowska. Also, practically the entire book trade business in Warsaw (especially the selling of new and used textbooks, as well as rare books) lay in Jewish hands and was concentrated on one street, Świętokrzyska, a narrow street that cut through Marszałkowska. Almost all the bookstores on this street belonged to Jews. Some of them had been there for over 100 years and had contributed much historically to the development of the Polish book trade. At the beginning of the school year, the street would be packed with students buying or exchanging new and used textbooks.

The *Oenerowcy* posted pickets in front of the stores on Świętokrzyska Street and in front of the Jewish stores on Marszałkowska, forcibly preventing customers from entering the shop, sometimes even falling upon the customers and beating them. The calls would come in from all sides to the Bund Secretariat asking them to come and help drive away the picketing hooligans, who were preventing Polish customers from entering Jewish shops. Storeowners would call, as well as ordinary people, appealing to the Bund to "do something." We took the position that this was not about securing the profits of the Jewish shopkeepers, but of protecting the civil rights of Jews. We decided to put up a fight against the hooligans and their antisemitic picketing of Jewish businesses.

We encountered many difficulties in carrying this out. The stores were open and were picketed during the day, at a time when our militiamen, who were, of course, all workers, were at work. Nevertheless when the pickets in a certain place became particularly numerous and aggressive and we received urgent phone calls asking for help, saying that something was about to happen, we relieved some of our militiamen from their jobs and sent them to fight off the hooligans. Such calls, however, were coming more and more often, and we couldn't take the militiamen away from their jobs so frequently: they were practically all family men and had to support a wife and children. Absenting themselves too often from their work could result in their losing their jobs.

True, the Jewish shopkeepers being picketed would gladly have paid the workers whatever they lost in pay, and even more. But we didn't want that—that would have had, we thought, a demoralizing effect. The resistance to the antisemitic attacks had to have a purely political and ideological character. The slightest breakdown in this particular could have brought a great deal of harm, and so we therefore categorically rejected any thought of taking financial help from the shopkeepers suffering from the boycott.

But we found a way out of this difficulty. We organized unemployed workers for this purpose. We kept them on alert all day in our *Arbeter Vinkl* on Przejazd 9, and we sent them out to mount a resistance against the pickets whenever we got an urgent call requesting help. But since we were keeping these unemployed workers in our meeting hall all day, we had to feed them, and even simple fare for several dozen people every day was a severe financial burden for our party treasury. We could have easily gotten help from the shopkeepers for this, but we didn't want to do that either. We met these expenses ourselves.

In this way we gave no peace to the picketers in front of the Jewish businesses. We did not permit them to carry out, undisturbed, their antisemitic terror and boycott action against Jews, and we often succeeded in driving them away.

CHAPTER 58

The "Ghetto Benches" in the Universities

Polish Hitlerism had an especially strong influence on the Polish university students. The gangs of hooligans that would attack Jews on the street consisted mainly of university students (with a considerable admixture of underworld characters). But in addition to their attacks on Jews in general, they threw themselves with especial rage on their Jewish classmates. They decided to establish a ghetto for Jews in the university classes. They set up several benches on the left side of the classrooms and tried to force the Jewish students to sit there on these so-called "ghetto benches."

The Jewish students strongly resisted. Instead of sitting on the "ghetto benches," they stood during the lectures. The antisemitic Polish students wanted to forcibly make them sit there. This led to dreadful scenes in the universities, culminating in frequent fights. They fell upon and beat the Jewish students, even women, till blood flowed. The university administrators, and most of the professors (some quietly, some openly), were on the side of the hooligans. The professors who had the courage to speak out against the attacks were subjected to insult, abuse, and even physical attacks.[1]

In the general battle that the Jewish students fought against the "ghetto benches," the Bundist student association, known in Warsaw by the name *Ringen* (*Links*, as in a chain) played an active role. *Ringen* was not very big, but they were a select group on a highly developed intellectual and political level. In addition, their student association gave us an additional source of pride. The grown children of our leaders that were university students all belonged to the Bund's *Ringen* group. The group not only participated in all the defense and protest actions of the entire Jewish student body, but also carried out its own. It clearly expressed the Bund's approach to the problem of struggle against antisemitism and fascism in Poland, working closely with the ZNMS (*Związek Niezależnej Młodzieży Soc-*

jalistycznej, Independent Union of Socialist Youth), the PPS's student organization. They were happy to work with the Bund's student youth association.

Often when our student group would come out on its own in a fight with the Fascist Polish students—an unequal battle against a huge mass of Polish antisemitic students—our party militia would come to their aid. One time, for example, the *Ringen* group decided to distribute a flyer at the entrance to the University of Warsaw with an appeal directed at the Polish students. It was clear that the antisemitic Polish students would resist the distribution of the flyers, and it would most certainly come to blows. The *Ringen* group, therefore, requested a group of Bundist militiamen at the entrance gate where the flyers were to be distributed.

On the morning of the day the flyers were to be distributed, a group of our militiamen went off to the university. In the quad on the other side of the gate were gathered small groups of anti-Jewish students who were in fact preparing to attack our young comrades. They noticed our group of militiamen, however, and probably understanding we were there to defend them, lost their courage to attack. In the meantime our group of students distributed all its flyers and left peacefully. As soon as they had gone, from a far corner of the university quad, a mob of students suddenly appeared. It turned out that a larger group of *Oenerowcy* had assembled in the auditorium and had readied themselves to attack our comrades. Fortunately, they were too late; we avoided a fight with them.

A similar situation occurred shortly thereafter at the Politechnika. But there it did result in a fight. The Bundist students distributed the flyers in front of the Polytechnic. Among them was Mikhl Klepfisz, the later hero of the Warsaw Ghetto Uprising. At the Politechnika the hooligans attacked our young comrades, and we defended them. A big fight broke out. The hooligan students outnumbered us greatly, however, and we barely escaped in one piece.

It thus often became necessary for the party militia to accompany our comrade-students, who were small in number, to help them fight off mobs of antisemitic Polish students.

Figure 109. Zalmen Frydrych addressing a *Tsukunft* meeting in Warsaw, 1930s. In July of 1942, disguised as a Polish railway worker, he smuggled himself into Treblinka, reporting back to the ghetto inhabitants what was happening to the Jews there. Fought in the Warsaw Ghetto Uprising; did not survive. From the Archives of the YIVO Institute for Jewish Research, New York.

Figure 110. *Tsukunft* cyclists during the first national *Tsukunft* convention in Warsaw, 1932. From the Archives of the YIVO Institute for Jewish Research, New York.

Figure 111. Zalmen Frydrych's Warsaw Ghetto identity card. From the Archives of the YIVO Institute for Jewish Research, New York.

Note

1. Among the courageous professors who were not afraid to defend the Jewish students, I remember the names of: Mieczysław, Szymanowski, Kridl, Kulczyński, and also Bartel, the former Piłsudski premier.—BG

CHAPTER 59

My Son at the Skif Camp

In the Summer of 1931, for the first time, both of our youth organizations, SKIF and *Tsukunft*, organized their summer camps in the scouting manner, living deep in a forest, sleeping in canvas tents, cooking on improvised stoves made out of stone, without any kind of service provided, that is, doing everything for themselves. Our young people had experienced summer camps for a long time, but this was the first time they were going to experience this kind of scouting summer camp.

Our summer camps were very popular with the entire Bundist youth. Every SKIFist or *Tsukunft*ist dreamt of going to one of our summer camps.

When the spring of 1932 arrived, my son, Janek, who was then 12 years old, requested permission to go to the SKIF summer camp. This decision was not an easy one for us. Janek was still, after all, just a child, our only child, raised tenderly and with much love. How could we now let him go so far away? True, he had already been many times to the Medem Sanitarium (see chapter 44), but things were different there: the children were under the supervision of teachers, pedagogues, caregivers, and a large number of personnel. But in this camp, the children lived in the woods, open on all sides, cooking and managing things on their own, and standing guard at night in the middle of the forest. Let me admit the truth: a father's heart trembled, as did his mother's. But we took courage. We allowed him to go.

A couple of weeks later, I went to the camp as a guest to visit my Janek. It was in a forest near Gąbin, not far from the Vistula. I went out past the town, following the directions. I soon came upon a thick pine forest. After walking for a time, I saw at a distance white canvas tents peeking out from between the pine trees. I picked up my pace. After all, for the first time, I was going to see a SKIF camp, about which such wonderful stories were being told.

The camp did in fact make a deep impression on me. The canvas tents were arrayed in a semicircle around a large clearing in the middle of the forest. In the center of the clearing, encircled by a little fence, stood a flagstaff topped with a red flag. Not far from the flagstaff was the campfire pit, surrounded by an amphitheatre with seating dug into the earth. Farther off I spotted tables and chairs constructed of raw lumber and supported on wooden legs set in the ground. A little farther off stood the "kitchen," constructed of rocks and bricks. Everything was decorated with greenery and fragrant with youth and freshness. Groups of friends, SKIFists, almost all of whom knew me, crowded around, encircling me, happy to see me. But all the while I was looking around, searching for my Janek.

Then I spotted him, and my heart sank when I saw his clothes: dirty, blackened, his shirt torn, his trousers in tatters. He ran right over to me. He could tell by my look what I was thinking. He defended himself, explaining that today he had drawn kitchen duty as cook. He had stood at the kettle by the fire and had not yet had time to change. I felt a little better. Then the Commander of the camp, Yoysef Brumberg, and the Vice-Commander, Emanuel Pat[1] (already then a medical student), approached. We talked about all the marvels of the camp.

I stayed the night. The Commander decided that that night Janek would stand the first watch with me, from 10 to 12 midnight (this was an exception—the younger children were not assigned watches at night). I spent time with the children around the campfire. The singing around the campfire, the songs echoing deep into the forest, and the tongues of fire reflecting onto the flag in the forest night all made a deep impression on me. The singing at the nightly roll call when the SKIFists were assembled standing at attention around the flag deepened my feelings of exaltation. I thought to myself: What a shame that neither I, nor any of the children of my generation, ever had such a childhood experience.

Everyone soon went to sleep in their tents and everything grew still. Janek and I took over the watch. I will never forget the feeling of pride in this child who, for the first time in his life, was given the duty of standing watch. Several times he asked me, "Bernard," (my son always called me by my first name), "do you have your revolver?" "Is it loaded?" "Give it to me to hold for a little." He was constantly warning me: "There are thieves in the forest. They can quietly steal their way in and take everything. We must be on our guard!"

All his senses were strained and his fantasy worked overtime. Every few minutes he would say to me, "Bernard, did you hear that?" "Yes, I heard it," I would answer. It was a little breeze that had whistled through the branches. He already imagined that someone was stealing through the trees. Soon, again, "Bernard, did you hear that?" A little branch had broken off a tree, or a little creature had run by, and in the stillness of the forest night it seemed to him that someone had leapt from a tree. At every rustle he imagined that now the thieves or murderers had made their final lunge to attack the camp, and he constantly wanted to grab his whistle to sound an alarm. I could barely restrain him.

In the course of two hours, as we walked around the camp that night, he told me about life at the camp. The camp was divided into groups, each group under the leadership of a SKIF assistant. He, Janek, belonged to Khayke Levine's group (she was one of the most interesting SKIF activists; she perished in the Soviet Union during the war). He also told me about the program of daily activities, about the tasks assigned, the discussions, the hikes, etc. He was very proud of it all.

The next morning I went off to visit the *Tsukunft* camp, only a few kilometers from the SKIF camp. Coming to welcome me was Pinkhes Rosenberg, an activist with the Bundist youth section of the Textile Union and a member of the Warsaw *Tsukunft* committee (his father, a long-time Bundist, was a member of the Board of Directors of the Printers Union and died in the twenties; he himself, Pinkhes, and his sister, Sarah—also a *Tsunkunft*ist—were working at the Medem Sanitarium during the war; both perished together with all the children of the Sanitarium in August 1942). He was in charge of purchasing provisions for the camp, so on his way back to the camp from shopping in town, he picked me up and gave me a ride to the *Tsukunft* camp.

The *Tsukunft* camp was arranged just like the SKIF camp. I was warmly welcomed. Henokh Russ, the Assistant Director, welcomed me (he perished while

Figure 112. SKIF youngsters in their Bund summer camp. From the Archives of the YIVO Institute for Jewish Research, New York.

attempting an escape from a Nazi concentration camp in Skarżysko-Kamienna). I responded to their greeting. I remember as if it were today what I said. I spoke of colors: of the blue shirts and blouses and the red neckerchiefs worn by the campers, reflected in the flag; of the greenery of the needles in the pine trees; of the lake (the *Tsukunft* camp was located on a high shore overlooking a small lake encircled by a thick pine forest).

In the evening I went back to Warsaw. The almost two days I spent in 1932 at the two Bund youth camps left a deep and lasting impression on me.

Note

1. Emanuel Pat became a physician with a practice in New York and remained a Bundist. He was the son of the distinguished Bundist leader and author, Jacob Pat.

CHAPTER 60

The Bakers Union Turns Away from the Communists; The Murder of Neuerman

The Communist attacks on the Bund and the wild strikes they were constantly calling against the will of the workers went on for a long time. Eventually this began to provoke a strong antipathy from the workers belonging to their unions. They became fed up with these strikes that made no sense, having not the slightest chance of success—strikes called for the sole purpose of breaking the Socialist unions and of sending glowing reports to Moscow. In those unions in which the Communists had no influence, their destructive work was resisted with every ounce of strength, but in those that were in their hands, it was they themselves that wrecked their own unions with their ill-considered strikes.

A great victim of these ill-advised Communist tactics was the Bakers Union, which, as a result, lost all control over the baker's labor market. The whole system of an organized distribution of *fayranter* (see chapter 23), for example, fell apart. Every worker did as he pleased. The bakeries were full of unorganized workers. Of course, there had always been bakeries over which their union had had absolutely no control. But now it had gotten much worse. The wages of the bakery workers fell sharply.

At this time, around the fall of 1931, a group of independent (nonparty-affiliated) bakery workers came to the Warsaw Central Council of the Jewish trade union asking them to take over the union and reorganize it. In other words, they requested the Bund take over the union again and put it back on its feet. It must be admitted that this suggestion did not, as it were, drop from the sky. The whole time the union found itself under Communist control, the Bundist group among them was in very active opposition. The Bundists did not leave the union, remaining loyal members and carrying out all the decisions of the union, but at the same time conducting a decisive struggle against Communist domination. At all the meetings they spoke out, unhesitatingly pointing out the ruinous effect of the erroneous dealings and decisions of the Communist leadership. The chairman of the Bundist group, Melech Tsiglman—along with Yankl Frimerman and other activist Bundists, along with Melech Teyvel's (Melech Friedman) an independent, nonparty member, now in America—never tired in their criticism of the harmful direction of the union. But it took quite a number of years before a large number of the bakery workers convinced themselves of how right the Bundists had been. They then came to the Bundist group suggesting they all go together to the Bund Central Committee and request to be taken back. (When the Communists captured the Bakers Union, under Communist Party pressure, the union had withdrawn from the Warsaw Central Council of Jewish Trade Unions.)

In the end, a meeting of the bakery workers was called, and a new Bakers Union was formed with its temporary headquarters at Leszno 19 (in the offices of the Leather Workers Union), later settling into the offices of the Retail Clerks Union on Mylna 7[1] (the Retail Clerks Union had in the meantime moved to larger quarters at Zamenhof 5). Salek (Zalmen) Lichtenstein—who had come to Warsaw in 1925 from Wloclawek, where he had been an active *Tsukunft*ist—was recruited to act as Secretary of the newly formed Bakers Union. In Warsaw he had thrown himself into trade union work and shown himself to be a capable and energetic trade union organizer. He had become Secretary of the Executive Board of the Printers Union, and after that, Secretary of the Leather Workers Union. Now he was being given the position of Secretary of the newly formed Bakers Union. He was confronted by a difficult task and a bitter struggle with the Communists. He carried out this task well. (He is now in America and an official of the Jewish Labor Committee.)

When the new Bakers Union was formed, the Communists fell into a terrible rage. They reacted in their usual manner, with a new series of attacks on the Bund and insulting tirades. When this had little effect, they began threatening that "heads would roll." It quickly turned out they meant this seriously.

The newly formed Bakers Union quickly reinstituted the old, normal, trade union activities. First, the union reestablished a just system of distributing the *fayranter* to the unemployed bakers (under the Communists this was no more than a fiction). To ensure that this was being observed, the members of the Executive Board of the newly formed union would visit the bakeries every night to make sure that the unemployed bakers that were sent to work there were in fact permitted to work. One of the most active members of the Executive Board, Avrom Neuerman—not a member of any party—on a Saturday night on the November 7, 1931, was doing the rounds of a series of bakeries for this purpose. Suddenly, as he emerged from a bakery on Miła Square, a band of Communists fell upon him, cursed and insulted him, and one Communist youngster (not a baker) smacked him hard and ran quickly off. This was clearly a warning that the Communists were preparing something more serious.

The next morning, Sunday, we were on the alert all day in the offices of the union. At nightfall word came that a gang of Communist strong-arms and street toughs were seen gathering on Miła Street near Tevye "Smoluch's" (Tevye Leszno's) bakery. Salek Lichtenstein and I went there, along with several others. We looked all around and saw no one. We entered the bakery and questioned the bakers. They said they had seen nothing at all suspicious. We went back to the union hall, glad to know it was a false alarm. But, in fact, it was not!

That same Sunday, after Saturday's attack, when Neuerman had ended his work at the bakery, he didn't head home, instead going again on his rounds to the various bakeries. It was around seven o'clock at night. When he emerged from Smocza Street onto Miła Street, he spotted a gang of Communists. He apparently understood they were probably waiting for him, so he quickly turned back to Tevye's bakery on Miła 59. And there, close to the entryway to the courtyard in which Tevye's bakery was located, he was struck by a hail of bullets, falling in the street in a pool of blood. Two of our comrades who happened to be near and heard the shooting, immediately ran over to the spot and, seeing Neuerman lying in a pool of blood, quickly hailed a taxi and took him to the hospital. He lost consciousness on the way there, and died as they were bringing him into the emergency room before a doctor could get to him. This innocent Communist victim was only 32 years old, leaving a widow and two small children . . .

The news of this terrible murder quickly spread to all the union halls. It is easy to imagine the kind of outrage this crime provoked. For a long time after this, I could not forgive myself for leaving so quickly from the spot we had been alerted to and where we had been told Communist thugs were seen gathering. We had a strong aversion to all these fights and were happy to find it was a false alarm. It did not occur to us that the Communists, having spotted us from a distance, hid themselves, lying in wait for their victim to appear.

The union, and also the party, was now confronted with a painful question. How to react to this cold-blooded murder?

After an exchange of views and discussion by Bund leaders, we came to the unanimous conclusion that this time we must reject revenge, no matter how just such an act might be, because it did not lie in the best interests of the whole movement. It was clear to us what the purpose of this coldly calculated murder was. They wanted to create a two-sided blood bath that would lead to chaos, to the demoralization and destruction of the newly formed Bakers union. Their goal was, that if the Bakers Union had left them, then it was better that there be no Bakers Union at all; let it drown in blood. Our goal, on the other hand, was a very different one. We wanted to strengthen the new Bakers Union. The Communists also wanted to frighten the workers that were leaving them, making them fear they might pay with their lives. The murder had just the opposite effect. The bakery workers left the Communist Bakers Union faster and in greater numbers than ever before, their union falling totally apart. Slowly and systematically the new union established itself firmly and brought back normal working conditions to the bakeries.

The police immediately began an investigation and sought the murderer. In the middle of December he was caught in Gdańsk (Danzig), where he ran right after the murder. He was a certain Simkhe Luksenburg (he was called "Simkhe Parkh"), a bakery worker, a "fourth hand" (see chapter 48), and a Communist. When he was brought back to Warsaw, he confessed to the investigators that he did in fact commit the murder, but that he did it on the orders of Melech Tsiglman, the chairman of the newly formed (Bundist) union, and by Fishl Kaufman, a nonparty member of the union. Despite how crazy this sounds, the police took these wild accusations seriously and arrested Comrades Tsiglman and Kaufman, charging them with organizing the murder of their own close comrade who had, together with them, organized the new union!

It took some time to demonstrate the absurdity of these wild accusations, and on December 24 Comrades Tsiglman and Kaufman were freed. The murderer Luksenburg was tried and sentenced to ten years in prison.

For a long time thereafter, the widow and orphans of Comrade Neuerman were supported by the Bakers Union.

Note

1. This street, near modern Nowolipie Street, no longer exists.—MR

CHAPTER 61

Nathan (Nokhem) Chanin's Visit to Warsaw

In 1928, during Nathan Chanin's[1] vist to Warsaw, he came to stay with me as my guest. He brought us regards from one of Lucia's relatives in America, the Secretary of the United Hebrew Trades,[2] Morris Feinstone.

In honor of Chanin, the Central Committee of the Trade Union Council organized a conference of the executives and trade commissions of the trade unions. The Communists decided not to allow Chanin to speak. They mobilized themselves mightily for the conference. This was not hard for them because in some of the unions the Communists had a vocal minority; also Communists sat on many of the trade commissions. By reason of this they had a legal right to be at the conference. In addition, they succeeded in smuggling in quite a number of Communists who had no official right to be there. They came, of course, with the sole purpose of creating tumult and passing a resolution that Chanin not be permitted to speak in Warsaw to any meeting of workers. They even put out a flyer saying that the "Social Fascist, Chanin," came to Warsaw to visit his "comrade Social Fascists, the Bundists," and that the "disgrace" of having this "Social Fascist" speak to a workers meeting should not be allowed to happen!

The conference, to which several hundred people came, was held in the union hall of the Transport Workers Union on Nalewki 2 (Simon's Arcade). When the chairman, Comrade N. Boymgartn announced that he was giving the floor to the guest, Comrade Chanin, an outcry arose. "He will not speak." Every time it quieted down somewhat and the chairman again gave the floor to Chanin, the shouting began anew. This lasted about 15 minutes. The chairman appealed to the Communists that they allow the conference to proceed peacefully, but they laughed at this.

At this point I got up on the platform and warned the Communists that if they did not immediately quiet down, they would be ejected from the hall, and

I gave them 5 minutes. When the five minutes were up, the chairman again gave the floor to Chanin, and the Communists again raised a tumult. We interrupted the meeting for ten minutes. We requested the whole audience to remain in their places. We used the time to scrutinize the hall so we knew who the main shouters were. We ejected them from the hall. The few professional thugs the Communists had brought along could do nothing because we asked the crowd to stay quietly in place, so the gang of thugs could not extricate themselves from the crowd to do their dirty work. They didn't dare beat up anyone openly in front of all these people. They were, after all, vastly outnumbered. Before long we had ejected all the Communist hecklers. The chairman called the conference back into session. Chanin could now speak undisturbed with no further interruption. There were still a few Communists remaining in the hall, but they now kept quiet. The conference concluded in an orderly fashion.

But this was not the end. One of our comrades, a militiaman, had a brother who was a Communist, and he told me that according to some talk he overheard from his brother, we should be prepared for the Communists to mount a serious attack on Chanin. Through other comrades with direct or indirect contacts in Communist circles through family and friends, I began to look into the matter. The planned attack was confirmed from many sources. I relayed this to our party leaders. We decided to guard Chanin, but we didn't tell him why.

Figure 113. H. Erlich and V. Alter with N. Chanin (standing to the right behind Noyekh, seated in the center), S. Dubnow-Erlich (to Noyekh's left), and the Kastelanskis.

With the excuse that I wanted to show him Warsaw, I spent entire days with him. He was, in fact, greatly interested in Warsaw. I showed him the poor Jewish neighborhoods, the great Jewish centers of commerce, the Polish quarter, and the interesting Warsaw old town. He never suspected that I was, in fact, guarding him. In addition, some of our militiamen were tailing us, and since he didn't know them, he didn't notice. When I had to leave him, the militiamen would stay and guard him, keeping their distance. At seven in the morning, several of our militiamen were already ready and waiting in the vicinity of his hotel. Several times a day, each group of militiamen would be relieved by a fresh group. Even when he was invited to a private party, they followed him at a distance. And so he was in fact well guarded. We never told Chanin about this, even at the time of his departure from Warsaw.

Chanin still had one more public appearance to make for us in Warsaw. It just so happened that during the time he was with us in Warsaw, a regional convention was to take place of the youth Bund organization, *Tsukunft*. Several thousand *Tsukunft*ists from a large number of cities and towns situated not far from Warsaw came together in Warsaw for several days. The festive opening ceremonies of the convention took place in the sports stadium of the PPS sports organization, SKRA (*Robotniczy Klub Sportowy*—Workers Sports Club). Chanin spoke to the thousands of young Bundists gathered there.

Notes

1. Nathan Chanin (1885–1965): Bundist from an early age; arrested several times; almost executed by firing squad in 1905 (he talked them out of it); put in irons and sent to Siberia for an 8-year sentence; escaped; arrived in NY in 1912. In 1921, in opposition to the Comintern, joined the *Jewish Socialist Farband of the Socialist Party of America*, becoming its General Secretary. Led the fight against Communist takeovers in the Workmen's Circle in the twenties. Delegate to the International Socialist Congress in Brussels, 1928. From 1936–1952, Educational Director of the Workmen's Circle. Elected General Secretary of the Workmen's Circle in 1952. Published many books and articles in Yiddish.—MZ
2. United Hebrew Trades, founded by Yiddish Branch 8 of the Socialist Labor Party and some Jewish unions in 1888. Morris Hillquit was one of its founding members. By 1910 it had 106 unions and 150,000 workers, growing to 200,000 by 1922, and to 250,000 by 1938. It joined with other unions and organizations in 1934 to form the Jewish Labor Committee, which was heavily influenced by the Bund, electing Bundist Baruch Charney Vladek as its first president.—MZ

CHAPTER 62

Three Bloody Attacks in One Day

The Communists now turned their attention to the Garment Workers Union. This was the largest trade union in Warsaw, and the political influence of the Bund on it was firm and decisive. This largest and strongest of the Jewish unions was, therefore, like a thorn in their side. As a result, they continually fomented strikes, one more senseless and galling than another.

A large garment factory in Warsaw belonged to a certain Wykinski. The factory had contracts with the military to produce uniforms, hats, etc. With over 100 workers, it was a large enterprise for Warsaw. All the workers in the factory belonged to the Garment Workers Union, with only two or three workers (truly, no more!) belonging to the competing Communist union. Miniscule and rickety, the Communists maintained it solely as a springboard from which to carry out their battles with the Garment Workers Union and the Bund.

In the winter of 1932 the Communists—in the name of their 2-3 hangers-on!—declared a strike in the factory, once again, over the heads of the factory workers and their union. Of course the workers in the Garment Workers Union did not want to hear of this Communist-imposed strike. The Communists came, therefore, with their thugs and—as at other of their similar strikes—tried to force the workers to leave work and go out on strike. During the first few days, as long as the conflict was being carried out internally, we did not get involved. But when we saw that the Communists were daily bringing their thugs—the coal haulers Simkhe Matshe, Dovid Milner, and Leybenyu Bereysh—to the factory in order to terrorize the workers of Wykinski's factory, the Bundist Militia, at the request of the Garment Workers Union, now had to get involved. The conflicts and hostile encounters around the factory occurred daily, growing more violent with every passing day.

On a certain morning, on February, 26, 1932, heavy fighting broke out close to the factory, on Żelazna Street. The fighting quickly escalated to shooting from street to street, lasting all day, until by dusk the fighting had moved all the way to Mariańska and Twarda Streets, a long way off from the factory.

The peculiar attitude of the police again became apparent. Despite the fact the fighting was going on in broad daylight and, in addition, in very busy streets, no policeman could anywhere be seen to put a stop to the fighting (see chapter 34).

At nightfall I came home, tired and exhausted, with my nerves very much on edge from the whole day's fighting and shooting. I was then living on Senatorska Street, near Miodowa Street. I shut myself in my room and lay down to sleep, but all night couldn't shut my eyes thinking about this tragic situation the Communists had dragged us into. Worker solidarity had always been a sacred principle among us, a fundamental precept in our credo—and now the Communists were forcing us to carry on a daily fight between worker and worker. Reason told us we could not act otherwise: the Communists wanted to defeat us and would stop at no means, not even at murder itself. It would have been more than foolish on our side to stand passively by and watch as the Communists wrecked our movement and pogromized our members: we had to fight back. But every time the Communists forced us to fight back in this manner, we did it with a heavy heart, with the greatest reluctance, as a bitter necessity from which we could not—although we would have wanted to—escape.

As I was lying thus thinking about this tragic situation, the door suddenly opened and Yosl Gutgold came in. I immediately understood that something serious had happened. In one breath, Yosl told me that just now the Communists had broken into our party club at Przejazd 9 (the *Arbeter Vinkl*—Workers Corner). They had attacked our comrades in front of the entrance and on the steps and had shot through the door to the club. We both immediately ran off to party headquarters. When we got to the end of Długa Street, across the street from Przejazd, we saw several well-known Communists on the street; when they saw us, they quickly disappeared.

What had happened was this:

At dusk, when there were still a few people there, the Communists attacked the Bund club. On the steps they encountered several young *Tsukunft* activists. The Communists attacked them. One of them (Shtaynman) received a deep stab wound and two bullet wounds; the other (Yablonke) received a bullet wound and no less than nine stab wounds. Fortunately, the bullets did not wound them severely. Their cries and the shots, heard from the stairs, caused an alarm in the *Vinkl*. The few people who happened to be there at the moment—Yankl Goldshal, an employee of the *Arbeter Vinkl*, now in Paris; Shepsl Mosak, who ran the buffet; Yosl Gutgold; and others—ran to the windows that looked out on the street and spotted the gang of Communists trying to break down the door. They ran to the door, locked it, and with all their strength, leaned against it to prevent the Communists from breaking down the door. The Communists did indeed try to break it down, but when they failed in that, they fired shots at the door, continued to make a scene, finally exiting to the street.

This was—except for the fighting around the garment factory—the first bloody Communist attack on this day.

Then came the second.

That same day, around eight thirty in the evening, Hershl Himmelfarb, the Secretary of the Garment Workers Union, was going, together with Benyek Vaytsman, a *Tsukunft* activist and Vice-President of the youth section of the union, to the union offices. At the corner of Przejazd and Nowolipki, the Communists fell upon Hershl from behind, stabbed him several times, and as he was lying on the ground bloodied, beat and stabbed him some more.

He was quickly removed to Menakhem Rosenboym's apartment, the Chair of the Warsaw Garment Workers Union (now in New York), on Karmelicka 6, near where the attack took place. A doctor was sent for immediately who administered first aid. Hershl's lungs missed being punctured by a hair.

But the Communists still were not satisfied.

Soon came their third attack. Sometime later they came upon Hershl Zegas on Nowolipki Street, a functionary of the Garment Workers Union (now in New York, an official of the Workmen's Circle) as he was heading to work at the union offices. They threw themselves upon him, beat him violently, stabbed him, and cracked his skull, leaving him lying there in that condition. Zegas was laid up for many weeks, his very life, in the beginning, hanging in the balance.

The news about these various Communist attacks, especially the attempt to kill Hershl Himmelfarb, spread quickly among the Jewish workers. Their wrath, especially among the thousands of garment workers, was enormous. The party had to exert enormous pressure to keep the Bundists from taking revenge. This question of revenge also was on the agenda at a session of the Warsaw Central Committee, because from all sides Bundists demanded vengeance. Despite some members of the Central Committee who were also voices for revenge, and although among the members of the Garment Workers Union there were also calls for revenge, the Committee decided to forbid any acts of vengeance. Also in the leadership of the union there was a strong mood to pay the Communists back for their terrible acts of terror. We, however, put pressure on the union not to allow it. The party took a firm stand that acts of revenge could only worsen matters, and that their murderous attacks strongly compromise the Communists, and that in itself was punishment enough.

And so it was in fact. No acts of revenge were carried out—just as before in the case of Neuerman.

We were a disciplined body.

CHAPTER 63

Temptations and Doubts

Every Bundist activist, every party professional, had his worries and his troubles. Everyone had to endure difficult struggles, and everyone was beset with dangers from every side. The particular circumstances in which I had to work unsettled me more than once.

I had no doubts about the importance and the justice of the task with which the party had entrusted me: to ensure the physical safety of our lives and of our movement against all our enemies. But I sometimes asked myself: Am I personally strong enough to carry out such a difficult task? Will my nerves hold out?

I was constantly in danger. There were continual fights, shootings, and chases. I lived in an atmosphere of fear and terror. I always imagined that someone was walking behind me who at any moment was going to jump me. I would get anxious, thinking I should turn around: perhaps it was the very last moment to fend off an attack.

But this feeling, no matter how disagreeable, was not really my main concern. I would have been ashamed if the physical dangers would have caused me to resign this party post. After all, someone else would have had to take over the work. Why should some other person have to risk his life more than I?

But what really weighed on my mind more than anything else was the moral danger I was in. I often dealt with people to whom money was nothing, people who drank, caroused, and for whom throwing their money around was a daily affair. People proposed partnerships with me in all kinds of businesses. I was offered money—great sums of money—ostensibly, as a "loan." People wanted to clothe me: "Look Bernard, how you are dressed. It's an embarrassment. Come to the store with me. I'll dress you so you'll look right. No one will know," and so on. Some, for example, the meat workers, said this without any improper intentions. They simply could not understand why I was such a fool and wouldn't take advantage of a comradely "favor." The temptation was even greater because I was always short of money and had barely enough to get by for my family. More than once I received support from my brother and my sisters in America.

I was afraid I wouldn't be able to stand up under the pressure—that I might cave in. Particularly, because I knew that it was enough to make just a small beginning, and . . .

People in similar positions working for other parties were frightening examples. Dr. Loketek, for instance, an educated person with a PhD. Look what became of him. And only because he did not have the strength to resist the pressure from the demimonde. How did I know *I* would have the strength? I must escape while I still can! After much thought and inner wrangling, I decided to go to the party and give up this post.

Whom should I tell? Comrade Noyekh, of course. I approached him, and we agreed to meet in a quiet café. It was just the two of us, so I poured out my bitter heart to him. I told him of my fears. I begged him, literally with tears in my eyes, that the Bund free me from this arduous and nerve-shattering work and give me some other function to perform. Comrade Józef, as we called him in Poland, listened attentively to me the whole time without interrupting me even once, and when I was finished, he said, in that way he had, calmly and slowly:

"If your condition is as you describe it, you will of course have to abandon this work, but I wonder if you should do that. You mentioned that something might happen to you physically. In that case, there is no option. You must be freed of this work. But you said yourself that this was not the main thing that troubled you, that the most important thing was that you were afraid you would be corrupted, compromised. But you see, about that *I* have no fears. I know it is possible, but it is good that it frightens you, for as long as it frightens you, it cannot pose a real threat. As long as you fear for your own corruption, you will never succumb to it. I guarantee it. I do not fear you will stumble!"

"How can you 'guarantee' that I will never lose myself, when I myself cannot be sure of it?" I asked him. "Perhaps you should, after all, try to get someone else?" "Well, okay then," he answered, "by all means, please suggest someone else as a candidate." So I named several people. Comrade Noyekh then said, "You know quite well they are not suited for this work." I argued that no party function should depend on one person. He answered this, counting every word, as he used to when he wanted to emphasize something: "No single party task must depend on one person. It will be carried out without you, without me, without others. When we are no longer around, *the Bund will still exist.* But as long as we are around, we must do our part." He continued, now at a somewhat quicker pace, "Bernard, our fate is bound up with the movement. It places each of us at our posts, and we all of us together bear responsibility for one another. We all know what kind of difficult work you do, and you know we have the fullest confidence in you. Strengthen yourself, get over this, continue your work!"

Why should I deny it: what he told me did in fact help me regain my confidence and my faith in myself.

But there was someone else who also gave me strength, very often, and that was Shloyme Mendelson.

CHAPTER 64

Shloyme Mendelson

Shloyme Mendelson became an important part of my life. For years we were bound together in an intimate friendship; it is impossible to imagine those years without him.

I first came to know him in 1925 during the second convention of TSYSHO. To help keep order at this convention, TSYSHO turned to the Bund Militia. I also had a closer contact with him on another occasion. It was when the Vilnius Yiddish Teachers Seminar came to Warsaw to perform an old play, "The Sale of Joseph into Slavery by his Brothers," under the direction of Max Weinreich. The instructors were performing this play in the Plac Teatralny, and TSYSHO again turned to our militia to help keep order.

Our close friendship continued to develop around the Plac Teatralny. I was a frequent theatergoer there and was well acquainted with many of the Yiddish actors. The theatre was at Leszno 1, and across the street, at Leszno 2, was the popular Gertner's Restaurant. The Yiddish Literary Club, as well as the Actors Union—where Yiddish actors, writers, and social activists congregated—were near Gertner's Restaurant. Many artists and activists were regulars there. After the performances, Shloyme Mendelson and his wife, the well-known actress, Klara Segalowicz, would often go to Gertner's restaurant. I, along with a couple of actors I knew, would do the same. It would often happen that we would go there together, and end up sitting together at one table. Our friendship developed and grew closer in this way.

I had always looked up to Mendelson. I would often frequent his public readings and marvel at his great talent as a speaker. His lectures on Peretz enchanted me. I knew Peretz when he was still alive, and like many Bundists, had a great liking for him. But Mendelson depicted Peretz as if he were placed high on a pedestal, and I began to see Peretz in a new light. At the table in the restaurant I now saw a different Shloyme Mendelson from the one I saw speaking from the platform. His humor and his sparkling vivacity engaged me. His intelligence and cleverness took me by surprise. No matter what we talked about, his remarks, his wit, his jokes, quickly illuminated and clarified things. His playfulness with words, his warm, clear voice, even his tone in speaking, was pleasurable. Sitting for an hour or two at a table with him presiding was a special experience for me.

I began to seek his companionship more and more often, exploiting various opportunities to sit at the same table with him. I noticed that he too began to show an interest in me. "Bernard, are you coming with us?" he would often ask as we exited the theatre. And with time, more and more forcefully: "Bernard, come!" After that he began inviting me to come see him during the day at the TSYSHO offices, so we could go have a bite together. We began to meet more and more frequently, just the two of us, spending many hours together. Before we knew it, there existed between us a strong friendship, a close bond.

What he was looking for from me, I don't know; what I was seeking from him, I knew: an uplifting of my spirits. When I met with him I felt as if I had suddenly been raised to a higher sphere. Whenever I was thinking something over, some issue, whenever I had doubts, was unsure, or if my position on a given question seemed to me unpersuasive—it was then enough for me to ask Shloyme and for him to tell me what I was thinking, in his warm voice and in somehow different words, for all my doubts to quickly vanish; all would become clear and sure, as clear as his words and as sure as his tone.

In the late twenties, Shloyme had already grown much closer to the Bund. In 1929 he officially joined the party. He would then want me to tell him stories about the party, not about positions taken, resolutions, and decisions—these things he knew without my having to tell him—but about the Bund's people, their dealings and happenings. He wanted me to tell him in greater detail about our labor activists, about the various events in the day-to-day life of the party.

He was greatly interested in heroic deeds, bold dealings by our comrades in the difficult battles we then (and after that time, constantly) had to endure, and about which he never tired of hearing. I became as a child when I was with him, listening to his talk. And he, it seemed to me, in turn became as a child when he was with me and listened to my stories—stories he loved, asking me to repeat them over and over again.

After every great clash or shooting, or whatever it was that totally unnerved me, I would run to him as one runs from some danger to one's mother. As soon as I closed the door behind me, I immediately felt calmer. He would receive me with a smile, a clever saying, a joke, or perhaps some witty remark, ostensibly about some side issue, but in fact, related to what had just happened. Or he would start in on some other topic, something pleasant, happy—and right away I found myself in another world, a loftier world, and everything that had happened earlier appeared distant, hazy, and almost as if it had never happened.

Sometimes I was too agitated and I wouldn't let him sidetrack me. I expressed my deepest repugnance at my fate: "Why do I have to be the 'enforcer'? Why do I have to be the one to do the shooting?" I shouted. To this Shloyme would answer, seriously now: "This is not a brawl, this is not a shoot-out, this is the struggle of a movement, an idea they want to destroy with a raised fist." Later, when the fights with the *Oenerowcy* occurred more and more frequently, he would emphasize: "We are not just fighting with hooligans or troublemakers. We are fighting for the rights of an entire people!"

"Easy for you to say," I would answer. "You sit here at your desk. You write, you busy yourself with intellectual matters." To this he would answer: "If only we could exchange our jobs, then I could do what you do, and I could then gladly give you my desk to do my work."

Always after a hard fight or shooting, when I would come to him to pour out my bitter heart, he would always find the right words to make clear to me what lay behind all this struggle. He was always able to show me the greatness that lay behind the day-to-day trivia. This strengthened me, helped me to endure, gave me courage.

He gave me the key to his apartment. I could go to there whenever I wanted. Often, when I was depressed, I would go to his place instead of heading home. Just the atmosphere of his apartment—its shelves of books, his cluttered desk—calmed me. And when he would come home and see me there, he immediately understood what I needed. I felt enveloped by such warmth and pleasant talk, that this in itself was enough to calm me.

Whenever I had to carry out some very dangerous mission, I would warn him that that day I didn't know what time I might come to see him. Nervously—I am quite sure of it—he would wait for my return, and as soon as I would appear at his place, he would meet me with his broad smile, with some appropriate saying, and my agitation quickly subsided. I would—as always—begin to pour out my troubled heart, and he would never tire of once again, and yet again, proving to me how much importance lay in this work of defending our lives and our movement from the assaults of our murderous enemies. Similarly, when he had to travel away from Warsaw for a couple of days to a meeting, a public reading, or, for example, to intervene with the governmental authorities about a TSYSHO school that had been shut down, I would wait impatiently for his return.

In time I also became a frequent visitor to the home of his mother and his older brother, Avigdor. At his mother's I was a most welcome guest. If I was a close friend of her Shloyme's, I was in her eyes one of the elect. I became one of her own, a member of the family.

In the Warsaw Ghetto I often had to visit Shloyme's mother. If I didn't show up for a few days, she immediately sent someone to get me. When she got sick, Doctor Kelson, who attended her, came herself to get me because Shloyme's mother demanded that she bring me to her. For a long time in the Ghetto, every Saturday, even in the worst frost, she would send me *tsholent* (a Sabbath dish of meat, potatoes, and beans) delivered by Shloyme's older brother, Avigdor. I would scold him, but he would simply say he had to do it, that "Mother said so."

I had to go to Avigdor's on the Sabbath and on Jewish holidays. If I didn't have time, I had to show up for at least half an hour. His wife, Feyge, happy and clever, as if born a Mendelson, made the house festive. They watched over their only daughter as if she were the apple of their eye. Right after the first days of the war a bomb fell on their apartment on Wielka Street and killed their daughter on the spot. Avigdor and Feyge perished later in the Ghetto.

When the Second World War broke out our paths diverged. Shloyme fought his way through, along with a number of members of the Central Committee of the Bund, to Vilnius and later to America. After a few days of wandering around, I made my way back to Warsaw. During the horrors of wartime, we heard reports of each other through the underground.

We met up again in 1946 when I arrived in New York, and our friendship was warmly revived. But sadly, not for long. Shloyme died suddenly in Los Angeles on February 8, 1948.

Figure 114. Henryk Erlich and Shloyme Mendelson, seated center, with leaders of the Romanian Bund and their cultural organization, *Morgnroyt*, in Cernowitz, 1929. From the Archives of the YIVO Institute for Jewish Research, New York.

CHAPTER 65

In the Trap of the "Shetshke Gang"

When the FRACs had gained control over a large segment of the Warsaw trade unions, their terrorist acts escalated, especially in the Transport Workers Union where the former American gangster, Shetshke (*Szeczka* in Polish), became Secretary of the FRAC's Transport Workers Union. Shetshke and his gang began to terrorize the workers, extorting money from them and driving away from their work those who wouldn't let themselves get pushed around.

One time a group of transport workers from the Danzig train station (near Muranów) came to our union hall with the complaint that Shetshke had driven them from their workstations with the pretext that it was for the purpose of changing their workstations. The truth was that he had sold their workstations, because the workers of our union had refused to pay him extortion money. He made several hundred dollars from the sale of a workstation. This dirty dealing was probably accomplished with the knowledge of the aforementioned Dr. Loketek. These workers came asking us to take their part. We stood up for them, several times sending our people to defend them and preventing them from being driven from their workstations. But Sheshke didn't give up easily. One time we were alerted that Shetshke had come again with his gang of toughs and was once again driving our people away from their workstations. We—Yoysef Lifszytz, "Bosak," the Secretary of the union, several others, and I—went there. It came to blows and shooting. Luckily no one was hurt. But Shetshke never bothered that group of transport workers again.

Some time later a similar situation arose at the East (Dworzec Wschodni) Station in Praga. A group of workers from whom Shetshke was trying to extort money would not allow themselves to be terrorized by him. They came to our union office asking us to defend them. Again in this case it came to a fight. Seeing there seemed no end in sight for these acts of terror, we sought to get somewhere with them in a civilized way, by talking to them. We approached Loketek about talking things over, and we agreed on a conference in their offices in Praga. I went there with Yoysef Lifszytz. When we entered the offices, their Secretary, Kelbasa, was sitting there. He asked us to sit in the reception area and wait; they should be arriving soon, he said. In addition to Loketek, Matraszek, the Chairman of the union, as well as Shetshke himself, were supposed to come. We sat down to wait. Soon various people came in, took a look at us, and left. After that, some of them stayed near us. We waited a long time. I began to suspect something was wrong. I said to Yoysef, "I am afraid we are in a trap here. We are not going to get out of this in one piece." He asked, "Maybe we should try to break out?" "We are surrounded," I answered. He asked again, "Do you have anything with you (he meant a gun)?" "Yes," I answered, "but we must wait a little. It is too risky now—they are watching us." I became terribly nervous; a shudder went through my body. I saw that we had no way out. I was certain we were surrounded by an armed gang that was watching us and wouldn't let us move from this spot.

Suddenly two tall young men entered the reception area. They approached us up close and looked into both our eyes. All at once one of them cried out joyfully, "Bernard*zie* (a Polish ending indicating endearment), *to ty jesteś?* (Bernard, is that you?)" I was totally relieved. I lifted my eyes up and saw the brothers Pawlowczyk, slaughterhouse workers who slaughtered pigs, whom I knew from the slaughterhouse for many years. "Come, Bernard," they said. We went out onto the street with them. They asked Yoysef to leave, and the three of us went into a restaurant. Here they told me they were supposed to give us *bates* (in their lingo, "beat us up badly"), but they weren't told who we were, just that two guys were sitting there that needed to be taught a "good lesson." But when they saw it was me, they didn't want to carry out this "assignment."

We sat for a while in the restaurant. One of the Pawlowczyks was continually running to the telephone, trying to locate Loketek. Finally, around ten o'clock in the evening, Loketek together with Matraszek, came into the restaurant. We told them what happened and I told Loketek openly, to his face, that I was sure he knew about the trap that was set for me and that is why he was "late." Loketek swore he knew nothing, and that he and Matraszek were very busy, and that's why they had come late. His explanation was that when Shetshke saw Loketek was not coming on time, and that I was waiting and was in his hands, so to speak, he exploited the situation, organizing an attack on me on the spur of the moment. Whether they were telling the truth or were partners to a prearranged attack on me—I will never know.

CHAPTER 66

The FRACs Try to Take Over the Newspaper Deliverers Union

The FRACs tried to capture the Newspaper Deliverers Union, a hard fight for us.

The Newspaper Deliverers Union numbered several hundred members. Its offices were on Nalewki 17. The Secretary was Pesakh Albert (now in Australia), a former *Fareynikter* (member of the Uniteds; see chapter 1, footnote 7), who, together with a group of leaders and activists from that party (S. Zusman, Isser Goldberg, S. Gilinsky,[1] and others) went over to the Bund in 1920. He was a calm, relaxed person, but a very effective activist.

A certain Mannes Marmurek was on the Executive Board of the union. A wounded World War I veteran, an invalid, he worked for a newspaper on Pańska Street. When the FRACs were at their peak, he joined up with them and took with him a small group of newspaper delivery workers. He then started up a new, smaller union under the FRACs, becoming the only one in charge. Like the other FRACs, he began to employ their well-known tactics of terror to force the other newspaper deliverers into his union. With the help of FRACist thugs, he began to terrorize the administrators of the newspapers to force them to favor his union members (i.e., give them more newspapers to deliver; give them the newspapers earlier than the others for distribution). The civil authorities favored his people when giving out the required newsstand concessions. He placed his newspaper vendors next to the activists of the old union or next to those who opposed his rule. In addition, he threatened to shoot and kill Pesakh Albert.

He also began to terrorize and beat up those who delivered the newspapers by special delivery to subscribers. For the most part, the people making these deliveries had other full-time jobs that didn't make them enough money, so to make a little extra cash, in the early hours of the day before they went to work, they delivered newspapers. They would get up around five in the morning, in summer and winter, and from around six to eight in the morning, deliver the newspapers. The union even accepted them as members, but Marmurek decided to chase them off. With his band of thugs he terrorized them, falling upon and beating them. He got the Secretary of the FRAC Transport Workers Union in Praga, Kelbasa, to help with this terrorizing. Kelbasa lent him one of his gangs of thugs for this work.

With all these workers falling into the hands of the FRAC syndicate, it got to the point that our union was in danger of disintegrating. The members of our Newspaper Delivery/Vendor Union were mostly older people, many among

Figure 115. Samples of the Bundist national press in Poland, including daily newspapers and periodicals. From the Archives of the YIVO Institute for Jewish Research, New York.

them women. They couldn't defend themselves against Marmurek and his thugs. When things got really bad, the union finally turned to our Militia for help. The Bund saw that the union was confronted by a real and immediate threat to its existence and was too weak to defend itself against the FRAC thugs. We decided to protect the union.

Characteristic of Marmurek's heartlessness is the following instance. In the Metal Workers Union there was a member by the name of Lerner. He had been an active Bundist since Czarist times. He was now quite old, and also rather sickly. He no longer had the strength to work with metal, so we were able to get him a spot as a newspaper vendor so he'd have enough to live on. Manes Marmurek deliberately set himself to deprive him of this living. He would come to his newsstand, berate him, and threaten to take his concession away, which he could easily get the police to do.

Several times we approached Marmurek through our militiamen in the Pańska neighborhood, who knew him, to stop his terror tactics. We tried to get him to desist by talking calmly with him, but it didn't help. On a certain morning, therefore, he found his newsstand totally wrecked.

It became clear to all that no one was afraid of him. His power among the newspaper deliverers and vendors began to diminish. It must be added, however, that this was also a result of Marmurek's dark dealings. The treasury of his little union lay in his pocket, and it became known that he didn't know the difference between his own money and the union's. In addition to this, he founded a cooperative with his members, and people began to talk that there was also disarray in that treasury. Even his own followers began to distance themselves from him. As a result of all this, his little union soon fell apart. The attempt by the FRACs to take over another one of our unions was defeated.

Note

1. Shloyme Gilinsky (1888–1961): Educator and founder of secular Yiddish schools, author of textbooks in Yiddish; later, Director of the Medem Sanitarium; Bundist Warsaw city councilman.—MZ

CHAPTER 67

The FRAC Transport Workers Union and Itshe "Zbukh"

It was a lot harder to stop the FRAC terror attacks on the porters in the marketplaces and bazaars. I have previously explained how the back porters were splintered among several different unions and various parties. The FRAC union became the strongest, not because it enrolled the most members, which it did, but because it installed a system of frightful terror. If some porters belonged to the FRAC union, they terrorized the other porters, even if the other porters were in the majority, forcing them to join their FRAC union. If they refused, they would begin to harass them, giving them a smaller share of the pool or pushing them out of work altogether. Often it happened that if one of those pushed out of work gave in and joined their union, he had to pay a large "penalty" to be allowed back to his old workstation. The strong-arms running the FRAC union divided this money among themselves.

The wildest of these FRAC thugs was Itshe "Zbukh" (his family name was Anders). He was the "chairman" of the FRAC Porters Union, but he was more like the leader of a gang of toughs than the chair of a union. He was a strong man, a wild thug, and a real "king" among the strong-arms, an underworld character down to the marrow of his bones. Using the power of the FRACs and the strength of his own gang, he terrorized everyone. As for his own work, he had a job at a fish market in Janusz's courtyard on Gnojna Street, near Krochmalna. There he was "king." Mostly he terrorized Bundists. One of the first he threw out of work was our comrade Shaye-Yudl, who also worked at the fish market in Janusz's courtyard. But Shaye-Yudl did not break down. He went around for a long time unemployed, but refused to swear allegiance to the FRAC union. Eventually he opened a small dairy shop on Krochmalna 17 and made his living there.

He did this largely because he got sick of the whole atmosphere the FRACs had introduced into the transport workers world.

In Janusz's courtyard there was also a station of handcart porters that belonged to our union. Among these porters was a comrade of ours, Zalmen Pipe, a Bundist and a member of our Militia. "Zbukh" tormented him. Once he beat him up in front of the whole group of handcart porters.

Now we were forced to act. If our members saw we were incapable of defending them even when they were being attacked and beaten, openly, on the street, they would leave us. What to do? Talk to Itche's conscience? He wouldn't understand. Call for a fight? In that case he would bring his FRACs and his thugs and they would surely win. There was only one thing left to do—somehow tear down Itche's prestige. I decided to do this on my own.

On a certain morning I went off to Janusz's courtyard to the spot where our handcart porters stood at their stations. I waited for the moment when Itche "Zbukh" stood encircled by a whole gang of porters, merchants, and "good fellows." They stood around calmly talking things over, Itche standing in the middle, talking like a boss. With rapid steps I approached, went into the middle of the circle, went right up to him and said to him, loudly, half as a question and half as a demand: "How long are you going to continue this beating and terrorizing?" And not waiting for an answer I delivered a resounding slap to his face.

I don't know whether my slap hurt him physically, but lifting a hand against the "king" of the thugs, the "chairman" of the FRAC Porters Union, was something nobody could have imagined. Everyone around became confused. He himself became pale and as if frozen to the spot. But he did not lift his hand to retaliate. He stood a moment, confused and lost. Suddenly, he turned and quickly left. All around things roiled and hummed as if in a beehive. The crowd dispersed and spread the sensational news that Itche "Zbukh" got slapped by Bernard. With this, the royal crown was knocked off his head.

I stayed there quite a while with our handcart porters. After that, when I had calmed myself down a bit—because the truth is I was scared; I knew this could end badly—I went back to the party offices.

That evening Dr. Loketek, the leader of the whole FRAC Militia, called. He wanted to see me, and we talked about when and where to meet. Before I went there, I told several acquaintances of mine, Polish labor activists, how I slapped Itche "Zbukh" and that I was now to meet with Loketek, probably because he wanted to talk to me about it. They strongly advised me to go meet with him. But it's good—they said—that you've told us about it. We will also go to the place where you are meeting him. Just in case—whatever—we'll be right there.

We had agreed to meet with Loketek in a restaurant near "Pod Blachą" (The Copper Roof Palace) near the Kerbedzia Bridge, next to the dock on the Vistula from which the ships departed. Loketek also brought along Matrashek, the chairman of the "zwirnikes," and several others. Loketek strongly complained about what I had done, that I had torn down the prestige of the FRAC union. He was not concerned about the honor of Itche "Zbukh;" what he was concerned about was the prestige of their union. I laid out my complaints to Loketek. I remonstrated with him about the things Itche did. He beat, he thrashed, threw people out of work, took "contributions" to let people come back to work. He is not a chairman; he is the boss of a bunch of extortionists. As I spoke I noticed that Matrashek was listening with great astonishment, as if he were hearing all this for the first time. In that case, I thought, I will tell him more. In greater detail I told more about the criminal behavior and criminal acts of Itche "Zbukh." Finally we agreed that if there were any further frictions or conflicts among the members of our two unions, the two unions would settle it between themselves.

Itche "Zbukh" was no longer "king." He no longer terrorized the porters as he had before. People were less afraid of him.

Eventually, Itche "Zbukh" came to a bad end. In the Warsaw Ghetto, he and his son, who had been a boxer in the Maccabi sports organization, became informers for the Gestapo. Their specialty was informing about smugglers who "illegally" brought food into the ghetto. Because of this, the ghetto smugglers attacked Itche "Zbukh," stabbing him to death.

CHAPTER 68

Returning Stolen Goods to a Leather Merchant

We also had to fight in altogether other ways against the immorality and lawlessness that was growing ever stronger under the influence of the FRACs.

One time, during a meeting of the Executive Board of our Transport Workers Union, the door opened and, slowly and somewhat shyly, a bearded Jew dressed in traditional Hasidic garb walked in and asked if he could speak to us. "Certainly, of course," we answered. "Say what you have to say."

He had a leather store on Franciszkańska Street, he said, and a few days ago he received a shipment of leather. While he was standing in his store reciting the afternoon prayer, the back porters, who had delivered the leather to his store, stole two bundles of his leather. He was ruined by this theft because he was not an independent merchant, but a middleman. He asked the union whether it could help him get his goods back, because if not, he was simply ruined. We promised to do all we could.

The next morning I went off to the station where the porters stood who carried the leather goods and sternly demanded they immediately make good the theft. They swore up and down they knew nothing about it. Secondly, they said, let the merchant swear we are the ones who stole his goods, and we will return them. So I went back to the merchant and told him, they deny stealing your goods, but if you swear you saw them take your two bundles of leather, they will pay the cost of the merchandise. The pious Jew answered, "How can I swear that I saw them take it? If I had seen it, I wouldn't have let them. While they were unloading the merchandise I turned to face the wall to say the 18 benedictions of the afternoon prayer, and during that time they stole the two bundles of leather. Who else could have done it? They were the ones who brought the leather into the store, and no one else came in after them. Even if I were to lose everything I own, I would not swear I saw them take the leather, when I didn't."

It was clear to me he was right. So I went back to the porters and demanded they return the leather goods or their value. I warned them that if they didn't return the goods, or their value, to the shopkeeper, then we would remove them from their work places. I told them, "If you didn't take it, then you must know who did. You must find the stolen goods and return them!" After a short while they did in fact locate the stolen leather and return it to the shopkeeper.

That same evening, however, they came to our union offices and threw down their work permits, declaring they were quitting our union and were joining the rival FRAC union. "We don't want to belong to a union that takes care of the shopkeepers instead of us. How is it your business to return stolen goods?" they shouted. "We will belong to a union that cares about us, not about shopkeepers."

But the impression this story had on the broader public, and among the workers, clerks, and shopkeepers on Franciszkańska Street, the Nalewki, Gęsia, and surrounding areas was extraordinary. The image of the Bund, and of the Bund unions, was greatly enhanced.

CHAPTER 69

Among the Retail Clerks; Another Worker Murdered

The Communists kept up their harassments, haranguing and assaulting of our comrades, attacking our meetings and unions, and continuing to call their futile strikes. After they lost control of the Bakers Union, they focused their attention on the Retail Clerks Union.

The Communists had learned nothing from their defeat in the Bakers Union and their senseless, coldblooded murder of Neuerman. They conducted their struggle to gain control of the Retail Clerks Union with the same violence they had used in trying to gain control of the Bakers Union. Here again they eventually lost, but this time the battle was more complicated and prolonged, because the retail clerks had a long Communist tradition.

Even back in Czarist times, the retail clerks in Warsaw had a union. Mostly white-collar workers had belonged to this union: bank officials, purchasers, bookkeepers, traveling salesmen, office workers, and so on, mostly from the assimilated segments of the Jewish population. Even before the First World War, their union had constructed its own attractive building on Zielna 25, near the Marszałkowska, and close to the wealthy Polish neighborhoods. Yiddish-speaking folk types from the Nalewki, Gęsia, and Franciszkańska neighborhoods were, with few exceptions, not allowed into these occupations. Politically, the SDKPiL and the PPS-Lewica (PPS-Left), two Polish Socialist parties, had a great influence on these workers. On the Jewish question, these parties took the assimilationist point of view. Influential as well were the nonpolitical assimilationists who simply could not stand it that Yiddish-speaking and Jewish folk types should have any entry into their "aristocratic" union.

Nevertheless, the Bund did have a strong group in the Retail Clerks Union. One of the most active Bundists there, who often gave brilliant public speeches defending the Bund's positions, was Comrade Lazar Epstein (now in New York and active in the Jewish Labor Committee[1]). The Bund faction continually demanded democratizing the union, letting in the "lower" sorts of employees, organizing literary readings in Yiddish (the official language of the union was Polish), and so on. After the First World War the Communists (the SDKPiL and the PPS-Lewica) took control of the union. But the Bundist faction also grew stronger at that same time, calling itself the "Grosser faction." Quite a number of Bundist activists became part of this faction, for example, Mayer Wasser, Vice-Chairman of the Central Committee of the Polish Bund; his brother, Gershn Wasser; Zygmunt Muszkat; Leon Michelson; Lutek Friedman; Jana Jojlson; and others.

Before the First World War a Yiddish-speaking union of manufacturing factory workers had also organized itself in Warsaw, including employees in the Nalewki neighborhood. After the war, this union fell under the influence of the Pa'ola-Tsiyon (Labor Zionist) Party, although the Bund had a strong following in the union, and once—for the election to the Warsaw Labor Congress—the Bund even acquired a majority.

The Bund then put forward a demand that the two unions be united. Both unions, in fact, passed such a resolution, but it was never carried out. The leadership of both unions sabotaged it. The manufacturing factory workers union grew continually weaker and smaller, and did not play a significant role. Around the general Retail Clerks Union at Zielna 25, however, the battle grew ever more intense.

The Bundist faction was especially energetic in putting forward its demand that the union organize the as yet unorganized. Mostly this meant the poorly paid employees (mostly girls) in the large covered markets and in the market squares around them (for example, "Gościnny Dwór," later "Wielopole," etc.). These workers were Yiddish-speaking folk people, who would have had a natural affinity for the Bund. The Communists, afraid that this new stream of members would cause them to lose their grip on the union, opposed letting them in. The battle around the issue of taking them into the union grew ever more intense. The Communist opposition kept growing more and more vehemently opposed; the Bund just as vehemently for. Objectively, justice was on our side: Why shut the doors of the union to a large mass of employees? Just because they might upset the reigning party? Or because they are of a "lower" sort, earn less, and do not speak an elegant Polish? These very poorly paid workers were, in that case, all the more in need of an advocate!

In the twenties a manufacturing worker in our faction arose who attracted everyone's attention with his energy and dynamism. His name was Dovid Wasserman. He was tall, broad shouldered, well-built, spoke with a deep bass voice, and was a person with a folksy sense of humor. He stemmed from a bourgeois family, and he himself had a well-paid position in manufacturing. He threw himself into the work of opposing the Communist leadership with all his exuberant energy. At every step of the way, as the Secretary of the Bundist faction at Zielna 25, he pointed out the unjust and antidemocratic conduct of the assimilationist Polonist-Communist union. The prestige and the following of the Bund faction continually grew. But as the influence of the Bund grew, so grew more intense the conflicts with the old Executive Board, mostly around the question of organizing the poorly paid marketplace workers. It went so far that the Communists excluded the representatives of the Bundist faction of the union to the Executive Board, for example, Comrade Chaim Wasser, Dovid Wasserman, and so on (the elections to the Executive Board were supposed to be proportional, according to the membership lists of the factions).

At this point the Bund stepped up independently to organize the workers the Communist union did not want to accept, for example, the Yiddish-speaking retail clerks of Gęsia and Franciszkańska Streets; the peddlers in the marketplaces and around the large covered markets; the fruit peddlers (fruit selling was also concentrated around the large covered markets), etc. Out of all these categories we created a new union. Dovid Wasserman quit his job on Gęsia Street and became the Secretary of the new union.

The newly founded union grew by leaps and bounds. Soon it rented its own large meeting hall (on Mylna 7). It quickly acquired a good reputation among the broad mass of retail clerks. Also manufacturing employees, leather workers, clerks in men's clothing stores, bookkeepers, and office workers all started coming round to the newly formed union offices.

The Communists made up their minds to destroy this newly formed union with every means at their disposal, even if it meant the spilling of blood, just as they had done with the Bakers Union. As a base for their bloody assault they chose the fruit market workers local, where they had some sympathizers, even though their union had refused to organize these workers.

The fruit workers were a unique element. They were half employees, half independent porters. As employees, they sold fruit to tradesmen wholesale, but, like independent porters, they also hauled baskets of fruit. They began working around three and four in the morning, when the fruit was brought in from the countryside to Warsaw, to the center of the wholesale fruit business in Mirowski Square, near the large covered markets. They worked hard both in summer and in winter, because even in the winter, aside from the winter fruits, there were also fruits from the hothouses.

At one point the wholesale fruit business lay completely in Jewish hands. Later Polish wholesalers also got into the business. The Jewish and Polish fruit wholesalers kept themselves apart from one another. The Polish workers belonged to the FRAC unions, which attempted to pull into their ranks the Jewish workers. Because of this there were often battles with our local union. The Communists, in order to wreck our local union, supported the FRACs. The Communists also gained the support of some of the Jewish bosses, who looked askance at the whole idea of their employees suddenly organizing themselves into a union.

It happened one time that one of the fruit workers went into business for himself, leaving a job opening for someone else. The fruit local of our union—to which everyone now belonged—decided to give the newly vacated job to an unemployed worker. At this point the Communists mixed in, deciding that this job opening should go to one of their people, the son of a fruit wholesaler, a boy who had never worked a day in his life at the fruit trade and was, of course, not a member of our fruit local. The Communists were seeking an excuse to foment trouble, rather than being actually interested in acquiring the job for this boy. He had received a call-up to serve in the reserves, in military exercises, and when this conflict flared up, he had already been called.

The Communists conducted the battle with their usual terror tactics. They disrupted a meeting of the fruit local with hurled insults and beatings. After that they shot into the apartment of our comrade, Simkhe Solnik, an active member of our fruit local. A few days later, in the afternoon, there suddenly appeared on Mirowski Square a band of Communists with their chief thug in the lead, and before we knew what was happening, they had let loose a heavy barrage of gunfire, not into the air to frighten us, but aimed straight at our comrades. The result was fatal: our Comrade Shejnowicz fell dead on the spot and comrade Simkhe Solnik fell, severely wounded.

These were not victims by chance. The Communists consciously aimed at them. At Shejnowicz, because he was a pillar of the fruit local; he had a large family, brothers, uncles, cousins—all of them fruit workers, and he brought them all into the union. At Solnik, because he was a member of the Bund Militia. In addition, the Communists committed the murder of an innocent bystander.

As soon as we heard the news about this new Communist murder, I went there with a group of our militiamen, but no trace of the Communist gunmen was anywhere to be found.

The union did some accurate investigations, and it was confirmed that several Communist members took part in preparing the bloody assault, and they were pushed out of their employment by the union.

We had great difficulties with the families of the two victims. Simkhe Solnik lay ill and recovering for a long time. The family members of the victims didn't belong to the Bund and were not interested in hearing anything about higher party and social issues. It cost us much effort and work to succeed in persuading the families of the victims to renounce any form of vengeance, because we wanted at all costs to avoid further bloodshed.

Note

1. Formed in 1934 by Yiddish-speaking immigrant trade union leaders and leaders of the Bund and Workmen's Circle in response to the rise of Nazism in Germany. Its

first president was the Bundist Baruch Charney Vladeck. Especially in the organization's early period, Bundist influence was significant. The JLC worked to support Jewish labor institutions in European countries, cooperate with American organized labor, assist the anti-Nazi underground movement, and combat antisemitism. After the outbreak of World War II, the emphasis focused on efforts to save Jewish cultural and political figures, as well as Jewish and non-Jewish labor and Socialist leaders facing certain death at the hands of the Nazis. The Committee succeeded in bringing over a thousand of such individuals to the United States, or to temporary shelter elsewhere.—MZ

CHAPTER 70

Auctioning Off the *Folkstsaytung*

Our daily newspaper, the *Folkstsaytung*, the central party organ of the Bund in Poland, was always struggling financially. It had almost no advertising, the most important source of profit for a newspaper. What firm would advertise in a newspaper read by poor workers who earned hardly enough for a piece of bread? Without advertisements, and subsisting only on pennies collected from periodic appeals to workers, it was really difficult for the *Folkstsaytung* to survive—it was always drowning in debt. Because of these debts, it was continually faced with being auctioned off, and more than once, it took a minor miracle to fend this off.

One time such an auction almost ended in disaster. A debt of around 40,000 zlotys had accumulated. The creditors refused to wait any longer, and the assets of the *Folkstsaytung* were to be auctioned off: the linotype, the rotary presses, and every last bit of property.

The bidders at auction, or as they were called in Warsaw, the "auction goers," were primarily from the underworld. They were a well-organized band, a mafia. They bribed the court officials, who would officially conduct the auction, and the police, and nobody but they, were permitted to buy anything. They divided the city up amongst themselves by neighborhoods. The auction goers of one neighborhood dared not come to an auction belonging to another neighborhood. These "auction goers" reigned over their fiefdoms without any kind of competition.

In the Jewish neighborhoods, the auction goers were Jewish, and they knew they couldn't mess with any Jewish political parties or social institutions. During an auction of the assets of a Yiddish school, or of the ORT, or of any Jewish social institution, one could pay off the Jewish auction goers for twenty zlotys or so. The institution would place their own people in the auction to buy up the assets for a pittance, and the institution could then carry on as before.

According to the law, an auction could be conducted three times. If the first time the bids were not judged high enough, a second auction could be conducted. If the second time the bids were again not sufficiently high, a third and last auction took place. This time the assets went to the highest bidder, no matter what.

The first two times, the auction of the *Folkstsaytung*'s assets went well. The Jewish auction goers of the neighborhood came, we gave them a little money, and they left. The third time we appointed Comrade Maurycy Orzech to "buy" the assets. He brought his lawyer with him, Schneerson, a good friend of ours (the father of our comrade, Issa Erlich). Another lawyer, Comrade Ludwig Honigwilll, represented the *Folkstsaytung*. On the day of the auction we were on time, waiting for the Jewish auction goers of the neighborhood to arrive so we could once again pay them off to go away. Orzech would then be able to legally "buy" the assets, and the *Folkstsaytung* would once again be saved.

Suddenly, at around eight o'clock in the morning, as we were waiting, ten Polish "buyers" come into the courtyard, all of them big men, "Goliaths," with Kazik Morawski in the lead. When I saw them my blood ran cold. Kazik Morawski was a giant of a man and one of the wildest thugs in Warsaw. He was a rich man, one of the top leaders of the auction goers. His "fiefdom" was a Polish one, and he only bothered with big deals, for example, bidding on houses, large machines, entire factories, etc. I immediately understood what had happened. The Jewish auction goers were afraid to mess with the Bund, but not wanting to miss out on such a fat profit, they sent the strong-arm Poles to buy up the assets of the *Folkstsaytung*. They would be silent partners in the profits.

I mustered up my courage and, approaching Morawski, I said in a polite and friendly way: "Listen Mr. Morawski, what is it you need to buy at this auction? This is after all the Bund, a Jewish workers party—we are workers, why would you want to harm us and take away our property? Go away and leave us in peace."

Answering angrily, he said, "I don't want to know anything about any party, about any workers. One can make some ten thousand zlotys here. Get off me! You want to be a partner? I can take you on as one, but that's all I can do for you."

So I began again to try to persuade him with the same arguments, and then again, and then once more. But he wouldn't budge. I saw I would not get anywhere with him by being polite and friendly. So finally I said to him, this time in a firm and decisive tone, "You will not buy here!"

With an ironic smile, he measured me up and down and asked, "What? You want to fight with me?"

I answered him with the same decisiveness as before, "No, we won't fight, but you will not buy anything here!"

He saw from my tone that this was not some little game, that it was not so easy to dismiss me with a wave of the hand, so his tone became a little softer, and he called me aside and said, "Listen, since I have come here, I must buy. This is no longer about money or profit. This is now about my reputation. Here is my gang.

They see everything. I cannot leave with nothing. If you want to be a partner, you can be a partner."

I answered him, "You are concerned about your reputation, but I am concerned about my very existence!" Apparently I said this with such desperation, that it impressed him. He grew silent, changed altogether, and suddenly said, "Come, let's go," and added a curse that is unprintable.

I answered him: "No, I cannot leave here with you alone, and you cannot leave here. You have to see to it that your people do not bid on anything. Sullenly, he then stepped back a bit to the side and signaled his people with a wink. They understood what this wink meant, and also stepped back to various sides.

The auction began. Comrade Orzech bid. Morawski and his buddies stood quietly on the sidelines, sullen but silent. The auction was quickly over. Orzech was the buyer.

Now that Orzech was the legal proprietor of all the assets of the *Folkstsaytung*, I went over to Comrade Noyekh, who had been standing the whole time, watching from a distance, and who understood all that was happening, and I said to him, that I needed 100 zlotys (about 20 dollars) to take the gang of Polish auction goers for a good lunch. Comrade Józef (Noyekh's other name) asked me with a touching, innocent naiveté, "100 zlotys? So much money? Wouldn't 50 zlotys be enough?" I was too aggravated to explain to him why no less than 100 zlotys were needed. I stubbornly insisted on the entire 100!

I took the money and went over to Kazik Morawski and told him I was taking him and his gang to a restaurant. We all went off without a word to a nearby restaurant. They all seated themselves around a big table and began to order. When I heard what they were ordering, I almost lost my composure once again. I went over to Murawski and whispered in his ear, "Mr. Murawski, I don't have enough money to pay for all this." Still sullen, he answered, "I don't need your money; I will pay myself!" They gorged and guzzled so much that it is even now hard for me to believe that Murawski paid almost 500 zlotys for this little luncheon. He most probably gave them all this food and drink because he wanted to erase the bad impression that he, Kazik Morawski, the *król* (king) of the Warsaw "auction goers," retreated from a bunch of weak kikes.

But Kazik Morawski did not pull back simply because of my firm and decisive attitude. He certainly thought things over during our dispute and understood that if he bid and bought, things would not go so smoothly for him. He well knew what the Bund was, and that it was friendly with the PPS, and that bidding might cost him more than it was worth.

When I brought back to Comrade Józef the 100 zlotys and told him the story, he gave me a happy smile.

Since I have mentioned Maurycy Orzech's name, I must go on to tell something about this comrade and his refined personality.

His family was one of the richest Jewish families in Warsaw. I had known him for many years, since he was fifteen. At that young age he was already a

Figure 116. Maurycy Orzech. From the Archives of the YIVO Institute for Jewish Research, New York.

member of the Bund. I became a young guest in his house. His grandmother, who lived with them, used to get angry with me, because when I would come into their house in the winter, I would often carry mud onto their shiny polished floors with my wet shoes (I had no galoshes at the time). Comrade Orzech later inherited a large fortune and became a partner in a large manufacturing business, partner to a large bazaar on Franciszkańska 19, with an interest in other enterprises as well. But his personal goodness, his refined persona, his loyalty to the Bund, did not diminish in the slightest.

When he would meet me, he would always ask if I needed anything for needy comrades—money or things. Quite often, in fact, I would tell him that an unemployed comrade needed a suit of clothes or a coat. He would then take me home with him, would open his closet, full of fine clothes, and tell me to take whatever I wanted. One time in such a moment he said the following: "You know what, Bernard, what do you need me for at all for this? I will tell my wife that you can take anything you want, whenever you want." And he asked his wife to come in and told her to always let me into the house and let me go to the clothes closet to take whatever I wanted from it.

I would actually quite often benefit from this privilege. And if a needy comrade was in need of some clothes, and was more or less the same size as

Orzech, I would go to his house and take whatever was needed, and clothe the comrade with it. His wife, who probably could not entirely grasp all this craziness of her husband, was, nevertheless, very loyal to all his work for the party.[1]

Figure 117. Henryk Erlich and some of the leading staffers of the Bundist daily newspaper, *Di Folkstsaytung*, in Warsaw. From the Archives of the YIVO Institute for Jewish Research, New York.

Note

1. After the outbreak of World War II, Maurycy Orzech fell into and then escaped from Nazi hands; he then entered into Nazi-occupied Warsaw, becoming the chairman of the underground Bund there. I have told about his death and that of his family in my book, *Finf Yor in Varshever Geto* (Five Years in the Warsaw Ghetto, translated as *The Stars Bear Witness,* New York, 1948, Viking Press).—BG

CHAPTER 71

A Defeat for the Priest, Father Trzeciak

In the thirties, at the time of the unending antisemitic assaults on the Jews in Poland, a certain priest named Trzeciak, an ideologue of the Hitlerite, Polish antisemites, was especially virulent.

Father Trzeciak was one of the most well-known Catholic priests in Poland. A raging antisemite, after Hitler came to power, he adopted Hitlerite tactics to incite the mob against the Jews. When he preached in the churches on Sundays, he would so inflame the crowd that after each of his sermons there was the fear of a pogrom. Several times he came to preach in the church on Bródno, and the surrounding Jewish population was in fear that on some Sunday, one of his inflammatory sermons would end in a pogrom.

Bródno was a small suburb of the larger Warsaw suburb of Praga. Located in Bródno, but serving Warsaw, was a large Catholic cemetery. There was also a Jewish cemetery there belonging to the Warsaw Jewish Community Council in which the Council buried paupers without any family, or whose family could not afford to pay for a plot in the Jewish cemetery in Warsaw.

The population of Bródno was for the most part Polish. But next to Bródno was a small suburb named Pelcowizna that was almost entirely Jewish. Between these two small suburbs was a piece of land called Annopol that had always been empty of people. There in Annopol, the city of Warsaw erected wooden barracks for homeless people—and after not too long a time, Annopol became its own little town, a town of "official" paupers, with its own character and its own kind of local patriotism.

The barracks were erected by the municipal Department for Social Welfare for homeless families, for people that had been evicted from their apartments and who couldn't afford to rent another. Also, the unemployed lived there, or unemployed workers who were employed by the city to perform public works, or unskilled workers—in short, the poverty-stricken population of Warsaw. The barracks themselves were long, large wooden boxes, divided into small rooms. In every little room lived a family. Around the barracks, in the small alleyways, were many small children in rags and tatters. Hunger reigned. Every day in the winter, the city would send hot kettles of soup to warm the hungry barrack residents. About eighty percent of the barrack residents were Poles; the rest, Jews.

The Bund had a party group there. At first we had wanted our comrades of the barracks to join the Bund group in neighboring Pelcowizna, but here their local patriotism came into play: "We are our own town, Annopol," the comrades argued, "and it is very important to us Jews of the Annopol barracks to have our own Bund group." The representative from the Bund to this group was Abrasza Blum, the later hero of the Warsaw Ghetto Uprising. Also our *Tsukunft* had a circle there, and their representative from the Bund was Yankele Mendelson, one of the most interesting folk types of our Warsaw youth movement. The PPS also had a group in the barracks with its own meeting place. They gave our Bund group the use of it.

On Sundays the Annopol Poles would go to the Bródno church, where the priest Father Trzeciak sometimes preached. One time our Annopol comrades and our Peltcowizna comrades came to us with the alarming news that on a certain Sunday, the priest Trzeciak would be coming once again to the Bródno church to preach, and that the mob, which had already been on previous occasions sufficiently inflamed by him, was preparing, after his sermon, to go into the street and beat up Jews.

The Presidium of the Warsaw Bund's Central Committee held a session at which it was decided to organize a resistance. I went off to the PPS locals in Praga and in Bródno and requested that their local Militia groups there help us raise a resistance to the hooligans preparing to assault Jews. They agreed. I also went over to the slaughterhouse and organized a group of Polish workers there who would, whenever I would ask, come and help us fight off the assaults on the Jews by antisemitic hooligans. The largest proportion of the resistance fighters, however, were our own comrades: Bundists from the Annopol barracks and from Pelcowizna (with Chaim Zucker, the meatworker, at their head) and members of our party militia.

That Sunday at eight o'clock in the morning, I was with the unit of militiamen in the offices of the PPS in Bródno, which had been set aside especially for us. In about half an hour we were all assembled. We wanted to be there early, because we weren't sure whether the hooligans might not begin their harassing and beating of Jews in the morning, when people went to church.

I divided our entire militia into three groups. One group, consisting only of Poles, I sent into the church to mingle with the crowd, sense their mood, and listen to what people were saying. We placed another group hard by the entrance to the church—this group also consisted only of Poles (if there had been among them any Jews, it would have been obvious and noticed, and would have aroused suspicion). The third group, the largest, was mixed, consisting of our comrades and some PPSers, gathered at a distance and hidden, so as not to be too obvious.

During the whole time of the service inside the church, reports were sent out to us that things in the church were quiet, but at around twelve o'clock, they let us know that the priest had already delivered his inflammatory sermon against the Jews and that groups were gathering at the doors of the church, preparing to go out into the streets and assault Jews. I had come to an agreement with the commandant of our brother PPS militia, who was with me the whole time, that we shouldn't wait till the hooligans began to harass the Jews, but that as soon as they emerged from the church with the cry, "Beat the Jews," we should stop them and engage them in a fight right by the doors of the church, so they wouldn't have the chance to harass and beat up any Jews in the street.

We sent instructions to our group in the church to stay close to the hooligans, get behind them, and come out together with them. As soon as they saw us attack the hooligans from the front, they should do the same from behind, so that the hooligans would suddenly be caught between two fires.

And that is what happened. When the hooligans ran out the doors of the church with their cry, we leapt at them and began teaching them a lesson. Our group behind them did the same. There was a fight and an uproar, shouting. Right away our third group also threw itself into the battle. For about a half hour, heavy fighting went on, until the police arrived. More of the hooligans than our people were beaten up, because we had surprised them.

The police began to disperse the crowd and make arrests. People from both their side and our side were arrested. But the hooligans were immediately let go. Those from our side were detained. Charges were brought against two of our Polish comrades, in addition to one of our comrades, a woman, a *Tsukunft*ist. They were put on trial. Several of the hooligans were witnesses for the prosecution. All three of our comrades were sentenced to a year in prison.

CHAPTER 72

Przytyk and the Protest-Strike on March 17, 1936

On March 10, 1936, Warsaw was shocked by the news of a pogrom that had broken out a day earlier in the province of Radom, in the small town of Przytyk.

Antisemitism in Poland had by then taken on intense forms. Physical attacks on Jews had become a daily occurrence. But it had never yet descended to an organized pogrom—until March 9, 1936.

The Bund's Central Committee convened and decided to call for a general strike on March 17 by all the Jews in all of Poland as a protest against the pogrom in Przytyk and against antisemitism in general.

In Warsaw we began hurriedly to prepare for the protest-strike. A strike committee consisting of the Bund and the trade unions was formed. The unions and the militia were given the job of seeing to it that the strike was a full on, general strike, and that the marketplaces, bazaars, and businesses would be shut down.

On the eve of the strike, on March 16, we held a meeting of the Militia, assigning the pickets for the following morning whose job it would be to ensure that the businesses were closed and that the goods in the street stalls and bazaars would not be displayed.

A day before the strike, Dr. Max Weinreich, the director of YIVO and correspondent for the New York Yiddish newspaper, *Forverts*[1] (Forward) came from Vilnius. I had been acquainted with him for a long time, going back to our Bund work in Czarist Russia. I first met him at a party convention in Kharkow in 1916, and subsequently at other party functions. Now he had come to Warsaw, saying he wanted to accompany me the whole day of the strike tomorrow wherever in the streets of Warsaw I would go. He wanted to see with his own eyes how the great general strike would take place. I warned him that we would have to go out into the streets early tomorrow morning, at six-thirty.

Dr. Weinreich showed up on time at the appointed place, and we went out into the streets together. First we went to the area behind the covered market in the neighborhoods of Zimna, Ciepła, Chłodna, Mirowska, in front of the Iron Gate and surroundings. The Bundist militiamen had already come a little earlier to these places and they—as well as the union pickets—went around among the stall keepers and the businesses demanding everyone close their shops and leave the marketplace. A great tumult arose, a sliding and scraping of shutters, a closing of doors, the shutting of locks and iron bars. Quite a number of police were also around. They noticed that people were constantly running up to me, then running off somewhere, and then returning to me. Several policemen approached Dr. Weinreich and me, declaring they were arresting us and taking us to police headquarters. When we protested they answered, "You can explain it all at police headquarters, but in the meantime you must come with us." They began to lead us away. The Jewish shopkeepers noticed that the police had arrested me and another person, so several of them went up to the policemen, whom they knew very well. These were police from that neighborhood that drew a nice little supplementary livelihood from these Jewish shopkeepers. They began quietly talking to them. I did not see whether or not the police were given something into their hands right there on the spot, or just the promise of something later. In any case, the police left and we were both free to continue on our way.

From there we went to Grzybowski Square and to Bagno Street where the famous commercial courtyard "Pociejów" was located. Old furniture, old iron goods, etc., were sold there. The same scene as took place in the covered market repeated itself there: workers, employees, and shopkeepers, began closing doors and shutters. Teamsters and coachmen began shouting to each other across the great Grzybowski Square, "Leave your stations! We're going home! *Jazda!* (Giddyap!)." You could suddenly hear the hoofbeats of horses over the cobblestoned pavements echoing over the whole square. The great Grzybowski Square, and all its surrounding streets, grew as quiet and empty as if it were a holiday.

Now we had to get to the second part of the Jewish neighborhood, to the Nalewki —"those other streets," as the Grzybów Jews called them; the Nalewki Jews referred to neighborhood of the Grzybów Jews' in the same way. We couldn't take a droshky there because that would be breaking the strike, so although it was quite a distance, we walked there. When we arrived, everything was in order—all the businesses and shops were shuttered and closed.

The same process was taking place in the workshops and factories. Groups of inspectors from the unions went to the workshops and factories and removed the workers from their jobs. Of course, these union inspectors did not have a difficult time of it. Either the workers didn't come to work in the first place, or they immediately left work as soon as a representative of the union appeared.

It must also be said that almost no difficulties at all in carrying out the protest-strike were encountered with the Jewish owners of the businesses, workshops, and factories. They gladly joined the strike. The whole Jewish community was deeply grateful to the Bund for taking the initiative in organizing such a resolute protest against the renewal of old Czarist pogroms in independent Poland.

In addition, almost all the students in the Jewish schools left their lecture halls and joined the strike. All the wailing and weeping of the school administrators that the students were ruining them, that the government might close down the school permanently, were to no avail. Even many of the Jewish children who attended the state elementary schools didn't attend school that day.

Around nine in the morning, the streets in the Jewish neighborhoods were full of people. The workers and employees did not remain sitting at home. Ev-

Figure 118. "Extra: Strike!" Special edition of the *Folkstsaytung* calling for a general strike of Jewish citizens in all businesses, factories, and workplaces to protest the pogrom in Pryzytyk in March 1936. From the Archives of the YIVO Institute for Jewish Research, New York.

eryone's mood was battle-ready. Pride and uplifted spirits were felt everywhere. The Jewish population protested with their heads held high. It was a mighty mass protest. At eleven o'clock in the morning the great protest meeting called by the Bund took place at Przejazd 9. The courtyard was large and crowded with thousands of people. The meeting took place for several hours, without interruption: speakers ascended and descended from the improvised platform, and the people in the crowd came and went continually, but the courtyard continued to remain packed with people. In this way, tens of thousands of people came to the meeting at one time or another. Only at around two o'clock in the afternoon did the meeting stop: the strike had been called for a half-day, from early in the morning until two o'clock in the afternoon. At two o'clock everyone returned to their everyday work.

But only superficially did everything return to normal. In fact, the protest-strike the Bund had called for and in which the whole Jewish population of Poland participated, left a deep impression. The courage with which large Jewish masses set themselves against further antisemitic acts of violence certainly had its roots in the mighty protest of March 17, 1936, which became a turning point in the continuing struggle, resistance, and rise of the Bund.[2]

Note

1. The first issue of *Forverts* ("Forward") appeared on April 22, 1897, in New York City. The paper's name, as well as its political orientation, was borrowed from the German Social-Democratic Party and its organ *Vorwärts* (it should be noted here that the standard Yiddish term for "forward" is *foroys*; *forverts* is nonstandard, considered a Germanism (*daytshmerish*)). By 1912 its circulation was 120,000, and by the late 1920s, the *Forward* was a leading US metropolitan daily with considerable influence and a nationwide circulation of more than 275,000, the largest daily Yiddish newspaper in the world.—MZ
2. "Three and a half million Jews went out on strike. At noon all Jewish workers left their work; all Jewish stores shut down; Jewish pupils walked out of school. The streets of Poland were filled with a fiery people, proud, and battle ready."—Lucy S. Dawidowicz, *The Golden Tradition* (New York: Holt Rinehart, and Winston, 1967, 80).—MZ

CHAPTER 73

The Pogrom in Minsk-Mazowiecki

The furor generated by the Przytyk pogrom had not even had a chance to calm down, when a second, even worse pogrom broke out.

On the May 31, a Jew from Kałuszyn, Yehuda-Leyb Chaskelewicz, shot and killed a Polish army sergeant, Jan Bojak. The shooting took place in broad daylight in the town of Mińsk-Mazowiecki.

Chaskelewicz was well known in Kałuszyn and the surrounding areas as psychotic, and his psychosis had something to do with this Polish officer, Bojak. Chaskelewicz had served in the Polish army, and his immediate superior had been Sergeant Bojak. The sergeant was a terrible bully. Many soldiers who were serving in the same unit as Chaskelewicz gave witness that Bojak had harassed Chaskelewicz unmercifully. While Chaskelewicz was serving in the army, he began displaying symptoms of mental imbalance, and he was discharged before his term of service was up. When he returned home, the idée fixe grew in him that the sergeant had caused his troubles, his mental illness, and that he must take revenge—shoot him to death. No one took this seriously, until the mentally ill Chaskelewicz actually acted on this delusion.

The Endeks and other antisemitic groups exploited this assault by a psychotic individual as a pretext to incite a murderous provocation against Jews. Chaskelewicz, they ranted, carried out this murder according to a secret order from the Jewish Community Council. Their incitement brought the desired result.

On the same day Chaskelewicz shot Bojak, a pogrom broke out in Mińsk-Mazowiecki carried out according to all the "rules" of this "art:" broken windows in Jewish homes, plundered Jewish shops, bloodied and beaten Jews.

When the bitter news arrived in Warsaw, the Bund Central Committee sent Yoysef Lifszytz (Secretary of the Warsaw Transport Workers Union) and Sholem Hertz (a writer for the *Folkstsaytung* and the editor of the *Yugnt-Veker*

(Youth-Awakener) to Minsk to make immediate contact with the Jewish population, lift their spirits, and try to organize a resistance if the pogrom should repeat itself. They were there for two days and came back with the report that there was great fear among the Jews there, and that they were running away in panic to Warsaw to wait until the Polish population in Przytyk calmed down.

A report then came that the funeral of the sergeant would be taking place soon, and that the Endeks were preparing to use that occasion for another pogrom. The Bund Central Committee now sent Comrade Yoysef Gutgold and me down to Minsk. We appealed to the PPS, and they sent one of their party activists to go with us. Together, we were supposed to seek any means of avoiding another outbreak, and to organize a resistance group in case another pogrom did in fact break out. Gutgold went because he was Secretary of the Central Committee of the Leather Workers Union in which both Poles and Jews were members, and in Mińsk-Mazowiecki there was a local of the union of Polish cobblers who knew Gutgold well because he worked on their labor issues for them, helping them with their battles and their strikes. The comrade from the PPS went with us to connect us with the PPSers there and to win their help to ward off another pogrom.

The three of us arrived together in Minsk-Mazowiecki. The city look deserted. No living soul was to be seen on the streets. The businesses in the center of the town were boarded up (they were all Jewish businesses). All the homes were shuttered. It was so empty and sad that, walking through the silent, empty streets, we were afraid of the echo of our own footsteps. Adding to our apprehension: our PPSer, who was a real Pole, looked like a Jew.

We went over to the office of the Cobblers Union. It was closed. We stood and waited. Soon a committee member came and opened the office. We stepped inside. In the course of about a half hour, the Cobblers Union committee members gradually gathered. We sat down to talk things over. Everyone was in a somber mood. The Polish cobblers stated that they didn't believe they would be able to do anything. The antisemitic fire the Endeks had lit was so great that there was no way you could talk to a Pole and appeal to his sense of justice.

I wanted to cheer things up a bit to dispel the somber mood, so I said: "We, that is, those of us who have just come from Warsaw, have not eaten yet, and you probably haven't either. Let's all go get a bite to eat." Soon food and drink were brought in (and some whiskey as well). We all sat down to eat, but it didn't do much good. We ate in silence. No one spoke. The general mood did not improve.

Suddenly we heard the ringing of church bells. Someone went out to see what was happening and came back with the news that a house was on fire. Antisemitic hooligans had set a Jewish home on fire and the church bells were ringing to summon the firefighters to put out the fire. In many Polish towns it was the practice, in case of a fire, to ring the church bells as a signal summoning the townsfolk to come and extinguish the blaze.

We all left the union office and went to where the fire was. A crowd was standing around the burning house, silently looking on. Fortunately, the house was empty, the Jewish residents having run away beforehand. But fire and wind know no difference between Jew and Pole: the fire quickly spread to a Polish house next door. When we arrived, the flames were licking ever more fiercely at the roof of the Polish house.

The onlooking townsfolk continued to gaze quietly at the fire. In an instance a thought occurred to me: What if there are people, Poles, inside the house, and something tugged hard at me. In a moment, I was inside the house. Once there, I did in fact find some people in a panic. Children were being saved. Suddenly I noticed an old, paralyzed woman who, in the panic, was forgotten. I grabbed the old woman and carried her out in my arms. A kind of rescue trance overcame me. I went onto the roof, shouting out for water. Now, finally, several people in the crowd ran and brought buckets of water and handed them up to me. I stood up there and threw buckets of water at the tongues of flame. The smoke was choking me, and the tin on the roof was burning the soles of my feet. The flames almost reached me, but I stood fast, pouring water on the fire.

Our group, Yosl Gutgold, the PPSer, and the cobblers, who were mixed in with the crowd, quickly oriented themselves to the situation, and one of them called out, pointing at me: "Paczcie, to Żyd! Żyd ratuje Polski dom!" ("Look, he's a Jew! A Jew is saving a Polish house!"). People in the crowd agreed: "Prawda, to Żyd!" ("True, he's a Jew!"). Our comrades became bolder and began talking and crying out to the crowd: "The Endeks will bring us nothing but misfortune. When they set a Jewish house on fire, all our houses will go up in smoke." Among the crowd, many agreed. At that point our people got up their courage still more and began crying out: "Down with the Endeks!"

The fire grew smaller and died out. I got off the roof and joined my comrades. The people in the crowd were eying me intensely, as if they were trying to decide if I really did look like a Jew.

Soon the news spread that a Polish home was burning and that a Jew had put out the fire and had rescued an old paralyzed Christian woman. The crowd got ever bigger and each person would tell another what had happened. People began to agree with our cobblers, who, having become ever more bold, said the Endeks were guilty of all kinds of evil doings. It became more and more apparent that the mood of the Polish crowd was changing. Then our group of Polish cobblers began demonstrating in the streets, crying out against the Endeks, and some of the people in the crowd joined with them, and a real anti-Endek demonstration took place. Seeing this, the two of us, Yosl and I, went off to the Jewish neighborhood. We banged on the shutters of the Jewish homes and shouted to them in Yiddish: "Come out, don't be afraid!" Shutters and windows began to open and people came out into the street.

For the rest of the day, the three of us, Yosl, the PPSer, and I, together with a group of the Polish cobblers, walked all around the streets of the town, observing what was going on, and listening to the talk of the townspeople. There were no more assaults, and no more antisemitic incidents in the town. Later that night we traveled back home.

The funeral of the sergeant was carried out peacefully; no further attempts were made to attack Jews in that town.

CHAPTER 74

Antisemitic Hooligans Kill a Jewish Child during a First of May Demonstration

The more intense the street battles with the *Oenerowcy* and the other Polish Hitlerites became, the more carefully we guarded our offices, meeting halls, clubs, public meetings, and, especially, our First of May demonstrations. In the thirties we so enlarged our militia that it practically encircled the whole First of May demonstration, and yet we weren't able to prevent a dreadful incident that occurred during the 1937 First of May demonstration.

In the later years, our First of May demonstrations had become ever larger, with many more demonstrators than in previous years. In protest against wild Polish antisemitism, the Jewish workers joined the demonstration in huge masses. So it was also in 1937. Both of the large courtyards at 34 Nalewki, the central gathering point of our First of May demonstrations, were jam-packed with people. The demonstration started out from Nalewki, wound its way to Muranowski Square, Miła, out to Smocza, and then through Nowolipki to Żelazna Street, where the Polish workers quarter began. The demonstration was so long that when its head arrived at Żelazna Street, the tail end was still at Miła, occupying four long blocks. Although we posted a tight and strong guard around the entire demonstration, we could not occupy every little corner of the several miles the demonstration stretched. On the way, near Smocza, a narrow street branched off, called Gliniana. Feiffer's large leather factory was located there. The whole time our lookouts kept reporting that the way ahead was calm and that there were no suspicious activities in the surrounding streets.

All at once, when about half of the demonstration had passed by Gliniana Street, there was a terrific boom, and suddenly a thick black cloud of smoke blocked out everything around as if with a heavy black curtain, walling off from view a large part of our demonstration. At the same moment, shots and screams were heard among the crowd of onlookers. The smoke obscured everything. We couldn't tell from our position where the shots were coming from. When the smoke lifted, we all saw that a bullet had struck a little boy whose mother was holding him as she looked on at the demonstration. Emergency first aid was immediately summoned, and the little boy was taken to the hospital. A short time thereafter, he died. His name was Avremele Schenker. He was five years old.

During the whole time of the panic and shooting our marchers stood in one place, not moving. Nobody broke ranks. The Printers Union band, which found itself close to the spot where the shooting took place, began playing loudly, and others began to sing loudly, because everyone seemed to understand quickly that some kind of terrible assault had taken place, and it was necessary to play and sing loudly to keep the panic from spreading to our other, more distant ranks. The demonstration was so long that neither the head of the demonstration, nor the tail end of it, had any idea of the terrible incident that had just taken place in the middle. One can imagine the agitation of the marchers when the news of the assault spread from mouth to mouth. Nevertheless, everyone maintained discipline, and the demonstration continued, ending in good order and according to plan.

We immediately began our own investigation into the attack. According to witnesses standing in the street watching the demonstration when the attack took place, this is the way it happened: At a certain moment two cars drove up from Gliniana Street. Several people jumped out, and in the blink of an eye threw a smoke bomb and began shooting. They then immediately returned to their cars and drove away in the direction of Okopowa Street.

The police began a formal investigation. After a few days a public notice appeared saying the ones guilty of the murder of the child had not been found. Every person, however, understood the character of the police investigation and the value of their notification.

That is how a murderous assault by Polish Fascists on Jewish workers was carried out, an assault that followed all the principles of a cowardly and vile attack from behind our backs and behind a cloud of smoke.

The Warsaw Bund's Central Committee and the Central Committee of the Youth-Bund *Tsukunft* jointly placed a tombstone on the little boy's grave with an inscription saying he fell victim to antisemitic hooligans.

The police would not allow a funeral.

CHAPTER 75

Oenerowcy Leaders Are Taught a Lesson

Since the police "investigation" into the attack on the Bund's First of May demonstration and the murder of the Jewish child, Avremele Schenker, had yielded no results, we decided that we would, on our own, pay back the *Oenerowcy* for the spilled blood of an innocent child: first, so they would feel on their own backs the punishment for their murder; and second, so they would not think that everything was now permitted and they could do as they pleased.

The PPS was, at the same time, also suffering at the hands of the *Oenerowcy*. True, the *Oenerowcy* did not dare to make such murderous assaults on them as they made against Jews, but they would disrupt PPS meetings and attack and beat up their activists. Among many PPS activists, therefore, the feeling grew that it was not enough to simply defend themselves against the *Oenerowcy* when they attacked, but that the *Oenerowcy* must also be attacked so as to diminish their enthusiasm for violence. Our Militia then came to an agreement with the PPS Militia, and we decided to show the *Oenerowcy* that we would not let them continue to terrorize us.

The *Oenerowcy* had their own daily newspaper, the *ABC*, a newspaper that daily conducted a vile, pogrom-inciting campaign against Jews in the Hitlerist style. The editorial offices of the newspaper were on Aleje Jerozolimskie. On that same street was a café belonging to a certain Miller. It was well known that the *ABC* editors, writers, and leaders of the *Oenerowcy* were regulars there: they had their own sort of café club there, and spent entire evenings in it. A group of our own militiamen and a group of PPS militiamen decided we would go there on a certain evening, around eleven o'clock, when there would be few, if any, non-ONR guests there (the café closed at midnight).

The café consisted of a store in the front, in addition to a side room, forming the letter "L." The *Oenerowcy* used to sit in the side room. We went into the café, not all at once, so it wouldn't look odd. Shaye-Yudl and I went into the side room where the *Oenerowcy* were sitting. The plan was this: Someone from the *Oenerowcy* would probably know me and would see me coming into "their" café with another Jew. They would not be able to contain themselves and would assault us. This would then provide a perfect excuse for our other group in the front room to enter the side room and take up the fight.

And so it was: As soon as the *Oenerowcy* saw me, they started to pick on me; one of them had already raised his hand against me. I grabbed a bottle off the table and threw it at him. Upon hearing the sound of breaking glass, our people ran in and began to throw bottles and glasses at the heads of the *Oenerowcy*. A fight began and we battered and bloodied them, teaching the Polish Hitlerite bandits a lesson for their wild misdeeds. We left immediately, so as to get out of there before the police arrived, but we stayed in the surrounding streets. Soon the ambulance arrived for the battered and bloodied, and after that the police arrived, closing off the streets and beginning to search. Fortunately, finding ourselves already outside the police cordon, we calmly looked on as the police bustled about, stopping people for questioning. We didn't stay there long—it was too dangerous. We left one of our Polish comrades behind to see what would happen next, so he could inform us later.

Shortly thereafter, in the afternoon Warsaw tabloid, *Kurier Czerwony* (*Red Courier*), there appeared an article about me by a journalist with a Jewish name: Seidenman. In the article he wrote that at night I could be seen in the elegant café *Adria* (a popular night spot for a segment of well-off Jews), dancing with women, giving them flowers, and so on, but that during the day, I was the "ruler of a band" that terrorized Warsaw. The article was, of course, inspired by the *Oenerowcy*. This fellow Seidenman, after writing the article, grew frightened that we might revenge ourselves on him, so he sent various people to clear up the matter and explain that he meant nothing bad by his article—quite the opposite, he was "praising" me as an elegant cavalier. We couldn't care less about Seidenman. Something else caused us much more concern: We found out that, as revenge for our attack on them, the *Oenerowcy* were preparing an assault on our *Folkstsaytung*.

CHAPTER 76

Guarding the *Folkstsaytung*

The information we had that the *Oenerowcy* were planning an attack on the *Folkstsaytung* caused us a great deal of concern.

It was relatively easy to mount an assault on the *Folkstsaytung*. Its print shop, located in the same place as the editorial offices, on the ground floor, in the courtyard of 7 Nowolipie, could be easily attacked. The rotary press was located next to the window, directly across the very narrow entry gate to the courtyard. One could enter the courtyard through this gate, and from there easily throw a bomb through the window. The windows on the other side of the print shop faced Miła Street, a very narrow alleyway running parallel to Nowolipie. The windows looked out onto a fence surrounding an empty lot that belonged to a church on Leszno Street. Right next to the low-set windows stood the linotype machines. One could easily approach those windows, shoot and kill a linotypist, or toss a bomb, destroying the machines and killing the workers at the same time. In short, from both sides, the print shop of the *Folkstsaytung* was an easy target. In addition to all that, we were not sure of the loyalty of the house super.

As soon as we got the information of an impending attack, we posted a permanent guard at the print shop. We guarded it night and day. One unit of our militia stood guard at the entry gate to Nowolipie 7, and a second unit stood guard on the Miła Street side.

It was fall, and the evenings were cold and often rainy. The nights were even colder. On the one side, the Nowolipie side, we stood guard until eleven o'clock at night, when the gate was closed and locked and the super was not supposed to let any unknown person in. On the other side, the Miła side, we stood guard until two or three in the morning, which was when the linotypists left work but several printers were still at work until five o'clock in the morning, when they finished printing the Warsaw edition. They worked inside the office, at a distance from the windows, not in any danger of attack. We provided them with guns, though, just in case . . .

We guarded the *Folkstsaytung* this way day after day, night after night, for many long months. Fall gave way to winter. Night fell earlier, the cold grew more bitter, rainstorms and snowfalls came more often, but we did not leave nor did we tire. We stood guard in every kind of weather. During the cold winter nights, we took turns warming ourselves in the empty rooms of the editorial and administrative offices, as if they were our barracks. We didn't leave for home to sleep until late at night, getting up the next morning to start the normal, hard-working day. All our militiamen were, after all, ordinary workers who, every day, worked hard for a living.

Things went on this way until late spring. This was perhaps the hardest task our militia ever performed. Often there were dangerous jobs asked of the militiamen, requiring them to risk their lives, but these were short-term assignments: the danger passed, and one could then go home and rest. In this case, however, one had to stand guard, night after night, for months, in very trying conditions. Although the same militiamen did not stand guard every night, relieving each other, nevertheless, every second or third night, the same militiamen had to stand guard. This was very stressful. But none of the militiamen ever complained. With the greatest loyalty and devotion, they guarded our proud, brave, and beloved fighter, the *Folkstsaytung*.

The days got longer with the coming of spring, and the threat of an imminent attack passed. We finally removed the guard.

CHAPTER 77

The Pogrom in Brisk

On the May 13, 1937, a pogrom against Jews broke out in Brisk. The direct cause of the pogrom was, again, the murder of a Pole by a Jew—this time, a Polish policeman. But the deeper, indirect cause of the murder was the economic antisemitism then raging, no less than the usual standard antisemitism of the nationalistic, right wing, hooligan variety.

An official, legal limitation on the production and sale of kosher meat was instituted in Poland at this time. Every city was allotted a certain quota of kosher slaughtering, but the quota allotted to each city was smaller than what was actually needed by the Jewish community. What to do then? In the smaller towns, where police oversight was light, more kosher meat was slaughtered than was allowed, and smuggled into the bigger cities as nonkosher meat.

On a tragic day in May, at the Brisk marketplace, a policeman caught such a shipment of "nonkosher" meat by a Jewish butcher, a certain Szcerbowski. A fight erupted between the policeman and the butcher and his family, and in the heat of the quarrel, the butcher's son grabbed a butcher knife and stabbed the policeman with it, who fell dead on the spot. The news of the murder spread with lightning speed throughout the city, and with the same lightning speed, a pogrom began. At first the mob wrecked and robbed the Jewish stalls in the market where the murder took place, then the violence quickly spread to the whole city. The police led the pogrom.

As soon as news of the pogrom reached Warsaw, the Presidium of the Bund's Central Committee met to determine what was to be done. Because of the nature of the issue, I was called in to attend. At the meeting, the gathering was informed that, according to swiftly spreading rumors in Brisk, the pogromists were planning to repeat their violent rampage following the funeral of the murdered policeman. It was proposed that I go to Brisk and try to organize a resistance, with the help of the Polish Socialist workers, if possible.

I told the comrades that the city was unfamiliar to me, that I didn't know anyone there, and that now, while the pogrom was still raging, I didn't see what I could accomplish. Nevertheless, the Central Committee decided that I must go, and that Leyzer Levine, a staff member of the *Folkstsaytung* and chairman of our militia, would accompany me (he perished in Kaunas, Lithuania, having fled there as a refugee in 1940). They also prevailed upon Jan Dombrowski to accompany us to Brisk. Jan Dąbrowski was a PPSer and a journalist. He was on the staff of the PPS's *Robotnik* and of their journal, *Tydzień Robotnika (Weekly Worker)*, whose editor-in-chief was Zygmunt Zaremba, a leader of the PPS and of the group of PPS activists that were in favor of working more closely and more openly with the Bund. Dąbrowski would often also collaborate on the Bund's Polish publications (e.g., the daily *Pismo Codzienne*, and, after that was shut down by the government, in the journals *Nowe Pismo*, *Myśl Socialisticna*, and *Nowe Życie*), ansd he gladly agreed to go with us and help us establish contact with the PPS organization in Brisk.

That night I was to get on the train to Brisk. I was in a very bad mood, because I could see no way in which I would be able to carry out my mission. As I usually did in such cases, I sought the counsel and encouragement of Shloyme Mendelson. He encouraged me: "You will find a way. Maybe you will find it there. You must try." We spent several hours together. He accompanied me to the train, which left at midnight. Only Leyzer Levine was with me. Jan Dąbrowski was to come on a later train.

A whole car full of Polish police reservists was traveling on the same train. Perhaps, I thought, they are also traveling to Brisk. But why? To further inflame the pogrom or to contain it? I didn't sleep all night, nor did Leyzer Levine. When we arrived before dawn at Terespol, one station before Brisk, several Jews from Brisk got on the train and related appalling details of the pogrom. They also told us that any Jew who gets off the train at the Brisk station is arrested.

Finally, the train arrived at the Brisk station. Brisk was an important train junction, so the trains stopped there for a longer time. Looking out the car window, I saw that the platform and the train station were full of police, and that they were, in fact, stopping people with "suspicious" faces. We both decided, therefore, to jump out the other side of the train; we then made our way over a network of rails, through a back way, past the railway workshops, and into the city.

We arrived in full daylight. It was a beautiful sunny morning, but on the streets we quickly saw snow—a snow of feathers and down and torn bedclothes. All around were broken windows and heaps of glass. We went to the place where the Bund activist Comrade Schneider[1] lived.

When we got to Schneider's place, his apartment was still full of rocks and shards of glass from the broken windows. Everyone in the apartment was dressed in a coat; packages and suitcases were packed, and they were all sitting on them.

Schneider and the others in the apartment were happy to see us. They told us all that had transpired in the couple of days of the pogrom. Today, things were calm in the city, but there was talk that Sunday, when the funeral for the murdered policeman was to take place, the pogrom would resume.

I talked things over with Leyzer Levine, suggesting that he go to the hospital, visit the Jews wounded in the pogrom, survey the destruction in the city, and send a report to the *Folkstsaytung*. I remained at Schneider's place. First, I asked Schneider to immediately call a meeting of the Bund activists in Brisk so we could determine what to do. The meeting did in fact take place in the apartment of the *Tsukunft* activist, Rifke Goldberg, a seamstress. At the meeting, besides Schneider, were Tannenboym, the dentist Lubelski, and several other comrades. First of all, I asked them if it was possible to organize a group that would be capable of mounting a resistance. They answered that many Jewish workers lived in the "Joint Barracks"[2] and that a resistance group could probably be formed there. They also told us that during the pogrom, Jewish blacksmiths and wheelwrights, who were concentrated on a certain street, put up a resistance (a couple of them were at the meeting). I posed a question to the gathering: If the pogrom resumes, could something effective be done to resist? They declared they were willing to resist, but alone, they were weak. If Polish workers would help, then something could be done. On the spot we put together a resistance group of 20 men. In addition, we decided to come to an understanding with the Jewish blacksmiths and wheelwrights, who were not present at the meeting, to see if they would join the resistance group.

Later that day, Jan Dąbrowski arrived. I explained the situation and the mood in the city, and that if there were a repetition of the pogrom, we would not be able to accomplish anything effective without the assistance of the Polish workers. I also told him it would be very useful if the PPS would put out a flyer to the Polish population.

We both went off to the chairman of the PPS's OKR (Executive Committee of the Region), a railroad worker. He told us that the mob was very inflamed. As to the suggestions we made to him, he said that, as for the flyer, he must have an order from the Central Executive Committee of the PPS in Warsaw, and as for creating a resistance group of Polish workers, he doubted that could succeed. We asked him to call a meeting of the OKR, or at least to call for a consultation with a few of their active members, to discuss the matter. Before we went off, things were left that, about the flyer, he would telephone the Central Executive Committee in Warsaw and ask them about it; as for a meeting with the OKR, he would call for a meeting tomorrow morning at nine o'clock.

After that I went off to Comrade Schneider's, where I met with Leyzer Levine. He had already phoned in a report to the *Folkstsaytung* about his talks with the injured Jews in the hospital and about the course of the pogrom. Dąbrowski went off to his room. All night he worked on a flyer addressing the Polish population. He wrote that the Polish people should not allow itself to be provoked by the antisemites, that it dishonors independent Poland to use the old Czarist methods of oppression of which Poland itself had been a victim;

that they should not imitate Hitlerite examples, because Hitler is the common enemy of both the Jews and the Poles, and so on. His flyer took a strong stand against antisemitism.

Next morning the meeting of the Polish workers took place. The full complement of the OKR was not present, but it was decided to put out the flyer that Dąbrowski had prepared (with a few small changes of a local character). It was also decided to try to organize a Polish resistance group that would help the Jewish group in the event the pogrom would resume.

In the evening a meeting of Polish workers took place in the union hall of the railroad workers. Mostly young people came to this meeting; a majority of them were *TUR*'s (*TUR* was the youth organization of the PPS). They said there were several hundred White Russians from the surrounding villages working in the railroad workshops at unskilled jobs, and that many of them had participated in the pogrom. Also the Polish police had participated in robbing the Jewish homes and businesses. If there were to be a repeat of the pogrom, they were all of the opinion that the police would have a hand in it. For that reason it was harder to organize resistance. Nevertheless the mood among the young people was better than that among the leaders. Right there on the spot, three groups were organized to help with the resistance, mostly consisting of the Polish *TUR* young people.

After the meeting I went for a walk with Dąbrowski through the Jewish quarter. It was Friday night, when Jews observe the start of the Sabbath with prayers and candle lighting. The streets in the Jewish quarter were empty. The doors were boarded shut, the windows shuttered. The Sabbath candles shone through the crevices of the closed shutters. These little candles threw an eerie light onto the dead streets. Our steps echoed loudly over the deserted streets. From time to time a door would open a crack and a frightened face would peer out to see who was passing by in the vacant street . . .

I explained to Dąbrowski the meaning of the Sabbath candles and how things look in a traditional Jewish home on a Friday night. And thus, deep in somber thought, we both walked silently through the pogromized, empty streets of Brisk—a Jewish and a Polish Socialist. Perhaps, I thought, hope resides in this, that we two, Dąbrowski and I, walk here together with a single purpose and a single will. He too remained silent the whole time. Perhaps he had similar thoughts.

The next morning I met with each resistance group separately. They received several instructions:

1. The Polish groups must distribute the Polish flyer that had been printed in several thousand copies.
2. One Polish group must go to the church early in the morning on Sunday, the day the funeral would be proceeding from the church. They must listen to the sermon and the talk to see if there was incitement to a pogrom.

3. A second Polish group must stand outside, in front of the church, and when the crowd emerged from the church, they must not mingle with the crowd, but stay together, somewhat to one side. If a part of the crowd tears off in the direction of the Jewish quarter, they must run with them and intervene if they start pogromizing.
4. The third group was split up as follows: part of them in the front part of the funeral cortege, and part at the end; they received the same instructions as the second group.

I dispersed the Jewish group into the side streets of the main street through which the funeral would proceed.

Sunday, reports kept coming to us from the church that all was calm, that no incitements were going on. The funeral in general was carried out peacefully. But at a certain moment—as we foresaw—a band of about 50-60 men tore off from the crowd. They went off into a Jewish side street (our comrade, the dentist Lubelski, lived on this street) and started throwing rocks into the Jewish homes and shouting, "*Precz z Żydami*" (Down with the Jews). Ten of our people, Jews and Poles together, went after them. We shouted at the pogromists to stop, but they threw rocks at us. I found myself in the midst of this group. I saw things were not going well; we were too few to stop the hooligans. So I stepped into the middle of the street, took out my revolver, and started shooting rapidly into the air. At the sound of shooting, the police immediately showed up, and the mob fled in panic. I quickly mingled with the crowd and the police did not see who had done the shooting. This ended the attempt to resume the pogrom.

We went up to the balcony of the dentist Lubelski's apartment and looked out onto the surrounding streets. It was quiet everywhere. The group of PPSers that helped us in the fight with the hooligans caught up with the funeral, joining the cortege so as to be on the spot in case there was another attempt to restart the pogrom. But there were no more attempts. The crowd that returned from the cemetery quietly dispersed. The rest of that Sunday passed peacefully.

That night we said a heartfelt farewell to our Polish comrades and to the Jewish resistance group and went back home.

Notes

1. During the Second World War, the Soviets arrested Schneider as soon as they occupied Brisk. It is not known in which Soviet prison Comrade Schneider perished. After 17 years of Soviet imprisonment, his wife Khaye was freed; she now lives with her children in Israel.—BG
2. Right after the First World War, when Brisk was in ruins, the "Joint" (Joint Distribution Committee) had erected temporary barracks to house the Jewish population. The barracks became permanent, and Jewish workers and the poverty-stricken lived there. People called the houses the "Joint Barracks."—BG

CHAPTER 78

The Bund's Warsaw Locales

For many years the Bund's address in Warsaw was Przejazd 9. With the years, this address became so identified with the Bund in Warsaw that it was often used as a synonym for it. In the same way, Nowolipie 7 became a synonym in Poland for the *Folkstsaytung* and the Bund's Central Committee.

Our location at Przejazd 9 acquired its popularity gradually, due perhaps in part to the centrality of narrow Przejazd Street where the various arterial streams of Jewish communal life in Warsaw came together. Right after the First World War, the Workers Aid Committee (*Arbeter-Hilf Komitet*) opened an inexpensive soup kitchen for workers there. Also after the war the Central Council of Trade Unions (*Tsentral-Rat fun di Profesioneyle Fareynen*) also took up its location there. During the Polish-Bolshevik war years, when, because of its antiwar stance, the Bund was declared illegal and its offices closed down by the Polish government, the Bund's Grosser Club on Karmelicka 29 was also shut down. It was at that time that the Bund quietly began using the location at Przejazd 9 for party purposes. The workers soup kitchen was still there, and people would often be entering and leaving, especially at lunch time, and so for that reason it was easier to conduct party business there without drawing the attention of the authorities. Also around 5,000 books from the library of the Grosser Club were brought there. When the Polish-Bolshevik war was over, the Bund's "General Worker Cooperative" (*Algemeyner Arbeter Ko-Operativ*), to whom the soup kitchen now belonged, created a Workers Corner (*Arbeter Vinkl*) there legally—a kind of tea café, where workers could come in the evening and have a cup of tea, eat a piece of bread and herring, and read a newspaper. In one of the rooms, a reading room was created with newspapers and journals (mounted on wooden sticks, as was the custom in Polish coffee houses). The Grosser Library was reopened there and began functioning again. Abram Stoller and I, who at that time worked in the party Secretariat of the Warsaw Bund, began to work on party matters there, under the protective mantle of the Workers Kitchen at the Cooperative.

In 1922, when the campaign began for the elections to the Polish Sejm (parliament), we set up the central office for it in the Workers Corner. The election campaign was now legal, so, as a matter of course, the Workers Corner stepped forward as an official Bund office, remaining so after the elections as well. In this way Przejazd 9 became the official address of the Warsaw Bund.

Along with the growth of the Bund and its party work, the activities in the Workers Corner also increased. The location became too small for the various branches of the Bund's activities. The Grosser Library[1] moved to its own large room at Leszno 36, the room belonging to an affiliate of the workers cooperative in that house, and the Workers Corner then became a purely party office. During the day, the Workers Soup Kitchen continued to function, as well as the Party Secretariat. In the evening the character of the place changed dramatically. It teemed with people. Bundists came there simply to have a good time, talk to their friends, or read a newspaper. In addition, all kinds of meetings and sessions would take place of party groups, *Tsukunft* circles, and all kinds of committees—some purely Bundist ones, others party trade union ones, and more. Often larger party meetings would take place there, as well as other events— mostly on Saturdays and Sundays—readings, literary evenings, and sometimes, simply, entertainments.

A vibrant life went on there 18 hours a day. At 6 in the morning the people who worked in the Soup Kitchen arrived. At around 9 in the morning the work of the Party Secretariat would begin. Around noon, lunch would be served and the rooms would fill up with workers who ate there. The lunch period would be over by three o'clock in the afternoon. The rooms would barely have been cleaned up, when at five o'clock, party people would begin to appear. From eight to eleven o'clock at night, all the rooms were occupied with meetings: in one of the larger rooms, sometimes two or three smaller groups would meet at the same time in the various corners of the room. Sometimes people who were just hanging around would have to be asked to leave so as to provide space for still another group meeting.

In this very stream of people that, evening after evening, filled up our Warsaw party premises, one person would always stand out, a central figure whom one saw threading his way through the thick crowds, and that was Comrade Abram. Abram Stoller was Secretary of the Bund organization in Warsaw, as well as Secretary of the Workers Corner. He was different from other secretaries. Normally a secretary stays seated at his desk and the clients come to him. Abram, quite the reverse, was a mobile secretary, coming to his clients. He was seldom to be seen in the office. He was always among the crowds in the various rooms, looking for his clients: the secretary of a party group, the representative of a craft committee, a member of a union Executive Board, a representative of *Tsukunft*, or SKIF, or YAF, or sometimes just an ordinary person who needed the help of the party with some personal matter. With a little notebook and the stub of a pencil in his hand, he would, in his own shorthand, write down all the action items that needed doing. At the same time, he was always embroiled in the personal concerns of people, always knew what headaches someone had, and never forgot to ask how things were going with this or that worry. He would listen, offer some counsel, write something in his little notebook—and then quickly run off to another corner of the room to grab yet another client. Again one would see him take out his little notebook and his stub of a pencil, and again write something there—only to watch him make his way through the crowd to someone else, and so on and on. Although he wrote everything in his little notebook, he seldom had to look at it. He navigated his way clearly through the labyrinth of hundreds of details; he had them all in his head.

The house where the Workers Corner was located was old. The gate was always wide open, because in the courtyard, in the so called "officine" opposite the entry gate, there was a movie theatre ("*Fama*") where we, by the way, often held meetings and Saturday morning events. The Workers Corner was located in the front building on the first floor. Wooden stairs, worn from uncounted thousands of feet that constantly climbed up and down on them, 16–18 hours a day, 365 days a year, led to the Club. The furniture in the seven-room premises was old and worn: simple wooden chairs and benches, ordinary square little restaurant tables that were left over from the early years of the Workers Soup Kitchen. But no one took any notice of that. Life seethed and bubbled in every room, and two streams of people never stopped their movement, one coming, one going, in and out, without interruption, from before noon until late into the night.

But the cramped quarters that were so beloved by us had become too small. We had to think of moving to a new location, a larger and more comfortable one. And not only that, but the landlord of Przejazd 9 had long wanted to get rid of the Bund, and he chipped away at this for so long that he eventually got an eviction notice from the court before we had a chance to find a new, suitable space. The Warsaw Secretariat of the Bund temporarily relocated to a small apartment on Nowolipie 3, where it stayed for almost a year. We finally found a suitable location on Długa 26, and in 1936 we moved there.

The house at Długa 26 was one of the well-known large buildings in the Jewish quarter. It had three large courtyards. The premises of the Bund were located on the first floor of the second entrance. The house already had some Bundist history behind it: it was the location of Hendler's Printshop where, for a time, in 1920, we printed our illegal literature. Also the Transport Workers Union rented a neighboring apartment.

The new location of the Warsaw Bund was much more spacious and attractive than the one at Przejazd 9, and we felt a renewed life. As before, the new locale was full of people. In addition to the party club and the Warsaw Party Secretariat, an array of other party institutions was also located in the new premises, including the soup kitchen of the Workers Co-op.

Note

1. At a certain point in time, the Grosser Library became a part of the *Kultur-Lige* (Culture League). Herman Kruk became its director and he began an energetic campaign to broaden its activities. The library burgeoned, containing tens of thousands of books. It then rented its own space on Leszno 13 where a study room was set up, as well as a large reading room with hundreds of journals and newspapers from all over the world. The library was free to all. It was the largest lending library in Warsaw and deserves an honorable place in a history of the cultural life of Warsaw Jewry.—BG

CHAPTER 79

A Bombing of the Bund Offices—And Our Answer to the *Oenerowcy*

In our Bund offies at Długa 26, on September 26, 1937, during *Sukes*,[1] between 5 and 6 p.m., we suddenly heard loud shots. Two bullets flew into the office where Shoshke Erlich (see chapter 51, footnote 3) was sitting. One bullet lodged itself in the heating oven near the door; the other flew past near Shoshke's desk and remained lodged in the wall. A few seconds later, there was a tremendous blast. The little transom window over the door was first brightly illuminated and then grew black with smoke. We went out into the corridor and surveyed a horrific scene. The front door was torn off its hinges. The glass panes in the doors were shattered. We counted ten bullet holes in the walls. The entire foyer was on fire. We quickly extinguished the blaze.

Opposite the door of the office was another door that led to a room belonging to YAF (*Yidishe Arbeter Froy*: Jewish Working Woman) where a Bund group happened to be meeting. Also on our premises at the time was a large group of comrades from the provinces who had come on an excursion to Warsaw. Because of the constant antisemitic unrest, they carried on their persons various iron weapons to defend themselves against the hooligans in case of an attack on the street. We were expecting the police to arrive, so we hustled our provincial comrades out the back door of the kitchen into the second courtyard. In a locked cabinet in the YAF room, our Militia had hidden two cases of rubber police truncheons we used in our fights with the hooligans in the parks and streets of the city.

The police came right away, entering our premises in the company of the super's son. We knew him to be an *Onerowiec*.[2] He went over to Abram and, pointing his finger at him, shouted to the police that he, Abram, had organized the shooting and that a bullet had struck his mother. As it later turned out, the attackers had started their shooting at the entry to the first courtyard, wounding our comrade Meyer Trombke, of the "Arkady" group,[3] along with others. In addition, a stray bullet had landed in the super's apartment, lightly wounding his wife. The super's son threw himself at Abram, shouting that he must take revenge for the wound to his mother. We all began to shout at the police that they should remove this wild young man and start looking for the real perpetrators. Instead, the police inspected the shot-up and burned corridor . . . and had us all stand in a row, searching each one of us, looking for a weapon. Luckily, our provincial comrades were gone, and even more luckily, it did not occur to the police to open the cabinet with the cases of rubber police truncheons.

During the attack, there were not many people on our premises, so that when the time bomb exploded, fortunately no one was in the corridor and there were no victims of the blast.

It was as clear as day to us that the *Oenerowcy* had set the time bomb under the door of our Bund premises. But when the police came to investigate—instead of pursuing the attackers—they inspected our premises, even searching the cellar to find out if the Bund wasn't hiding some weapons and dynamite down there.

The next morning a meeting was held of leading Bundist comrades, and it was decided not to let this attack go unpunished. As for the idea that the Polish police would punish the attackers, that was out of the question and, therefore, not even mentioned. The matter was turned over to the party militia.

The offices of the *ONR* were located at Bracka 17, not far from Jerozolimskie Street, in the heart of the strictly Polish quarter. We organized a group of our Bund Militia, as well as some Polish workers from the PPS, and on a certain evening we went to the offices of the *ONR*. We stormed into their premises, and before they knew what had hit them, we were breaking their furniture to pieces and wrecking anything we could lay our hands on. There were about three dozen *Oenerowcy* in their office at that time. After a few minutes they came to their senses and started to mount a resistance. A big fight broke out in which they got well beaten up. We taught them never again to think of attacking a Bund office. Several *Oenerowcy* were badly hurt during the fight.

Knowing full well the police would be arriving at any moment, I urged our group to finish and leave as quickly as possible. But not everybody succeeded in getting away before the police came. The police managed to detain one of ours, the Polish worker Stanisław Wojciechowski. A few of us and I remained in the neighborhood not far from our revenge attack on the Polish Fascists to see what would happen next, and to see whether the *Oenerowcy* might not now send a band of theirs to attack a Bund locale.

Soon we got the news that one of the wounded *Oenerowcy* that was taken to the hospital died as soon as they brought him home. This now made our situation very dangerous. The police were holding one of our people. They might put him on trial for participating in a murder. What was to be done? I was totally confused and distraught, as were the few comrades with me.

One of us went off to the police station and tried to bribe the freedom of our arrested comrade. But the police sergeant on duty said he couldn't do it because he was responsible for the people arrested that are delivered to him. At this moment Leon Andruszek, a Polish worker who often went with us to help us fight off the Polish Fascists, came up with a good plan: we should exchange the arrested man for another man. The police sergeant went along with this (for good money, of course). Andruszek and Romanowski, the secretary of the Construction Workers Union, went off to the offices of the FRACs on Jerozolimskie 6, not far from where we were at the moment. There they sought out an acquaintance of theirs—a worker who had a job at a government armaments factory and had just returned from work—and persuaded him to trade places with Wojciechowski at the police station. The worker had a good alibi: the time card from the factory time clock was stamped with the time he left work, the very time we were making our attack on the *ONR* offices.

We then went back to the police station. The police sergeant let Wojciechowski go free and, for the promised amount of money, let us put in his place the worker from the armaments factory. At night the district attorney came. The worker argued that the police had arrested an innocent man, that while he was coming from work, he happened to be passing by the spot where the fight was going on. He showed the district attorney his stamped time card, showing that at the time of the attack, he was at work in the factory.

The whole night we wandered about in the streets. No one could go home to sleep. We were frightened of the possible consequences in case the plan did not work, but luckily everything went well. In the morning witnesses for the *ONR* came. They did not recognize the one "arrested." His alibi was accepted as credible and he was immediately released.

Note

1. Modern Hebrew pronunciation, *Sukkot*, a joyful Jewish holiday; historical (commemorating the 40 years the children of Israel wandered in the desert) and agricultural (a harvest festival); traditional Jews build temporary shelters and take their meals there for seven days (referred to in English as "The Feast of Tabernacles").—MZ
2. Member of the antisemitic, fascistic party, the *ONR (Obóz Narodowo-Radykalny* or National Radical Camp).—MZ
3. Named after Arkady Kremer (1865–1935), "father" of the Bund, it was made up of individuals who had been raised in orthodox environments and had studied in yeshivas and other religious institutions, but had been drawn to the Bund. The Arkady Group had nearly 250 members in Warsaw (Jack Jacobs, *Bundist Counterculture*, 15).—MZ

CHAPTER 80

An *Oenerowcy* Attempt to Murder Comrade Henryk Erlich

But the *Oenerowcy* did not give up so easily.

One time, in the fall of 1938, we received a warning from the PPS that the *Oenerowcy* were preparing to assassinate Comrade Henryk Erlich. They had obtained this information from their informers among the *Oenerowcy*. When, where, and how the assassination was to take place, they didn't know. They could only tell us that the information came from their regional organization in Grochów, a suburb of Warsaw and Praga.

I immediately went off to Grochów and talked to the right people, who agreed to try to find out for us the most accurate details possible about the planned assassination. A short time thereafter I received a disturbing message from the PPSers that the time and the place of the attempt on Comrade Erlich's life had been decided, along with the two people appointed to carry it out. Their plan was as follows: They were going to telephone Comrade Erlich and make an appointment to meet with him at ten o'clock in the morning to consult with him about a legal matter (Comrade Erlich was also a practicing attorney). When they were alone with him in his office, they would carry out the assassination.

Receiving this information at noon, I did not lose a moment. I immediately notified the Presidium of the Warsaw Central Committee. We decided not to tell Comrade Erlich anything about it (why alarm him and his family), but to immediately get to work to block the planned assassination.

Comrade Erlich's apartment was located on Nowomiejska Street, a quiet, strictly Polish neighborhood, somewhat removed from the center of the city. There was not much activity on the street, and there were very few people to be seen. Coming there in the morning with a group of Jewish workers would attract too much attention, so I organized a group of Polish workers, arranging to meet them at eight o'clock in the morning at a certain spot. At the prearranged time, I went there with Comrade Eisenberg from our militia—he was blond and looked like a Pole (now in Montreal, Canada).

I split up the group as follows: One group of Polish workers I placed by the entry gate to the building; a second group, in the courtyard, hidden in an entryway, but not in the one containing the stairs to Erlich's apartment; and a third small group and I hid on the stairs a half-story up from Comrade Erlich's apartment, positioning ourselves so we could not be seen from the door of Comrade Erlich's apartment, but we could still see the door. The group at the front gate was instructed to let the *Oenerowcy* through the gate to the building's courtyard, but to shut the gate as soon as they heard anything suspicious—for example, shots, an alarm, shouting, or any kind of commotion—so as not to allow the murderers to escape into the street. I instructed the group hiding in the courtyard that, as soon as they saw the *Oenerowcy* climb the stairs to Erlich's apartment, to follow from behind, but not too closely, so as not to arouse suspicion that they were following them—but if the assassins tried to run down the stairs, they should be stopped immediately. I and my group, up some stairs from Erlich's apartment, were positioned so that with one leap we could be at the door just at the moment the *Oenerowcy* rang Erlich's doorbell and attempted to enter his apartment.

At precisely 10:00 p.m. I received a signal that two people were on the street and moving in the direction of Erlich's residence. We tensed. I heard the footsteps of the two men on the stairs. Now they were at Erlich's door. I heard the steps of someone in the apartment coming to open the door. As soon as I heard the door being unlocked, in one leap from a half-story of steps from above, I found myself at the door. Lightning fast I stuck my foot into the crack of the door before the person inside had been able to open it fully. It was Comrade Erlich himself. I said to him quickly: "Close the door; I'll be right back!" I then turned to face the two men. In that moment they saw the others that had been hiding above and who had immediately come down behind them. They probably immediately understood they had failed, so they put on a pious and innocent expression and said, in an elegant and refined Polish, typical of the Polish intelligentsia, that they apologize and that they apparently rang at the wrong door. They started descending the stairs, with us right behind them. In that moment our group down below came up the stairs. The two assassins saw they were surrounded on all sides. They paled and began to tremble. We all descended silently. They did not speak, nor did we, but we kept them surrounded on every side.

Downstairs, in front of the exit to the courtyard, Leon Andruszek, one of ours, took out his revolver and, putting it right in their faces, commanded: "Hands up!" Pale and trembling, they did as they were told. Andruszek searched them both, confiscating their revolvers. He then demanded they hand over their passports. We copied down their names and addresses as they appeared on their passports. Then I drew out my revolver. "You see this?" I said to the *Oenerowcy*. "Remember, we now have your names and addresses, and we can easily find you at any time. If anything happens to Erlich, even if it's not of your doing, you will pay with your lives. Remember this well!" and we let them go.

When they were gone, we waited a bit. I went up to Erlich and I told him everything that had happened. He was in fact sitting and waiting for two people who had telephoned him yesterday and had arranged for a visit at ten o'clock that morning. He was even somewhat suspicious at the time, because the person who called would not tell him clearly what it was he wanted, but he didn't think too much of it, as it often happened that people were reluctant to discuss their legal matters over the telephone. I then went right back down to my comrades. We went off to a restaurant for breakfast—we hadn't eaten since early that morning.

After that, in accordance with a decision by the Party Presidium, we guarded Comrade Erlich for many long weeks, wherever he went, without his knowledge.

Some of our comrades complained that we let the assassins get away without breaking their bones. But to this day I think we did the right thing. Of course we could have broken some bones and even led them off to some abandoned spot and killed them. But what would have been the result? Revenge actions would then have taken place from both sides, and we would never have known how it would all end. About these issues, my position and the position of our militia was always for restraint. We never allowed ourselves to be provoked—not by the Communists and not by the antisemites or Fascists—never to go farther than was absolutely necessary in any given case in order to defend our very existence. We preferred to avoid a fight or a battle, rather than to win one. But when our feeling of social responsibility dictated that we take on a fight, we did so, no matter what the risk.

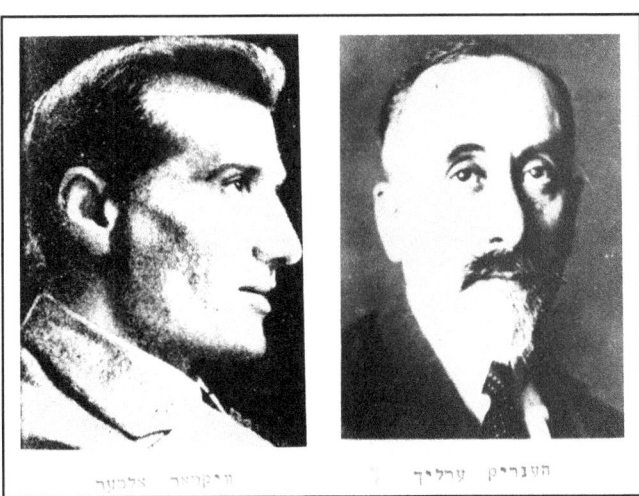

Figure 119. Erlich and Alter; both perished in a Soviet prison in 1941, accused of "anti-Soviet activities." From the Archives of the YIVO Institute for Jewish Research, New York.

Figure 120. Solidarity, the movement to overthrow the Polish Communist regime, issued this commemorative stamp, illegally, in 1988, to honor the memory of these two Bundist leaders. From the Archives of the YIVO Institute for Jewish Research, New York.

CHAPTER 81

December 18, 1938

We lived to see a day that every political party dreams of. A day when the people freely follow you and bestow upon you their boundless loyalty. So it was for the Bund in Warsaw on December 18, 1938, when the elections for the City Council of Poland's capital city took place, as well as in a large number of other cities in Poland. Of 20 Jewish Councilmen that were elected in Warsaw (out of a City Council of 100), the Bund, and its allied trade unions, won 17 seats. All the other Jewish parties—various Zionist parties, Po'ale-Tsiyonistn (Labor Zionists), the Orthodox, merchants, artisans, and others, who presented two tickets or blocks—together received only three votes. The overwhelming majority of the Warsaw Jewish population voted for the Bund.

Quite a number of weeks before the election, while we were campaigning house to house, we sensed how strongly the sympathy for the Bund was growing among the Jews in Warsaw. Our house-to-house campaigners were warmly welcomed in the poor Jewish homes with the greatest friendliness (we didn't campaign among the rich homes at first). Even more symptomatic was the often friendly welcome our campaigners were met with at the homes of the Jewish professional intelligentsia: doctors, lawyers, dentists, engineers, and others. In Poland—among Jews as well as Poles—this sort of person, in their vast majority, were followers of bourgeois parties, so if they sympathetically welcomed Socialist campaigners, this was certainly a bit of a surprise. We also encountered many instances where assimilated Jewish intellectuals living in the strictly Polish neighborhoods showed a great interest in the Bund's election campaign (they would, for example, telephone the Secretariat of the Bund and ask if we had election literature in Polish, asking us to send it to them).

But even the warmest reception to our election campaign, even though they presaged our victory, could not be compared to what happened on the day of the elections. It is impossible to forget what the Jewish streets looked like on that day. Big and small came out for the Bund. There was a sharp frost on that day. It was, according to the American thermometer, close to zero degrees Fahrenheit, but who cared about that? Right in the beginning, thousands of campaigners, Bundists, *Tsukinft*ists, and older SKIFists, who were placed in our Party locales, took their bundles of Bund ballots, and ran to their assigned polling places. Early reports were favorable. The Bund ballots were eagerly torn from their hands. That was still not, it was thought, a sign of victory. After a few hours, reports from the streets kept coming that did signify something. In the Jewish homes, housewives came out with hot tea kettles and distributed cups of tea among our campaigners, who, after standing a couple of hours in the street in the frost, were half frozen. From all streets came the same reports: Jewish women they didn't even know were bringing hot tea out onto the streets to warm our Bund campaigners.

Right after that, another sign came of the prevailing mood on the Jewish streets. Around noon large crowds of children gathered in the heavily Jewish streets, on Smocza, Miła, Gęsia, and surroundings (it was a Sunday, when the children were not in school), pulled out red kerchiefs from somewhere, hung them up on sticks, and marched through the streets, shouting, "Hooray for the Bund! Long live the Bund!"

On that Election Day, our party militia had a responsible task. Rumors were going around that the *Oenerowcy* were going to attack the Jews, terrorize them, and keep them from voting. The experiences of the last few years had taught us to take such rumors seriously.

In addition, the City Council had prepared various harassments. For a large part of the Jewish population of Smocza, Gęsia, Wołyńska,[1] and the surrounding areas, the City Council assigned a polling place near the Jewish cemetery, almost outside the city limits. In order to vote, one had to traverse a field, and on top of that, it was in a Gentile neighborhood. It was, after all, winter, and nightfall came around four o'clock. The way to the poll was poorly illuminated and sparsely inhabited. The governmental authorities figured that the Jews would be afraid to go there to vote for that reason. In addition to that, it was in a Polish neighborhood, an abandoned one, where underworld types, taverns, and drunks were not lacking. What were we to do? We lined the way with our militiamen, and we let the Jews of that precinct know—mouth to mouth—that the path was safe, that the Bund was guarding it, and one could pass through to vote without fear. And in fact, Jews were not frightened away, and they went, in that forlorn corner, in their masses, to vote.

In addition, our militia also had to guard our election campaigners out on the streets, because the danger they would be attacked by the *Oenerowcy* or plain antisemitic hooligans, and even plainclothes policemen, was great.

It also fell to the militia to guard our movement against another danger: false Bund ballots that our opponents (apparently the Jewish National bloc) had printed in order to invalidate the votes for the Bund. What happened was this:

On election day, first thing in the morning, a bookbinder came running to us at the election committee headquarters and told us that at Smocza 4—he gave us the exact address—there was a warehouse full of forged Bund ballots. The falsifying of the ballots consisted in that, for the Bundist ballots of a given region, the names of candidates from another region were printed. In the bookbindery where this man worked all day, he was cutting to size the sheets of paper with the false Bund ballots printed on them. In the morning the boss told him to deliver them to a certain address. He came right from there to warn us about this.

We sent two men to the bookbindery immediately to see if the information was correct, and they came back with a confirmation. At that point a large group of militiamen and I went to the address. When we came into the apartment, the boss was already burning the forged ballots. I dressed him down for what he had done, warning him that we would report him to the courts. He defended himself, saying he didn't know they were false ballots—he was recommended by the housing administrator of the building in which he lived to people who came to rent a place in which they could store election documents. He didn't even look at the documents to see what they were. Secondly, he said, the two men we sent earlier promised him that if he wouldn't let anyone remove the documents till they returned, we wouldn't do anything to him, and, he continued, "As you see, I have kept my word." So we let him alone. Nevertheless we sent people out to all the election offices to make sure that no false Bund ballots were being distributed.

A little later came a second alert about falsified Bund ballots. This time our campaigners caught a boy who was distributing false Bund ballots. They surrounded him and warned him that if he wanted to return home with all his bones in one piece, he should show them where he had obtained the false ballots. He defended himself, saying he didn't know they were false ballots. Apparently he was telling the truth: he was just a poor Jewish boy who had been hired for a couple of zlotys to distribute ballots, so that's what he did. He led our campaigners to Długa 25, to a certain Waxman, and our comrades confiscated a whole warehouse full of false ballots they found there. Then we sent out people again to make sure that no more of these false ballots were being distributed. Did we prevent all these false ballots? We cannot know.

Jews produced these false ballots, and according to all the signs, they were people from the "National Bloc" to whom it was clear, even before the elections, there was going to be a great victory for the Bund, and they wanted to ruin this outcome. As a result, on the day of the election we were, because of this, very much agitated, and we thought we would not let this go without letting it be known. In the morning, however, under the impact of our extraordinary victory, we forgot all about it.

The great victory of the Bund at the Warsaw municipal elections was not simply a local phenomenon. The victory of the Bund was just as large in the municipal elections—some held earlier, at the same time, or later—in many other cities: Lodz, Vilnius, Białystok, Lublin, Tarnów, Piotrków, Włocławek, and Kutno.

At the darkest moment in their battle for elementary civil and national rights, and face to face with an intense, daily struggle for their physical safety and existence, the broad folk masses of Polish Jewry proclaimed their great trust in the Bund.

Figure 121. "Vote! Agitate! For the Bund and the Trade Unions!" A Bund election poster. From the Archives of the YIVO Institute for Jewish Research, New York.

Note

1. Now Lewartowskiego Street.—MR

CHAPTER 82

A Final Look at Our Youth

July 1939. The spectre of the Second World War was already menacing Poland. Amidst the general uneasiness and tension, Comrade Mikhl Merlin and his wife came on a visit from far-away America, from Atlanta, Georgia. Shloyme Mendlsohn, who was acquainted with them from the time of his mission to America in 1935, guided them around Warsaw. He showed them the Medem Sanitarium, our schools, our Grosser Library, the Party offices, and our trade unions. Now, prior to their departure, he wanted to show them something they would long remember. He led them to our youth camps, SKIF and *Tsukunft*, located in the neighborhood of Włocławek. For the last few years, since the intensification of the attacks on Jews, the camps had been relocated near one another so that, if it should become necessary, one camp could come to the aid of the other. Shloyme asked me to come along. Also accompanying us was Moyshe Kligsberg (in his role as "expert").

We first went to the SKIF camp, where they gave Merlin a comradely reception. SKIF-ists with little red flags and in their full dress uniforms (blue shirts and blouses with red kerchiefs) were lined up along the forest road three or four kilometers before the camp. They greeted our auto with their little flags. Through such a highway of young heralds we arrived at the camp. At the edge of the wood, the camp leader welcomed us—Teacher Shifris from Grodno. (When the Bolsheviks occupied Grodno, they arrested him, since he was an active Bundist. They imprisoned him in a Soviet jail and killed him. His wife and daughter now live in America.)

Shifris mustered the SKIF-ists to attention around the camp flag. The SKIF hymn was sung and short speeches begun. Speaking were: Mendlsohn, Shifris, and, at the end, Merlin, the guest. He looked all around several times, at the canvas tents, at the tables and benches cobbled together from plain, unfinished boards, at the "kitchen" made of stones, at the "amphitheatre" around the campfire, at the tall mast of the red flag that waved among the green branches of the tall pine trees, and at the two columns of SKIF-ists, and he began:

"We in America also have 'camps,' better, more comfortable than yours. But what you have here, we don't have"—and at this point he had tears in his eyes.

In the two columns of "anonymous" young SKIF-ists, arrayed around the flag, stood: Yurek Blones, Janek Bilak, Tobshe Davidovich... who could then have imagined that here stood before us the future heroes of the Warsaw Ghetto Uprising!

From there we drove over to the *Tsukunft* camp, located in a wood right by the shore of the Vistula. The director of the camp was at that time Yoylke Litewka, the secretary of the Warsaw *Tsukunft* organization (now with his family in Los Angeles). There we spent the rest of the day.

At dusk we drove home. None of us imagined that we had just seen for the last time the flower of our Jewish youth in Poland in its full loveliness and radiance...

A few days after that, the Polish government ordered us to liquidate both our camps. No reasons were given. But we knew that on the spot where the camps were located, military fortifications were to be built. With heavy hearts we lowered the flags, folded up the tents, and drove home.

A short time later, Hitler's troops marched across the borders of Poland.

The Second World War had begun...

Figure 122. Author Bernard Goldstein's grave in New York. It reads: "Comrade Bernard, leader of the self-defense militia, fighter in the Warsaw Ghetto Uprising, dedicated his life to the Bund. 1889–1959." Photograph courtesy of Victor Gilinsky.

Glossary of Terms, Names, and Acronyms

Numbers in parentheses—in addition to the dates—indicate chaper where the item first appears in the text.

Abramovich, Raphael Rein (1880–1963) (8): A member of the Bund and a leader of the Menshevik wing of the Russian Social-Democratic Workers Party (RSDRP).

Alter, Viktor (or Wictor) (1890–1943) (52): One of the two beloved Bund leaders in the interwar period in Poland (the other being Henryk Erlich). An engineer by profession, active in the Polish Bund starting in 1913, exiled to Siberia, escaped to England where he was a conscientious objector during World War I, went to Russia after the February Revolution, came back to Poland where he served on the Central Committee of the Bund and rose to prominence. Executed by the Stalinist regime in the 1940s.

Ansky (Shloyme Zanvl Rappoport) (1863–1920), (27): Author of "the Oath," the Bund anthem, and the famous Yiddish play, *The Dybbuk*.

Arbeter Vinkl (52): Workers Corner. A kind of tea café, where workers could come in the evening and have a cup of tea, eat a piece of bread and herring, and read a newspaper. In one of the rooms, a reading room was created with newspapers and journals (mounted on wooden sticks, as was the custom in Polish coffee houses.

bibke (50): A small, intimate get-together of friends and acquaintances, with refreshments, at a home.

Blum, Abrasza (1905–1943) (46): A leader of the wartime underground Bund and young hero of the Warsaw Ghetto Uprising. By profession, a structural engineer. Beginning in 1930, a director of the *Folkstsaytung*. In September 1939, participated in the defense of Warsaw, helping to organize all-Jewish detachments. When Warsaw fell, most of the Bund's senior leadership evacuated the city: they were too well-known; the leadership of the party fell to the Youth-Bund *Tsukunft*ists. Abrasza worked in the ghetto brush factory, 1942–1943. He was Bund representative to the Jewish Fighting Organization (ZOB). Escaped the burning ghetto through the sewers, hiding in the apartment of the Bund courier, Władka. The janitor reported him to the Gestapo. Abrasza escaped through the window on a rope made from bedsheets but broke his legs in the fall from the third story; captured and murdered by the Gestapo in 1943.

Brisk (54): Yiddish name for *Brześć* or *Brześć Litewski* or *Brześć nad Bugiem* (Polish) or *Brest-Litovsk* (English). Now part of Belarus. Once a center of Jewish scholarship: followers of the famous Brisk Solveitchik family of rabbis were called "Briskers."

Chanin, Nathan (1885–1965) (61): Bundist from an early age, active in various strikes and assassination attempts; arrested several times; almost executed by firing squad in 1905: his fiery and impassioned speech talked the soldiers out of firing; put in irons and sent to Siberia for an eight-year sentence; escaped; arrived in New York in 1912; became a cap maker, joined their union, and became Vice President. During World War I, joined the Jewish Socialist Federation; in 1921; in opposition to the Comintern, joined the *Jewish Socialist Farband of the Socialist Party of America*, becoming its General Secretary. Led the fight against Communist takeovers in the Workmen's Circle in the twenties, in the Cap and Millinery Workers Union, in the ILGWU Cloakmakers Union, in the Furriers Union, House Painters Union, Leather Workers Union, etc. Delegate to the International Socialist Congress in Brussels, 1928. From 1936–1952, Educational Director of the Workmen's Circle. Elected General Secretary of the Workmen's Circle in 1952. Publishes many articles in *Folkstsaytung, Veker, Forverts, Fraynd, Undzer Shul, Kultur un Dertsiyung, Tsukunft, Kinder-Tsaytung*. Published many books, among them, *Sovyet Rusland: Vi Ikh Hob Zi Gezen; A Rayze Iber Tsentral un Dorem Amerike; Berele.*

Di Shvue (27): "The Oath," the Bund's anthem, written by S. Rappaport (Ansky), author of the famous Yiddish play, *The Dybbuk*. The lyrics in Yiddish and English translation of the first two stanzas and refrain:

Brider un shvester fun arbet un noyt,
   Brothers and sisters of toil and of poverty
Ale vos zaynen tsezeyt un tseshprey,
   All who are scattered and dispersed,
Tsuzamen, Tsuzamen,
   Together, together,
Di fon zi iz greyt,
   The flag is ready,
Zi flatert fun tsorn,
   It flutters with rage,
Fun blut iz zi royt
   With blood it is red,
A shvue, shvue,
   An oath, an oath,

Oyf lebm un toyt.
        On our lives, on our deaths.
        (refrain)

Himl un erd vet unz oyshern,
        Heaven and earth will hear us out,
Eydes vet zayn di likhtike shtern,
        The bright stars will bear witness
A shvue fun blut, a shvue fun trern,
        An oath of blood an oath of tears,
Mir shvern, mir shvern,
        We swear, we swear,

Mir shvern tsu kemfn far frayhayt un rekht,
        We swear to fight for freedom and right
Mit ale tiranen un zeyere knekht,
        With all tyrants and their slaves,
Tsebrekhn, tsebrekhn di finstere makht,
        To smash, to smash the dark power,
Oder mit heldnsmut tsu faln in shlakht.
        Or to die in battle with the courage of heroes.

        (refrain)

Himl un erd.

din toyre (46): Lawsuits brought before a rabbinic court.

droshky (46): A low, four-wheeled, horse-drawn carriage.

Dubnow-Erlich, Sophia (1885–1986) (51): The daughter of the historian Simon Dubnow, wife of the preeminent Bundist leader, Henryk Erlich, and mother-in-law of Shoshke Erlich. In addition to her Bundist activism, she was a poet, critic, translator, biographer, and memoirist.

Endek (15): Fascist antisemitic National Democratic party of Poland ("Endek" from the name of the letter *N*, the initial letter of the first word of this party's name, *Narodowa Demokracja* + *-dek* (from the *d* and *k* in *Demokracja*).

Erlich (or Ehrlich), Henryk (1882–1942) (52): A lawyer by profession, the other of these two beloved leaders of the Polish Bund between the wars. He was a member of the 1917 Petrograd Soviet, then later in Poland, a member of the Warsaw City Council and a member of the Executive Committee of the Second International. Perished in Stalinist imprisonment in the 1940s.

Fareynikte or Uniteds (1): *Fareynikte Yidishe Sotsyalistishe Arbeter Partey*—United Jewish Socialist Workers Party, a unification (*fareynikung*) in 1917 of the Zionist Socialist Workers Party and the Jewish Socialist Workers Party. The Uniteds, like the Bund, believed in fighting for civil rights and cultural autonomy in Poland and the Ukraine, but also, unlike the Bund, in seeking to create a Jewish state in any available territory (not necessarily in Palestine).

Fayranter (23): Overtime hours. In several trades the established custom was that the fully employed workers would give up their overtime hours to their unemployed comrades; it was an especially old tradition among the bakers.

Leon Feiner (1885–1945) (42): A lawyer and Bund activist. While living as a Pole on the "Aryan" side of Warsaw under the assumed name "Berezowski," was a leading figure in the Jewish underground, meeting with couriers, distributing funds, acquiring arms for the uprising, finding hiding places for Jews on the "Aryan" side, etc. He was the author of most of the communiqués of the Bund from Poland to the Western allies, in which he described the Nazi terror, brutality, and genocide. Served as a guide for the Polish courier Jan Karski inside the Warsaw Ghetto (they both crossed into the ghetto through the Warsaw sewers). Survived the war and the uprising; died of throat cancer in Lublin in 1945.

Folkstsaytung (21): "People's Newspaper," the Bund's daily newspaper.

Forverts (72): The first issue of *Forverts* ("Forward") appeared on April 22, 1897, in New York City. The paper's name, as well as its political orientation, was borrowed from the German Social-Democratic Party and its organ *Vorwärts* (it should be noted here that the standard Yiddish term for "forward" is *foroys*; *forverts* is nonstandard, considered a Germanism (*daytshmerish*)). By 1912 its circulation was 120,000, and by the late 1920s, the *Forward* was a leading US metropolitan daily with considerable influence and a nationwide circulation of more than 275,000, the largest daily Yiddish newspaper in the world.

FRAC (20): PPS-Revolutionary Faction *(FRACcja)*, a breakaway party from the PPS, formed in 1906 by Pilsudski, who wanted a more militant nationalism (including a war of liberation against Russia), a position rejected by the 1906 PPS Congress.

Frydrich, Zalmen (1911–1943) (36): Member of the Bund and the Jewish Fighting Organization (ZOB) in the Warsaw ghetto. World War II drafted into the Polish army, fought the Germans and fell prisoner. After his release, returned to Warsaw, where he got involved in underground activities. In early August 1942, during the Great Aktion (mass deportations from the Warsaw ghetto) he went on a mission for the Bund to follow up on the deportees to Treblinka to find out exactly what was happening there. He brought the information back to the Warsaw ghetto. On September 20, 1942, the Bund's underground newspaper *Oyf Der Vakh* (On Watch) published an article, "The Jews of Warsaw are Being Murdered in Treblinka," based on his testimony. During the Warsaw ghetto uprising, Friedrich served as a courier between the fighters and ZOB Headquarters. On April 30, 1943 he escaped the burning ghetto via the sewers to the "Aryan" side of the city. In May, while accompanying a group of fighters to a village hiding place, he fell in combat.

Gabai (27): Title of the administrative manager of a synagogue; overseer; trustee.

Gilinsky, Shloyme (1888–1961) (66): Educator, founder of secular Yiddish schools, author of textbooks in Yiddish; later, Director of the Medem Sanitarium; Bundist, Warsaw city councilman.

Grosser, Bronisław (1883–1912) (69): A Bundist writer and theorist on Jewish nationalism. A lawyer by profession, he was recognized as one of the party's most articulate defenders of Jewish national-cultural autonomy. Defining himself as a Polish-Jewish Socialist whose task it was to defend the interests of the Jewish workers in Poland, he became a Bundist legend, with several cultural, educational, and health institutions established in his name in interwar Poland, including the renowned Bronislaw Grosser Library in Warsaw.

Grosser Library (78): The Grosser Library, named after Bundist theoretician Bronislaw Grosser, became a part of the *Kultur-Lige* (Culture League). Herman Kruk became its director and he began an energetic campaign to broaden its activities. The library burgeoned, containing tens of thousands of books. It then rented its own space on Leszno 13 where a study room was set up along with a large reading room with hundreds of journals and newspapers from all over the world. The library was free to all. It was the largest lending library in Warsaw and deserves an honorable place in a history of the cultural life of Warsaw Jewry.

gymnasium (17): European secondary school at about the level of the American community college.

Haller, Jozef (1873–1960) (5): Polish general, military hero; member of Polish parliament, 1922–1927. Because of his nationalist views, considered one of those responsible for the antisemitic riots in Czestochowa, 1919.

Hallertchikes (5): Soldiers in General Haller's army.

Hashomer Hatzair (42): Hebrew for "The Youth Guard," a Socialist-Zionist, secular Jewish youth movement founded in 1913 in Austro-Hungary. By 1939, it had 70,000 members worldwide, with its membership base in Eastern Europe. In contradistinction to the Bund, Hashomer Hatzair believed the liberation of Jewish youth could be accomplished by immigration to Palestine and living in kibbutzim.

Hasidism (22): A mystical branch of Orthodox Judaism, stressing joy, dance, song, drink, and festivity. It arose around 1700 among Ukrainian Jews, spreading in great numbers among the Jews of Eastern Europe. Various sects of Hasidism, usually named after their town of origin, owe fervent allegiance to their particular founding rabbi and, often, to his descendants. In its beginnings, it was bitterly and actively opposed by the *misnagdim*, traditional, orthodox Jews who believe in the deep study and mastery of holy texts and commentaries, as opposed to the joyful and mystical excesses of the Hasidim and their wonder-working rabbis.

Hazomir (22): Founded in the early 1900s by the classic Yiddish writer, I. L. Peretz, to replace the Yiddish Literary Society banned by the Czarist government. Chaired by Peretz, it became an important cultural center in Warsaw, featuring his readings, speeches, and his famous "question-and-answer-box" evenings.

Ispolkom (chapter 1): *Ispolnitelniy Komitet*—Executive Committee.

Janek Jankliewicz (1887–1920): Typesetter. Led illegal typesetting, printing, and distributing of Bund underground press. Member of Central Committee. Selected as delegate to the Bund's planned 8th convention in Vienna in 1914. Executive Secretary of the Central Bureau of the 20-craft association of trade unions (1915). Arrested by Germans in 1916. 20,000 Jewish workers attended his Warsaw funeral.

Jewish Labor Committee (69): Formed in 1934 by Yiddish-speaking immigrant trade union leaders and leaders of the Bund and Workmen's Circle in response to the rise of Nazism in Germany. Its first president was the Bundist, Baruch Charney Vladeck. Bundist influence was significant, especially in the organization's early period. The JLC worked to support Jewish labor institutions in European countries, cooperate with American organized labor, assist the anti-Nazi underground movement, and combat antisemitism. After the outbreak of World War II, the emphasis was on efforts to save Jewish cultural and political figures, as well as Jewish and non-Jewish labor and Socialist leaders facing certain death at the hands of the Nazis. The Committee succeeded in bringing over a thousand of such individuals to the United States, or to temporary shelter elsewhere.

Joint Distribution Committee ("Joint") (77): The largest nonpolitical organization dedicated to helping Jews in distress all over the world. Founded in 1914, it was generally known as the JDC or "Joint" and headquartered in New York. The Joint began its work in Warsaw in 1919. The JDC Overseas Unit in Warsaw was staffed by dozens of American experts. They organized urgently needed sanitary and medical aid, as well as childcare. The JDC's appropriations for the relief of Polish Jewry in 1920 alone totaled almost $5 million.

Kahan, Borukh Mordkhe (Virgili), (1883–1936); beloved Bundist activist, labor leader; also active in organizing and supporting the Yiddish secular school movement; 20,000 Jewish workers attended his funeral in Vilnius.

Kehilla (21): Official Jewish Community Council.

kest (13): The old traditional Jewish custom of the parents of the bride supporting a newlywed couple for several years.

khale (22): Braided, holiday bread, also transliterated as *challah* or *hallah*.

khesedl (51): *khesedl*, diminutive of *khesed*, literally means, "favor, mercy, clemency, grace;" the Yiddish expression *mit khesed* means, "it could be worse"; street vendors.

Klepfisz, Mikhl (58): Young Bundist; Warsaw Ghetto Uprising hero; an engineer who manufactured grenades, bottle bombs, and mines for the fighters and died a heroic death during the fighting by throwing himself on a German machine gun to save his comrades. His then little daughter, Irena Klepfisz, survived and is now an acclaimed poet in America.

Kremer, Arkady (79) (1865–1935): Known as the "father" of the Bund. In September 1897, Kremer and his comrades founded the General Jewish Workers Union (Bund) in Vilnius. Kremer was one of three members of its first Central Committee and was widely respected as the Bund's leader. Just a few months after the Bund's founding, Kremer was also one of the main organizers of the Founding Congress of the Russian Social-Democratic Labor Party (RSDLP), which would later (in 1903) split into Bolsheviks and Mensheviks. His death in 1935 was commemorated with massive marches and heroic obituaries in the Bund's party press.

Kruk, Herman (42) (1897–1944): Director of the library in the Vilnius Ghetto; chronicler and author of *The Last Days of the Jerusalem of Lithuania: Chronicles from the Vilnius Ghetto and the Camps, 1939–1944* (New Haven, 2002). He buried his journal on September 17, 1944, a day before he and almost all the other prisoners in a Nazi concentration camp in Estonia were forced to carry logs to a pile, spread them in a layer, and lie down naked on them so they could be executed and burned in a massive pyre.

Kultur-lige (42): "Culture League." Founded in Kiev in 1918 and supported by various Yiddishist parties, it encompassed all spheres of culture: drama, music, lectures, libraries, concerts, press, books, periodicals, education (playing an active role in TYSYSHO), as well as hiking and camping. In Poland in 1925, the leadership of the Kultur-lige was taken over by the Bund and became its "cultural section."

Landrat (16): Jewish Trade Union National Council.

Lebns-Fragn (2): "Issues Affecting Our Lives," the Bund's daily newspaper.

Literary Club (1916–1939) (31): *Fareyn fun Yidishe Literatn un Zhurnalistn in Varshe*: Association of Yiddish Writers and Journalists in Warsaw, a trade union, advocacy group, and social meeting venue for writers. Its initial location was at 13 Tłomackie Street, an address associated with the Yiddish secular cultural movement. The premises functioned as a social meeting place not only for members, but also for actors, artists, teachers, guests from abroad, and others who were interested in Yiddish secular culture. In addition, the Association offered a large variety of literary and other activities, both for its members and for the general public.

Masuvke, First of May (53): "Meetings to prepare," that is, the pre-First of May meetings.

Matse (4): Usually rendered as *matzoh*—unleavened flat bread eaten during Passover, tothe exclusion of ordinary bread with leavening.

Medem, Vladimir (1879–1923) (5): The main theorist of the Bund and its most famous and celebrated leader, revered and beloved by Bundists.

Medem Sanitarium (44): Founded in 1926 in Międzeszyn near Warsaw, it was an educational and clinical facility for children and young adults at risk for tuberculosis. Named after the Bundist leader Vladimir Medem, it was the pride of the Bund. Until World War II, it was recognized internationally for its reformist pedagogical approach and its social-democratic, secular orientation. On August 22, 1942, over 100 of its children, their teachers, and staff were brutally rounded up by the Germans, taken to Treblinka, and gassed to death.

Mendelson, Shloyme (1896–1948) (22): Well-known Bundist leader, writer, speaker, and public intellectual; member of the Polish Bund's Central Committee; "A kind of spiritual leader inside the movement . . . elected to the Warsaw City Council in 1938 . . . considered by his colleagues an inspiring orator and prolific writer . . . a giant in the movement . . . thousands attended his funeral in New York City, demonstrating how popular and influential a figure he was " (David Slucki, 180).

Henoch Mendelsund (1911–1994) (35): Worked as a mechanic and attended Warsaw University. Arrived in the US in 1941 as one of 1,500 Bundist labor leaders and intellectuals rescued from the Nazis through the efforts of the ILGWU and the Jewish Labor Committee. Joined the ILGWU as a sewing machine operator. While working in the shop during the day, attended the New School for Social Research at night, earning a master's degree in economics and sociology. Served as a member of the National Coat and Suit Recovery Board staff, and in 1949 became secretary of Cloak Finishers Local 9. In 1953 became assistant general manager of the ILGWU New York Cloak Joint Board, and then general manager in September 1959, a post he held until 1973. Also served as ILGWU Vice President and director of the International Relations Department from 1968–1980.

Michalewicz, Bejnisz (1876–1928) (53): One of the most important Bund theoreticians in the 1920s. Forty thousand Jewish workers marched in his funeral profession. Three hundred and thirty-nine wreaths were laid at his bier on behalf of various labor and social-democratic delegations, both foreign and domestic. The national idea of the Bund, he wrote, was that every nation does not necessarily need a separate state and that every state does not necessarily need to be inhabited by one nation. A state of nations was the way of the Bund—a large, open state, accommodating diverse nationalities.

Mir Kumen On (46): "We Are On Our Way," a documentary directed by Aleksander Ford, one of Poland's leading young directors in the thirties, with a script by the well-known Polish novelist, Wanda Wasilewska, produced 1935 by the Bund and the Medem Sanitarium. Banned by the Polish government and not permitted to be shown in Poland, it was screened in Paris, Brussels, and New York. It is now available in DVD format with the title

Children Must Laugh from the National Center for Jewish Film, Brandeis University, Waltham, MA.

Mizrachi (18): Religious Zionist organization founded in 1902 in Vilnius that believed the Torah should be at the center of Zionism.

Morgnshtern (36): "Morningstar," the Bund's sports organizations, the largest such organization in all of Poland, Jewish or Polish.

Narovtses (50): Members of the virulently antisemitic, Fascistic party, the *ONR (Obóz Narodowo-Radykalny* or National Radical Camp).

Nowogrodzki, Emanuel (1891–1967): General Secretary of the Polish Bund's Central Committee. In America by chance in 1939 when the war broke out. Founded the Bund Representation and the Bund Coordinating Committee in America. Editor and writer for the Bund's monthly in New York, *Undzer Tsayt*. Author of *The Ghetto Speaks* (Warsaw, 1936?), *Individual, Rank and File, and Leader* (Warsaw, 1934), *Henryk Erlich and Victor Alter* (1951), and *The Jewish Labor Bund in Poland 1915–1939* (2001), later translated into Polish as *Żydowska partia robotnica Bund w Polsce 1915–1939* (2005).

Noyekh (sometimes also known as Jozef), Yekusiel Portnoy (1872–1941), leader of the Bund in Poland, a charismatic paternal figure with enormous moral authority.

Oenerowcy (57): Members of the ONR (which see).

Ogniwo (58): See *Ringen*.

ONR (56): A virulently antisemitic, Fascist party, the *ONR (Obóz Narodowo-Radykalny* or National Radical Camp), its members usually referred to as *Narovtses* or as *Oenerowcy*.

ORT (22): *Obshchestvo Remeslennago i Zemledelecheskago Truda Sredi Evreev v Rossii* (The Society for Handicraft and Agricultural Work among the Jews of Russia: ORT). Established in 1880 in Russia to support craft education in schools and workshops to encourage Jews to become artisans and agriculturalists. Branches were active in almost every Russian city having a substantial Jewish population. After World War I, ORT began to work outside of Russia.

Orzech, Maurycy (1891–1943) (55) (70): Polish-Jewish economist, journalist, politician, and leader of the Bund in interwar Poland; one of the Bund's commanders during the Warsaw Ghetto Uprising. Captured and murdered by the Nazis.

Pasharnyes (3): Farms where chickens were raised for shipment to Warsaw.

Peretz, I. L. (1852–1915) (31): Considered the "father" of modern Yiddish literature, one of the three great founders of modern Yiddish literature whose home in Warsaw drew many new young Yiddish writers seeking his imprimatur.

Petliura, Vasylyovych (1879–1926) (1): Publicist, writer, journalist, Ukrainian politician, statesman of the Ukrainian People's Republic, and national leader who led Ukraine's struggle for independence (1918–1921) following the Russian Revolution of 1917. On May 25, 1926, Petliura was slain with five shots from a handgun in broad daylight in the center of Paris by the Jewish-Russian anarchist, Sholem Schwartzbard, to avenge Ukranian pogroms against the Jews.

pletsl (48): Little plaza or square.

Po'ale Tsiyon (81): Labor Zionist.

Pomocniki (23): Bakers assistants.

PPS (3): *Polska Partia Socjalistyczna*—Polish Socialist Party.

Red Falcons (55): The name of various Socialist children's organizations, popular in Europe and the United States, emerging during the First and Second World Wars; the first such group was founded by Anton Tesarek, an Austrian Socialist educator.

Ringen (58): "Links," as in a chain; a Bundist organization for Jewish university students (Polish name, *Ogniwo*).

RM'O (8): Acronymn (pronounced "Ramu") for Rabbi Moses (Moyshe) Isserlis, 1520–1572), Talmudist, famous for his decisions in Jewish law; renowned author of *ha-Mapah*, a commentary on Jewish law.

Robotnik (32): *Worker*, the PPS newspaper and central organ of the party.

Schutzbund (55): In full, *Republikanischer Schutzbund* (German: "Republican Defense League"), paramilitary Socialist organization active in Austria between World War I and 1934.

SDKPiL (3): *Socjaldemokracja Królestwa Polskiego i Litwy* (Social Democracy of the Kingdom of Poland and Lithuania); founded in 1893; originally the Social Democracy of the Kingdom of Poland (SDKP); Marxist; in 1918 merged into the Communist Workers Party of Poland; Rosa Luxemburg most famous member.

Sejmowiec (15) or *Sejmist*: A member of SERP (the Jewish Socialist Workers Party), which called for the establishment of an extraterritorial Jewish diet for all of Russian Jewry, with national, political, and cultural autonomy.

shtadtlan (46): Traditionally, a public intercessor for the Jews with the authorities; has acquired pejorative implications.

shtibl (52): A small Hasidic place of prayer, often an apartment in a building.

Shulman, Victor (1876–1951) (7): Noted journalist, leading figure of the Bund, joining in his early youth. Exiled to Siberia. Escaped. From 1915, resided in Warsaw where he was managing editor of the *Folkstsaytung*. During Nazi invasion, escaped to Lithuania and, in 1940, among a handful of political refugees permitted to enter the United States.

Shvue, Di (27): "The Oath," the Bund anthem, written by Ansky, author of the famous Yiddish play, *The Dybbuk*.

Shvues (27): In Sephardic Hebrew, *Shavuot*, a Jewish holiday celebrated seven weeks after Passover, to commemorate the giving of the Torah at Mt. Sinai.

SKIF (50): *Sotsyalistishe Kinder Farband*: Socialist Children's Union, the Bund's organization with programs for children, founded in 1926.

SKRA (55): *Robotniczy Klub Sportowy*—Workers Sports Club, the PPS's labor sports association.
Socialist Zionists (17): Founded in Odessa in 1905 as the Zionist Socialist Workers Party and committed to territorialism (the idea that Jews should seek to found a state anywhere in the world it might be possible to do so).
SRs (13): Revolutionary Party, or Party of Socialist Revolutionaries (the SRs, or "Esers"), a major political party in early 20th century Russia and a key player in the Russian Revolution.
Tabaczinski, Benyomin (1896–1967) (42): Active Bundist in *Białystok*. Emigrated to America in 1938 where he became Executive Secretary of the Jewish Labor Committee and a leading figure in the World Yiddish Culture Congress, YIVO, and Workmen's Circle; also a member of the Bund's Representation to Poland and the World Coordinating Committee of the Bund.
TOZ (36): *Towarzystwo Ochrony Zdrowia Ludności Żydowskiej* Society for Safeguarding the Health of the Jewish Population. Established in Warsaw in 1921; by 1939 in charge of 368 clinics and institutes in 72 towns, employing 1,000 physicians, nurses, and residents.
Tsayt (23): Pre-World War I Bundist newspaper in St. Petersburg.
Tsholnt (23): A special dish (meat, potatoes, legumes) for the Sabbath meal, prepared the day before and stored Friday night in Bakers' ovens so it could be picked up and served warm on the Sabbath, when no cooking is allowed.
Tsukunft or *Yugnt-Bund Tsukunft in Poyln* (3): "The Future" or "Youth-Bund Future in Poland," the Bund's youth organization.
TSYSHO (8): Acronym for *Tsentrale Yidishe Shul Organizatsye*—Central Yiddish School Organization, which created and administered a network of secular Yiddish schools under Socialist auspices, led primarily by the Bund and the Left Po'ale Tsiyon (Labor Zionists).
TUR (72): *Towarzystwo Uniwer- sytetow Robotniczych,* Workers University Association, the youth organization of the PPS.
United Hebrew Trades (61): Founded by Yiddish Branch 8 of the Socialist Labor Party and some Jewish unions in 1888, Morris Hillquit one of its founding members. By 1910 it had 106 unions and 150,000 workers, growing to 200,000 by 1922, and to 250,000 by 1938. It joined with other unions and organizations in 1934 to form the Jewish Labor Committee, which was heavily influenced by the Bund, electing Bundist Baruch Charney Vladek as its first president.
Uniteds or United Jewish Socialist Workers Party (1): See *Fareynikte*.
Weinreich, Max (1894–1969) (56): Born in Kuldiga, Latvia, then part of Russia; completed his doctorate in linguistics in 1923 at Marburg University; Yiddish linguist, literary scholar, public intellectual, the driving force behind YIVO; the impetus behind an impressive series of academic publications

in Yiddish by himself and others; author of a monumental *History of the Yiddish Language* in Yiddish; member of the Bund.

YAF (51): *Yidishe Arbeter Froy*—Jewish Working Woman, a special division of the Bund to conduct political agitation among Jewish women and to provide them with counseling and cultural enrichment.

YIVO (48): Acronym for *Yidisher Visnshaftlekher Institut* (Yiddish Scientific Institute). Founded in 1925, it became the leading institution for scholarship in Yiddish and about the history and culture of East European Jews and their emigrant communities. Now in New York, renamed the *YIVO Institute for Jewish Research*.

Yugnt-Veker (38): "Youth Awakener," Bund periodical for youth.

ZNMS (58): *Związek Niezależnej Młodzieży Socjalistycznej*, Independent Union of Socialist Youth, the PPS's university student organization.

ZOB (36): *Zydowska Organizacja Bojowa*; in Yiddish, *Yidishe Kamf Organizatsye* (Jewish Fighting Organization), underground Jewish military group established in the Warsaw Ghetto to resist deportations of Jews to extermination camps. The ZOB was formed on July 28, 1942, during a two-month wave of deportations to Treblinka. During the deportations of the summer of 1942, the ZOB appealed to the ghetto's Jews to resist. However, the Jews did not heed their call. In addition, the ZOB was made up of different political factions who had trouble cooperating, and the group did not have enough weapons. Thus, the ZOB was unable to execute any effective attacks at that time. When the deportations ended, ZOB members saw that they needed to settle their differences and shape up in order to be of any help to the Jews of the ghetto. Many new members joined under the leadership of Mordecai Anielewicz, who became head of a revitalized ZOB in November 1942. They prepared for the next onslaught by the Germans, and executed those Jews in the ghetto who had helped the Nazis carry out the deportations. In January 1943, they resisted Nazi attempts to round up Jews. The ZOB then organized the Warsaw Ghetto Uprising and when the revolt broke out in April 1943, ZOB members fought heroically to the bitter end.—Shoah Resource Center, The International School for Holocaust Studies.

Zygielbojm, Shmuel-Mordkhe (1895–1943) (10): Party name "Artur." In 1924 elected to the Central Committee of the Bund in Poland, serving in that capacity until leaving Warsaw in 1940. Chairman of several leading Bundist institutions and trade unions of Polish-Jewish workers. City Councilman in Warsaw (1924–1936) and in Lodz (1936–1939). Participated in the defense of Warsaw against German invaders in 1939, helping to organize the Jewish fighting battalions and acting as a member of the general Warsaw Defense Committee. Volunteered to be one of 12 hostages demanded by the Germans in 1939, later becoming a member of the Judenrat. Member of the first Warsaw committee of the underground Bund. Only member of Judenrat to urge the Judenrat to defy the German order for the Jews to enter a walled ghetto. He followed this with a speech to a mass of Jews outside the Judenrat building, calling on them to refuse to go voluntarily into the ghetto. The Bund leadership, in January 1940, asked Comrade Artur to smuggle himself out of Poland to the free world and to tell them what was happeining to the Jews of Poland. He made his way across Nazi Germany and occupied Europe to America and finally to England, where he became a member of the Polish Government in Exile representing the Bund. Failing to arouse the free world to come in any way to the aid of the Jews of Poland, on May 11, 1943 (after the heroic Warsaw Ghetto Uprising), he committed suicide, leaving a letter in which he stated that perhaps with his death he would succeed in arousing the free world to the plight of the Polish Jews when he was unable to do that while living. The note said, among many other things, "I cannot live while the remnants of the Jewish people in Poland, whom I represent, continue to be liquidated."

References

Aronson, Gregor, et al., ed. *Di Geshikhte fun Bund, Vol. 1–5.* New York: Unzer Tsayt Farlag, 1960, 1962, 1966, 1972, 1981. (Volume 1 edited by S. Dubnow-Erlich et al.; Volume 5 (1926–1932) written by I. S. Hertz.)

Auerbach, Ephraim; Moyshe Shtarkman; Yitsrok Charlash, et al. *Leksikon fun der Nayer Yidisher Literatur* (Biographical and Bibliographical Lexicon of Modern Yiddish Literature, 8 volumes). New York: Congress for Jewish Culture, 1956–1981.

Celemenski, Yankev. *Mitn Farshnitenem Folk.* New York: Undzer Tsayt Farlag, 1963.

Dawidowicz, Lucy S. *The Golden Tradition.* New York: Holt Rinehart, and Winston, 1967.

Dubinsky, David and A.H. Raskin. *David Dubinsky: A Life with Labor.* New York: Simon and Schuster, 1977.

Farlag Undzer Tsayt, ed. *Henryk Erlich un Victor Alter.* New York: Undzer Tsayt, 1951.

Gitelman, Zvi Y. *The Emergence of Modern Jewish Politics: Bundism and Zionism in Eastern Europe.* Pittsburgh: University of Pittsburgh Press, 2003.

Goldstein, Bernard, translated by Leonard Shatzkin. *The Stars Bear Witness.* New York: Viking Press, 1949.

Hertz, I. S. *Der Bund in Bilder: 1897–1957.* New York: Undzer Tsayt Farlag, 1958.

———, ed. *Doyres Bundistn, Vol. 1, 2, 3.* New York: Undzer Tsayt Farlag, 1956, 1968.

———. *50 Yor Arbeter-Ring in Yidishn Lebm.* New York: WC National Executive Committee, 1950.

Hundert, Gershon David, ed. *YIVO Encyclopedia of Jews in Eastern Europe.* New York: YIVO Institute for Jewish Research, 2008.

Jacobs, Jack. *Bundist Counterculture in Interwar Poland.* Syracuse: Syracuse University Press & YIVO, 2009.

———, ed. *Jewish Politics in Eastern Europe: The Bund at 100.* New York: New York University Press, 2001.

———. *On Socialists and "The Jewish Question" after Marx.* New York: New York University Press, 1992.

Jacobs, Jack and Gertrud Pickhan. "New Research on the Bund." *East European Jewish Affairs* 43, no. 3 (December 2013).

Johnpoll, Bernard K. *The Politics of Futility: The General Jewish Workers Bund of Poland, 1917–1943.* Ithaca: Cornell University Press, 1967.

Kazhdan, H. S., ed. *Medem Sanitorye Bukh.* Tel Aviv: Hamenora, 1971.

Medem, Vladimir. *The Memoirs of Vladimir Medem.* Translated and edited by Samuel A. Portnoy. New York: KTAV, 1979.

Meed, Vladka. *On Both Sides of the Wall.* Translated by Moshe Spiegel and Steven Meed. Tel Aviv: Beit Lohamei Haghettaot & Hakibbutz Hameuchad Publishing House, 1973.

Melzer, Emanuel. *No Way Out: The Politics of Polish Jewry, 1935–1939.* Cincinnati: Hebrew Union College Press, 1997.

Mendelson, Ezra. *Class Struggle in the Pale: The Formative Years of the Jewish Workers Movement in Tsarist Russia.* London: Cambridge University Press, 1970.

———. *On Modern Jewish Politics.* New York: Oxford University Press, 1993.

Michels, Tony. *A Fire in Their Hearts.* Cambridge: Harvard University Press, 2005.

Nowogrodzki, Emanuel. *The Jewish Labor Bund in Poland: 1915–1939.* Rockville, MD: Shengold, 2001.

Pikhan, Gertud. *Gegen den Strom: Der Allgemeine Judisher Arbeiterbund "Bund" in Polen 1918–1939.* Munich: DVA, 2001.

Portnoy, Samuel A., ed. *Henryk Erlich and Victor Alter: Two Heroes and Martyrs for Jewish Socialism.* Hoboken, NJ: KTAV and Jewish Labor Bund.

Prager, Leonard. *Yiddish Literary and Linguistic Periodicals and Miscellanies: A Selective Annotated Bibliography.* Darby, PA: Norwood Editions, 1982.

Ravel, Aviva. *Faithful Unto Death: The Story of Arthur Zygielbaum.* Montreal: Workmen's Circle, 1980.

Segalowicz, Z. *Tlomatske 13.* Buenos Aires: Tsentral Farband fun Poylishe Yidn in Argentine, 1946.

Slucki, David. *The International Jewish Labor Bund after 1945: Toward a Global History.* Piscataway, NJ: Rutgers University Press, 2012.

Tobias, Henry J. *The Jewish Bund in Russia: From its Origins to 1905.* Stanford: Stanford University Press, 1972.

Trachtenberg, Barry. *The Revolutionary Roots of Modern Yiddish, 1903–1917.* Syracuse: Syracuse University Press, 2008.

Index

A

ABC (newspaper), 369–370
Abramovich, Raphael, 49, 50n2, 291–292, 293n3, 397
Abram the Lady, 106–107
Actors Union, 327
Alter, Victor, 54, *207,* 267, 268, *274,* 282, 283, *292, 316, 389,* 397
   death of, 50, 51n3
   trade union unification and, 83
Alter-Ivinska, Esther, 237–238
Ambaras, Berl, 17, 190, 198
Anti-Semitism
   boycotts of Jewish businesses and, 301–302
   Brisk pogrom and, 373–377
   Father Trzeciak and, 355–357
   "ghetto benches" in universities and, 303–306
   Jewish Labor Committee and, 344, 347n1
   medical schools and, 91
   Minsk-Mazowiecki pogrom and, 363–366
   murder of Jewish child at First of May demonstration and, 367–368
   Onerowcy newspaper and, 369–370
   Poland under Hitler and, 295–300
   Przytuk pogrom and, 359–362
   Warsaw City Council and, 24–25
Arbeter Vinkl, See "Workers Corner"
Arciszewski, Tomasz, 91, 161
Arkady Group, 384, 385n3
Arsenal, the, 15, 16
Assassination attempts on Bernard Goldstein, 205–207, 227–229
Autonomy, cultural, 83–84

B

Back porters, 101–102, 191
   met by Bernard Goldstein, 105–109
   mutual aid by, 103–104
Bagel bakers, 129–131
Bagiński, K., 192
Bakers Union, 63, 123–127, 201
   bagel bakers within, 129–131
   communists and, 126, 311–314
Bass, Alter, 125
Berczikes family (slaughterers), 97–98
Bereza Kartuska, 299
Berman, Dina, 233
Berman, Leybetshke, 205
Bilak, Janek, 396
Blones, Yurek, 396
Blum, Abrasza, *233,* 234n1
Bolsheviks, 9–10, 41–42, 43, 379, 395

Boycotts of Jewish businesses, 301–302
Brisk, pogrom in, 373–377
Bródno suburb, Poland, 355–357
Brojde-Heller, Anna, 50, 196, 220
Brumberg, Yoysef, 220, 308
Bund, the, 1. *See also* First of May demonstrations; Goldstein, Bernard; Militias, Bundist; Newspapers; Trade unions; *Tsukunft* youth organizations
   Central Trade Union Council, 17–18
   club, 10, 22, 25, 27, 35, 36, 64, 81, 116, 143, 232, 233, 242
   Club closure in Praga, 35–36
   Commissar Cechnowski and, 153–154
   Communists and, 63–64, 126, 167–169, 189–190, 197–203, 311–314
   convention for unification of Polish and Galician organizations, 41–45
   Cracow Convention, 41–45, 57
   cultural awakening and, 253–264
   Danzig Convention, 57–61
   election of 1922 and, 75–82
   electoral victories, 2
   Janek Jankelewicz and, 37–39
   Kombundishe FRAKtsye faction, 57–61, 63–64, 126, 156
   locales of, 379-382
   members' sympathies with the Bolsheviks, 9–10
   office bombing in 1937, 383–385
   Polish labor movement and, 4, 5
   Polish persecutions of, 47–50, 143–144
   in Praga, 22–25
   schools built by, 4, 6, 44–45, 45n3, 215–216, *217–218,* 232, 258
   sports movement, 175–183, 289–293
   underground press, 53–56
   unification of all trade unions and, 83–87
   unification with Galician Bund, 41–45
   unions and, 254, 258
   uprising in Kieve, Ukraine, 1918, 9–12
   Warsaw locales of, 379–382
   weapons obtained by, 195–196
   World Coordinating Committee, 213n4, 407
Bund City Council, 265–272
   December 18, 1938, election and, 391–394
Bundist Youth Militia, *66*

C

Cechnowski, Commissar, 25, 153–154
Central Committee, 13n4, 37, 39, *41,* 44, 51n3, 54, 56n1, 56n2, 58, 59, 64, 65, 83, 84, 85, 87n1, 98, 101, 108, 120n5, 145, 146, 153, 157n1, 160, 167, 168, 191, 198, 203, 226, 276, 277, 282, 283, 296, 312, 315, 321, 330, 344, 356, 359, 363, 364, 368, 373, 374, 379, 387, 397, 402–405, 408
Central Congress of Trade Unions, 37, 379
Central Provisions Administration Office, 24–25
Chanin, Nathan, *207,* 315–317, 398
Chaskelewicz, Yehuda-Leyb, 363
Ciołkosz, Adam, 192
City Council, Warsaw, 24, 25, 47, 48, 50, 97, 120, 160, 163, 190, 237, *255,* 260, 265–271, 335
College students, Jewish, 303–306
Communist International, 57
Communists
   assassination attempts on Bernard Goldstein, 205–207, 227–229
   attack on Medem Sanitarium, 219–226
   attacks on night schools, 215–216, *217–218*
   Bakers Union and, 126, 311–314
   election of 1922 and, 75–81
   First of May demonstrations and, 31, 284–285
   Henryk Erlich and, 50
   Kombundishe FRAKtsye, 57–60, 63–64
   Krochmalna Street, 231–234

Nathan Chanin's visit to Warsaw and, 315–316
physical violence used by, 64, 73, 102, 167–169, 189–190, 197–203, 312–314, 319–321, 343–347
shooting at workers convention, 171–173
trade union unification and, 85–86
Transport Workers Union and, 189–193
the underworld and, 71–74
unification of Bunds and, 45
warfare against Bund, 60
wildcat strikes and, 197–203
Cracow Convention, 41–45, 57
Cultural autonomy, 83–84
Cultural awakening among workers, 253–264
Czechoslovakian Labor Sports Organization, 185–187
Czompel, Mayer, 71, 72, 73–74n1, 168

D

Dabie Concentration Camp, 49
Dąbrowski, Jan, 374, 376
Danzig Convention, 57–61
Daszyński, Ignacy, 47, 50
Davidovich, Tobshe, 396
Dembitser, Peysakh, 42
Dembitser, Yoyl, 42–43
Dembski, Moniek, 108–109, 195–196, 207
Der Moment, 54, 56
Di Naye Tsayt, 144
Di Shvue, 398
Dorfman, Hershl, 105–106, 171
Dubinsky, David, 293n2
Dubnow, Simon, *260*
Dubnow-Erlich, Sophia, *260, 316*
Dzontses, 191

E

Eikhl, Lazar, 179
Elections
1922, 75–82
1938, 391–394
Eliasz, Manye, 48
Endek Party, 295–296, 363, 364–365, 399
Epstein, Lazar, 344
Erlich, Alexander, *256, 260*
Erlich, Henryk, 49, 59, *207, 256, 260, 266, 267, 274, 275, 282, 283, 292, 316, 330,* 399
anti-war speech, 47, 48
assassination attempt on, 387–390
Bundist city council and, *266*
Congress of the Socialist Internationale and, 291
First of May Bund demonstrations and, *144,* 146
Folkstsaytung and, *353*
at joint meeting of Jewish and Polish Workers, *84*
persecutions of the Bund and, 47–50
Erlich, Shoshke Rukhl, *260,* 383
Erlich, Sophia-Dubnow, *207, 260*
Erlich, Victor, *260*
Etkes, Tsvi, 22

F

Falk, Y., 23
Fama (movie theatre), 381
Fareynikte. *See* Uniteds (United Jewish Socialist Workers Party)
Fat Yosl, 235–239
fayranter, 123, 125, 127, 311, 312, 400
Feiner, Leon, 42, 181, 210, 213n3, 400
feminism, 256
Finf Yor in Varshever Geto [Five Years in the Warsaw Ghetto], 6–7
First of May demonstrations
1920, 31–33, 66

1923, 143–147
1931, 151
joint PPS and Bund, 1931, 287–288
murder of Jewish child during 1937, 367–368
under the Piłsudski regime, 273–285
Flaczaz, Yankl, 90
Flamenboym, Avrom, 201
Flatshazh, Yankl, 135, 298
Fligl, Rachel, *256*
Flug, Aba, 57, 60–61
Folkstsaytung, 113, 143, 144, 171, 185, 186, 193, 212, 232, 234, 237, 257, 267, 283, *361*, 374, 375, 379
   on assassination attempt against Bernard Goldstein, 228–229
   auctioning off of, 349–353
   guarded against attacks, 371–372
   "Khaskele Hunchback" and, 241
   Saturday editions of, 149–151
Food Workers Union, 24, 63
Ford, Aleksander, 238, 239n3
Forverts, 359, 362n1, 400
FRAC (PPS-Former Revolutionary Faction), 160–161, 190–193, 295, 385, 400. *See also* PPS (Polska Partia Socjalistyczna)
   militia, 163–165
   Newspaper Deliverers Union and, 333–335
   Porters Union, 337–338
   stolen goods and, 341–342
   terrorist acts by, 331, 337
   Transport Workers Union and, 164, 331, 337–339
Frankel, Nathan, *48*
Frimerman, Yankl, 125, 312
Frydrich, Zalmen, 181, 182n4, *305, 306*, 400

G

Gajewski, Geniek, 137–139
Galician Bund, unification with, 41–45
Galsworthy, John, 210
Garment Workers Union, 23–24, 63, 144, 153, 168, 172, 189–190, 269
   Communist attacks on, 319–321
General Food Workers Union, 115–121
General Polish Union of Food Workers, 137
German Social Democratic Party, 291
Germany, Nazi. *See* Hitler, Adolf
ghetto benches, 182, 303–306, 400
Gilinski, Mordkhe, 220, 223
Gilinsky, Shloyme, *216*, 220, 333, 335n1, 400
Gnojna Street, 235–239
Goldberg, Issar, 190, 333
Goldstein, Bernard, 1, 3, *146, 264*. *See also* Bund, the
   appointed to head Bund sports movement, 176
   arrested, 18
   assassination attempts on, 205–207, 227–229
   assigned to work in Praga, 21–26
   doubts about work with the Bund, 323–325
   First of May demonstration, 1920, 31–33, 66
   First of May demonstration, 1923, 144–147
   grave in New York, *396*
   Henryk Erlich and, 49–50
   imprisonment of, 58–59
   invited to parties and celebrations with meat workers, 141–142
   leadership of, 3–7
   return to Warsaw in 1918, 11–12
   Shloyme Mendelson and, 327–330
   shot at by Communists, 200
   travel through Czechoslovakia, 185–187
   underground Bund press and, 53–56
   unification of trade unions and, 86
   work with the Central Trade Union Council, 17–18

Yankl Levine and, 58
    in Zakopane, 209–213
Goldstein, Janek, 40, 196, 212
    at SKIF camp, 307–310
Goldstein, Lucia, 11, 15, 40, *228*
Gotthelf, 26
Grochów, Poland, 25
Grosser, Bronislaw, 13n5
Grosser Club, 10, 13n5, 16–17, 48, 379
Grosser faction, 344
Grosser Library, 13n5, 379–380, 382n1, 395, 401
Gutgold, Yosl, 280, 298, 320, 364, 365

H

Hairdressers Union, 63
Haller, Jozef, 32, 33n1
Halpern, Leivik, *16*
Hashomer Hatzair, 210, 213n2, 401
Hasidism, *42*, 43, 116, 120n4, 149, 150, 151, 262, 268, 341, 401, 406
Hazomir, 119, 121n10, 402
Hendler's printshop, 381
Hertz, Sholem, 53, 56n1, 185, *292*, 363–364, 411
Himmelfarb, Hershl, 42, *264*, 321
Hitler, Adolf, 61, 293, 295–300. *See also* Anti-Semitism
Holocaust, the, 2–3, 309–310
Honigwill, Ludwig, 200, 228, 350

I

Isaacson, Itshele, 237–238
Iron Gate, 32, 102, 297, 298, 360
Iwinska, Esther, 267

J

Jakubowicz, Shmuel, 107–108, 251
Jankliewicz, Janek, 17, 18, 37–40, 155, 157n1, 402

Janusz's Courtyard, 26, 235, 337, 338
Jaszunski, Grisza, 210–212
Jewish Labor Bund. *See* Bund, the
Jewish Labor Committee, 344, 347n1
Jewish life. *See also* Bund, the; SKIF (Union of Socialist Children); *Tsukunft* youth organizations
    boycotts of Jewish businesses and, 301–302
    Bund locales and, 379–382
    captured in writing, 2–3
    cultural awakening among workers and, 253–264
    Diaspora, 3
    education in, 4, 6, 44–45, 45n3, 215–216, *217–218*, 232, 258
    "ghetto benches" in universities and, 303–306
    under Hitler in Poland, 295–306
    labor movement and, 4, 5
    landlord/tenant relations and, 268–270
    Tsukunft youth organization and, 23, *77,* 97, 114, 119, 124, 125, 145, 179, 190, 232–233, *234*
Jewish National Bloc, 392, 393
Jewish Porters Union, 164
Jewish Trade Union National Council, 83
Joint Distribution Committee, 18, 19n5, 375, 377n2, 402
Jutrzenka, 182n2

K

Kahan, Borukh Mordkeh, 13n6
Kahan, Mordkeh (Virgili), 11, 13n6, 402
Kalmen the Bootmaker, 155–157
Kamashnmakher, Kalman, 57
Kamenev, Lev Borisovich, 90, 93n2
Kastalansky, Abraham, *94*
Kautsky, Karl, 292
Kazimierz, Kazik, 58–59
Kehilla, 18, 40, 270
"Khaskele Hunchback," 241–243

Khayetshkes family (slaughterers), 96–97, 141, 142, 249–251
Kiev, Ukraine, uprising of 1918, 9–12
Kirschenzweig, Khayim, 206–207
Klepfisz, Mikhl, 18, 304, 402
Kolnitshansky, Anshl, 89, 95–96, 135, 142
Kolnitshansky family (slaughterers), 89, 95–99, 142
Kombundishe FRAKtsye, 57–61, 126
    final splitting off from Bund, 63–64
    Kalmen the Bootmaker and, 156
Kremer, Arkady, 385n3, 403
Krisztal, Czilba, 15, 196
Krochmalna Street, 241, 242, 245, 248, 253, 258, 264
    Communists and, 231–234
    Fat Yosl and, 235–239
    Meatworkers Union, 232
    Transport Workers Union, 232
Królikowski, Stefan, 58, 61n2
Kruk, Herman, 209, 213n1, 283, 382n1, 403
Kultur-lige (Culture League), 209–210, 232, 382n1, 403
Kurier Czerwony, 370

L

Labor Sports Internationale, 185, 289
Labor Zionists, 191, 344
Leather and Haberdashers Union, 116
Leather-Haberdashers Union, 63
Leather Workers Union, 57, 63, 85, 190, *248,* 312, 364
Lebns-Fragn, 15, 48
Leivik, H. *16*
Lestchinsky, Yankev, 89
Leszczyński, Stanisław, 25
Levine, Leyzer, 207, 374, 375
Levine, Yankl, 15, 58
Lichtenstein, Dovid, 22, *84*
Lichtenstein, Israel, *266, 292*
Lichtenstein, Salek, 312, 313

Lichtenstein, Zlatke, 22
Liebknecht, Karl, 9, 113
Lifszytz, Rueben, 213
Lifszytz, Yoysef, 17, 57, 332, 363–364
Likhtenshtayn, Yisroel, *38*
Literary Club, 49, 157, 403
Litewka, Yoylke, 396
Łokietek, Dr., 163–164, 331–332, 338
Lumber Workers Union, 63
Luxemburg, Rosa, 9, 113

M

Macz, Simkhe, 167, 168, 169, 171, 173
Majerowicz, Mania, 15
Malematke, 245–248
March to Kiev, 47
Marmurek, Mannes, 333–335
Maroko, Yekhiel, 113–114
Masaryk, Thomas, 185
masuvke, 277
Matraszek, Geniek, 297–298, 331–332
Mayer, Dovid, 83
Mayn Yingele (poem/song), 124
Meat Workers Union, 97, 102, 103, 133, 142, 190, 202, 232, 281, 298. *See also* slaughterhouses
Medem, Vladimir, 15, 16, 18n1, 32, 40, 42, 43, *43,* 57, 116, 403
    unification of Bunds and, 42, 44
Medem Sanitarium, 44–45, 118, *131, 216,* 219–226, 238, 239n3, 307, 309, 335n1, 395, 401, 404
Mendel Beilis Trial, 119, 121
Mendelson, Shloyme, 220, *228,* 325, 327–330, 395
Mendelsund, Benyomin, 116–118
Mendelsund, Golde, 116–117
Mendelsund, Henoch, 172, 173n1
Merlin, Mikhl, 395
Metal Workers Union, 63, 144, 190, 202
Meyer, Dovid, 176

Michalewicz, Bejnisz, 15–16, 18n3, 42, 146–147, 282
Michalowicz, Jerzy, 181
Military coup (1926), 159–161
Militias, Bundist, 5, 6, 65–69, 144, 190
    assassination attempt on Bernard Goldstein and, 206–207
    bombing of Bund offices and, 384
    communist assaults on, 171–173, 197
    election of 1922 and, 77
    election of 1938 and, 392
    FRAC, 163–165
    guarding of the *Folkstsaytung*, 371–372
    "Khaskele Hunchback" and, 241–243
    "Malematke" and, 246–247
    Poland under Hitler and, 296–299
    Przytyk protest strike and, 359–362
    Warsaw City Council and, 265–272
    weapons and, 195–196
    wildcat strikes and, 197–203
Milner, Dovid, 71, 72, 171, 197, 319
Milosna Wood, 27
Minsk-Mazowiecki, pogrom in, 363–366
Mir Kumen On, *131*, 238, *239*, 239n3, 404
Mlotek, Dina, 233
Moment, 54, 56
Moraczewski, Jedrzej, 47
Morawski, Kazik, 350, 351
Morgnroyt, 330
Morgnshtern (sports organization), 175–183, 185, 274, 282, 289, 291, 405
Myśl Socialisticna, 374

N

Nalewki, 72, 101–103, 111, 113, 144, 145, 171, 178, 186, 283, 301, 315, 333, 342–344, 360, 367
Narovtses, 249, 297, 298, 300, 405. *See also Onerowcy*
National Association of Jewish Labor Unions, *84*
Nationalism, 47–50

Naye Folkstsaytung, 276
Nayman, Yekhiel, 57, 60
Nazism, 346–347n1. *See also* Anti-Semitism; Hitler, Adolf; Holocaust, the
Neuerman, Avrom, 312–314
Newspapers
    on assassination attempt on Bernard Goldstein, 228–229
    Deliverers Union, 333–335
    Folkstsaytung, 15, 48, 144, 171, 185, 186, 193, 257, 283, 349–353, *361*, 371–372, 374
    New York Yiddish, 359, 362n1
    Oenerowcy, 369–370
    Robotnik, 91, 160–161, 288, 374
    struggles over Saturday edition of, 149–151
    Yungt-Veker, 193, 363–364
Niedziałkowski, Mieczyslaw, 91
Nowe Pismo, 374
Nowe Życie, 374
Nowogrodzki, Emanuel, *10*, 10–11, 13n4, 53, 59, 146–147, 202, 203n1, *264*, *274*, *292*, 405
Noyekh (Portnoy, Yekusiel), 16, *17*, 19n4, 59, 60, 202, 203n1, 207, *207*, *220*, *266*, *274*, 282, *292*, *316*, 324, 405
    Folkstaytung auction and, 351
    Medem Sanitarium and, 220
    shoemakers union and, 202
    Uniteds and, 102

O

Oenerowcy, 295, 297, 300n2, 302, 304, 329, 367, 369–370, 385n2, 392, 405, 412
    attack on *Folkstsaytung* threatened by, 371–372
    attempt to murder Henryk Erlich, 387–390
    bombing of Bund offices and, 383–385
Ofman, Yoshke, *84*
Olympiad, 185, 289

ONR, 251n1, 298, 299, 369, 384, 385
ORT, 119, 211, 349, 405
Otwock, 12, 141, 142, 219, 222, 223
Orzech, Mauricy, 42, 48, 292, *292,* 293n4, 350–353, *352,* 405

P

Paderewski Park, 297
Paper Workers Union, 57, 63
Pasharnyes, 25–26, 405
Pat, Emanuel, 308
Peasants' Party, 192, 287
Pelcowizna, Poland, 25
Perenson family, 205–206
Peretz, I. L., 40, 156, *156,* 157n2, 327, 405
Persecutions of the Bund movement, 47–50, 143–144. See also Police, Polish
Petliura, Vasylyovych, 9, 12n3, 13, 405
Piłsudski, Jozef, 159–161, 164–165, 191–192, 236
  First of May demonstrations under regime of, 273–285
Pismo Codzienne, 374ŁŁ
Pizhits, Chaim, 185, *228, 292*
Plac Teatralny (Theatre Square), 143, 271, 274, 283, 284, 327
Pogroms
  Brisk, 373–377
  Minsk-Mazowiecki, 363–366
  Przytkyk, 359–362
Poland. *See also* Praga suburb, Warsaw, Poland; Warsaw, Poland
  Bernard Goldstein's return to, 11–12
  boycotting of Jewish businesses in, 301–302
  election of 1922, 75–82
  Emanuel Nowogrodzki on the Bundist movement in, 10–11, 13n4
  evolution of Jewish community in, 1–2
  Hitlerism in, 293, 295–306
  independence in 1918, 47
  Jewish Socialist students of, 80–81
  mass murder of Jews in, 1
  nationalism and persecutions, 47–50
  newspapers, 15, 48
  Piłsudski military coup against, 159–161
  police (*See* Police, Polish)
  typhus epidemic, 38
  unification of trade union movement in, 83–87
  workers parties, 25
  during World War II, 395–396
Poliakowicz Cigarette Factory, 18
Police, Polish
  bagel peddlers and, 130
  Bund office bombing and, 383–385
  clashes with funeral attendees, 39–40
  closure of Bund Club in Praga, 35–36
  election of 1922 and, 78–79
  First of May demonstrations and, 31–33, 143–147
  Henryk Erlich and, 49–50
  persecutions of the Bund movement, 47–50
  wildcat strikes and, 201–202
pomocnik, 112, 123
Porters Union, 254, 258–259
  FRAC, 337–338
Portnoy, Noyekh Yekusiel. *See* Noyekh (Portnoy, Yekusiel)
PPS (Polska Partia Socjalistyczna), 25, 31, 50, 58, 65, 83, *84,* 287, 304. *See also* FRAC (PPS-Former Revolutionary Faction)
  Brisk pogrom and, 374–376
  in Bródno suburb, Poland, 356–357
  election of 1922 and, 77
  First of May demonstrations and, 151, 273, 277, 282–283, 287–288
  Lewica, 343, 344
  Oenerowcy and, 369–370
  Piłsudski coup and, 159–161
  Robotnik newspaper, 91, 160–161
  slaughterers and, 90–91, 96, 137–138

teamsters and, 106–107
Praga suburb, Warsaw, Poland, 19n6. *See also* Poland; Warsaw, Poland
   Bund Club closure by police in, 35–36
   Bund Club in, 25
   Central Administration of Provisions in, 21
   Commissar Cechnowski in, 153–154
   First of May demonstration, 1920, 31–33
   Goldstein leads Bund work in, 18
   Goldstein's work in, 21–26
   police (*See* Police, Polish)
   teamsters, 27–29
   thieves of, 27, 28
Press, underground, 53–56
Printers Union, 63, 312, 368
Prostitution, 71, 73, 168, 261–264
Protest strike, Przytyk, Poland, 359–362
Przytuk, pogrom in, 359–362

R

Rafes, Moyshe, 58
Red Falcons, 291, 293n1, 406
Religious holidays, 104
Retail Clerks Union, 73, 312
   murder of worker in, 343–347
Rifke the Cow, 168
Ringen, 282, 303–304, 406
Robotnik, 91, 160–161, 288, 374, 406
Rope and handcart porters, 111–114
Rosenberg family (slaughterers), 96–97, 249–251
Rosenboym, Menachem, 17, 321
Rosenthal, Anna, 210–211, *292*
Rozental, Anna Heller, *242*

S

Sanacja Party, 295
Saxon Gardens, 297, 298
Schneider, Comrade, 374–377, 377n1

Schools, Yiddish, 4, 6, 44–45, 45n3, 215–216, *217–218*, 258
   Krochmalna Street and, 232
Schwalbs, 28
Schwartz, Pinkhas, 181, 185, 284
Scwartzbard, Sholem, 13n3
Sczerba, Yankl, 28
SDKPiL, 25, 26n1, 343, 344, 406
Segalowicz, Klara, 327
Sejmist, 81, 406
Sejmovic, See *Sejmist*
Sejm, 190, 380
Self-defense militias. *See* Militias, Bundist
Shapiro, Bella, *255, 266*
Shatzkin, Julek, 38, *39*
Sherer, Emanuel, *2*, 7, 277, *292*
Shetshke gang, 331–332
Shifris, 395
Shoe-Leather-Cutters-and-Stictcher Union, 85–86
Shoemaker Union, 85–86
Shoshke. *See* Erlich, Shoshke Rukhl
Shtern, Shaye, 259–262
Shulman, Victor, 15, 18n2, 37, 264, 267, 406
Shutzbund, 291, 292, 406
Shvartsnobel, Srul, 90–91
Shveber, Sarah, *84*
Shvue, Di, 142, 246, 398, 406
SKIF (Union of Socialist Children), 114, 117, 124, 151, 242, 258, 274, *276*, 282, 381, 392, 406
   bakers and, 124
   establishment of, 114n2
   eve of World War II, 395–396
   Golde Mendelsund and, 117–118
   "Khaskele Hunchback" and, 242
   Khayim Ejno and, 233
   Korchmalna Street and, 232
   summer camps sponsored by, *242*, 307–310
Skoropadskyi, Pavlo, 9, 12n1
SKRA, 289, 317, 406

slaughterhouses, 21–22, 26, 298
   families, 95–99, 249–251
   Jewish and Polish workers working in, 137–139
   "Malematke"'s work in, 245–248
   Meat Workers Union and, 103, 133
   parties and celebrations among workers in, 141–142
   power of, 98–99
   typical day in, 133–136
   union, 89–93, 96
Smocza, 264, 299, 313, 367, 392, 383
Smuggling of foodstuffs, 102
Socialist Internationale, 289, 291–293
Socialist-Zionist Party, 89–90, 95, 102
Soviet Union, the
   Bolsheviks and, 9–10, 41–42, 43
   Danzig Convention and, 58–59
   imprisonment of Erlich and Alter, *389*
   Mikhl Merlin killed in, 395
   war between Poland and, 54
Spivak, Buzi, 80, 82n4
Sports movement, Bund
   Czechoslovakian Labor Sports Organization and, 185–187
   Morgnshtern sports organization and, 175–183
   Vienna events of 1931 and, 289–293
SRs, 407
Stavnikes, 112
Stoller, Abram, 79–80, 81, 380
Strikes, worker, 26, 197–203
Sztrigler, Elye, 17, 124
Szumolewizna, Poland, 25

T

Tabachnik' Coffee House, 262
Tabaczinski, Benyomin, 212, 213n4
Tabaczinski, Krayndl, 212
Tasiemka, 163–164
Teamsters, 27–29, 101–102
Textile Workers Union, 60–61, 63

Tlomatskie, 13, 157
Toller, Ernst, 210
TOZ, 175, 176, 182n1, 407
Trade unions. *See also* FRAC (PPS-Former Revolutionary Faction); specific unions
   bakers, 63, 123–127, 311–314
   Bund Central Trade Union Council, 17–18, 315
   cultural awakening and, 253–264
   food workers, 115–121
   garment workers, 23–24, 63, 144, 153, 168, 172, 189–190, 269, 319–321
   newspapers deliverers, 333–335
   slaughterers, 89–93, 96, 103, 133
   unification, 83–87
Transport Workers Union, 101–104, 105–109, 107
   back porters and, 102–109
   Communists and, 189–193
   FRAC and, 164, 331, 337–339
   National Convention, 171–173
   rope and handcart porters and, 111–114
Traugutta Park, 297, 299
Trzeciak, Father, 355–357
Tsalke, Comrade, 266–267
Tsiglman, Melech, 312, 314
Tsukerlekhmakher, Fishl, 119
Tsukunft youth organizations, 22, 23, 56, 77, *91,* 97, 105, 114, 119, 124, 125, 145, 151, 206, 210, 234, *234,* 250, *275,* 288, *290, 305,* 307, 309, 317, 356, 357, 368, 375, 380, 392, 395, 407. *See also* Bund, the
   Bund sports movement and, 179
   chorus of, 215
   Communist attacks on, 190, 215–216, *217–218,* 320
   dramatic group, 215
   "ghetto benches" in universities and, 303–306
   "Khaskele Hunchback" and, 242

Krochmalna Street and, 232–233
militia of, 206
schools for, 215
under the Piłsudski regime, 274–282
TSYSHO (Tsentral Yidishe Shul Organizatsye), 44, 45n3, 114, 117, 119, 120, 178, 196, 209, 215, 217, 218, 232, 258, 327–329, 407
Tuberculosis, 219–226
TUR, 376, 407
Twenty-One Conditions, 57, 60, 61n1
Tydzień Robotnika, 374
Typhus epidemic, 38

U

Underground Bund press, 53–56
Underworld, the
bakers and, 124
Communists and, 71–74
Korchmalna Street and, 231–234
Unification of Polish and Galician bunds, 41–45
Union of Coal Carriers, 171–173
Union of Domestic Workers, 156
Union of Newspaper Distributors, 171
Union of Socialist Children. *See* SKIF (Union of Socialist Children)
United Hebrew Trades, 315, 317n2, 407
Uniteds (United Jewish Socialist Workers Party), 11, 13n7, 89, 101, 333, 399, 407
University of Warsaw, 303–304

V

Vaser, Khayim, *48, 84*
Veker, 215
Venger, Moyshe, 112–113
Vienna, Austria, 289–293
Vladeck, Baruch Charney, 347n1

W

"Walczący," Hershl, 71–72, 73–74n1
Warsaw, Poland. *See also* Bródno suburb, Poland; Poland; Police, Polish; Praga suburb, Warsaw, Poland
Arsenal, 15, 16
Bernard Goldstein's return to, 11–12
boycotts of Jewish businesses in, 301–302
Bund locales in, 379–382
Central Provisions Administration Office, 24–25
City Council, 24–25, 48, 237–238, 265–272, 391–394
Ghetto Uprising, 18, 53, 54, 181, 233
Grosser Club, 10, 13n5, 16–17
Lebns-Fragn newspaper, 15, 48
Praga suburb, 21–26
prostitution in, 71, 73, 168, 261–264
slaughterhouses, 21–22, 26
Warsaw Fund for the Sick, 25
Warsaw Labor Council, 10
Wasilewska, Wanda, 233n3
Wasser, Gershn, 344
Wasser, Mayer, 344
Wasserman, Dovid, 344–345
Weinreich, Max, 296, 300n3, 327, 359, 360, 407
Wildcat strikes, 197–203, 311
Witos, Wincenty, 159, 192
Wojciechowski, Stanisław, 159, 384
Workmen's Circle, 213n4
Workers Corner, 107, 202, 320, 262, 263, 271, 283, 302, 379–381
World War II, 395–396
Woyland, Zalmen, 42

Y

YAF (Yidishe Arbeter Froy), 226, 254, 257, 264n1, 276, 277, 283, 381, 383, 407
"Yankl Szczerba," 28–29

"Yankl the Lion," 27
Yiddish Literary Club, 156, 157, 157n3, 327
Yiddish schools, secular, 44, 45, 45n3, 48, 64, 106, 114, 117, 118, 119, 124, 125, 135, 143, 178, 210, 215, 216, *217*, 232, 255, 276
Yiddish theatre, 210, 253
YIVO, 213, 243n1, 296, 300n3, 359, 407, 408
Youth organizations. *See Tsukunft* youth organization
Yugnt-Bunk Tsukunft. See Tsukunft youth organization
Yukele, 249–251
Yungt-Veker, 193, 363–364, 408

Z

Zakopane, Poland, 187, 207, 209–213
Zaremba, Zygmunt, 374
Zawrat, 212
"Zbukh," 337–339
Zegas, Hershl, 321
"Zelig the Carpenter," 27–29
Zelmanowitch, A. L., *292*
Ziegleboym, Artur, 54, 56n2, *84*, 277, 408, 409
Zilbershteyn, Shaye-Yudl, 106, 171–173, 207, 337, 370
Zionists, 86, 89, 95, 104n1, 191, 273, 344, 391, 407
Zlatke, 22
ZNMS, 303, 408
ZOB, 408
Zuckerman, Rubin, *24, 48, 85*
Zusman, Shloymke, 89, 333
Zygielbojm, Artur, 56n2
ZZZ (Zwiqzek Zwazkow Zawadowych), 164

www.ingramcontent.com/pod-product-compliance
Lightning Source LLC
Chambersburg PA
CBHW070542230426
43665CB00014B/1779